ECONOMICS IN THE PUBLIC SERVICE

By Edwin G. Nourse:

AMERICAN AGRICULTURE AND THE EUROPEAN MARKET

AMERICA'S CAPACITY TO PRODUCE

INDUSTRIAL PRICE POLICIES AND ECONOMIC PROGRESS

PRICE MAKING IN A DEMOCRACY

THE 1950'S COME FIRST

Economics
in the Public Service

ADMINISTRATIVE ASPECTS OF THE EMPLOYMENT ACT

EDWIN G. NOURSE

Harcourt, Brace and Company

NEW YORK

COPYRIGHT, 1953, BY
EDWIN G. NOURSE

first edition

Library of Congress Catalog Card Number: 52-13769

PRINTED IN THE UNITED STATES OF AMERICA

TO MY SISTERS

MARY AUGUSTA NOURSE
historian of the Far East

ALICE LOUISE NOURSE
novelist—"Alice Tisdale Hobart"

Foreword

In the present volume, I am frankly stepping out of my primary role as economist and assuming that related role of political scientist to which the economist must frequently turn if he is to do an adequate job of economic analysis and prescription. The line between economics and political science is in fact shadowy, and it is my belief that workers from each side can profit from exploratory journeys into the territory of the other, rather than accentuating the line of demarcation or stooping to "jurisdictional quarrels."

If the political scientist is to advise wisely as to machinery of administration, he must understand the economic content of public policies and the economic forces with which we have to deal in devising the governmental structures of an economy and in formulating administrative procedures to effectuate desired policies and assure compliance with laws, old or new. Likewise, if the economist is to advise wisely as to programs of action—or of inaction—he needs a reasonable working knowledge of the realities of executive, legislative, administrative, and citizen behavior in political structures. He must be aware of the administrative problems involved in the actual functioning of economic institutions. He must be realistic about these political forces and limitations in his formulation or evaluation of economic policies.

As first chairman of the Council of Economic Advisers, set up under the Employment Act of 1946, I felt it incumbent on me to study carefully the administrative problems involved in the operation of this new agency in the executive branch of the Federal Government. In fact, in the first annual report of the Council to the President in December 1946, the opening section was entitled "The

Political Philosophy of the Employment Act," and "The Economic Philosophy of Sustained Employment" was reserved to Part II.

After more than three years of service in the Executive Office, I retired to a position where I could consider these problems from the vantage point of an outsider. During the last three years, I have been mulling over my experience and the comments and criticisms that have been made concerning the work of the Council and of the Joint Economic Committee of Congress. I have pondered also the future possibilities of both these agencies for implementing the Employment Act.

In the present volume, I shall offer my personal interpretation of the national policy enunciated in the Employment Act, set this policy in its historic perspective, and discuss the steps that have thus far been taken to bring the Council of Economic Advisers to a position of usefulness consonant with the terms of the act and worthy of the purposes which it was designed to express. In somewhat less detail and from a necessarily less intimate experience I shall discuss the parallel work of the Joint Congressional Committee on the Economic Report of the President.

Some two years ago, Professor Stephen K. Bailey of Connecticut Wesleyan University published a book under the title *Congress Makes A Law*. It was a trailbreaking attempt to show in rich detail the human and political realities that lie back of the process by which a Federal statute comes into being under our Congressional system. The method developed in that monograph met with such a favorable response in the profession that the American Political Science Association awarded Professor Bailey its Woodrow Wilson prize.

Fortunately for the present writer, Bailey chose the Employment Act of 1946 for the purpose of demonstrating his method of analyzing the legislative process. His book recounts the "dramatic story of the birth, growth, and metamorphosis of a public policy" in that act. Without wishing to engage in a battle of metaphors, I might suggest that public policy was in fact born only after the conference committee reconciled or compromised the provisions of S. 380 and H. R. 2202, when both Houses overwhelmingly voted for the synthesized product and President Truman signed Public Law 304 of the 79th Congress on February 20, 1946. During the year that preceded that occasion, there had been flirtation with a policy (or

several policies), courtship between ardent but coy factions, and
eventual marriage of Senate and House in a tolerably peaceful
union, from which a living policy was born.

Now granting that the policy delivered on February 20, 1946 was
a congenitally healthy and quite promising infant, the question
remained, and in fact still remains: What sort of postnatal care will
it receive? Will the promise of its innate potentialities be realized?
Or will it struggle along, puny and neglected, mistreated, or even
cast off entirely by the infanticidal revulsion of a subsequent
Congress?

The present volume extends the story of how Congress made this
law to the no less dramatic and human story of the men who have
undertaken during the first six years to administer it—of their theoretical slants and their behavioristic leanings. It has been their responsibility to interpret the broad intent of the Congress in making
such a policy statement as they did and to make this interpretation
in the context of the fast-changing situations with which the country has been confronted during these years. The book examines
some of the practical problems that have arisen in attempting so to
administer the law as to achieve most fully the purposes the people
were reaching for and which Congress sought to promote.

I shall begin by giving briefly the background of the Employment
Act. In so doing, I shall not be content merely to summarize the
story that Professor Bailey has assembled with infinite patience and
great originality of approach. I shall go a little farther afield to
trace some lines of descent that seem to me significant but which
lie outside the scope of Bailey's narrative.

To make clear the nature of this redrawing of the background of
the present statute, it is necessary to introduce here a brief critical
comment on the frame of reference used by the author of *Congress
Makes A Law*. This relates to the question: what policy was embodied in the Employment Act? It would seem natural that I as an
economist might think of it solely as establishing an economic policy
for dealing with massive unemployment or, more broadly, as stabilizing the nation's economic activity. It might seem also that Professor Bailey as a political scientist would naturally be preoccupied
with any change in government structure or definition of government functions made by this law.

In fact, however, these roles or lines of approach have been, in considerable measure, reversed. The emergence of national policy which Professor Bailey traces in so much detail is primarily an economic issue of how to cope with business depressions or threats of prolonged stagnation. He is in the main concerned with the adequacy of private business agencies to handle these matters or the economics of government action in such situations. Hardly at all does he invoke political science principles to shed light on how far or in what way it may be safe, effective, or expedient for the Federal government to intervene in these economic matters. Nor does he give professional attention to the executive role of the President in the area of economic statesmanship or to needed or desirable staffing to meet these responsibilities. Neither does he analyze the nature of Congressional organization and procedures as bearing on the problem of securing integrated and internally consistent policy for dealing with the complexly related aspects of national economic affairs—fiscal, monetary, agricultural, labor, industrial, or what not.

It was admirable for Bailey as a political scientist to study how the Congress is politically and emotionally conditioned when it comes to grips with the economic phase of a piece of legislation which has great historic importance. But it would also be enlightening to trace the legislative debates and the extracurricular activities of Senators and Representatives as they bear on the question of how both the executive branch and the legislative branch of the Federal government are being shaped for their roles of policy-making for the economy. Perhaps some day Professor Bailey will perform this complementary task. Such explanation is all the more important because of the fact that the final action of Congress had the purpose and effect, as I shall explain in later chapters, of deleting practically all economic doctrine from the Employment Act and making it essentially a political, that is, a structural and procedural, statute. I shall not attempt to delve into the reasons why or the process by which the various Senators and Representatives brought this change about. I shall try rather to explain what the statute is and how we undertook to carry out that intention.[1]

Part I traces several aspects of the concept of national economic policy and how its growth gave rise to institutional changes which

[1] I hope to embody in a subsequent volume under the title "The Road to Full Employment—without Serfdom" my analysis of the central economic problem with which both the Council of Economic Advisers and the Joint (Congressional) Committee on the Economic Report of the President have to wrestle.

culminated in the Employment Act of 1946. Part II is an account, narrative in form but with some running analysis, of operations under the act from July 1946 to the present. Part III represents my personal interpretation of the significance of these events—problems which have emerged in these initial years, and possibilities for the future.

In the writing of this book I have been the beneficiary of two most fortunate circumstances. First, so much of the history I have undertaken to recount and to analyze is so recent that most of the actors are still living. Many of them I have known personally and with not a few of them I have worked more or less directly from time to time over the years. Whenever I have approached them for information and for criticisms as my writing proceeded, all have been most generous and stimulating in their suggestions. I refrain from mentioning names, not from any lack of appreciation but simply that no one shall be embarrassed by being identified with a book which is bound to evoke some controversial reactions.

A second source of help has come to me through the generous gift of the John Simon Guggenheim Memorial Foundation. The grant made to me shortly after I "retired" from government service and later extended has helped greatly in facilitating the studies of which this volume is a partial product. I have been able to maintain a small workshop in downtown Washington, in convenient contact with the persons and the source materials essential to my work. Most important, I have been able to retain the services of Miss Margaret Quill, who was my personal secretary during the whole of my service on the Council of Economic Advisers and who had also been my assistant for some years previously at the Brookings Institution.

December 30, 1952   EDWIN G. NOURSE

Contents

Appendixes

PART
I

Economic Science and Practical Policy

INTRODUCTION

This book was conceived primarily as a simple story of people in action—a narrative and descriptive account of one particular effort of free government to make itself better government, of free business enterprise to make itself more fruitful. This experiment—the Employment Act of 1946—was not, however, something that sprang full-blown from the head of any one man or group of men. Nor was it newly invented in 1945, with letters patent issued in 1946. It had some relation to the thinking of our times and to earlier attempts of free Americans to devise "a more perfect" frame of government.

Being who I am and what I am, I cannot look at the twelve Economic Reports of the President and the six years' record of the Council of Economic Advisers and the Joint Economic Committee of Congress as acts in a spiritual vacuum or "an Island detached from the Main." I have therefore set down in the following six chapters what seem to me some significant and illuminating features of the philosophical and historical background out of which the Employment Act emerged.

CHAPTER ONE

Human Ends and Scientific Means

The central proposition around which this book is written is that the Employment Act of 1946 constitutes an attempt to bring the tools of economic science, in this modern day, to bear more effectively in the formulation of practically successful policies for the conduct of the nation's business. If we are to see clearly just what is proposed and to judge fairly what has been accomplished—and what yet needs to be done—a few opening pages may well be given to examining the meaning of each of the terms in the title "Economic Science and Practical Policy." What is a policy and when is it practical? What are the methods of science in the economic field?

A POLICY IS A PHILOSOPHY OF LIFE

I hold this truth to be self-evident: that the envisioning and implementing of policies of individual and group action (including that of government units) make up a major part of the serious or disciplined thinking of adults. Whoever really ponders the meaning and ends of human life begins, at least subconsciously, to formulate policies for living it. Policy-making is an accomplishment limited to civilized and mature people. The savage reacts spontaneously to the immediate pressures of hunger, danger, the biologic urge, and other sensuous stimuli. Even in advanced societies "a boy's will is the wind's will." But those men, both civilized and mature, who claim the right of self-direction in a democracy want to see actions in their relations and their sequence.

"Policy" is a key word in our modern thinking about the problem of preserving and perfecting a system of free enterprise within a scheme of democratic government. Today farmers talk of farm policy. Workers talk in terms of union policy and their officers consider wage policy, strike policy, and their policy of political action or neutralism (even John L. Lewis formally convenes a "policy-making group"). Businessmen debate trade policy, price policy, and their policies toward organized labor. Statesmen and politicians hold forth not merely on debt management policy; tax, tariff, and transportation policy; but also on the governmental aspect of all the policies that impinge on the business affairs of the manufacturer, the merchant, the banker, and the citizen.

We have abandoned the complacent reliance on *laissez faire* as the comfortable doctrine that we can give the old Adam free rein and the Unseen Hand will cause our untutored and self-seeking acts to add up to an acceptable or even tolerable result. On the other hand, we are not ready—most of us—to have our choices made and our actions governed by an authoritarian power that presumes to direct our labors and apportion our rewards. In a golden mean between these two extremes, free men assert the right to make their own choices, and accept responsibility for working out with each other ways of directing the organizations and practices of voluntary economic life.

To this end, we must be constantly shaping and reshaping economic policies to guide the action of groups—large and small, private and public. We cannot let ourselves drift with the tide of habitual or imitative behavior or thoughtless whim. We must, with some grown-up realization of the importance of both ends and means, take a good hard look at three basic and ever-recurring questions: Just what is it that we really want to accomplish? Are present business structures and practices moving us as steadily and rapidly as possible toward these goals? What permanent changes or temporary adaptations are needed to put me as an individual, my group as a business organization, or all of us as a democratic government on a better line or in a faster tempo toward what we really seek?

An economic policy is a sophisticated—that is, an intellectual rather than emotional—way of defining ends to be sought and adopting promising means of pursuing those ends. Perceiving business life as a complex social process about which, in spite of its vagaries, we have some hard-won understanding, policy-making expresses a faith that we can have some measure of control over the outcome. This will be only in proportion as we learn the arts of communication and of co-operation.

It was in the Employment Act of 1946 that we the people of the United States first explicitly stated a national policy of co-operation between business and government to maximize our national production. That act is novel too in that it declares a policy about policy-making, namely that the methods and tools of modern social science be used by the official makers of national economic policy. The goal of the economic process was stated in the Employment Act in terms to which there would presumably be almost universal agreement—maximum production, with that fullness of employment and abundance of real economic purchasing power (or consumption) which are its logical accompaniments. It invites our subsequent thought and effort to the devising of means for attaining this general end. To validate free enterprise and representative government, we must hammer out management policies, labor policies, financial policies, farm policies, fiscal, monetary, and regulatory policies of government which will work together to promote that commonly desired end of sustained high production of the materials and services prerequisite to an advancing culture. Such is the challenge to the individual as an aspiring personality and as a tractable but dynamic member of organized groups and, finally, as citizen.

ECONOMICS IS A SOCIAL SCIENCE

Natural scientists, even the biologists, have been disposed to look down their professional noses at the use of the term "science" in connection with social studies. But science is merely "organized knowledge" and its form will differ from one problem field to another. The conditions encountered and the criteria that can be applied are not the same when we pass from the realm of inorganic nature on to the realms of plant and then of animal life. And as we enter the universe of social structures and the actions of men in society, both methods of work and the end product of scientific study must be considerably different. We pass from law and control to behavior and incentive. Precise quantification gives way to statistical sampling and grouping, to averages and indexes. Natural laws are superseded by interpretations of probabilities and trends— inevitably touched with the subjective qualities of both the observer and the observed.

The first feature that strikingly distinguishes the science (that is, the systematized knowledge) of human society from the science of nature is its much greater complexity and changeableness. The "behavior" of 16 million wage earners within the structure of their unions and under the incentives, frustrations, frictions, and pressures of their domestic, political, business, and cultural relations can never be predictable as can the "reactions" of sixteen million units of a chemical element or physical compound fed into a processing machine under given conditions of heat, pressure, electric force, or in the presence of a catalyst. The natural scientist can to a great extent, though not always fully, isolate that aspect of his problem on which he wishes to get basic and quantified knowledge. But isolating a single aspect of social behavior is not merely a methodological impossibility; it is a logical contradiction. No economic action can be read "out of context"—for us the infinitely complex social context of an institutionalized market and a representative government.

A second difference and major handicap of the social sciences concerns the matter of "controls." What we will tolerate, or what we seek in the social realm is utterly dissimilar or indeed contrary to what is permitted or sought in the natural realm. This applies both to methods of gaining knowledge and to methods of using it. The natural scientist is free to follow experimental methods in any way that his exploring mind suggests. The physicist may select specimens at will, subject this material to any degree of heat, pressure, or other treatment he likes, with no protest from the material and no disapproval from the public. The chemist may tear down molecules, bind atoms in new syntheses, or split atoms to their actual destruction or transmutation—and they can't talk back. The biologist may starve, overstimulate, sterilize, frustrate, vivisect, or even kill living experimental material. Some religious sects decline to participate and ardent dog lovers disapprove, but the law does not intervene nor society frown.

Without their laboratory controls and their guinea pigs, natural and biologic scientists feel utterly lost. But true "laboratory conditions" cannot be set up in the economic world, and "no guinea pigs" is a rule that from the start cramps the social scientist's methodology. What he learns he must get the hard way. He cannot select his human material, requisition it, put it under rigid controls of his own devising, and manipulate it as his problem requires. No, he must deal with the complex processes of social life "on the wing," studying unstandardized units in unstable and ever-changing combinations. Even if he arrives at findings that he is convinced have a reliable scientific basis, he can demonstrate them or apply them in practice only as the people who are the material of his science understand these findings and accept the ends which would be a "solution" of the problem as scientifically conceived.

While the social scientist cannot be as dogmatic as the natural scientist about what *will* happen, he can have illuminating and helpful insights as to what *may* happen, what may be brought about in the lives and associations of men who claim the divine right of freedom and who are endowed with the godlike attribute of judgment. The social scientist can make practical suggestions to his brethren in other walks of life as to how to promote conditions in society which they regard as desirable, how to avert the harmful, or adapt to the inevitable. He can contribute solutions to these problems only as he can persuade the minds of men.

If economic science is to make its maximum contribution to the shaping of practical policy in the free world we hope to preserve, we must show a lively realization that the economy is not a great automatic machine whose cogs mesh together in inexorable interaction. Economic life is a vital but ever-changing relationship among men and women. To produce a satisfactory national result, through the organized efforts of private business and government, we must honor people's aspirations, assuage their rebellions, ease their frustrations. We must fuse the dynamic spirit of competition and the no less dynamic spirit of co-operation. Both are inborn in the hearts of men. Both must be used in the great social process by which we organize our own productive energies to lay a broader and richer material foundation on which to erect the intellectual and spiritual superstructure of free America.[1]

In all this, those who shape policy must have scholarly understanding of the nature of the forces with which they are dealing in the economic world and of the principles according to which they work. As an old professor of mine used to say, "There is nothing so practical as a good theory"—that is, a generalization based on wide and precise observation rather than the limited personal experience and snap judgments of the "practical" man.

While every economist must be an analyst, a generalizer, a theorist, there is a wide range in the degree of generalization which

[1] A few of these sentences are drawn from my earlier book *The 1950's Come First.*

to one or another seems necessary, possible, or useful. Some economists aspire to get principles of economic action so broad in their
application as to give us a "general theory" that will cover all cases
and approximate the universality and perpetuity of a "natural
law." But the common denominator of what is true under such
widely differing circumstances and over such span of time is so
small as to make the statement trite as to any actual situation in
which workers and citizens want the diagnostic service of the economist. Most of our card-carrying members renounce the ambition to
build a pure science of economics abstracted from local or temporal
reality, and prefer to limit their generalizations about the economic
process to the behavior of specific groups of producers and consumers operating particular mechanisms—in the main those we now
have but find not altogether adequate. Insofar as they come to
understand what is actually going on in this limited universe, they
can speak with practical helpfulness about real shortcomings and
possibilities of improvement.

ECONOMIC FORCES

Science in general deals with the nature of basic forces which
operate within its particular field of interest, of what results these
forces produce, and how. These may be the cosmic force of the
astronomer; the force of light, heat, and mechanics with which the
physicist deals; or the inter-atomic and now intra-atomic forces
slowly being mastered by the chemist—in new partnership with the
physicist. They may be the force of cell growth, of hereditary continuity, or of environmental change that still baffle the biologist
and, in spite of that or because of it, keep him persistently hunting
for answers and means of control. To the psychologist science means
understanding of the human mind and the spiritual forces that
sometimes add up to genius or nobility and sometimes fall into such
disorder or defiance as to produce the maniac or the criminal.
Through knowledge gained, the scientist hopes that desired effects
may be brought about or undesired results be eliminated or
curtailed.

Economists have not been much disposed to draw up a formal list
of economic forces and to lay out a comprehensive plan under which
there would be an orderly and coherent division of labor among
members of the profession in studying them. It has become a popular

usage in recent years to talk of economic forces in terms of "propensities." Three such basic economic forces are man's propensity to
work or to produce, his propensity to consume—or just to acquire—
and his propensity to save. Each one of these propensities is a dual-
istic and at times even contradictory force.

The propensity to produce runs all the way from love of work for
its own sake—the "instinct of workmanship," "the grandstand play"
—through the strictly economic area of making a minimum of work
produce a maximum of product, on to the merely negative aspect
of avoiding work in every way one can and still "get by." In a free
society we cannot undertake to salvage this productive resource
through forced labor.[2] Instead of beating with a stick, we dangle a
carrot, seeking to galvanize propensity to work through the use of
incentives. Indeed incentives are of major significance at every level
of the working force, from common laborer to top executive. They
become the mechanism through which the propensity to work is
gauged and directed as a basic economic force.

Man's propensity to consume is obviously related to the older
phrase "insatiability of human wants," but it is not synonymous with
it. Some people are avid in their desire for more and better things
to eat, wear, play with, or just own. Others "have simple tastes" and
may even dislike being burdened with worldly goods. Still others
are soon cooled in their consumptive desires by the sacrifice necessary to acquire the means for their satisfaction. Long-run expans-
ibility of consumers' wants is no more significant economically than
short-run satiety. Natural limitations on the public's propensity to
consume are well attested by the emphasis given in the training of
commercial salesmen to "want creation" and by the derogatory
phrase "high-pressure selling."

Furthermore, there is some kind of psychological balance to be
struck between the propensity to consume and the propensity to
produce. In a really rich and productive country, all the people
some of the time and some of the people all the time arrive at the
point where what they want most to consume is leisure. Indeed a
considerable amount of leisure must be provided if they are to use

---

2 The Employment Act of 1946 saw this complex character of the propensity to
produce quite clearly. When some people voiced a captious or an honest fear that
the goal of "full employment" might mean a loss of personal freedom or lead to
involuntary servitude, drafters of the act defined the social purpose clearly and
simply as "employment opportunities for those able, willing, and seeking to work."

and enjoy their pleasure cars, television sets, parks and playgrounds, athletic equipment, and similar goods. And it is through the replacement of old and the expansion of new leisure-time goods that many employers make profits and many workers get jobs.

Completing the eternal triangle of our economic life is the propensity to save. It may be a provident instinct of taking care of oneself and one's dependents in the future. It may take a perverted and negative form in mere hoarding or become an economically constructive force as capital formation and well-calculated investment. But nominal investment may be distorted into ill-considered ventures or wasteful gambles.

These three basic economic forces or propensities—production, consumption, and saving-investment—are characteristic of a civilized society. But they by no means spontaneously fall into good working equilibrium, much less into optimum adjustment, one to another. We hear much of overproduction, underconsumption, and oversaving as causes of the unhealthy booms that lead to our recurrent depressions. We hear of underproduction, overconsumption, and overinvestment as leading to inflation. The great practical problem to which both private and public policies need to be scientifically directed is how to curb or prod consumers' desires and producers' activities, how to gauge saving and guide investment so that there shall be a ready market for all the goods produced, job opportunities for all who wish to work, and such a rate of advance in technology and improvement in equipment as will most fully exploit the economic resources at our command.

In a static economy or even during "normal" times—if such there are—in a dynamic world, the working out of such adjustments and securing the acquiescence or positive support of a myriad of individual free agents would be a difficult matter enough. In fact, modern man has never been permitted time to perfect a set of principles and practices that would adjust these economic forces scientifically to any particular set of economic circumstances. Public and private policy with reference to economic propensities is always relative to the times.

During most of the nineteenth century, it was good policy to hammer away on maxims in praise of diligence like "Early to bed, early to rise" and "The bookkeeper who stays at night to finish his work will be tomorrow's boss." Good practical policy too to hammer

away on maxims designed to strengthen the propensity to save—
from Benjamin Franklin to Samuel Smiles. "A penny saved is a
penny gained." "Thrift is the road to riches." Self-denial was ex-
tolled as a virtue in itself, in contrast to the "waste" of income "on
selfish indulgence." I remember as late as 1921 the applause with
which a business audience greeted the story of the banker who
would make a loan to a farmer only on condition that he leave at
the bank the four wheels of his automobile as collateral security.

In recent years, however, we have heard much more of the need
for full mechanization of farm no less than factory. As the nation
has progressed in wealth and productivity, we hear employers
preaching the economic soundness of high wages and a moderate
work week as conditions needed for dynamic balance of our highly
equipped and intensively organized industrial economy. Pressed by
the circumstances of war, reconversion, and post-Korean rearmament, we have been so assiduous at capital formation that, in the
years ahead—assuming that we escape World War III—the prime
concern of economic policy might quite possibly be to give freer
rein to the consumer propensity.

These are the very problems that disturb organized labor and
organized management as they meet at the collective bargaining
table or as they clamor for representation on the Wage Stabilization
Board or other defense agencies. Management feels a trustee's responsibility for the preservation and improvement of the capital
plant on which high and ever-rising productivity must rest. Union
representatives are the spokesmen superficially for the consumers'
Oliver Twist complex "More, More!" In a deeper sense, however,
they are the spokesmen for the fundamental requirement of a
healthy market, to wit, that there shall be current purchasing power
for all the consumer goods produced under conditions of full
employment.

The interrelations among basic economic forces must be carefully
studied also as we try to adjust policies for our national life to the
fact of our rise in recent decades to a position as the world's great
creditor nation. In particular, shall we work hard and effectively,
turn out a great product, and cash in on it only through rapidly
rising standards of living and ample capital formation at home?
Or shall we follow also a carefully-weighed policy of substantial gifts
and/or large investments abroad? Might our ineptitude at devising

practical programs for pursuing either of these courses in proper measure result in frustration of our own people's propensity to work? Stupidity or gross selfishness among policy makers, private and public, might produce a stagnation like that of the thirties. Then more government intervention might be resorted to to stimulate a faltering private business leadership. There might be an irresistible demand even to supersede private enterprise. There is anything but full agreement on how to implement the policy declaration for "maximum production, employment, and purchasing power" set forth in the Employment Act of 1946.

It becomes the central responsibility of the economist, the practical businessman, and the government administrator to judge when one or another economic force is, in the peculiar circumstances of the time, relatively overemphasized or underemphasized in the habits and philosophy of the people and how it is facilitated and encouraged by existing economic institutions or how it is impeded or discouraged by them. It is the task of social science both to detect and to measure these departures from an optimum relationship. It is the task of practical policy, private and public, to devise means of stimulating the lagging force and of restraining the one that is too active.

In this connection, it needs to be emphasized again that the great economic forces with which we deal do not operate in a vacuum or in a structure of Nature but through mechanisms of our own devising. It is only through study of how these mechanisms operate that we can arrive at valid judgments as to which need acceleration, which need retardation, and how they can be brought to a more steadily workable balance.

ECONOMIC MECHANISMS

All branches of science deal both with intangible forces and with tangible structures—the planets and stars; wheels, levers, and electronic devices; plant and animal bodies; or the brain, nervous system, and sense organs—through which these still mysterious forces operate. The economic scientist deals with intangible forces that make men tick in their individual efforts and their group activities. He deals also with the "social structures"—such as property, contract, the market, and government—through which these grouped-individual efforts to "make a living" are carried out.

Basic economic forces come to expression spontaneously in the behavior, in the demands and responses (under existing institutions), of the mass of the people. As economic sophistication proceeds, however, economic theorists or analysts (both professional and lay) begin perfectionist redesigning of old or inventive designing of new institutional mechanisms to harness these native economic propensities to do a better job.

It is clear that men did a good deal of trading before they formulated even the simplest principle of mutual exchange or conceived of money as a means of facilitating it. Men cannot carry on any but the most primitive productive work except as part of a group organization; but it was only in 1776 that Adam Smith set down a rationale of the "division of labor" and functional specialization. Even since that time we have been pretty slow in developing adequate understanding about the forces of economic competition and economic co-operation which we are trying to bring to mutual expression in the modern corporation, the trade union, and other mechanisms.

It is a matter of common knowledge and frequent comment that our economic mechanisms have been and are undergoing constant and rapid change. After the slow creep of status and habit over the centuries, the economic world has now entered an epoch of change no less sweeping than the revolution in mechanisms and technology which has been taking place in the processes of physical production. Changing concepts and laws of property right—tangible and intangible; the apparatus of progressive taxation as determining the distribution of wealth; the explosive growth from a few company pension plans to a ubiquitous pattern of social security, mostly governmental; the burgeoning of simple trade unions into a gigantic federation and an industrial "congress," with the "disaffiliation" of war lords and the intervention of government; the surge of money management and Federal credit agencies—these make up only a partial catalogue of new features introduced into our economic machinery largely within a period of four decades.

Economic theorists have done a great deal of work in recent years in the area of private business in analyzing the "economics of the firm." Of no less importance is the economics of the economy, that is the total economic process, which involves public as well as private institutions, practices, and policies. This is often hailed as a return to the "political economy" of an earlier day before the onrush of industrial development brought preoccupation with the business corporation, the labor union, and our rapidly evolving mercantile and financial institutions. Passage of the Employment Act not only constituted a formal recognition of the integral character of the economics of the economy, but also set up a specific machinery for dealing with this problem in the spirit of science, with the best tools that economic science can provide, and with trained scientific personnel.

WHEN IS POLICY PRACTICAL?

In what has been said thus far about scientific means of arriving at economic policy, there may have seemed to be a latent implication that such policy could or should be an idealistic picture drawn by the economist in an ivory tower. My title, however, is "Economic Science and Practical Policy." In closing this chapter, therefore, I turn briefly to the question: What is a "practical" national economic policy, and what is the relation of economic science to such a policy?

First, the economist as such is not the proper instrument for making actual policy for the nation[3]—or for the firm. Policy-making passes beyond the role of the economic scientist to that of someone who can best be called an "economic engineer." Scientists studying the economic process are tireless in their effort to understand the motives and responses of men in their business relations—not mankind, but the specially conditioned population of some particular economic universe, for instance present-day United States, middle-income consumers, or, more narrowly, union labor or professional corporation executives. Tireless they are too in seeking to learn how to measure the actual performance of the economic mechanisms with which these people work or through which these forces operate. But there is another type of man—less contemplative, more dynamic. He would keep touch with the scientific student but he would choose for himself the task of using the scientist's findings in the active process of operating our economic mechanisms or of building new ones. He is the economic engineer.

The partnership between the applied scientist and the engineer is close and indeed the line of demarcation is not always clear. The economic engineer employs the concepts, measurements, and tools supplied by economic scientists. With these aids he seeks to develop a better technology in the use of the economic machine. This technology is embodied in our economic policies and practices, public

[3] Compare pp. 413–14.

and private. The economic engineer and scientist seek at their top level to re-form technology as to both practice and structure. It seems an anomaly that the business world uses "reformers" as such a term of opprobrium when the same attitude and purpose on the part of the industrial scientist and engineer are awarded highest praise and support.

The economic scientist excludes from his consideration all factors that are noneconomic—aesthetic, ethical (except as it has a bearing on productive efficiency), "subjective," or broadly (and to a great extent quite properly) "political." The economic engineer, like the industrial engineer, must, to be competent, have a good basic training in science and technology. He must keep up to date as to scientific knowledge about the economic process. But his primary task is to decide what, in the light of current knowledge, is the course of action which will direct practices or modify structures in such a way as to promote economic stability and progress, taking into account such other factors of the human process as he or his employer thinks it desirable to have recognized.

As economics has been brought in recent years more actively into the service of private business—the corporation, the union, the financial institution, and the farm organization—posts of "economic adviser" have been manned, sometimes by one of these types of economists, sometimes by the other. Broadly speaking, the economist has been looked to as the applied scientist analyzing cause and result sequences or probabilities, or at most as "consulting engineer" with decision and implementation retained in the hands of professional executives. Likewise economists have come to be used as advisers to government executives. But the same distinction holds as between the technical adviser and the responsible executive.

Economic policy in the full sense must make choice among conflicting values and come to a synthetic judgment as to what is "best" in the total situation. A practical policy thus means a workable policy. The competent policy-maker must not only give technical advice but also must have fundamental understanding of and patience with the varied and often capricious human material with which he is dealing. He must also have a realistic appreciation of how present institutions have emerged as the machinery through which the economic process operates. But it is toward the present and the future rather than the past that our national policies must be beamed.

Thus practical economic policy must reflect a nice sense of balance between stability and progress. It must adjust its pace to the rate at which a society or group can assimilate social change. To be really workable or practical in the long run it must not make compromises with economic principles to serve some special purpose or selfish end. Certainly practical policy does not mean corruption or rationalization of economic principles in the cynical sense of *realpolitik.*

Establishment of a Council of Economic Advisers in the Executive Office of the President and a nonlegislative joint committee in the Congress raises the question of what kind of service economics could render toward improving the quality of national policy and what kind of economist could render the most useful service. The functional difference between the economic scientist and the economic engineer is important for our subsequent consideration of the operations of the President and the Congress, the Council of Economic Advisers and the Joint Economic Committee, and the staffs of the Council and the Joint Committee respectively, all working together to effectuate the sophisticated purposes envisaged in, or at least potential under, the Employment Act of 1946. Broadly speaking, I think we should have economic scientists in the Council posts and in the staffs of both Council and committee, economic engineers (of varying degrees of professional competence) in the person of the President and members of the Joint Committee, the real formulators of national policy. In general, Congress would be analogous to the executives and board of directors of the operating firm, which takes or modifies the action program of the engineer.

Obviously, these lines are blurred, particularly in the Congressional area, since Congress is itself the real maker of policies and programs, whereas the Joint Committee merely suggests or criticizes. The distinction, however, does hold with reference to the committee staff, Council staff, and the Council itself and it will be elaborated as the book proceeds. The term "engineer" may seem inept or strained in this connection since we habitually talk of people in these relationships not as engineers but as politicians. To my mind, however, it is helpful to use the concept of the engineer in approaching this question of the economic aspect and responsibilities of the politician's role. The succeeding chapter will consider the policy-making function further in terms of the more familiar usage—that is, "politician."

CHAPTER TWO

Economics and Politics

The previous chapter has dealt with economic science and practice at three levels, namely pure science, applied science, and engineering. In this chapter, I pass on—or, if you prefer, proceed downward—to the consideration of a fourth level under the title "Economics and Politics." First a word about the relationship between political science and practical politics.

THE PROFESSION OF POLITICS IS A CREATION OF DEMOCRACY

Political science deals with the legislative and administrative structures and functions of group life in whatever schemes of rule-making and rule-enforcement men devise and maintain. Broadly, these structures fall under two heads, autocracy and democracy. Autocracy tries to deal with the problem of government the easy way or by the short-cut method. In the dynastic monarchy it relies on hereditary power whose roots may run back to an allegedly divine origin and which has been strengthened by gaining control over revenues and a military force. In the revolutionary dictatorship, the "strong man" relies on violent seizure of power, on arbitrary choice of succession, on personal judgment or that of a small elite as the source of rules, and on police power as the means of rule-enforcement.

Democracy attacks the problem of government the hard way—that is, the most fundamental way. Instead of dividing society into two sharply differentiated classes, the rulers and the ruled, it seeks maximum participation by free and (so far as possible) qualified citizens in a flexible and (presumably) improving system of self-government. This system must rest upon rules acceptable to the majority and on

compliance by the minority. The natural restiveness of this minority
is assuaged by the knowledge that they have at their disposal every
peaceful means for changing a rule which in practice can be shown
to be ill-conceived or to have been outmoded by changing circumstances.

It is in this democratic system of government that politics becomes a regular full-time trade and has its opportunity for development into a learned and an honored profession. It also runs the
risk of sordid and destructive debasement.[1] In a democracy, the
profession of politics is itself an integral part of the process by which
rule-making and rule-enforcement is carried on. It provides the
distinctive means by which the rank and file of citizens can make
their thinking influential in the shaping of group policies and in
the adaptation of the institutional structure to the better realizing
of their aspirations.

Democracy, in choosing the long, hard road to a stable but not
static government of the people, by the people, for the people, starts
from two distinctive premises: (a) that the wishes, hopes, and fears
of all persons shall be given full and equal expression and consideration in the formulation of policies and the taking of action, and
(b) that the governing staff of both public and private bodies shall
be drawn from the whole reservoir of its human resources. The role
peculiar to the professional politician in a democracy is to nominate
himself from wherever he may happen to be born in that great
human mass; to sense its physical, intellectual, and spiritual needs;
to qualify himself to be the interpreter of these needs; and then
to secure the choice of himself to be the representative of these
other people.

THE ECONOMIC POLITICIAN AS SALESMAN OF POLICIES

The function of the economic politician is comparable to that of the
commercial salesman in our industrial world, with its basic reliance
on scientists and engineers.

At his best, the commercial salesman may use the methods of
science scrupulously and skillfully. With their aid he may learn
what are the needs or wants of consumers or users of the various

[1] Since man is by nature a political animal, there will, of course, be "palace
politics" under even the most autocratic system. But this is merely an incidental
avocation of persons whose prime business is to promulgate the general rules of
conduct or the particular directives of the ruler or the ruling group.

kinds of goods and equipment. He may likewise seek to understand and to expound fairly and effectively the scientific reasons why a given character or quantity of these goods and services will best serve the real needs of the potential consumer. He is the "honest broker" raised to the nth power.

On the other hand, the commercial salesman may debauch the vocabulary and even the methods of science to promote such transactions as give him the easiest, quickest, and largest personal gain, regardless of consequence either to the ultimate welfare of the buyer whom he persuades or the long-run prosperity of the industry which he is supposed to serve.

Similarly, the economic politician, as salesman of public policies or measures, at his best performs highly useful, indeed essential, functions. First, he may get sound and accurate knowledge of what our citizens in various categories want and/or need for achievement of the good life. Second, he may, conscientiously and with scientific understanding, help them to find out what means or mechanisms, public and private, are available to the gaining of these ends and how this social apparatus can be procured, installed, and operated.

On its highest plane the role of the economic politician may be ancillary to, if not co-ordinate with, that of the scholar—both teacher and research worker. He may, by being an accurate reporter and gauger of popular aspirations, quicken the economic engineer and the economic scientist to devise new mechanisms or improve old ones for serving these ends. He can contribute important concrete materials both for the inspiration and the testing of the scholar's theories, and he will make experimental uses of their product which will demonstrate its actual usefulness or show its limitations. He may, by becoming an expert popularizer of somewhat abstruse economic principles, help the plain citizen to play his part in our enterprise system with better responses and fewer frustrations.

At his worst, the economic politician may whip up or distort the demands and expectations of the public or the members of his particular group for economic results that are unsound or unattainable. He may enlarge the market for economic nostrums and encourage the belief in spurious, disappointing, and even harmful economic wares. He may, like the unscrupulous promoter, use a superficially scientific patter and pseudo-scientific "evidence" to secure a following. All this he does to the end of personal aggran-

dizement rather than conscientious and expert service to his constituents or to the economy.

Economic politics may be divided horizontally into good politics and
bad politics. It seems strange that we have coined so few phrases
to describe good politics. As to bad politics, a dozen epithets almost
at once occur to the mind—cheap, corrupt, peanut, or dirty politics;
ward, machine, or logrolling politics; partisan, racial, or sectional
politics; and so on. For good politics, on the other hand, we rely on
a single word—"statesmanship."

Through the terms of derogation run three notes: (1) dishonesty,
(2) craftiness, (3) narrowness. For the purpose of this discussion we
can discard the issue between honesty and dishonesty. We are all
against sin. But as to craftiness and narrowness, the issues are not
so simple. It will pay us to look a little further into these words and
the qualities they describe.

To be crafty means literally to be skillful in the practice of a
craft. The word is used today largely to describe human relationships, and its meaning has been debased till we think of the crafty
man as one who is sly and cunning. The line is fine, however, between these qualities and the shrewdness that comprehends the
nuances of human behavior and deals skillfully, artfully, or craftily
with people as we find them. Certainly we are not against political
and economic sophistication among those who ply the craft or profession of leaders of men. This is an important role, which requires
technical competence and is no place for the politically and economically naïve. Democracy demands political functionaries whose
art of statecraft includes the skillful leadership of run-of-mine voters
and qualities of shrewd judgment and astute evaluation of how far
they can be led, how fast they can be educated, and what lines of
argument will appeal to their better qualities or anesthetize their
selfish or venal intentions.

A somewhat similar discrimination must be made with reference
to the matter of desirable breadth or narrowness on the part of the
economic politician. It is easy to dismiss the matter by saying that
we want utmost breadth of view and purpose. But the expansive
outlook and diffuse interest of the utopian reformer are just as bad
in their way as the narrowness of the special-interest partisan. The

optimum for the economic politician is that he shall be focused down to an intensive familiarity with local, specialized, and personal situations that need to be taken into account in synthesizing total policy. That does not mean that he shall become the attorney for these interests, whatever they may be. On the contrary, he should have the broad objectivity that enables him to weight these constituent issues, to subordinate them properly to over-all considerations, and even compensate for these particular biases and resistances in the legislation through which our economic mechanisms are shaped.[2]

Statesman is the antonym for demagogue. A statesman is a man whose outlook is as broad as the state and whose concern is for the general welfare, not personal nor partisan gain. The demagogue's concern is as narrow as the interests of his particular clients or indeed his own personal advantage, if only he can persuade some group to advance it even at their own loss. Etymologically, demagogue means "leader of the people" but, through bad association, it has come to mean an "orator upholding a popular faction" or "a popular leader who plays on the passions, prejudices, or ignorance of the populace to further his own interests." Finally, the dictionary defines the demagogue as an "unprincipled agitator." Note in these several definitions the emphasis on oratorical equipment and reliance on "the populace"—common people, inferiors.

Even the best economic politician may have to be a bit of a demagogue to win his chance to be a statesman. He may have to use all his forensic powers to attract and hold a local following, persuading these people that what is good for the country is good for them. This he must do without being either cynical or supercilious. The technologically competent servant of the people must display a sense of concern for the less richly endowed majority. He is animated by a desire to see how fine a social product can be created from the available raw material. Such is the "sense of workmanship" or political artistry in this particular field, comparable to what we find in physical technology.

As to this opprobrious term "agitator," the economic politician operates at the front lines where the destinies of our economic system are being determined, not in a library, a study, or an ivory tower, where finespun theories are being adumbrated. I have referred to

2 A vivid illustration of this issue is to be found in the cynical aphorism of the late nineteenth century, "The tariff is a local issue."

the definition of the demagogue as an "unprincipled" agitator. The statesman, on the other hand, can properly and should as a matter of duty be a principled agitator. That is to say, with the best mastery of economic principles he can gain, he should consistently agitate for their acceptance by the mass of voters and their embodiment in legislation by the voters' representatives. It was principled agitators like Cobden, Peel, and Pitt, who secured the repeal of the Corn Laws and passage of the Factory Acts in England. It took principled agitators in our own country to get laws to restrict child labor, to safeguard competition, and to pioneer in social security legislation. The principled agitator as economic statesman seeks popular support for means of promoting a total good in which he, his fellows, and his children will continuously share.

As agitator for progress, the economic statesman must have a fine "time sense" and be patient withal. While eager to advance the tempo at which the average voter gains understanding of, and is willing to support, sound economic policies, he must be a patient as well as a diligent gardener waiting for the bud to unfold and the fruit to ripen.

THE POLITICIAN AS ECONOMIC NEGOTIATOR

Here we strike one of the most subtle and most persistent problems in the laboratory of democracy. Progress or even social stability demands that the ranks of professional politicians be filled from the cream, not the dregs, of the total population. How then shall we bring about the acceptance of a statesman as a legislative representative by men who are themselves economic illiterates, many of whom are willing to live by the practice of business mayhem? A partial answer is that we must continue to rely on the ubiquitous school and the militant church to lessen consumer resistance to high-quality political wares. Beyond that, we who think we are better equipped than the average voter, must honor and reward in tenure the economic politician who shows patience, sagacity, astuteness in the practice of his craft of human leadership. And, finally, the professional politician must give the voting mass a justifiable feeling that their needs or desires have been both understood and taken into account in the process of actual legislation. Democracy must rely upon the politician-statesman to find practical settlements which will incorporate as much as possible of good social economics and still gain the acceptance—even if grudging—of the not inconsiderable number who are primarily motivated by a craving for short-run acquisitive advantage—the "gimme spirit."

Infinite patience and warm tolerance must be manifested by the economic politician in the discharge of his legislative and administrative duties. He cannot hold out for a rigid formula of what he is convinced the country ought to want, however high his ideals or however great his competence for judging what would in fact be good public policy. He cannot ignore what his constituents deeply feel they must have, even if in his better trained judgment it would be bad for the country or even bad for them. And he must give equal consideration to the demands and the reasons advanced by the representatives of all other constituencies. It is a common saying among the more philosophically conditioned members of Congress that in our legislative process one cannot hope to achieve the answer that is "right" or really good. Legislators can aspire only to achieve what is "the least bad." In this process it is necessary that the economic politician show himself to be a shrewd and able negotiator, conceding nonessentials to gain or protect basic principles, yielding where he must, cutting his losses, living to fight another day.

The economist who yearns to make economics as exact as a natural science or to find social laws as capable of quantification and of as great predictive value as natural laws, makes models of the economy which aspire to make it work with the mechanical perfection of an automatic machine. To do this he abstracts from reality by starting from an impressive array of arbitrary and simplified assumptions. But human behavior neither recognizes these assumptions nor obeys laws based upon them. Hence the economic engineer and the economic politician, without losing the value of this rigorously logical analysis must find some way either to curb these behavioristic deviations or to utilize, harmonize, and guide them. Two answers are being proposed. One is negotiation. Of that we have spoken. The other is "planning."

The technique of the economic politician grown statesman will seem, it must be admitted, a somewhat "messy" process from the view of the natural scientist and physical engineer in their tractable world. And many a social scientist and social engineer wish they could tidy up their job to a like extent. Although tolerant of the ignorance and selfishness of his constituents, the economic politician is shrewd and sagacious in finding workable but also basically sound compromises among rival claims and pressures. He may, however, find himself tempted by the escapist philosophy of "economic planning."

In seeking to recruit our economic politicians from the cream of the population we must not fall into a particular form of "the aristocratic fallacy" which has had many proponents among us in recent years. It is a blend of "do-goodism" and intellectual arrogance. Science is by its very nature an aristocracy of brains. But men sometimes become so "brainy" that they show a rather patronizing attitude toward ordinary folk and would presume to do their thinking and decide their values for them.

Of course we all want planfulness in our national economic affairs and the several parts of our institutional structure consistently related one to another. But this is something very different from fixing goals and values. I see no justification for the belief that there is some objective concept and formulation of "the common good" which has validity. Instead, there can be an infinite variety of subjective views. They amount to no more than saying, "This is the kind of economic world that I would like to live in, that would best fit my criteria of workability and my standards of right, beauty, or fitness which must not be subordinated to sheer economic efficiency." Plan economy at its worst becomes autocracy. That of course is "out of bounds" for this discussion. Even at its best, as "democratic planning," it starts from the idea that central government has or can gain a clear and acceptable concept of "the common good" as something which can be formulated, dated, reduced to an operating program, and effectuated by politically chosen administrators.

The concept of the politician-statesman as economic negotiator rather than as planner of a centrally rationalized economic system has its counterpart in the philosophy of collective bargaining, which by many is looked to as the road to peaceful progress in the world of private business. If space permitted, we could trace out the increasing service of the economic scientist, the economic engineer, and the economic politician or negotiator in that large area where spokesmen for management and spokesmen for labor hammer out policies and actions that go far toward determining the success or failure of our modern economy. If we are to achieve economic stabilization under free enterprise, this adjustment apparatus of the private market must be perfected just as truly as statesmanship must be achieved in the world of governmental politics.

It seems to me encouraging therefore to find someone who has been a leader in this process giving an expression of belief that the broader viewpoint and the more fundamental principles that give a scientific foundation to practical business relations is coming to wider acceptance. Speaking before the Society for the Advancement of Management, the vice president of one of our leading industrial companies said:

I am assuming that we here tonight are interested in reaching conclusions only as to what is the sound economics, and not as to what is the expedient politics, involved in the wage stabilization question. I take it that none of us is running for office at the moment, and that we are willing to leave to the politicians any compromises with the truth they feel is necessary in the face of what they believe to be the lack of information or lack of character on the part of the *majority* of our citizens.

Incidentally, I don't believe good economics and good politics are anything like as far apart as some presumed leaders apparently continue to think. I believe the public has already ferreted out for itself the major fallacies in the something-for-nothing school of economics and politics. I am confident the public is more than ready to accept and act on *more* of the truth as to what we should all do—no matter to what degree that further truth is unpleasant or runs counter to the easy preachings of the last few years.[3]

We shall always have politics as a major factor in our economic process so long as we have free economic enterprise and free representative government. But the question is: "Shall we have blind leaders of the blind?"—venal leaders of a rapacious clientele? Or shall we have intelligent spokesmen for the common man and well trained and courageous analyzers of the economic process for their constituents—who must be educated or persuaded if progress is to be made.

As will appear more fully as this book proceeds, it is my belief that the Employment Act of 1946 took a significant step forward by institutionalizing a channel of communication through which the conscientious and scientifically oriented political functionary can draw upon the intellectual resources of the realistic economic scien-

[3] L. R. Boulware (vice-president, General Electric Co.), "Wage Stabilization and Inflation," *Employee Relations News Supplement,* Jan. 9, 1951.

tist and the technician of applied economics can project his labors forward into the action realm of the nation's economic life. We need to have economic scientist, economic engineer, and economic politician teamed in conscientious joint enterprise to find ways by which we can live and work together most harmoniously and most productively in free association.[4]

[4] In this chapter, the chapter which precedes, and the first part of the chapter which follows I have drawn freely on material presented at the University of North Carolina as the Weil Lectures in February 1951.

CHAPTER THREE

Economic Enterprise and National Planning

In our opening chapter, we talked of economic forces in terms of three "propensities" of economic man and the mechanisms through which these forces may most productively be directed. Nothing was said of "the spirit of enterprise," which sometimes is thought of as the master force of economic life in free countries. Nor was much said about the agencies of government as economic mechanisms which, in civilized times, have always played at least a conditioning and sometimes a very active role. The real value and the desirable limitations of this government role have been brought under recurrent if not constant review. They were major issues in connection with the New Deal and will be major problems of the new Administration if it is confronted with a depression threat or as it undertakes, under whatever conditions, to carry out the declared policy of the Employment Act.

This act makes a vigorous reaffirmation of the principle of "free competitive enterprise" and, at the same time, a positive declaration of enlarged Federal responsibility in the economic sphere. Hence this chapter will undertake a brief restatement of the problem of economic forces and mechanisms in terms of the concept of economic enterprise. This discussion will deal with "enterprise" not merely as a global activating or regulating force in economic life but will differentiate its two hemispheres, one of which can properly be called private business enterprise and the other, no less properly, public enterprise.

THE "SPIRIT OF ENTERPRISE"

Business enterprise has generally been identified with proprietorship or the managerial function. As such it connotes not only the diligence of the productive worker but, still more, the ambition, the planning ability, and the daring of the man who feels competent to organize a working group and to direct its labor and the marketing of its product. This of course means that he is magnifying his chances of gain but also is taking on himself additional risks. The pattern of small independent proprietorship survives in vigorous form in the family farm and the small store and shop of the merchant and mechanic. But modern commercial, industrial, and financial development has caused the individual proprietor to be superseded over wide areas by the corporate organization, attaining at times a size of billions of dollars of assets and hundreds of thousands of employees. This development has been accompanied by important emancipations and frustrations of the spirit of enterprise as it motivates the actions and determines the rewards of a large part of our population.

The advent of modern industrialism and the coming of the corporation opened the door of opportunity to the creative and ambitious individual. The principle of limited liability enabled him to break the bonds of his own capital and credit limitations and to become the administrator of other people's money. Modern technology opened the door for more productive use both of other people's money and of other people's labor. These developments, taken together, multiplied the scope and power of the profit motive in the hands of the aggressive promoter as never before.

Thus the first epoch of modern industrialism witnessed great growth in personal power and personal wealth for an able and daring group. There was a sort of elephantiasis of individual business enterprise that gave us the "tycoon," the "captain of industry," the industrial Napoleon. These upstarts were able to gratify a love of money and/or power to a degree undreamed of before by anyone not "born to the purple."

Along with the public benefits of this private enterprise there were popular resentments against the pre-emption of natural resources, monopolistic tactics in the market, and the "exploitation" of labor. We are still far from having come to general agreement as to how we can suitably protect and reward capital savers and capital managers respectively and yet ensure the optimum progress in technology and proper recognition of the needs and rights of workers and consumers.

By the time the Industrial Revolution rounded out its first century of progress, we had concluded that business enterprise could be too free. As private capitalism developed the industrial, commercial, and financial corporation as its major mechanism, the public, jealous of its rights, proposed many a curb as it felt that its interests were being prejudiced. It tightened the loopholes in laws that had been quite adequate to control small proprietorship. From the Interstate Commerce Commission Act of 1887 and the Sherman Antitrust Act of 1890 through "trust-busting Teddy" and scholarly Wilson to the present time, there has been a reinterpretation of capitalist-manager enterprise and re-examination of the institutions and practices through which we hope to keep its dynamism and avoid its abuses. The verdict has not been that the large corporation must be destroyed, taken over by the state, or put under rigid control. General standards have been laid down for quality of product or service and for business practices, but wide latitude has been left for innovation and for growth.

But what is equally important is that, besides sharp challenge from the outside, there has also been self-examination from the inside. Company managers have been using the tools of analysis to see just how corporations, big and little, actually function in organizing the use of resources, natural or human, and what is the impact of their policies and practices on the economy as a whole. Even before the modern corporation comes to maximum size for operative efficiency, it is brought by public prodding or the searching of its own experience to a realization that the very nature of its being calls for high standards of performance and a large measure of public service, not maximum short-run acquisition by either its owners or its managers. The large corporation has become a semipublic institution, not merely a personal venture. For such an institution to be permanently successful, it must formulate and follow enlightened policies not only in the technological and managerial sense but also as to its administration of the stream of wealth that flows through its hands, that is, price policies, wage policies, investment policies, and dividend policies.

In the old theory of capitalistic enterprise, it was held that the entrepreneur should use his bargaining power fully to push prices as high as possible and costs of labor, materials, and equipment as low as possible so that his capital would grow at the maximum rate. The practice of this theory accelerated capital formation in the hands of entrepreneurs, to be plowed back into existing companies or used to launch new ones. It resulted also in the amassing of great private fortunes. The newer theory of managerial enterprise is focused much less on acquisitions of great personal wealth in the hands of strategically placed capitalists. It is concerned rather with developing a system of private economic administration in which professional corporate managers see to it that the process of wealth creation and distribution shall go on steadily because the system is directed both with scientific skill and with a high sense of responsibility for the efficient continuation of the process of production and sale.

The spirit of enterprise of these professional administrators is gratified by a sense of technical achievement, by social prestige, and by places in the top bracket of professional salaries. The mechanics of corporate management permit them pretty much to write their own salary ticket, and they are not inclined to be modest as to the value of their services in top administrative posts. But the amount of the total product which is drawn into their hands under current practices is small indeed compared with the amounts acquired by the proprietary or promotional entrepreneurs of the nineteenth century. Both their salaries and the profits that they succeed in making for the company are subject to high levies as a source of tax revenue.

Under both the older proprietary theory and the newer professional-salaried theory of capitalist enterprise, the country enjoyed rapid economic progress from the Civil War to World War I or indeed until the decade of the thirties. This in spite of interruptions from time to time by frequent mild and occasional severe periods of depression and unemployment. Capitalist business leaders had full confidence in their own ability to achieve brilliant success not merely for themselves but for the economy and, by and large, workers and consumers were ready to "go along" in spite of minor socialist or other utopian grumblings. But when, after the collapse of 1929, we failed to get the quick recovery that we had enjoyed after all previous depressions, three new notes were struck in American thinking.

(1) Businessmen rushed to Washington to invoke the aid of government, apparently ready to admit that the forces with which they were then contending were too great for even the largest and most capable private management. (See p. 56.)

(2) Reinforcing this pressure was a demand on the part of labor and the public that some way be found for getting the economy back into vigorous operation through public enterprise if private capitalist and managerial leadership had faltered or had been outgrown. One theory was that private enterprise is adequate only to the pioneer or adolescent country, that we had now attained economic "maturity" and that, from this time forward, responsibility must shift in larger measure to the central government for the maintenance of prosperity and progress, with private management held accountable only for operative efficiency.

(3) At this time also there was explicit expression and wide popular acceptance of the doctrine that it was no longer necessary for us to have recurrent periods of slack production and low consumption. The people and the times demanded that we so modify our institutions and practices as to permit or indeed assure the continuous employment of the whole working population and capital equipment. This demand was eventually expressed in tempered form in the Employment Act of 1946. If we are to accomplish the purpose of the act, we shall need to give both opportunity and incentive to all the parties to the economic process.

THE PARTNERSHIP OF PRIVATE BUSINESS ENTERPRISE

In the early days of the Industrial Revolution, the disappearance of many small proprietorships and the increase in the number of hired workers led to the charge—with much justice—that their enterprise was being extinguished or superseded by "wage slavery." History, however, has amply demonstrated that the spirit of enterprise does not die that easily among the national or racial strains that have gone into the melting pot of industrial America. We think of freedom of economic choice, private property rights, and the profit motive as the major economic forces that animated the small proprietor and that have carried over into corporate business, large and small. As many erstwhile small proprietors (and yeoman farmers) found themselves recast in the role of wage workers, they found ways of reasserting these tenets of free enterprise.

Looking at the matter comparatively, it is easy to see similarities between the enterprise of the employer and that of the employee. Proprietary enterprise demands freedom to enter any line of production or trade which looks most promising and to pursue it by methods that produce the most profitable output. It demands the right to buy materials in the cheapest market and sell products wherever buyers are most numerous and affluent. It demands the right of ownership in intangible as well as tangible property acquired or created in the process. In this freedom to seek business opportunity and to retain the fruits of his labor and acumen, the proprietor is animated by the profit motive.

This has a fair counterpart in the motivation of the worker. As the proportion of proprietors has shrunk and the ranks of factory, store, and office workers have grown, the individuals have not been content merely to preserve their freedom of choice in shifting from one kind of employment to another or of improving their position in the labor group as they advanced in training or education. Beyond this, they have preserved, retained, or revived the spirit of economic enterprise in their ranks in three distinctive ways: (1) through effectuating a claim to as large a share as possible of such increased productivity as commercial and industrial progress brings about; (2) by asserting their right of "belonging" to the economic process in the productive and directional sense rather than being mere cogs in the industrial machine or accepting the theory that "labor is a commodity"; (3) more recently, by acquiring something of a capitalist role of their own and thus resuming a proprietary position and the functions of economic enterprise in the more conventional sense.

To say that "they," the labor group, have done all this means, of course, that leadership individuals amongst them have, in varying degrees, done so. From local union officers or even active members, up to the presidents of the great union federations, these leaders of the group express a spirit of business enterprise from the employee side, even as the corporate hierarchy of big and little managers express it from the employer side. The spirit of business enterprise on the proprietary side has manifested itself in the building of corporations, in effecting mergers, and in developing intercorporate relationships of subsidiaries, affiliates, and less permanent contract relations. A similar spirit of enterprise among workers led to the organization of unions, the development of bargaining methods, the elaboration of wage structures, working rules, and seniority rights. These have been the mechanisms through which the worker's spirit of enterprise has continued to find expression in an economic society in which the avenue of proprietorship was closed to him.

As to bargaining for wages (and better working conditions), the unions first nibbled at such small gains as they could get with their limited power. Now they have moved on to greater strength and larger claims and have pressed the principle of "ability to pay" to the point where, if fully successful, they would become in fact the "residual claimant" to profits as such. In the matter of management, they have at times established working rules which in effect invoke product restriction as a distributive principle. On the other hand, they have at times made themselves a factor toward better productivity (as in the garment trades) and have made claims that if they were allowed to participate on a freer basis in the laying out and conduct of productive operations they could increase production importantly. This would be in part because of their intimate knowledge of operative conditions and in part because of a latent productivity that would be released by this incentive—to the advantage of both parties. Such recognition of the worker's spirit of enterprise is to a degree recognized in practice through opportunities for promotion to foremanship or even executive position and to a limited but increasing extent through financial rewards to "employee suggestions." But, in general, management looks on this ferment of employee enterprise as "an invasion of the prerogatives of management."

It should be recognized, however, that labor is actually participating in management every time it collectively bargains a wage contract. It asserts its power against the authority of management and on behalf of its own spirit of enterprise. At times it forces the employer to introduce more efficient management to recoup the cost of a wage advance. At times its raising of labor cost constrains him to recoup by adjusting his prices or by curtailing the capital formation that resides in his profit margin. When unions bargain for security provisions, working rules, or an annual wage, their participation in business management is even more marked. The question is, will they show capacity to use this power in such ways as to contribute to economic progress? Or will they use it so blindly or stupidly as to impair the employer's ability to give jobs?

The third way in which we noted that workers gain an avenue for the expression of their business enterprise is by acquiring enough capital within their own treasury so that the labor organization as such becomes a business enterprise in the more conventional sense. Familiar illustrations are the entrance of unions into the banking business, the ownership of office buildings, or occasionally of productive plants. Union accumulations were first referred to as their "war chest" to finance strikes. But as the exchequer grows and strikes are avoided, the union finds itself with a generous reserve or endowment fund which needs to be invested. As pension funds under union control (such as the United Mine Workers') grow to large proportions, so do the possibilities that the union may acquire a capital stake as well as a labor stake in the business in which it is employed or in some other. Only a few months ago the newspapers reported the incident of employees of a butcher-shop chain using their accumulated pension fund to acquire ownership of the corporation.

Finally, organized labor today is demanding not only a voice in private management but also a voice in public policy-making. The worker's spirit of economic enterprise, of "belonging" not only to the company but to the economy and of being entitled to an active voice in its direction comes to its largest expression in the demand for labor representation in state or Federal administrative agencies and on national policy-making boards or commissions. This claim has now received considerable recognition in both peace and war agencies. The former president of a national craft union sits today in the President's Cabinet.

In fact, it is often said that we have now developed a system of laboristic capitalism, in which government as well as management must respond to the demands of organized labor. It has not been alone in response to labor dictation but also to broad public sentiment that government has been so active in recent decades in establishing health and safety requirements, limitations in women's and children's labor, the eight-hour day, and the minimum wage. Management, labor, and government all have made their contribution to the growth of our present still-inchoate system of social security, and new frontiers of discussion and action have been opened up in terms of "the annual wage" and government-guaranteed "full employment." Management has by no means seen its way clear to bring the annual wage into its private practices. Nor did the 79th Congress see its way clear to write a commitment of full employment into Federal law. These are the growth frontiers which we must still explore in trying to find ways in which, under modern technological conditions and financial institutions, the enterprise of the whole people—that is, their desire to apply their labor with high efficiency to the satisfaction of their wants—can be realized.

This involves not merely an understanding and peaceful partnership between capital and labor, employer and employee, giant corporation and massive union. It involves also the relation between the co-ordinated partners of private enterprise and the government as a parallel or complementary agency through which national resources, labor, and capital may be efficiently employed in rendering services and in facilitating the production of goods for our people. While the expression "public enterprise" has not come into any such general usage as has "private enterprise," it is in fact a logically co-ordinate aspect of free economic enterprise.

ECONOMIC ENTERPRISE OF THE CITIZEN

When we have gloried that America is the land of the free enterpriser and the home of the businessman brave enough to take capital risks, we have not claimed that government had no part in the economic process. *Laissez faire* meant that the proprietor, the worker, the saver, and the consumer should be let alone to make their business choices within a structure—of security and often of aid—provided by the state. Government was looked to to protect the economic man against conquest from without and violence from within, to provide a sound and adequate currency, an equitable legal structure, and various consumer facilities such as post offices and public roads, harbors and lighthouses, statistical information, and commercial standards.

By and large, it has been our national and state policy to allow the private enterprise of property owners and workers to organize itself freely for the actual production of practically all goods and most services. Such regulation of private business practices as has been undertaken was designed to prevent fraud or undue restraint of others' enterprise, not to stifle individual initiative or choice.

Though, generally speaking, we have given the individual and the privately organized group the first chance to perform a given economic service and to reap its gains, this doctrine has not been followed to ideological extremes. When it has become clear that private resources were insufficient or private venturesomeness too feeble or the terms of private trade incompatible with social need, we have quite freely invoked community organization, state activity, or Federal aid or outright operation. Sometimes—as in the carrying of the mail—the people have prejudged the case and launched a public agency without giving much opportunity for private business to show what it could do. Sometimes, on the other hand, the public has put up with poor service because of a feeling that the field should, as a matter of principle, be left to private exploitation.

In a surprisingly large number of economic functions we have organized along parallel lines of private and public activity. We have accelerated or checked the expansion of postal, highway, education, health, power, forest, and amusement services as local and temporary circumstances seemed to require. It is nonsense to say that we have had any consistent or rational policy or economic or social theory in these matters. We have been opportunists trying to get something done, and to *preserve freedom of action of the citizen as well as the business enterpriser* in the process of getting it done.[1]

Two familiar cases are quite adequate to illustrate the point. From Colonial times forward, we have had a lively realization that providing every child a good opportunity to develop his abilities and talents for productive work and to prepare himself for citizenship was essential to the soundness and the progress of the country. From "the little red schoolhouse" to the superb "consolidated schools" of today, we have gone on to make public education free up to high school commencement day. And state colleges and universities make advanced general, technical, and professional training available on a low-cost subsidized basis up to the top limit of formal education. But have private schools, parochial schools, academies, seminaries, institutes, and endowed colleges been liquidated or denied the right to be born and live? Everyone knows

[1] Edwin G. Nourse, "Public Administration and Economic Stabilization," *Public Administration Review*, Spring 1947, vol. vii, No. 2, p. 85.

better. Though many a youngster has even learned to fox trot or rhumba in a public school or college, the private enterprise of Arthur Murray—and many a lesser dancing master—is doing all right. A boy can learn a trade or a girl can take a secretarial course in a public high school. But thousands of trade schools and "business colleges" flourish from Portland, Maine to Portland, Oregon. The stream of free competitive enterprise flows strongly and harmoniously through both public and private channels.

My second illustration comes closer home to the businessman. He may not think of education as a very important field for business exploitation, and may be well satisfied that government is taking major responsibility for giving basic training to the labor force that the employer draws upon. But how about transportation? Government always has carried responsibility for a system of military roads, depots, and transport suitable to the time. But, beyond any potential military need, we have always expected government to supplement private enterprise in seeing to it that there was a local and national system of highways, railways, waterways, and now airways that gave private producers and traders quick and adequate means of moving materials, personnel, and product.

If, to cite a single case, we had not shown the public enterprise, as the automobile age burst upon us, to push the whole country over from dirt and gravel to concrete, growth of the automobile industry—and the vast industrial structure that depends upon it—would have been stunted. County road commissioners had to give way to State Highway Commissions. A Federal agency had to coordinate a national system of primary highways and, at strategic places, super channels or freeways. Uncle Sam put many millions into overhead cost and aid to states. States and even counties spent as they had never spent before and bonded themselves, often to the legal limit. That's "deficit spending" in any man's language.

In spite of local mistakes, wastes, or even abuses in the rush of this big economic development, I think we all agree in retrospect that it was good business all around. Government did not "invade" the transportation business. It played a necessary "facilitating" role but did not get into the operative field. The roads were built by private contractors, and their orders made profitable business for cement and steel mills, machinery manufacturers, and many others. As the roads were made available, bus and truck companies arose and flourished, the farmer's marketing problems and costs were eased, and the whole manufacturing and distributing system benefited.

As the twentieth century has unfolded, problems of the proper or desirable role of government and particularly the Federal government, in economic areas have increased in number and become more controversial in character. In the early years of the century the issue of government action or "control" centered largely around questions of the conservation of natural resources. To this issue, which still plagues us, have been added the complications of our participation in wars of world-wide scope and our precipitation into a depression of great depth and greater persistence than we had previously experienced. And while these developments were taking place, we were passing from a largely automatic money-credit system with a gold standard and an almost free banking business over to a central bank organization and "managed money." Finally came active espousal of a national policy of sustained "full employment," though it remains to be seen whether this concept is to be interpreted fantastically or realistically.

All five of these challenges to more aggressive governmental action have become mutually involved in complex ways. The strain of war involves the question of adequacy of resources and policies for their conservation or development, particularly the provision of plant capacity. Both war and depression tempt, if they do not actually require, more active participation by government in financing, in risk-taking, or even in the actual provision of facilities. Full employment as a social goal tends to run beyond the risk-taking propensities of private enterprisers.

Public concern about conservation led to extensive withdrawal—particularly by Theodore Roosevelt—of forest lands from private ownership and to an active program of fire prevention and reforestation on government lands or on private lands in co-operation with the government. Both the reclamation of arid lands and the desire to accelerate the development of hydroelectric power and to prevent its monopolization led to a program of dam-building which was both ambitious and costly according to previous standards of Federal public works. These developments inevitably were involved with transportation problems and revived the perennial public interest in "cheap" water transportation.

The depression of the thirties provided an effective link between (1) those who wanted to see all types of resource development aggressively pushed, (2) those who wanted to have government leadership or direction of soil conservation, forest preservation, water transportation, public power, and the protection of wildlife "integrated" into a single government program, and (3) those who felt that the recurrence of deep depression demanded that the Federal government take a new or at least more decisive role of public entrepreneurship. Thus the Tennessee Valley Authority was born as a comprehensive government plan of integrated leadership in dealing with the whole congeries of problems of co-ordinated economic production as part of a bold action program for leading the country out of depression.

This is not the place to analyze the sweeping ramifications and implications of the TVA development or of subsequent proposals of like but larger scope for the Columbia River valley and the Missouri River valley. By some enthusiasts this kind of development was intellectually projected to include the smaller as well as the greater river valleys down to the Kennebec and the Penobscot. Since all our land drains into some river system, the logical end of this road would be an integrated or planned administration of the economic resources of the whole country under a series of Federal Valley Authorities which would be superimposed upon or even supersede municipal, state, and even Federal authorities as we have known them.

Whatever the future may hold as to any such recasting of the politico-economic structure and practices of the United States, the TVA serves admirably for the purposes of this book to illustrate the issues as to the scope of public enterprise and its relation to private enterprise and the several types of "action programs" that the government has been pressed into by the demand of the people under stress of war or depression during recent years. The conservation and development of natural resources is linked with the problem of public works. The magnitude and timing of public works is in turn linked with the problem of business cycles and the possibility that government activities could become a significant or even decisive factor in promoting the recovery of general business. That raises the problem of how public spending is to be financed. The question of how much money we undertake to channel from

private pockets and corporate treasuries into the public coffers and
out again to create facilities and services of general usefulness links
in turn to the question of fiscal policy, public debt, and the reinterpretation of private property rights. Our ideas of the most
desirable interplay of public and private enterprise have been very
much in flux for the last twenty years.

FREE ENTERPRISE AND ECONOMIC PLANNING

Undoubtedly the frustration of millions of people, able, willing,
and seeking to work during the early thirties heightened popular
dissatisfaction with our "mixed system" of predominantly private
business enterprise and complementary public enterprise as it was
working out. There was deep resentment about "the planlessness"
of a situation that had allowed the country to come to such a state
of demoralization. There was a demand that some top leadership
come forward with a comprehensive plan for getting things going
again—and so they would stay going. Thinking along these lines
had in fact been going on abroad as well as at home for almost two
decades before the depression of the thirties broke upon us. It had
developed under the name "economic planning" or, more ambi-
tiously, economic and social planning.

The general idea had two phases. One was simply the better application of constantly improving methods of statistics, accounting, and
economic analysis to any and every business operation. In the field
of private business, planning in this sense had always been practiced
at least in some rudimentary or amateur way. The growth of industrialism caused it to take on systematic and formal development
in the "scientific management" movement. This movement sought
to link engineering and economics in the "rationalization" of
industry. In its full aspect, the planning idea emphasized co-ordination of detailed plans and working programs with general business
or economic policies adopted for the individual company or the
industry.

On the public side, economic planning involved assistance and
some guidance by the government to private industry in its efforts
of co-ordination, and particularly, co-ordination of recognized
government functions (monetary, fiscal, labor, social, etc.) in such
a way as to develop a consistent national program for sustained
and balanced economic growth. While this came to be designated as

"central planning," its exponents did not advocate either a more centralized form of government or the elimination of private enterprise. They were strongly opposed to any form of authoritarianism. What they had in mind was to use the democratic forms of the American government to give direction to the unco-ordinated trends and policies which were impinging on the economy. They hoped in this way to facilitate changes toward greater stability, fuller use of all resources, and equitable distribution of the product. In other words, the planners quite generally sought more active leadership, and even some more control, in economic affairs on the part of government than had been considered necessary in the past but in line with basic American democratic traditions.

Those who were anxious to see broader patterns of industrial management developed in the private sphere, more systematic handling of public affairs, and a better articulation between the private and the public sphere were at considerable pains to distinguish American "planfulness" in business affairs from the Russian Five-Year Plan or other developments toward authoritarianism in Europe. Herbert Hoover, as Secretary of Commerce, had devoted his engineering talents toward promoting "simplification in industry" and, as President, had tried to captain a voluntary recovery movement of private business when depression got under way early in his Administration.

In June 1931, President Hoover adroitly entitled an address at Indianapolis "A Twenty-Year Plan for America." He repudiated the idea that "we should use force instead of co-operation in plans and direct every man as to what he may or may not do." He aligned himself with "our American system, which holds that the major purpose of a state is to protect the people and to give them equality of opportunity, that the basis of happiness is in the development of the individual, that the sum of progress can only be gauged by the progress of the individual, that we should steadily build up co-operation among the people themselves to these ends." As to specifics, he said:

I am able to propose an American plan to you:

We plan to take care of 20,000,000 increase in population in the next twenty years. We plan to build for them 4,000,000 new and better homes, thousands of new and still more beautiful city buildings, thousands of factories; to increase the capacity of our railways, to add thousands of miles of highways and waterways; to install 25,000,000 electrical horsepower; to grow 20 per cent more farm products.

We plan to provide new parks, schools, colleges and churches for these 20,000,000 people. We plan more leisure for men and women, and better opportunities for its enjoyment.

We not only plan to provide for all the new generation, but we shall, by scientific research and invention, lift the standard of living and security of life of the whole people.

We plan to secure a greater diffusion of wealth, a decrease in poverty, and a great reduction in crime.

And this plan will be carried out if we just keep on giving the American people a chance.

President Hoover, however, did not interpret "giving the American people a chance" as meaning that the Federal Government must limit itself to the functions it had exercised prior to March 4, 1929 or to the institutions it then had. Three important extensions of Federal responsibility for economic revival or stabilization secured his support as we shall note more fully in the next chapter. But Hoover never went out for any general planning or economic policy-making agency. (See pp. 52ff.)

Not so some of the "progressive" members of the Republican party. Early in 1931, Senator Robert M. LaFollette, Jr., introduced a bill (S. 6215, 71 Cong. 3 sess.) to establish a "National Economic Council." "The bill," he said, "breaks away from the stereotyped idea of restricted production, in the direction of enhanced consumption . . . the question of national economic planning in the United States of America has left the realm of theoretical discussion and become an issue of practical politics."[2]

The LaFollette bill proposed a National Economic Council with specific powers for fact-finding and recommendation. The Council was to be composed of nine members, appointed by the President and confirmed by the Senate. They should be men of deep understanding of national economic problems and include at least one expert in each of the following fields: finance, transportation, labor relations, agriculture, scientific management. The term of office was four years, the salary $15,000 (equivalent to that of Cabinet members), and each member was to give full time to his office. The

[2] The idea of economic councils was stimulated by the writings of Lewis L. Lorwin whose booklet on Advisory Economic Councils was published by the Brookings Institution in 1931.

Council was to make an annual report, on or before the first Monday in December, to the President or the Congress, together with recommendations for legislation or other action, and special reports as they saw fit.

In February 1932, a similar bill was introduced in the House by Mr. H. S. Person of Michigan. While neither of these bills passed even in the chamber in which it was introduced, they brought forth lengthy and unusually well-organized hearings and a great volume of discussion.

Both management and labor were, in this depression period, intrigued by the idea of planning for recovery and for subsequent stabilization of the economy. The Chamber of Commerce set up a Committee on Continuity of Business and Employment. Its report, recommending "a rational program of production and distribution, to be initiated by business itself," was adopted by a large majority of the chamber's membership in a referendum vote (1931). It stated that, "Planning by individual concerns and even by whole industries,—while it offers very definite promise as a means of eliminating waste, curtailing excess production, anticipating seasonal fluctuations and maintaining a scheduled rate of production throughout the year,—may not suffice to remedy such a severe lack of adjustment between production and consumption as we are experiencing." The committee doubted that a Planning Board, with "power to assemble the facts and then direct the people and resources into the various activities where they would be most useful . . . would, in view of the extreme complexity of our industrial organization . . . be a satisfactory way out of our difficulties."

On the other hand, advisory "planning on a national scale seems to be urgently needed." The chamber therefore recommended a National Economic Council of three to five members "of the very highest ability and integrity [with] experience and background which will enable them to understand sympathetically the circumstances of all the essential elements of our industrial life, but they must think and act for the country as a whole, and be without obligation to any particular constituency." Appointments were to be made by an appointing board chosen by the Chamber of Commerce to represent the various interest groups—agriculture, manufacturing, banking, railroads, public utilities, distributive trades, the law, engineering, and professional economists, the United States

Department of Commerce, and the chamber itself. The council was to co-operate closely with existing trade associations and encourage them to establish strong central committees or economic (trade) councils.

The general purpose of this proposal was "to retain the benefits of private initiative and at the same time to supply, if possible, some degree of control or influence that will help to maintain a better balance and thus reduce the severity of business fluctuations. . . . In the methods by which industry brings science and engineering to its aid with physical problems, we have a clue to an appropriate procedure for dealing with economic problems: to use and control the great research establishments as an effective tool for guiding engineering advance, to charge scientists with the problems, to support them liberally, and to act with courage to make their findings effective." The chamber report specifically explained that it used the term National Economic Council rather than Planning Board "because of the implication of detailed plans with autocratic powers of control which the latter carries and which we oppose."

From the business side, there was also forthcoming at this time the widely publicized "Swope Plan." Gerard Swope, president of the General Electric Company, presented this suggestion in a paper before the National Electrical Manufacturers Association in December 1931 under the title: "Stabilization of Industry." Mr. Swope argued that "Industry exists basically for serving the needs of the people. Consumption is by the mass of the population, not by the few. These, the wage earners, must be sufficiently assured of the future to feel that they are safe in spending their money."

In order to "correlate into a comprehensive whole the present undirected efforts of forward-looking business enterprise toward stabilization, Mr. Swope recommended that "all industrial and commercial companies with fifty or more employees may form a Trade Association under the supervision of a Federal body," either the Federal Trade Commission, the Department of Commerce, or a special supervisory agency. There was to be a General Board of Administration of each trade association, with three representatives of the employer, three of the employees, and three of the public. The associations were to collect and distribute information on volume of business transacted, inventories of merchandise on hand, simplification and standardization of products, stabilization of prices, and like matters. This plan did not win the full support either of management or of labor, and the powers proposed include several that have been consistently denied to trade associations under our antitrust laws.

Labor, on its part, also gave support to the planning idea. The American Federation of Labor urged the calling of a National Economic Conference by the President of the United States. The AF of L pointed out (Vancouver Convention, 1931):

We have everywhere throughout industry very successful attempts at planning by industrial undertakings, by industries, by unions, by communities, by states, and by geographic sections. But this is not adequate—there must be comprehensive planning by all the groups which affect each other. . . . The principles of balance in industry are the key to sustained progress. . . . Balance is not a result that can be obtained by arbitrary decision; it comes through working with laws in the light of knowledge and facts. . . . The interchange of information through reports, documents and conferences is basic to developing balance. . . . Unless organized labor is in the councils, national planning and balanced progress are impossible. . . . To accomplish teamwork by the whole industry and teamwork between all industries there should be comprehensive planning by an advisory body, representative of all production and consumer groups. Such a National Economic Council should plan the machinery for achieving economic equilibrium, and undertake to secure the co-operation of voluntary associations and government agencies in a co-ordinated undertaking.[3]

Such was the general background of American thinking about the government's role in economic affairs as brought about partly by the growing size and complexity of the economy but, in perhaps larger part, by the severity of the depression following 1929 and the persistence of special problems such as those of agriculture

[3] Matthew Woll, vice president of the American Federation of Labor, called upon the National Civic Federation to summon a great American Congress of Industry representing all forms and characters of industrial organizations in the country "to outline a recovery and stabilization plan." As to a general approach, he said: "There is a growing conviction that unless industry finds and applies a remedy, the Federal Government will attempt to find and apply a remedy. But it is the conviction of organized labor in America that political government lacks the competency to govern industry. Industry must find and apply its own measures of guidance. Permanence of machinery is vital to industry's salvation from an onslaught of state political control, which cannot be avoided in the absence of self control."

after World War I. The very word "planning" was anathema to many people,[4] whereas others saw it as the key word to near-term recovery and long-term progress. Quite independent of this explicit and general "planning" philosophy, the Federal Government had been setting up agencies in several areas of the economy which expressed policies as to how the operations of the economy might be stabilized or at least how particular destabilizing forces might be dealt with.

[4] "The word 'planning' has been widely and loosely used. It has meant different things to different people. To crusaders it has been a Holy Grail leading to the sunlit hills of a better day. To conservatives it has been a red flag of regimentation heralding the dawn of collectivism and the twilight of the old order of free private enterprise and the democratic way of life. But to the humble practitioners of the art, viewing the matter with the cold eye of engineering rationality and a matter-of-fact indifference either to crusades, Red hunts, the class struggle, or the omnipotent state, it has been merely a process of co-ordination, a technique of adapting means to ends, a method of bridging the gap between fact-finding and policy-making. Planning is the opposite of improvising. In simple terms it is organized foresight plus corrective hindsight. . . . In peacetime the aim of American planning is to promote progressively rising material and cultural levels of living for all the American people through reasonably full use of the productive resources of the nation. In time of war the common aim is victory." George B. Galloway and Associates, *Planning for America*, pp. 5, 8.

CHAPTER FOUR

Successive Expressions of Stabilization Policy

Formal acceptance of responsibility for protection of the economy and sustained search for stabilization policies is a quite recent development in the life of our Federal Government.[1] Woodrow Wilson had declined to summon a conference on economic adjustment after World War I, but by the fall of 1920 President Harding felt moved to set up an Unemployment Conference. It extended its sessions into 1921, but industrial rebound came so promptly that no considerable program was even proposed.[2] Harding himself in

[1] Although Congress had made *ad hoc* inquiries into the causes of various crises or depressions during the nineteenth century and, following the great depression of the nineties, set up the very pretentious National Industrial Commission in June 1898. This Commission's report appeared in nineteen volumes, published from 1900 to 1902. The letter of transmittal of the final volume commented on "the immensity and complexity of the industrial life of the nation and . . . the fact that nearly all kinds of business have undergone almost revolutionary changes in recent years. It would now seem impossible to legislate wisely or conduct business prudently without obtaining knowledge of these new conditions. . . . A bureau in a permanent department of the government would have all it could do to keep trace of the mutations of business—a subject which is quite apart from the scientific and statistical work now well performed by other bureaus and departments." Surely a modest estimate of the task of economic analysis and policy-making as it has developed during the fifty years since that report! Indeed the Departments of Commerce and of Labor date only from 1913, and the Federal Trade Commission from 1914.

[2] President Harding's Unemployment Conference did, however, lead to three national surveys of economic problems, first a study of Business Cycles and Unemployment, second a study of Seasonal Operation in the Construction Industry, and third an extensive survey of Recent Economic Changes conducted under the

the report of this President's Unemployment Conference remarked: "There has been vast unemployment before and there will be again. There will be depression and inflation just as surely as the tides ebb and flow. I would have little enthusiasm for any proposed remedy which seeks either palliation or tonic from the public Treasury."

As agriculture, in spite of general business recovery, continued in a depressed state, the President called an agricultural conference in January 1922. Its purpose and result were to head off the more radical proposals then being made for government intervention in behalf of agriculture. Instead of showing any trend toward central planning or toward establishing institutions or practices of comprehensive policy-making for the economy, Federal legislation continued for some time to be directed to particular situations or economic areas.[3] Such particularized attacks on national economic problems, of course, dated back a very long time in our history—as in the case of public land policy, transportation policy, and foreign trade policy (eventually institutionalized in such agencies as the Interstate Commerce Commission and the Tariff Commission).

---

auspices of the National Bureau of Economic Research with funds provided by the Rockefeller Foundation. The latter was published commercially as a two-volume work in the spring of 1929 under the title *Recent Economic Changes in the United States*. Herbert Hoover, then Secretary of Commerce, had been the chairman of the committee which sponsored this study.

Following the survey of Recent Economic Changes, a similar but even more extensive survey of Recent Social Trends in the United States was conducted under the auspices of the President's Research Committee on Social Trends. In his foreword to the published report (October 11, 1932) President Hoover said: "This study is the latest and most comprehensive of a series, some of them governmental and others privately sponsored, beginning in 1921 with the report on 'Waste in Industry' under my chairmanship. It should serve to help all of us to see where social stresses are occurring and where major efforts should be undertaken to deal with them constructively."

[3] Some exception to this generalization may be made as to Woodrow Wilson's administration. The doctrine of the "New Freedom" on which he took office was based on a broad concept of modeling our economy on a more consistent basis of free competitive enterprise. The features of this program included freer trade under the Underwood Tariff Act, clearer definition of antimonopoly policy through the Clayton amendment to the Sherman Antitrust Act, and setting up the Federal Trade Commission. On the credit side, it included sponsorship of the Federal Reserve Act of 1913 and the Farm Loan Act of 1916. These developments will be discussed presently as "segmental policies," but the point is that in Wilson's mind they unquestionably were parts of a comprehensive national economic policy.

SEGMENTAL POLICY-MAKING, 1913–32

In the establishing of the Federal Reserve System in 1913 a very broad policy area of great significance to the functioning of the economy was dealt with in a fundamental way and a carefully designed institution was set up for continuously implementing the declared policy under ever-changing conditions. The Federal Reserve Act was a response to the growing belief that a more adaptable currency and credit system would help the economy to weather safely or avoid altogether such financial panics as had occurred in 1907–08 and at numerous earlier times in our history. It looked to a nonpartisan, technically competent board and staff to formulate and execute policies of financial stabilization under the general control of Congress. The Federal Reserve Board of Governors was not made responsible to the President.

Hard on the heels of the Federal Reserve Act came the Federal Farm Loan Act of 1916. This law expressed a national policy of providing more ample mortgage credit in agriculture on terms better suited to the character of the farming industry, thereby helping to stabilize farmers' production and marketing operations. The system was headed by a Federal Farm Loan Board—first attached to the Treasury Department—and twelve regional land banks. During the period of agricultural distress following World War I, the Federal Government extended its activities in the credit field to include "intermediate credits." The Agricultural Credits Act of 1923 authorized twelve Federal Intermediate Credit Banks paralleling the regional Land Banks under supervision of the Federal Farm Loan Board. Particular purposes of this development were the better financing of livestock operations and aid to co-operative marketing associations.[4]

A second segmental development of national stabilization policy occurred in agriculture when farmers suffered a severe depression following World War I and lagged behind in the general recovery that followed 1921. There arose a continuing agitation for measures

[4] During the 20's, there was a good deal of discussion of monetary policy and credit institutions as a factor in guidance and stabilization of the economy. The "Strong bill" was a focus of the philosophy of central bank policy as a national stabilization force. It was introduced by Representative James G. Strong of Kansas and opposed by Benjamin Strong, Governor of the Federal Reserve Bank of New York.

which would protect agriculture against the recurrence of such conditions. It was argued—with considerable exaggeration—that agriculture is such a "fundamental" industry that the advent of depression there would produce a general collapse or that failure to cure farm distress would preclude industrial recovery. Congress responded by twice passing an agricultural support measure (the McNary-Haugen bill), but it was on both occasions vetoed by President Coolidge.

Eventually, the Agricultural Marketing Act of 1929 gave expression to the demand that the Federal Government assume responsibility for some stabilization of this segment of the national economy by lessening the volatile character of the farm commodity market. The violent shifts in these prices and hence in farmers' incomes was disproportionate to the ability of small-scale operators to "average out." This attack on the problem was somewhat less drastic than that proposed in the McNary-Haugen bill. It emanated from the Business Men's Commission on Agriculture, sponsored by the Chamber of Commerce of the United States and the National Industrial Conference Board.[5] In signing the act (June 1929), President Hoover endorsed the

declared . . . policy of the Congress to promote the effective merchandising of agricultural commodities in interstate and foreign commerce, so that the industry of agriculture will be placed on a basis of economic equality with other industries . . . by aiding in preventing and controlling surpluses in any agricultural commodity, through orderly production and distribution.[6]

The statute is interesting for two reasons. First, it embraced a specific plan for stabilizing the agricultural industry, namely government financing and manipulation of crop carry-overs. Second, it set up a Federal Farm Board of eight members to act as a top economic strategy body for the industry. The act provided that in appointing members of the Board the President and the Senate should "give due consideration to having the major agricultural commodities represented." In practice, this composition of the board lent itself to logrolling among the several members, seeking maximum advantage for their respective commodity groups rather than taking a broad view of the interests of agriculture as a segment

[5] Business Men's Commission on Agriculture, *The Condition of Agriculture in the United States and Measures for Its Improvement* (1927).

[6] 46 Stat. 11.

of the total economy. Furthermore, the nature of the remedy provided and the scope of resources through which the general policy was to be carried out were so disproportionate to the strain imposed by general depression during the next few years that, by 1932, the experiment was conceded to be a failure.

After the crash of 1929, depression gripped the nonfarm area and an effort was made to attack the problem of industrial unemployment. This took the form of the Employment Stabilization Act of 1931, "an Act to provide for the advance planning and regulated construction of public works, for the stabilization of industry, and for aiding in the prevention of unemployment during periods of business depression." This measure had first been proposed (as S. 4307) by Senator Wagner on May 1, 1928 in the hope of averting the crash of 1929, which he already foresaw. Not till the depression was two years old did he secure passage of the bill in modified form.

The act declared it

to be the policy of Congress to arrange the construction of public works so far as practicable in such manner as will assist in the stabilization of industry and employment through the proper timing of such construction, and that to further this object there shall be advance planning, including preparation of detailed construction plans, of public works by the construction agencies and the Board.

To carry out these purposes, there was set up an Employment Stabilization Board consisting of the Secretary of Labor, of Agriculture, of Treasury, and of Commerce, with the latter as chairman. The board's function was to investigate the volume and timing of all public works and to assist in advance planning of construction so that government building would help to offset private unemployment. Nine executive departments and six independent Federal agencies were to prepare and present to the board a six-year plan of their construction projects. The board was to keep the President informed as to these plans and the general trend of business activity. If depression developed, these public works were to be accelerated or even supplemented by additional appropriations for public buildings, flood-control projects, river and harbor improvements, or highways and bridges.

There was in the act, however, no suggestion of a comprehensive and integrated policy to promote recovery and assure economic stabilization thereafter through co-ordination of fiscal, monetary, industrial, labor, and agricultural institutions and practices—public and private.[7]

The measure was inaugurated at an advanced stage of business recession and near the close of an administration. It soon was engulfed by the more sweeping program of the New Deal.[8]

During the last year of the Hoover Administration, a policy of government aid to combat depression and promote recovery was expressed in two other measures, both designed to give easier access to credit in areas where private institutions found the risk too great or their resources inadequate. The first of these credit measures was the Reconstruction Finance Corporation Act of January 1932. The second was the Federal Home Loan Bank Act of July 1932.

The Reconstruction Finance Corporation was authorized to make loans of somewhat hazardous character to commercial banks and other financial institutions to aid in the liquidation or reorganization of closed banks or to enable institutions in distress to avoid closing. Loans also were made to industrial corporations, construction companies, and agricultural associations to enable them to continue in operation or undertake new commitments, thereby helping to lessen unemployment. Special emphasis was placed on financial assistance to small business organizations. Besides a capital of 500 million dollars provided from the Treasury, the corporation

[7] President Hoover's initial strategy in 1930 and 1931 was to seek to rally the voluntary recovery efforts of private businessmen to a continuation of operations while the process of readjustment of over-extended positions or faulty direction of productive or distributive activity went forward—a sort of "business-as-usual-during-alterations" policy. But businessmen soon showed a lack of confidence in each other's ability to take such calculated risks. They lapsed into a general scramble for individual security in a market thus made insecure for everybody. Thereupon Mr. Hoover supported the Reconstruction Finance Corporation and other measures whereby Government would "bail out" private business. By 1933, the demand of businessmen for government rescue operations went much farther, as was attested particularly by the National Industrial Recovery Act. These developments are discussed in the following chapter.

[8] President Roosevelt abolished the Economic Stabilization Board on June 10, 1933, but action was deferred until such time (March 1, 1934) as its functions and personnel could be transferred to the Federal Employment Stabilization Office in the Department of Commerce. The former director of the work of the ESB was appointed Federal Emergency Administrator of Public Works under the National Industrial Recovery Act, and these operative functions were continued under the Public Works Administration. This agency was, in due time, merged into the Federal Works Agency. The planning functions of the ESB, which were first transferred to the Federal Employment Stabilization Office, were later transferred to the National Resources Planning Board in the Executive Office of the President.

was authorized to secure additional funds by sale of its own notes, debentures, or bonds.

Under the Home Loan Bank Act, a Home Loan Bank Board was authorized to secure funds through the issuance of bonds, debentures, or notes, in addition to some 100 million dollars of capital provided from the United States Treasury. It was to make loans to savings and loan, building and loan, and homestead associations; savings and co-operative banks; and insurance companies. A special objective was to make and service loans to veterans.

NEW DEAL POLICIES AND THEIR CO-ORDINATION

In the election of 1932, the country turned to another political party, which initiated a "New Deal," featured by a varied group of "action" programs designed to attack depression in all its major sectors. No statutory machinery was set up for the integration of these programs. Reliance was placed rather on the administrative intuition and fast footwork of the President with the counsel of a personal staff of "brain trusters."

The Agricultural Adjustment Act of 1933 superseded the Agricultural Marketing Act of 1929. Its broad policy was stated to be:

> To establish and maintain such balance between production and consumption of agricultural commodities, and such marketing conditions therefor, as will re-establish prices to farmers at a level that will give agricultural commodities a purchasing power with respect to articles farmers buy, equivalent to the purchasing power of agricultural commodities in the base period [August 1909–July 1914]. . . . To protect the consumers' interest by adjusting farm production at such level as will not increase the percentage of the consumers' retail expenditures for agricultural commodities . . . above the percentage . . . August 1909–July 1914.[9]

This measure invoked a much enlarged panoply of governmental direction and Federal subsidy of production as well as marketing activities. The idea of an administrative board was abandoned in favor of

[9] 46 Stat. 11.

Viewing the Agricultural Adjustment Act as reflecting a Federal policy for dealing with a "sick" industry, one finds its counterpart in the Bituminous Coal Act of 1937, "which provided for the stabilization of the bituminous coal industry." This act by its terms was limited in operation to a period of four years from the date of its enactment. Successive legislation extended the act to August 24, 1943, on which date it expired" (*U. S. Government Organization Manual 1951–52*, p. 587) although many of its functions were transferred to the Bituminous Coal Division of the Department of the Interior.

a single Administrator, heading an organization which was separate
from, though closely related to, the Department of Agriculture.[10]

The National Industrial Recovery Act (June 1933) was designed
to stimulate employment, increase wages in the low brackets and
standardize and co-ordinate business activities and practices.[11] By
Section 1 it was

> declared to be the policy of Congress to remove obstructions to the free
> flow of interstate and foreign commerce which tend to diminish the amount
> thereof; and to provide for the general welfare by promoting the organiza-
> tion of industry for the purpose of co-operative action among trade groups,
> to induce and maintain united action of labor and management under ade-
> quate governmental sanctions and supervision, to eliminate unfair com-
> petitive practices, to promote the fullest possible utilization of the present
> productive capacity of industries, to avoid undue restriction of production
> (except as may be temporarily required), to increase the consumption of
> industrial and agricultural products by increasing purchasing power, to re-
> duce and relieve unemployment, to improve standards of labor, and other-
> wise to rehabilitate industry and to conserve natural resources.[12]

The Public Works Administration set up under Title II of
NIRA was designed to stimulate pay rolls and the purchase of
materials. The Farm Credit Administration consolidated and expanded the work of several agencies for both mortgage and short-
time credit to farmers and farmer co-operatives. The Home Loan

[10] No specific machinery for administering the Agricultural Adjustment Act was
set up in the statute. Blanket authority was given the Secretary of Agriculture to
"appoint such officers and employees . . . and such experts as are necessary to
execute the functions vested in him by this title."

[11] The sense of historic development was heavy on the President as he signed the
act. He wrote: "History will probably record the National Industrial Recovery Act
as the most important and far-reaching legislation ever enacted by the American
Congress. It represents a supreme effort to stabilize for all time the many factors
which make for the prosperity of the nation and the preservation of American
standards. Its goal is the assurance of a reasonable profit to industry and living
wages for labor, with the elimination of the piratical methods and practices which
have not only harassed honest business but also contributed to the ills of labor."

[12] As in the case of the Agricultural Adjustment Act, no administrative machinery
was set up in the statute, but the President was "authorized to establish such
agencies, to accept and utilize such voluntary and uncompensated services, to
appoint . . . such officers and employees, and to utilize such Federal officers and
employees . . . as he may find necessary [and to] delegate any of his functions and
powers under this title to such officers, agents, and employees, . . . and may establish
an industrial planning and research agency to aid in carrying out his functions
under this title."

Bank System was designed to refinance and extend urban credit. The Emergency Relief Administration was to give temporary support to the consumptive needs of the unemployed, and there was also in the New Deal a program of credit easing and "money tinkering."

To effect some degree of administrative co-ordination of policy and practice in the ambitious New Deal program, the President by executive order set up in July 1933 an Executive Council composed of Cabinet officers and the heads of AAA, NRA, PWA, and other recovery agencies. It met each Tuesday to review figures on economic developments, iron out conflicts in those figures or in the philosophy and activities of the various agencies, and co-ordinate future plans. Apparently the temperaments of many of the prima donnas in the group robbed the council of any great objectivity or co-operation.

Within a few months the Executive Council was replaced by a National Emergency Council of generally similar character but somewhat different composition—fewer ex officio department heads and more chiefs of "recovery" agencies, with the President as chairman. The Emergency Council was set up for the particular purpose of "co-ordinating and making more efficient and productive the work of the numerous field agencies of the government." It set up regional offices and appointed state chairmen. These branches were intended to serve as eyes and ears for the national council, to effect co-ordination between local and national parts of the several recovery plans and programs. The effort fell flat from the beginning. In October 1934 the Executive Council was consolidated with the National Emergency Council under the latter name. This council was abolished under the Reorganization Plan of July 1939, and its functions and personnel transferred to the Office of Government Reports in the Executive Office of the President.[13] Apparently,

13 One other development of this period, little remembered but possibly of considerable significance, was the establishment by President Roosevelt late in 1938, of a Fiscal and Monetary Advisory Board. It consisted of the Secretary of the Treasury, the Chairman of the Board of Governors of the Federal Reserve System, the Director of the Bureau of the Budget, and the chairman of the National Security Resources Board. Under the chairmanship of the Secretary of the Treasury, this board was intended to discuss questions of fiscal and monetary policy and to attempt to arrive at consensus and voluntary action within their respective areas of administrative discretion or of recommendations for the President, either with reference to his executive role or Administration policy in dealing with Congress. This board quietly disappeared after about a year, when internal disagreement developed and the chairman ceased to call further meetings. The underlying idea, however, is not dead. (See p. 72.)

however, two policies can be traced back to the National Emergency Council—opening the closed banks and establishing the Federal Housing Authority.

It was during this period that the concept of the Executive Office of the President as a formal institution for the organization of the greatly expanded functions of the Presidency took shape. It was an outgrowth of studies conducted by the President's Committee on Administrative Management and was given statutory recognition in the Reorganization Act of 1939. Its creation was a response not merely to the growing scope of the President's executive responsibilities but also to the need for greater co-ordination among the multifarious programs of the various government agencies.[14] This need had been inadequately met by *ad hoc* bodies set up by Executive Order such as the National Emergency Council.

Toward such co-ordination an important step had been taken in 1921 with the passage of the National Budget and Accounting Act and the setting up of a Bureau of the Budget in the Treasury Department. This agency became a major staff arm of the President, guiding the budget-making work of the several departments and commissions in accordance with the President's general policy. It has eight functions:

(1) To assist the President in the preparation of the Budget and the formulation of the fiscal program of the Government.

(2) To supervise and control the administration of the Budget.

(3) To conduct research . . . and advise the executive departments and agencies of the Government with respect to improved administrative organization and practice.

(4) To aid the President to bring about more efficient and economical conduct of Government service.

(5) To assist the President by clearing and co-ordinating departmental advice on proposed legislation and by making recommendations as to Presidential action on legislative enactments, in accordance with past practice.

[14] "The most important administrative event of [the past quarter-century from the standpoint of giving the President staff help in developing government policy] was the creation in 1939 of the Executive Office of the President. This office was set up on the theory that the President should not only be the political and ceremonial head of the government, but be staffed to discharge his executive responsibilities as its general manager. . . . The President needs in his Executive Office a staff and procedure by which he can direct his department heads in building up a unified program, and adjust differences between them." Don K. Price, "Staffing the Presidency," *The American Political Science Review*, Vol. XI, No. 6, pp. 1158, 1154.

(6) To assist in the consideration and clearance and, where necessary, in the preparation of proposed Executive Orders and proclamations. . . .

(7) To plan and promote the improvement, development, and co-ordination of Federal and other statistical services.

(8) To keep the President informed of the progress and activities by agencies of the Government with respect to work proposed, work actually initiated, and work completed, together with the relative timing of work between the several agencies of the Government; all to the end that the work programs of the several agencies of the executive branch of the Government may be co-ordinated and that the moneys appropriated by the Congress may be expended in the most economical manner possible with the least possible overlapping and duplication of effort.[15]

The Bureau of the Budget has been given responsibilities for promoting improved administrative management throughout the executive departments, improving and co-ordinating statistical services, clearing departmental advice on proposed legislation, and recommending Presidential action on enrolled bills sent to him from the Congress. Since the Director of the Bureau of the Budget felt that he could not advise the President competently on broad matters of spending policy without a comprehensive and intensive view of the economic conditions and trends in the economy, he set up in 1940 a Division of Fiscal Analysis in charge of an Assistant Director. This division went a considerable distance in developing the lines of statistical and analytical service subsequently called for under the Employment Act of 1946.

THE NATIONAL PLANNING ASSOCIATION AND THE
COMMITTEE FOR ECONOMIC DEVELOPMENT

The "planning movement" discussed in Chapter III came to expression in 1934 in the establishment of a private study and promotional group known as the National Economic and Social Planning Association.[16] This body, with modest headquarters in Washington, carries on studies of current and emerging economic problems through a small staff supplemented by consultative committees. The association seeks, through its board of trustees and standing committees to get well-balanced representation of academic, business, labor, and agricultural views. The post of

---

[15] *United States Government Organizational Manual,* 1951–52, p. 60.

[16] Organized by Lewis L. Lorwin, George Soule, Marion Hedges, and others. Reorganized in 1939 as the National Planning Association.

chairman of the board of trustees has been successively held by
prominent businessmen—William Batt of SKF Industries, Charles
E. Wilson of General Electric, and H. Christian Sonne of Amsinck,
Sonne and Company.

Departing somewhat from the planning concept of its founders,
the NPA in recent years has focused its attention on consideration
of economic problems of current interest such as labor-management
relations, farm policy, and postwar stabilization. It has combined
staff studies and committee consultation with informal luncheon
and dinner conferences of representative leaders. It has sought to
arrive at formulations of policy which are in the public interest and
which therefore would be accepted by special economic groups as
being, in the most fundamental sense, also in their own long-time
interest. Publications of the association have in the main taken the
form of small, simply written pamphlets designed to reach a broad
audience, though there have been a few book-length reports. As
World War II progressed, the National Planning Association gave
attention to such issues as settlement of war contracts and disposal
of surplus plants, and to taxes, savings, investment, and fiscal policy.
In 1945, the association published a study, *National Budgets for
Full Employment* which unquestionably sparked a great deal of the
thinking which led up to passage of the Employment Act of 1946.

As far-seeing individuals began to consider the nature of the
problems which would confront the country after World War II,
another private agency for dealing with national economic policy
in the over-all sense was set up. This was the Committee for
Economic Development. Its immediate concern was with the peacetime utilization of productive facilities built for or converted to
war uses, and the prompt re-employment of war workers and returning military personnel in order to avoid a postwar slump. To
this end, the committee organized an extensive program of field
work in conjunction with local Chambers of Commerce, but at the
same time launched also a research program for the study of broad
questions of government and private business policy. As reconversion proceeded smoothly, the Committee for Economic Development made research and policy statements their sole activity.[17]

[17] National Economic policy in the over-all sense was also being considered by
other nongovernmental research agencies. For example, the Brookings Institution,
which had made intensive studies of the agricultural, industrial, and monetary
programs of the New Deal, published a number of pamphlets and books devoted

The studies of the CED are conducted under direction of a research and policy committee instructed to "initiate studies into the principles of business policy and of public policy which will foster the full contribution by industry and commerce to the attainment and maintenance of high and secure standards of living for people in all walks of life through maximum employment and high productivity in the domestic economy." The studies are made by outstanding research scholars drawn mostly from our leading universities under instructions that all "research is to be thoroughly objective in character and the approach in each instance is to be from the standpoint of the general welfare and not from that of any special political or economic group." Significant titles in the early period included: *Production, Jobs, and Taxes; International Trade and Domestic Employment; Postwar Taxation and Economic Progress; Jobs and Markets;* and *International Trade and Domestic Employment.* More recent have been books on *Monetary Management; American Monetary Policy,* and *National Security and Individual Freedom.*

Besides research volumes by outside scholars, the CED issues timely "Statements on National Policy" based on studies by the committee's own staff but formulated by a group of eminent businessmen who constitute the Research and Policy Committee, any one of whom is free to dissent from or qualify the group statement as he sees fit. Among such pamphlets may be mentioned: *Economic Policy for Rearmament; National Security and Our Individual Freedom; Monetary and Fiscal Policy for Greater Economic Stability; Toward More Production, More Jobs, and More Freedom; International Trade; Foreign Investment and Domestic Employment; The Threat to Our National Security.*

Both the CED and the National Planning Association thus serve in a very real sense the basic purpose of a "national economic council" for fact-finding and policy recommendations such as was proposed in Senator LaFollette's bill in 1931 (p. 44) and again during

to problems of postwar reconversion and of permanent peacetime stability and "economic progress." Significant book titles include: `Controlling Factors in Economic Development; A National Transportation Policy; A National Labor Policy; The United States and Foreign Investment Problems; Government Costs and Tax Levels; Postwar Fiscal Requirements* and also such prewar publications as *The New Philosophy of Public Debt; Capital Expansion, Employment, and Economic Stability; Income and Economic Progress; Government and Economic Life; America's Capacity to Produce* and *America's Capacity to Consume.*

consideration of the Murray "full employment" bill of 1945 (p. 69) except that they are privately constituted and supported.

THE NATIONAL RESOURCES PLANNING BOARD

Besides these private expressions of the economic planning philosophy, the 1930's saw it come also to further public expression. Under the Public Works Administration, there was established in July 1933 a National Planning Board to "advise on the preparation of a comprehensive program of public works, through development of regional plans, service, and research, and correlation of effort among Federal, state, and local agencies." The following year this board was, by Executive Order, given a larger and more independent status as the National Resources Board. As such it made technical studies of land, water, mineral, and energy resources and their economic use. In June 1935, this board was rechristened the National Resources Committee, and in 1939 it became the National Resources Planning Board in the Executive Office of the President. It was authorized to "collect, prepare, and make available to the President with recommendations, such plans, data, and information as may be helpful to the planned development and use of national resources." By an Executive Order of June 1940, the board was assigned duties in co-operation with the Bureau of the Budget for the development of a six-year program of Federal public works.

The National Resources Committee consisted of the Secretary of the Interior, of Commerce, of Agriculture, and of Labor; the Administrator of PWA; and two private members, Frederic A. Delano and Professor Charles E. Merriam. Secretary Ickes was chairman and Mr. Delano vice-chairman. There was also an advisory committee under the chairmanship of Mr. Delano and with Professor Merriam, Henry S. Dennison, president of the Dennison Manufacturing Company, and Beardsley Ruml as members.[18] The National Resources Planning Board consisted of Mr. Delano, chairman; Professor Merriam, vice-chairman; George F. Yantis, a lawyer from the state of Washington, as member; with Henry Dennison and Beardsley Ruml as advisers, all serving on a per diem rather than full-time basis.

Both the National Resources Committee and the National Re-

[18] Professor Wesley C. Mitchell was a member of the National Planning Board and of the National Resources Board, 1933 to 1935.

sources Planning Board interpreted their mandate rather liberally. Though not limited to the engineering and physical planning concept, they made broad studies of resources use, regional and city planning and technological development, but they also studied population trends, the structure of the national economy, consumers' incomes and expenditures, and national economic policy. Both operated through a staff of professional economists and statisticians, with consultative assistance from top echelon economists in other agencies.

The National Resources Planning Board, in a publicity pamphlet dated May 1, 1941, described its own role in the following terms:

The National Resources Planning Board is the planning arm of the Executive Office of the President. Its function is to prepare and make available to the President and the Congress plans, programs, and information that may be helpful to the wise use and fullest development of national resources. In carrying on its activities, the Board consults and co-operates with agencies of the Federal Government, with States and municipalities, and with public or private planning or research agencies and acts as a clearing house and means of co-ordination for planning activities.

The board set up field offices to deal with state planning boards and, through them, with city planning bodies. The major purpose of these field offices was to co-ordinate the work of local agencies into specific developmental programs for the "region." Several regional studies (of which the Southeast was the most ambitious) were issued by the board, designed to fit into a long-range national program of economic development. Pursuant to the Employment Stabilization Act of 1931 (see page 53), the board made quarterly reports to the President on employment trends, and in March 1943 delivered to him a voluminous report entitled "Security, Work, and Relief Policies" and a somewhat shorter one on national resource development. These he transmitted to Congress, but neither in the executive nor the legislative branch were they given any great attention.

In fact, the National Resources Planning Board was notably unsuccessful in making itself effective as an advisory agency in national policy making. Except for the administration of the six-year public works program, which was done jointly with the Bureau of the Budget, the Planning Board's functions were not made part and parcel of the policy-making machinery on the executive side. There was no organic relationship between the board's recommendations and the President's program.[19]

Over a considerable period of time the National Resources Planning Board itself avoided any direct comment or commitment upon the studies which it published. These studies usually represented the conclusions of a committee of government or other technical experts. On some occasions the studies were largely the work of a single individual. Only in the last years of its existence, mainly after 1941, did the board itself indicate its own collective attitude about various issues of public policy. The introduction to the *Report on Security, Work, and Relief Policies* was the first of its kind.[20]

This move toward a more positive role was ill-starred. The thinking of the National Resources Planning Board had by this time fallen under the sway of Professor Alvin Hansen, who was serving as special economic adviser to the Federal Reserve Board. His fiscal policy doctrines dominated the pamphlets, *After Defense—What?* and *After the War—Full Employment,* published by the board in 1942. These views were anathema to many members of Congress as was also anything which bore the label "planning." To this we must add a vague feeling that the Resources Planning Board was operating in an ivory tower without participation of or consultation with Congressional committees and the desire of some congressmen to take a slap at President Roosevelt. At all events, the board was terminated as of August 31, 1943 by the action of Congress in denying it any further funds.[21]

[19] Several persons who were familiar with the experience of the Resources Planning Board were influential in drafting the Employment Act of 1946 and sought, in setting up the Council of Economic Advisers, with specific advisory responsibility in connection with the Economic Report of the President, to remedy this defect.

[20] John D. Millett, *The Process and Organization of Government Planning,* p. 21.

[21] In terminating the life of the National Resources Planning Board, Congress stipulated that none of its functions should be transferred to any other agency. "Planning" was out! However, an executive order promptly announced that certain functions that had been the joint responsibility of the board and the Bureau of the Budget would thereafter be the sole responsibility of the bureau. These tasks related to "carefully planned and realistic long-range programs of public works and improvement projects" (at least annually revised). All departments and executive establishments of the executive branch of the government were to report fully to the Bureau of the Budget on such plans and programs "in order to facilitate budgeting activities." The bureau was instructed to "report to the President from time to time but not less than once a year, consolidated estimates and advance programs in the form of an over-all advance program for the Executive Branch of the government." (Executive Order 9384, Oct. 4, 1943.)

WAR POLICY-MAKING AND POSTWAR FEARS

After the outbreak of World War II, several new co-ordinating agencies were set up by the President or Congress. The Office of Emergency Management was established by Executive Order in 1940 to serve as a major device for organizing the war program. Under it there was established an Office of Economic Stabilization in October 1942, with James Byrnes as Economic Stabilizer, followed by Fred Vinson.[22] Another Executive Order created the Office of War Mobilization in May 1943, which became the Office of War Mobilization and Reconversion under an act of October 1944. Vinson was the first director and was followed by John Snyder and then by John Steelman. This office was to "develop unified programs and establish policies for the maximum use of the nation's natural and industrial resources for military and civilian needs, for effective use of national manpower not in the armed forces and for the adjustment of civilian economy, and to formulate reconversion plans to meet problems arising out of the transition from war to peace." The director was to make quarterly progress reports to the Congress and the President.

The OWMR employed a small professional staff and, during 1945 and 1946, issued a series of reports which discussed the economic problems involved in winning the war and of liquidating the war effort and securing a prompt and vigorous resumption of peacetime activities. The reports included recommendations of general policy. The major issues centered around the relaxation of controls, termination of war contracts and disposal of surplus property, and the re-employment of workers. The need for atomic legislation was noted, and the establishment of a Federal research agency was proposed.[23]

[22] This Office was abolished in September 1945, and its functions transferred to the Office of War Mobilization and Reconversion.

[23] The War Mobilization and Reconversion Act (October 1944) resembled the Employment Act of 1946 as finally passed more closely than did the Wagner Full Employment bill in that it called upon the director (after consulting with state and local governments, industry, labor, and agriculture) to formulate plans for meeting the problems that might arise in the transition from war to peace. The original form of this bill (S. 1893) contemplated an agency which would go beyond the immediate reconversion period and deal with problems of maintaining employment and business prosperity over a longer time. The director was to unify the programs and activities of Federal agencies concerned not only with war

Attached to the OWMR was an Advisory Board consisting of twelve members—three representatives from business, three from organized labor, three from agriculture, and three from the general public. This advisory board met with the director semimonthly to give him and his staff such counsel as they saw fit. The meetings were also attended from time to time by military and civilian officials for discussions of problems in which they were directly interested. Early in its life, the board drew up a statement of objectives for the postwar economy and another covering reconversion principles.

The chairman of the Advisory Board appointed a subcommittee to plan a study of the proposal for a guaranteed annual wage, which was being pressed by labor as a security measure after the war. For carrying out this study, the board secured a special grant of $250,000. Murray W. Latimer, chairman of the Railway Retirement Board, was put in charge of this study, and late in 1946, a voluminous report, largely of a factual nature, was filed with the Advisory Board.[24]

Of this board, the director said in his Fifth Quarterly Report: "In many instances I have sought the Board's advice and recommendations on specific problems. Frequently the Board itself has originated studies which have been particularly helpful. . . . Before issuing Executive Order 9651 redefining the government position on the wage-price question, the President consulted with the Advisory Board at the White House."

The last quarterly report of OWMR appeared in October 1946, after the Council of Economic Advisers had been appointed and begun its work. Three months later, with the Council's assistance, the President sent to Congress his first Economic Report under the Employment Act. Thus there was neither gap nor overlap in the series of periodic reports from the Executive Office on the state of the economy.

---

mobilization but also with "peacetime production and employment." In this early draft, there was set up a "Bureau of Programs" to review government and private plans, current and projected, and survey continuously the necessity for additional programs or legislation "to promote peacetime full production and employment." Although the OWMR, as finally established, had a less ambitious role, the degree to which the final form of the Employment Act of 1946 resembled the "reconversion" proposals of 1944 is striking.

[24] When OWMR was abolished at the end of 1946, the Advisory Board commended this report to the attention of the Council of Economic Advisers.

CHAPTER FIVE

The Employment Act as Capstone

The Employment Act of 1946 should be seen in the perspective of earlier developments, public and private, toward formulating national economic policies that would make for stabilization. So viewed, it may properly be regarded as the capstone of such an arch of earlier and partial building stones. This figure of speech is, I think, valid, since the Employment Act does not propose to supersede these other efforts toward policy-making, nor itself to furnish comprehensive and detailed bases for policy-making in the various areas. It does, however, attempt to tie together and complete an arch of policy-making agencies or organizations, deriving its strength from all other members of the supporting structure.

The distinctive character of the Employment Act was that it accepted responsibility on the part of the Federal Government to make systematic study of its several policies and programs to see that they move consistently toward maintaining the health of the economy and continuous high-level utilization of the nation's resources. Such study is to be continuous but its findings are to be formally reviewed and publicly reported on by the President each year as a new session of Congress gets to work.

An outstanding feature of the act is that it invokes the aid of professionally trained economists as technical advisers at the policy-making level as a means of raising the quality of economic statesmanship, both in the Executive Office and in the Congress, in approaching the task of economic stabilization. The dual implementation of the Employment Act in such a move to exploit the resources of economic science in national policy-making embraces a Council of Economic Advisers in the Executive Office and a Joint Committee in the Congress.

TOWARD POSTWAR NATIONAL POLICY

It has always been one of the shortcomings of our Congressional system that it makes so little provision for any comparative analysis and winnowing of legislative proposals as they appear spontaneously from the drives of individual Senators and Representatives or from the leadership or pressure of the executive branch. Numerous standing committees weigh the merits of bills of differing character within their particular jurisdiction. Sometimes the outlook of the committee members may be wide enough to consider adequately the impact of legislation in a particular area upon the functioning of the whole economy. But there was prior to 1946 no committee in either house—and still less any standing joint committee—specifically charged with the task of examining pending legislation from the standpoint of its cumulative implications or mutual consistency.

From time to time both Senate and House undertake to remedy this shortcoming by setting up special committees in broad problem areas. This took quite an ambitious turn in the case of the Temporary National Economic Committee of 1938–41. The same thread of development was picked up again as Congress began to think of the difficulties of economic reconversion after V-Day. As early as January 1941, Senator Wagner introduced a Joint Resolution to establish a Postwar Emergency Economic Advisory Committee (S. J. Res.16, 77 Cong. 1 sess.). In February 1941, the House set up a Special Committee on Postwar Economic Policy and Planning under the chairmanship of Representative Colmer of Mississippi. A year later, the Senate established a special committee of the same name under the chairmanship of Senator George. These special committees were to supplement the work of the regular standing committees, not to usurp their legislative functions. They were "to investigate and report to Congress upon all matters relating to postwar economic policy and problems . . . to the end that Congress may be . . . in a position to formulate solutions with respect to them." Both committees reviewed a large amount of legislation that was introduced for dealing with postwar technical and economic problems and submitted a series of special and annual reports to their respective Houses.

There were also other committees or subcommittees whose fields of study came to embrace a pretty wide area of general postwar economic policy. This was notably true of the War Contracts Subcommittee of the Committee on Military Affairs of the Senate, which consisted of James E. Murray, chairman, Harry S. Truman, and Chapman Revercomb. It was from these approaches that Senator Murray moved to the drafting of his "full employment bill." At about the same time, Senator Kilgore, from his activities on the War Mobilization Subcommittee of the Military Affairs Committee, became impressed with the need both for some comprehensive type of postwar legislation and for some permanent means of co-ordinating the consideration of postwar economic legislation in Congress.

"Starting in 1943, [he] had set his staff to work on an omnibus reconversion bill which would place special emphasis upon an administrative and planning mechanism in the Federal Government to oversee the orderly liquidation of the war economy, ease the human side of reconversion, and plan for the future."[1] He introduced a bill on March 29, 1944 which recommended giving OWM over-all responsibility for reconversion. A similar suggestion was made by Bernard Baruch who, with John M. Hancock, submitted a *Report on War and Postwar Adjustment Policies* to Mobilization Director Byrnes in February 1944. Senator Murray and many of his colleagues were out of sympathy with the Kilgore and Baruch approach on the ground that it by-passed Congress and put too much influence in the hands of administrative agencies responsible to the President. Even there, entrusting leadership to a Bureau of Programs would put an important policy-making function in the hands of a group removed by two steps from the seat of responsibility.

The War Mobilization and Reconversion Act won out over Kilgore's War Mobilization and Adjustment bill and the Murray Full Employment bill (S. 380), introduced shortly afterward, restored emphasis to the prerogatives of Congress in policy-making. By its terms the core of national economic policy was to be found in a National Production and Employment Budget. This was largely a statistical compilation and estimate of the Bureau of the Budget but called for policy conclusions derived from the estimates of production, employment, and public and private spending.

When the National Production and Employment Budget was transmitted to Congress, it was to be referred to a Joint Committee on the National Budget composed of the chairmen and the ranking

[1] Stephen K. Bailey, *Congress Makes A Law,* p. 31. A detailed account of these developments is given on pp. 28–36.

minority members of the standing committees on Appropriations, Banking and Currency, Education and Labor, and Finance (Ways and Means in the House) and additional members appointed by the President of the Senate and the Speaker of the House of Representatives. This Joint Committee was to study the National Budget and report to the Senate its findings and recommendations "together with a joint resolution setting forth for the ensuing fiscal year the general policy with respect to such National [Production and Employment] Budget to serve as a guide to the several committees of Congress dealing with legislation relating to such National Budget."

A NATIONAL ECONOMIC COMMISSION IS PROPOSED

As the "full employment" bill went through the process of Congressional consideration, its basic philosophy was substantially modified, and this change was reflected in the implementing machinery finally provided. As first introduced in the Senate by Senator Murray of Montana (with Wagner, Thomas, and O'Mahoney as cosponsors), it placed major reliance for stabilization action by the government on the balancing of a "national production and employment budget." To effect this balance, three steps were proposed: (1) The President, with the aid of various administrative agencies of government should annually take a statistical measure of the gap between prospective volume of private expenditure and the volume of total expenditure needed to sustain full employment. (2) The government was then to take such steps as seemed feasible toward so improving general business conditions as to raise the level of non-Federal investment and expenditure. (3) If the results were deemed insufficient to provide a full employment volume of production, Congress should undertake such "Federal investment and expenditure as will be sufficient to bring the aggregate volume of investment and expenditure . . . up to the level required to assure a full employment volume of production."[2]

[2] On the other hand, "if the estimated aggregate volume of prospective investment and expenditure for any fiscal year or other period, as set forth in the National Budget . . . is more than the estimated aggregate volume of investment and expenditure required to assure a full employment volume of production . . ." the President should propose and Congress act upon "a general program for preventing inflationary economic dislocations, or diminishing the aggregate volume of investment and expenditure to the level required to assure a full employment volume of production, or both."

In this Murray Full Employment bill, it was proposed that the preparation of the National Budget and the program for balancing aggregate investment and spending with full employment needs should be done "under the general direction and supervision of the President, and in consultation with the members of his Cabinet and other heads of departments and establishments."

The implication of this language might seem to be that the economic advisers to department or agency heads would have reconciled the special interests and claims of agriculture, labor, business, or other interests with the needs of the economy as an integrated whole, or that such reconcilement would take place through the process of Cabinet discussion or in the head of the President himself. It might seem to imply also that the existing staff of White House aides would have the time and technical qualifications needed to reduce the statistical estimates and the program recommendations to the form of a state paper which the President could send to the Congress at the beginning of each regular session or at times of special need as the expression of his economic statesmanship covering stabilization policy.

While this bill was under debate in the Senate Committee (Banking and Currency), minority members strongly advocated "an Office of Director of the National Budget" on the ground that "planning of this economic program is extremely complicated and cannot possibly be done by the President himself. It should be done by an identifiable group responsible to the Congress and the people, as well as to the President, and not by an anonymous group of economic planners." Against this view, sponsors of the bill argued that "before there has been any experience in the development of a national production and employment budget, there can be no sound basis for establishing a specific administrative framework, within which the President should operate. The wiser course is to allow the President to work out this problem in consultation with his Cabinet."

This line of argument may have reflected a view on the part of some sponsors that the bill itself prescribed the character of the stabilization policy to be followed, leaving to the President only the routine task of preparing the financial estimates which would be the basis on which Congress would authorize stabilization expenditures and taxes. The fight over the bill in both houses produced a progressive de-emphasis of this specific stabilization device in favor of a policy of comprehensive study of all sources of weakness or instability in the economy and synthesis of a comprehensive program embracing remedial actions of many sorts integrated into a consistent whole. It became increasingly clear that, for the preparation of such a report, the drafting services of the White House staff or the Bureau of the Budget and the discrete and politically conditioned consultation of Cabinet officers would be quite inadequate. Hence proposals for some special agency in the form of an economic commission or council were pressed from various quarters.

The metamorphosis of the pending bill was clearly stated by George Terborgh, research director of the Machinery and Allied Products Institute, in his testimony before the House Subcommittee. He said: "The Bill should be purged of its remaining vestiges of the right-to-a-job idea, its qualified but still persistent reliance on government spending as a panacea, and the surviving remnants of its mandate for long-range (fiscal-year) forecasting. Relieved of these incongruous carry-overs from earlier drafts, the bill would boil down . . . [to acceptance of Federal] responsibility to foster private enterprise . . . and promote a high and stable level of employment . . . to develop and pursue consistently an appropriate economic program"—for the President to evolve such a program and the Congress to review it. He thereupon pointed out that the President would need a professional staff specifically assigned to assist him in his task, what he called a National Economic Commission.

The bill, he said:

makes no real contribution to the organization and administration of national economic policy in the executive branch of the Government. It states merely that "the National Budget shall be prepared under the general direction and supervision of the President. . . ." Obviously, the President himself cannot give major attention to these activities. They must be delegated, therefore, to officials who remain anonymous in the bill. . . .

In consequence, both the economic analysis and the economic policy may be prepared and promoted by men unknown to the public, whose appointment has not been confirmed by Congress, and who have no formal public responsibility. This set-up invites behind-the-scenes manipulation by Presidential advisers of the moment, possessed, it may be, both by a passion for anonymity and a passion for controlling national economic policy. However able and high-minded these advisers may be, the arrangement is bad. If the Federal Government is really serious about developing and implementing a full-employment policy—as it should be—it ought to make better organizational provision than is made in this bill.

What is needed, in our view, is a small independent commission, appointed by the President and confirmed by the Senate, whose responsibility it should be to make continuous study of the art of business stabilization through Federal action. Appointment to this commission should be for a long term of full-time service and should carry a sufficient prestige and emolument to command the highest talent in the Nation. Provision should be made, of course, for an adequate staff, and for the full co-operation of other Federal agencies and departments. The commission should be required to issue periodic reports to the President, the Congress, and the public, giving both its findings and its recommendations for Federal policy, accompanied by a full statement of dissenting views.[3]

What Mr. Terborgh was here proposing was not a staff aid to the President in determining the outlines of his economic statesmanship and drafting his economic report. Instead, he proposed that an entirely detached body, somewhat in the nature of a British Royal Commission, present Olympian findings against which the President's recommendations and the legislative actions of Congress could be weighed—and found wanting. The paragraphs in which this recommendation was made follow hard upon one in which Terborgh had derided the "papa-knows-best tradition established during the last decade and a half" and deprecated the "abdication of the proper responsibility of Congress." This conception of the proposed commission is made pretty evident in the very next paragraph of Terborgh's testimony:

We believe that an official commission of this character, insulated so far as possible from political pressure, and commanding the attention and respect of the Nation, can make an invaluable contribution to public understanding of the complex and difficult art of economic stabilization, and can have a most salutary influence on public policy, now too often dominated, in the absence of popular comprehension of the problems involved, by the self-seeking demands of minority pressure groups and by the opinions and philosophies of a changing coterie of Presidential advisers, operating in the obscurity of the Executive Offices.[4]

[3] *Full Employment Act of 1945* (79 Cong. 1 sess.), Hearings before the Committee on Expenditures in the Executive Departments on H. R. 2202, Oct. 23, 1945, pp. 612–13.
[4] The same.

Terborgh's suggestion was seconded by the United States Chamber of Commerce. Pointing out that "there are no simple and pat remedies for instability and unemployment," the chamber continued:

The issues are so controversial and complicated that we recommend the appointment by the President of the United States, by and with the advice and consent of the Senate, of a permanent Economic Commission, composed of outstanding experienced citizens of unquestioned ability and integrity. These persons should be drawn from fields dissociated from politics and the interested parties. They should be appointed on a reasonably long-term basis, with staggered terms and subject to reappointment, and with adequate compensation in order to draw the very best talent available.

This Commission should be required to make quarterly reports as well as an annual report, with minority opinions in case of disagreement, to a joint committee of the House and Senate and to the President, especially with a view toward recommendations as to the inner consistency of government policies. . . . The Commission should be completely independent and its recommendations should be of an advisory character. The joint Congressional Committee and the President should be free to call on the Commission for recommendations on any matter pertaining to the problem of full utilization of resources.[5]

The idea of a National Economic Commission was also endorsed by the C.I.O. and had earlier been advocated by various officials of the AF of L. (See p. 47.) Members of the House Committee were impressed with the argument that the Employment Act should be provided with a permanent and professional staff organization for broad and continuous study of all elements of economic instability. However, they considerably changed the form of the proposed agency.

DUAL IMPLEMENTATION OF THE EMPLOYMENT ACT

In spite of this extensive sponsorship, the proposal for a National Economic Commission to advise both the President and the Congress did not gain the support of either the Senate or the House.

To invoke the aid of formal economic analysis and of trained economists in the making of practical policy, Congress provided dual implementation of the Employment Act. It included a three-man Council of Economic Advisers in the Executive Office of the Presi-

[5] Chamber of Commerce of the United States of America, *A Program for Sustaining Employment* (Report of Committee on Economic Policy), pp. 31–32.

dent. This Council was to have a small but high-quality staff and to draw upon the work of professional economists throughout the government and outside.

In Congress itself, the act provided for a joint committee on the Economic Report, consisting of fourteen members, seven from each House. It also was to have a small analytical staff and, of course, would be able to draw much professional assistance from the Legislative Reference Service of the Library of Congress. It was thought that assignment to this committee might be sought by legislators of superior economic training and business experience. It was to report its findings to the Congress, but its role of leadership in legislation was somewhat less than that expressed or at least implied in the Murray bill.

How this attempt to bring economics more fully into the public service has worked in practice will be examined in considerable detail in Parts II and III of this book. Some light on the nature of the operative problems involved and on reasonable criteria of success may be gained by first examining some earlier efforts within our Federal Government to use economists and statisticians as economic advisers either as technicians on operative problems, as advisers to Cabinet officers or agency heads concerned with segmental policy-making, or in some circumstances as advisers on the integration of segmental policies in the White House or in the Congress.

CHAPTER SIX

Precedents for Economic Advisership

In the preceding chapter we traced a number of steps which, over some years, moved the Federal Government progressively in the direction of a general statute embodying a national policy of economic stabilization—the Employment Act of 1946. It was a distinctive and novel feature of that act that it set up in the Executive Office of the President a Council of Economic Advisers to give professional assistance to the Chief Executive in this task of economic policy-making. That, however, was not the first time that economic advisers of professional training had been used in one capacity or another in the Federal Government. In the present chapter, therefore, we shall undertake to see how economic advisers had in the past been structurally or functionally introduced into Federal Government operations, and shall consider what changes or expansions of economic advisership were contemplated in the new statute.

This chapter will traverse much the same historical ground as did the previous one, but the emphasis will be different. From economic stabilization as an end of national policy we turn to professional staffing as a means toward sounder policy-making. We are not concerned with operational activities of the different agencies but with their analytical and policy-making activities. We shall examine those places in the Federal Government at which some individual or some group has been assigned, either by legislative or by administrative action, the task of reviewing the consequences of past economic policies or programs and projecting the probable consequences of alternatives proposed for future action. In a word, to what extent had economic staffing progressed within the structure of the Federal Government prior to the two organizational devices set up in the

Employment Act—in the Executive Office, the Council of Economic Advisers, and in the Congress, the Joint Committee on the Economic Report of the President. We can then see that act as the latest step in a development that goes back many years.

MR. ECONOMIST GOES TO WASHINGTON

It has been a matter of frequent and often plaintive comment by economists that their professional services were but little in demand in the Federal Government prior to World War I. Others might say that economists had little to offer in the field of public affairs. At all events, Professor Irving Fisher devoted his presidential address, at the annual meeting of the American Economic Association in December 1918, to this matter. His comments were in part congratulatory and in part a challenge to the profession.[1]

Fisher began by noting that not less than 120 economists had been called to Washington for government service during the war just closed! Of course there had for years before that time been many more than 120 persons of greater or less economic training scattered through the various departments and bureaus of Washington. By and large, however, they had functioned as technicians on limited

[1] Fisher's address contains much that is of interest in the light of subsequent developments. He said in part:

"Of the many effects which the war has exerted on the minds of men, one of the most notable is the keener desire which we all now feel to be of genuine public service. . . . During the impending world-reconstruction, economists will probably have more opportunity to satisfy this impulse than most students in other departments of human thought; for the great problems of reconstruction are largely economic. It therefore becomes each of us, as we pause on the threshold of a possible 'new world,' to consider what are the new opportunities and what the new duties which lie before us. . . .

"A generation ago many economists thought it beneath their dignity to engage at all in practical affairs except to cry: '*Laissez faire.*' They believed that a scientist should be simply an observer, compiler, and interpreter of facts, not a guide, counsellor, and friend of humanity. Their attitude of academic aloofness not only failed to give to economic study, in the eyes of the world, that status of a 'true science' which they claimed for it but, on the contrary, brought it into disrepute and provoked a vigorous reaction. . . .

"If we are to succeed [in rendering public service] it will be because we perform our task with wisdom, unselfishness, and impartiality. As economists in public service in a democratic world, we are pledged not to serve simply our local community, our own country, or our own time, but to serve rather all humanity throughout the world and throughout future generations." Irving Fisher, "Economists in the Public Service," *American Economic Review Supplement*, March 1919, pp. 5, 21.

phases of economic activity and had not been relied upon to any considerable extent at the policy-making level. That function was pretty generally reserved for the political appointees who headed up the several agencies.

There were some notable exceptions, however. Dr. Adolph Miller, who was a charter member and served long on the Federal Reserve Board, was an economist of distinction. Professor Taussig was brought in to render special service to the Tariff Commission at the policy level, and, during World War I, served in a similar capacity with the Price-fixing Committee of the War Industries Board. David Houston, who served as Secretary of Agriculture in Wilson's Cabinet, had had graduate training in economics and government and been president of a land-grant college in Texas.

In line with the "New Freedom" philosophy of Woodrow Wilson, Secretary Houston declared: "We have unmistakably reached the place where we must think and plan. We are suffering the penalty of too great ease of living. . . . We have been so bent on building up great industrial centers by every natural and artificial device that we have had little thought for the very foundations of our industrial existence."[2]

As an aid to his thinking and planning for agriculture, Houston turned to his old friend, Thomas N. Carver of the Department of Economics at Harvard University, who had been making studies of rural life with the financial support of the General Education Board of the Rockefeller Foundation. Carver was Director of Rural Organization Service in the Department for one year (1913-14) and continued as "Adviser in Agricultural Economics" during 1914-15. His recommendations led, among other things, to the establishment of the Bureau of Markets in 1917.

In 1922, Henry C. Wallace, as Secretary of Agriculture, brought Dr. Henry C. Taylor, an outstanding agricultural economist, to head up the Bureau of Agricultural Economics, into which were consolidated the Bureau of Markets, the Bureau of Crop Estimates, and the Office of Farm Management. Secretary Wallace thereafter continually turned to Dr. Taylor for advice on economic matters.[3]

[2] *Report of the Secretary of Agriculture*, 1913, p. 19.

[3] Besides recruiting an able staff of economists in this bureau, business, labor, and academic economists were brought in as consultants to guard against too narrow or partisan a view of agriculture's functioning in the economy. This practice began as early as 1923 in connection with the Outlook Conferences held each fall by the bureau.

Other departments, as they grew, were constantly enlarging their staffs of professionally trained economists and statisticians. These staffs, however, served largely on technical problems such as the preparation of the census, the current review of business statistics and trends, or of employment, unemployment, and labor market conditions. It would depend upon the temperament and outlook of each Cabinet officer or agency head as to whether or to what extent he would use the professional staff within his agency as a means for guiding his departmental policy or advising the President or Congress.

At best, there was an innate tendency for the economic work of each department or agency to be strongly influenced by the interests of its particular group of clients or constituents. Even if the agency head sought his staff's counsel for the purpose of integrating departmental policy into national welfare, it generally transpired that the advice was politically processed to a lower plane or narrower viewpoint before the voice of the Cabinet officer or agency head was heard by the President or the Congress. Anyone well acquainted in the professional staffs of Washington must know of instances in which research reports objectively beamed to national welfare rather than to group advantage were suppressed or editorially revamped before publication was permitted. At the same time, there have been staff economists who were willing rationalizers for their chief or protagonists for "causes" of their own.

In recent years, however, there have been an increasing number of instances in which objective economic analysis has been sought at a high policy-making level. Likewise the ways in which the problems are set and the kind of answers that are sought are, more frequently, those of national economic well-being in a broad context.

ECONOMIC ADVISERS TO AGENCY HEADS

Formal economic advisership to a Cabinet officer or the head of an independent board or commission emerged first in the case of the Federal Reserve System. The very nature of the functions performed by the Federal Reserve Board demanded an extensive staff of economic and statistical technicians. Its role as a central bank required also that it should take a very broad view of the whole economy and make intensive studies of its functioning as a guide to national credit policy.

Dr. H. Parker Willis, who had been an active participant in the process of drafting the Federal Reserve Act, became the first secretary of the Federal Reserve Board. He found a need for much fuller and more accurate statistics if the Board was to comply with the requirement of the act to make periodic reports to Congress on the financial condition of the country and to make the analyses necessary to the intelligent shaping of Federal Reserve policy. He directed various staff workers in the task of devising suitable report forms, and in September 1918, this project of reports and statistics was amplified into a Division of Analysis and Research.[4] Four years later, Walter W. Stewart became director of this division and its work was expanded and put on the very highest professional plane. Under subsequent directors,[5] this staff has continued to grow, to attract economists of first-rate ability, and to afford them favorable and congenial conditions for doing scientific work.[6] It has been the practice not only for the director of the division but for top staff members to sit in board meetings, where they could note the progress of policy discussions and contribute information or comment as called for.

When Thomas McCabe became chairman of the Board of Governors of the Federal Reserve in 1948, he brought in Dr. Winfield Riefler under the title "Assistant to the Chairman." An economist of unusually wide experience in policy matters, he not only advises and assists the Chairman as to economic developments and policies but also serves in a senior staff capacity on various matters for the Board and for the Open Market Committee.

The next year Thomas was given the title "Economic Adviser to the Board." He is expected to advise the Board on matters relating to its monetary and credit policies, and has particular responsibility for the Board's activities with respect to open market operations. In this

[4] "Thus was completed the general system of reports which had been provided for in the original Federal Reserve Act, and in the report of the Technical Committee on Organization, which had recommended most of the actual steps afterward agreed on. A foundation has thus been laid for regular banking self-analysis." H. Parker Willis, "Ten Years' Experience in Business Statistics," *Journal of the American Statistical Association,* June 1924, p. 209.

[5] Dr. E. A. Goldenweiser held this post from 1926 to 1945, Woodlief Thomas from 1945 to 1951, and Ralph Young since that time. The division is now known as Research and Statistics. There is also a Division of International Finance under the able direction of Arthur W. Marget.

[6] See E. A. Goldenweiser, *American Monetary Policy,* particularly Chapter VI, "Economic Intelligence."

capacity he serves also as economist for the Open Market Committee. In addition, he is a member of the Editorial Committee, which has charge of the publication of the Board's *Federal Reserve Bulletin*. He is chairman of the system's Research Advisory Committee which is composed of heads of research of Federal Reserve Banks, and has certain responsibilities for co-ordination of research and statistical activities within the Board's staff and throughout the system.

Besides its full-time economists, the Board has from time to time engaged special economic advisers to assist on particular topics or issues, notably Alvin Hansen during the period from 1940 to 1945. Lauchlin Currie, who served as assistant director of the Division of Research and Statistics from 1934 to 1939, thereafter became one of the "anonymous" assistants to the President until Mr. Roosevelt's death in 1945.

Turning to the field of agriculture, we find the Federal Farm Board, in 1929, taking a second step in the direction of using outstanding economists as advisers to its top policy-making officers. This agency presented the first instance of a board of strategy for the whole of a basic industry. As such, its members felt a need for the services of economists and statisticians of broad experience and outlook to aid them in dealing with over-all issues of policy for the industry as a segment of the whole economy. The Board brought in one of the most distinguished agricultural economists of the country—Dr. Joseph S. Davis of the Food Research Institute of Stanford University—as "chief economist." Following him, Dr. John D. Black of Harvard University served in a similar capacity until the Board was superseded by the Agricultural Adjustment Administration in 1933.

"Triple A" unlike the Federal Farm Board was established as part of the Department of Agriculture,[7] but with a separate organization

[7] In the first annual report of the Agricultural Adjustment Administration, Chester Davis, as Administrator, described the act as "the first step toward the attainment of a national policy for agriculture" and said of his report: "It supplements the outline of general information contained in Secretary Wallace's annual report with a complete and detailed description of what has been done toward effectuation of these policies and the purposes of the Agricultural Adjustment Act. . . . The Administrator wishes to acknowledge the assistance of Department economists and others in providing source material for this report. Experts and economists of the Bureau of Agricultural Economics, of other bureaus of the Department, and commodity sections of the Agricultural Adjustment Administration contributed much time and effort in its preparation." United States Department of Agriculture, *Agricultural Adjustment, May 1933–February 1934*, p. xi.

under an Administrator, a Co-administrator, and three Assistant Administrators, each in charge of a division. Of these three divisions, one was designated the Program Planning Division. Its task was "to relate all programs and activities under the Agricultural Adjustment Act to a general attack on the whole front of the agricultural situation, to correlate the programs for all commodities and to shape the entire program into a coherent whole which will constitute an advance through emergency measures to an established and lasting agricultural industry to the ultimate benefit of the whole nation."[8]

There were also in the AAA set-up four administrative assistants, of whom one was designated Consumers' Counsel. He was in effect an economic adviser to the Administrator with reference to the impact of control programs on the consumer.[9] The Consumers' Counsel thus became a second economic adviser to the Administrator, complementary to or a check upon the economic advice given by the head of the Program Planning Division. In addition, Louis Bean was designated economic adviser to the Agricultural Adjustment Administration from 1933 to 1939. The Bureau of Agricultural Economics served as a powerful source of statistical and analytical material and the advice of its chief was also sought by the Adjustment Administrator upon occasion. After 1939, Bean was designated counselor to the chief of the bureau. Chester Davis, who followed George Peek as Administrator of AAA, was himself something of a lay economist and was succeeded as Administrator by Howard Tolley, formerly chief of the Bureau of Agricultural Economics and subsequently head of the Program Planning Division of the Agricultural Adjustment Administration.

Henry Wallace designated Dr. Mordecai Ezekiel[10] as Economic

[8] The same, p. 15.

[9] "The primary interest of the Consumers' Counsel has been to see that an adequate supply of farm products for the consumer is maintained, and that such measures as would cause an undue spread between farm and retail prices, are avoided." To this end, "the staff of the Consumers' Counsel has participated in the economic analyses and in the conferences and hearings that have preceded the adoption of control programs for basic commodities, and the establishment of marketing agreements, licenses, and orders covering other commodities." *Agricultural Adjustment, 1933 to 1935,* p. 79.

[10] Ezekiel had been assistant chief economist to the Federal Farm Board under both J. S. Davis and John D. Black. When Wallace became Vice-President (1944), Ezekiel was designated Economic Adviser to the Bureau of Agricultural Economics.

Adviser to the Secretary. Professor Rexford G. Tugwell of Columbia University, one of the "brain trusters" brought to Washington by President Roosevelt in 1933, was assigned the post of Assistant Secretary of Agriculture and advanced to be Undersecretary the following year, when that post was created. He brought Dr. Gardiner Means into his office as "Economic Adviser on Finance." M. L. Wilson, who followed Tugwell as Undersecretary of Agriculture, was well known as an agricultural economist. All in all, the use of professional economists by top-level policy-makers in the Department of Agriculture at this time surpassed anything seen before in any Federal department.[11]

In 1947 Secretary Anderson brought Bean back (from the Bureau of the Budget) as staff assistant in his office, dealing with broad economic matters, not merely agricultural issues. The immediate problem was that of steel prices, which concerned Anderson not merely in terms of the cost of agricultural implements and other farm supplies but also as a Cabinet officer considering general industrial relations.

While Wallace was Secretary, the BAE had been specifically designated as the planning agency for the Department, thus to a degree taking the lead in agricultural policy-making out of the Secretary's office. This has now been changed. A Program Board, consisting of the Secretary, Undersecretary, and Assistant Secretary, and the heads of some half dozen major staff agencies has become the center of policy-making. Secretary Brannan had no one designated as "economic adviser in his office but turned to the chief of the Bureau of Agricultural Economics, the head of the Office of Foreign Agricultural Relations, the Director of the Production and Marketing Administration, or other staff agencies as he found them most useful for the particular question under consideration.

The Department of Commerce had, ever since its establishment as a Department of Labor and Commerce in 1903 (and much earlier in the case of the Census Bureau and other of its constituent parts), been building up one of the largest and most competent staffs of economists and statisticians in Washington. They had contributed in many, though not any formal or co-ordinated, ways to the economic thinking and policy-making of successive Secretaries. While

11 For a detailed discussion of staff organization in the Department of Agriculture, see John M. Gaus, Leon O. Wolcott, *Public Administration and the United States Department of Agriculture,* particularly Chaps. 3, 4, and 15.

Herbert Hoover was Secretary of Commerce, Dr. E. Dana Durand was Director of the Division of Statistical Research, and Hoover designated him "statistical assistant to the Secretary." Since Durand was well known as economist as well as statistician, this is probably the first instance of a Cabinet officer formally establishing the post of economic adviser in his department. At this time also, Dr. Julius Klein, who had been trained as an economic historian, was head of the Bureau of Foreign and Domestic Commerce. Secretary Hoover looked to him for assistance on many economic problems. In 1929, Klein became Assistant Secretary of Commerce.

Ten years later, Harry Hopkins brought Willard Thorp (formerly of the Bureau of Foreign and Domestic Commerce) back into the Department as "economic adviser to the Secretary of Commerce."[12] Thorp assembled a group of some eight young economists in a research and advisory group. Their first assignment was to prepare and present materials to the Temporary National Economic Committee, then making an extensive investigation of "the concentration of economic power." From this task, Thorp's group passed on to a very broad field of inquiry relating to recovery and stabilization policies. After about a year, Thorp left and was succeeded by Richard Gilbert as head of the group. Its members were often referred to around Washington as "the spark plug boys." Hopkins had a broad concern in the relation of business policy and practice to the functioning of the economy. But ill health precluded his giving real attention to the work of his department.

Jesse Jones had little if any interest in this kind of staffing and some members of Congress took a rather dim view of the purposes of the group and the qualifications of its members. With the departure of Hopkins from the Department, it faded into oblivion. Over a period of years, Dr. Amos Taylor, as chief of the Division of Research and Statistics and as Director of the Bureau of Foreign and Domestic Commerce performed important functions of economic advisorship to successive Secretaries, to recovery and war agencies, and on interdepartmental committees.

When Henry Wallace, who had had an "economic adviser" in the Department of Agriculture, became Secretary of Commerce, he established (March 1946) by Department order an "Office of Program

[12] He had been commuting from New York, where he was director of the research staff of Dun and Bradstreet.

Planning." It has continued to the present, with a small staff. It is a purely advisory body, having two functions: (a) to examine the programs of the various bureaus and other operating agencies of the Department[13] and (b) to analyze national and international economic issues in which the Department is concerned and make recommendations as to a desirable policy for the Department with reference to them. In general, the two functions are co-ordinate, but under one Secretary dominant emphasis may be given to the internal administrative program of the Department itself, whereas under another Secretary the advice which he seeks or accepts from this office may be primarily with reference to the functioning of the economy and the concerns of businessmen or "management" with reference to these broad economic policies.

Secretary Harriman made effective use of departmental conferences, in which the heads of appropriate bureaus or divisions and their top technicians (as well as members of the Office of Program Planning) would seek to get a well-rounded view of economic situations or problems that involved national or international policy.[14] From 1948 to 1951, an economist (Thomas C. Blaisdell, Jr.) was assistant secretary for Foreign and Domestic Commerce in the Department of Commerce. He had served previously as economic ad-

[13] The remark made with reference to the Department of Agriculture—"We are not a Department; we are a family of bureaus"—is no less true of the Department of Commerce, which embraces fifteen operating bureaus and offices. These bureaus include: the Weather Bureau, Bureau of the Census, the Bureau of Standards, the Coast and Geodetic Survey, the Inland Waterways Commission, the Patent Office (sic), and the Civil Aeronautics Administration, Maritime Administration, and the Bureau of Public Roads.

Whereas bureaus ordinarily have highly specialized functions and a good deal of operative autonomy, an "office" is generally advisory and is directly responsible to the department head. Four operative offices—Business Economics, Field Service, Domestic Commerce, and International Trade—have grown up in the Department of Commerce through subdivision of the Bureau of Foreign and Domestic Commerce, which still continues as a bureau of the Department. The fact-finding and analytical work of these offices is of basic importance to the Secretary in the making of departmental policy and in any attempt to relate it to national policy.

[14] On matters of domestic policy, the Secretary also consults the Business Advisory Council. This council was organized by the Secretary of Commerce in June 1933 and consists of a representative group of businessmen who are invited to serve without compensation for a one-year term. The council meets in Washington or at some convenient outside point bimonthly to discuss problems which they wish to bring to the attention of the Secretary or President or that have been referred to them for their views.

viser in various branches of the government[15] and tended during the period of his secretaryship to become one of the top economic advisers to the Secretary or the Secretary's representative in various interagency conferences at the policy-making level. This situation is comparable to that noted in the Department of Agriculture (p. 83), and the Department of State (p. 87).

The Department of Labor has grown by the addition of various operative and regulatory branches to a fact-finding and statistical bureau which was established in 1884 and which still constitutes the major element in the Department. The statistics which it gathers cover a wide range of economic activities besides employment and wages—such for example as consumer expenditures, construction activities, and industrial productivity. The head of the bureau is designated as Commissioner of Labor Statistics and is the staff official whom the Secretary normally consults on matters of economic policy. Likewise he frequently represents the Secretary in interagency conferences involving economic questions.

In addition to the role of the Commissioner of Labor Statistics as economic adviser to the Secretary, there was established in the Department of Labor by Secretary Frances Perkins an economic advisory group which still continues, with a small full-time staff and designation as an "office"—that is, reporting directly to the Secretary.

Here, as elsewhere, the character and significance of an economic advisory post depends both on the personality of the Secretary and on the training and temperament of the man occupying the subordinate post. When Isador Lubin became Commissioner of Labor Statistics in 1933, issues of recovery policy were pressing. He had had considerable experience in policy-making positions,[16] and Secretary

[15] Assistant director, consumers' counsel, Agricultural Adjustment Administration; executive director, Consumers Advisory Board, NRA; economic adviser to the administrator of the Resettlement Administration; assistant director, Bureau of Research and Statistics, Social Security Board; assistant director, National Resources Planning Board; member of the Planning Committee of the War Production Board; director of the Bureau of Plans and Statistics, Office of War Mobilization and Reconversion; and chief of the Mission for Economic Affairs to London (with rank of minister).

[16] Economic adviser to various Congressional committees, chairman, Labor Advisory Board, Federal Emergency Administrator of Public Works; vice-chairman, United States Central Statistical Board; President's Economic Security Commission; U. S. representative on the governing body of the International Labor Organization; member of the Temporary National Economic Committee, and U. S. representative on Allied Reparations Commission to Moscow (with rank of minister).

Perkins was eager to make the Department contribute as actively as possible to the formulation of policies and programs which would promote absorption of a large number of unemployed. Lubin and his deputy commissioner, A. Ford Hinrichs, not only were economic advisers to the head of their department, but also were active contributors to interagency conferences in which all phases of national economic policy were being considered. He brought into his bureau staff not only statistical technicians but competent economic analysts.

In 1941, Lubin was moved into a position on the White House staff as one of the "anonymous assistants" to the President. In his absence, Hinrichs served as acting commissioner. After Lubin left he failed of promotion to the commissionership because of labor union resentment over the objective and independent manner in which he had discharged the duties of this difficult post. But he waged a gallant battle to retain control as acting commissioner until confirmation could be secured for a man of proper qualifications and character—the present incumbent.

In the Department of State, a post of economic adviser was specifically designated as early as 1922 and has been occupied by economists of recognized standing. Dr. Herbert Feis held this post from 1931 to 1937, after which his title was Adviser on International Affairs until 1943, when he became "special consultant to the Secretary of War." In 1934 Henry Grady, a well-trained economist, formerly dean of the College of Commerce of the University of California, and vice-chairman of the United States Tariff Commission from 1937 to 1939, was made chief of the Trade Agreements Division of the Department. With Alvin Hansen (then serving as economic adviser to the Department) and others, he had the task of implementing the trade agreements program based on the Trade Agreements Act of 1934. This division developed an interdepartmental organization and did much to formulate a new United States commercial policy, which was crystallized in the "general provisions" of the agreements and has now become thoroughly integrated with our international economic policy.

Leo Pasvolsky, on leave from the Brookings Institution, joined this Trade Agreements Division in 1935. The following year, he became special assistant to the Secretary of State, Cordell Hull, whom he served in a close personal relationship until the latter's resignation in 1944. His field of work expanded to include a considerable range of research in the Department, and he was, at various times designated chief of the Division of Special Research, supervisor of the Division of Political and Economic Studies, and Executive Director of the Committee on Postwar Programs. He continued his services to the Department under Secretaries Byrnes and Stettinius. Because of previous specialization in monetary problems and his facility in the use of the Russian language, he played an important role in the Dumbarton Oaks Conference and at the San Francisco conference launching the United Nations.

From 1939 to 1941, Henry Grady served as Assistant Secretary of State in charge of Economic Affairs, followed by Willard Thorp, well known as an economist and statistician. The staff of this division came to embrace some 300 persons, its particular function being to analyze the impact of domestic economic developments on foreign relations and the impact of our foreign policy on domestic affairs. In the fall of 1952 Thorp resigned this post to return to academic life.

The Treasury Department, unlike some others, has a fairly well integrated function—financial and hence basically economic in character. Though of course it harbors a few orphans like the Bureau of Narcotics and the Coast Guard, its central problem is fiscal policy and management. Treasury's use of advisers from professional ranks goes back to the days of T. S. Adams and R. M. Hale, and in recent years includes such well-known economists as Walter Stewart, Jacob Viner, O. W. M. Sprague, Carl Shoup, and Roy Blakey. Harry White entered the Department as an economist in the research division of which, in the process of time, he became director. Thereafter he was made Assistant to the Secretary and then Assistant Secretary.

Henry Morgenthau used the staff conference (with some outside consultants) as a means of getting pretty broad analysis of economic and financial matters which had an impact on Treasury policy and operation. But, particularly with a national debt of present size, the Treasury has been prone to feel that its "needs" are paramount in matters of national economic policy.

The Department of the Interior is one of the most miscellaneous agglomerations of bureaus or services to be found in the Federal Government. It has never developed a permanent philosophy or organization of economic policy-making or consideration of the part which should be played in the national economy by the industries or activities which it represents. It has a small Office of Program

Analysis, but the activities of the office are devoted largely to consideration of internal administrative co-ordination rather than the economics of land reclamation, power development, or the development and use of other natural resources in relation to the total economy. During the years of the National Recovery Administration, Secretary Ickes had charge of the Public Works Administration, whose operation was deeply involved in the question of re-employment and the broadest questions of stabilization policy. During the war, the Petroleum Administration for War, and now the Petroleum Administration for Defense have been located in the Department of the Interior.

As the Council of Economic Advisers sought to integrate issues of national resource use and development into its analyses of national policy, Interior moved to set up or reactivate a planning group in the office of the Secretary. But many of the bureaus of this Department have their own statutory authorizations and direct relations with Congress. Real policy integration under these conditions is extremely difficult.

ECONOMIC ADVISERS TO RECOVERY AND WAR AGENCIES

The growth of old departments and the appearance of several new "independent" agencies of the Federal Government was accompanied by an increasing use of professionally trained economists as advisers at the policy-making level and not merely as technicians at the operative level. This advance from the tactical to the strategic role had, prior to 1933, however, been limited largely to consideration of the strategy of a segment of the economy—the attack on the problem of economic stabilization on a single front, such as the credit or monetary policies of the Federal Reserve or the agricultural adjustment policies of the Federal Farm Board.

War always serves as a unifying influence, however temporary or misguided, and so World War I had brought some measure of integration among segmental policies. The War Industries Board was at first expected to be adequate to the task of directing the economy in time of war. But, gradually, it was supplemented by a War Trade Board, a War Labor Board, a Food and Fuel Administration, and numerous satellites or offshoots. Bernard Baruch, whose role came closest to being that of Economic Stabilizer of World War I, was an astute and nimble stock market trader rather than a business statesman or an economist. "Even after the War Industries Board was given sweeping powers in March 1918, its activities were still governed by 'expediency in individual instances' rather than 'by an established policy for which the whole administration took responsibility.' "[17] Likewise, the Price-fixing Committee set up to deal with prices and wages operated by methods of negotiation, opportunism, and sheer bluff rather than having any thought-through policy or principle to use as a bench mark—from which the nature and necessity of compromises could be measured.

As mentioned previously, a number of distinguished economists were brought in during the war for consultation or for continuous work. But they were closer to the level of operational tactics or segmental strategy than to the top administrative command and its grand strategy for the economy. Over-all integration of economic policy depended on the strength of the Cabinet, and the leadership of Woodrow Wilson. The President had no great admiration for scholars in government, and, of course, at this time the statistical fact-finding and analytical work of the government was still in a quite rudimentary stage.

The Great Depression made a new demand for integration of national economic policy. It was pointed out in Chapter IV that the recovery program launched by the President and Congress in 1933, although it had at least five major manifestations, was in fact conceived as a related or comprehensive program for the economy. It launched an attack in the province of the Department of Agriculture through the AAA; in the province of the Department of Commerce through the Code Authorities; in the province of the Labor Department under the banner of the "Blue Eagle"; in Interior's province through the Public Works Administration; and in the province of the Treasury and the Federal Reserve through a series of fiscal, monetary, and credit measures.

In the preceding section of this chapter, we have noted the increasing use of professional economists as economic advisers to the administrative heads of most of these departments or agencies. This use was far from systematic though some approach toward coordination was effected through informal conference among these economic advisers or the more formal device of the interdepartmental committee. Something of an intellectual clearing house for

[17] Joseph Dorfman, *The Economic Mind in American Civilization (1865–1918)*, Vol. III, p. 477.

total policy was obtained also through the "brain trust" of personal confidants of the President. Most of them found "a local habitation and a name" in executive departments closely related to the recovery program—such as Undersecretary Tugwell in Agriculture. Adolph Berle as Special Counsel of the Reconstruction Finance Corporation, Thomas Corcoran as Assistant to the Attorney General, and Benjamin Cohen as Associate General Counsel to PWA. Raymond Moley, presiding genius of the group, was appointed Assistant Secretary of State. Judge Rosenman bore the title "Special Counsel to the President."

A more formal device for group discussion and policy co-ordination was afforded through the Executive Council and its successor, the National Emergency Council. (See pp. 57–58.) The Executive Order establishing the Executive Council described it as designed "for the orderly presentation of business and to co-ordinate inter-agency problems of organization and work of the new government agencies." A second Executive Order created the office of Economic Adviser to the Executive Council, and this post was filled by Dr. Winfield Riefler, chairman of the Central Statistical Board.[18] Later he continued as economic adviser to the National Emergency Council.

This office was abolished by the Reorganization Plan of July 1, 1939, which established the Executive Office of the President. Within this Office, President Roosevelt appointed ten "anonymous" assistants to the President, several of whom were economists and/or statisticians of broad training and experience. This staffing, together with such advice as came to the President from the National Resources Planning Board, set the pattern of economic advisership in

[18] Statistical services had, over the years, grown up, Topsy-like, in many Federal agencies, with the result that there were gaps, overlaps, and contradictory or at least ambiguous statistics emanating from the different sources. Under the good offices of the Social Science Research Council and on the neutral ground of the Brookings Institution conference room, the heads of the several agencies were brought together with nongovernment statisticians, not without considerable struggle, in May 1933. This meeting discussed defects and means of improving government statistics and set up an interdepartmental committee on government statistics. Spade work by the committee led to the establishment of the Central Statistical Board in August 1933 under authority of the NIRA. This board was to "plan and promote improvement, development, and co-ordination of Federal and other statistical services." After six years of useful work, the functions of this board were transferred to the Division of Statistical Standards of the Bureau of the Budget.

the Executive Office of the President in 1945 when the Employment
Act was first proposed. Though the President's uncle was chairman
of the NRPB and its members and staff had high hopes as to its
advisory role, it never succeeded in becoming really influential.

ECONOMIC ADVISERS TO THE PRESIDENT AND TO CONGRESS

Three decades or more of varied and expanding use of economists
in the Federal Government, both its executive and its legislative
branches, gave Congress a rich body of experience to draw upon in
providing suitable implementation for the Employment Act of
1946. We noted in Chapter V that the central objective of this act
was to shape national policy toward the end of economic stabilization
and to integrate the policies of the several administrative agencies
and the various legislative directives to this end. To promote this
purpose, two agencies of central and permanent economic advisership were proposed. The Employment Act established, in the
Executive Office of the President, a Council of Economic Advisers,
to serve as a staff arm to the President in the preparation of annual
and special economic reports to the Congress which would embody
a consistent economic program. The Act also set up a joint committee of the Senate and House to perform a similar leadership and
co-ordination function with reference to economic legislation.

It was not specifically stated that members of the Council of Economic Advisers should have had professional training as economists
but that each "shall be a person who, as a result of his training,
experience, and attainments, is exceptionally qualified to analyze
and interpret economic developments, to appraise programs and
activities of the government in the light of the policy declared [in
the Act], and to formulate and recommend national economic policy." Without superseding such economic advisership as was already
provided in various government agencies, the Council would furnish
a means of comparative and integrating study of segmental policies
with a view to assisting the President in charting a course which
would promote the well-being of the whole economy. The staff provided for the Council was to be small, being limited to a synthesizing function and relying upon existing agencies in the government
and outside for factual material and preliminary analyses.

While there are obvious differences between the role assigned the
Council of Economic Advisers and that assigned the Joint Com-

mittee, there is also an underlying similarity. Since membership in the committee is not at all dependent on a man's position as chairman or ranking minority member of any committee, it could draw to its ranks any person who has special interest in or fitness for its duties. The phrases used to guide the President in his appointment of members of the Council of Economic Advisers might well guide the President of the Senate and Speaker of the House in making their selections of members of the Joint Committee. A member might be "especially qualified" as the result of academic training, business experience, public service, or a combination of all these avenues of preparation. Since the party representation was "as nearly as feasible to reflect the relative membership of the majority and minority parties in the Senate and House," the committee would presumably have a bipartisan or unpartisan character.

Its composition and the fact that it had available to it the methods of public hearing, questionnaire, and easy means of consultation with all government personnel and private spokesmen for economic interests would put it in a position to play a role not too dissimilar to that proposed for a National Economic Commission. Printed and mimeographed materials prepared by the committee, the participation of its members in the work of other committees, and the voices of members raised in Congressional debate on matters touching national economic policy would make it in a very real sense a committee of economic advisers to the Congress—and to the country.

The Joint Committee on the Economic Report was given a small staff of its own but would be in a position to secure almost unlimited assistance from the staffs of the various executive departments and from the Library of Congress. The Legislative Reference Service of the Library has a sizable staff of competent economists and statisticians, some of whom are assigned full-time to the work of the Joint Committee, whereas others are available for special tasks.

Thus the door has been opened for the use of economics in the public service or of economic science in practical policy-making on a plane never possible before.

PART
II

We Start to Administer the Employment Act

INTRODUCTION

Part I undertook to examine something of the philosophical background of national economic policy in the United States and to trace the steps by which we moved to the position taken in the Employment Act of 1946. Although that measure was under Congressional debate for more than a year and was passed in the House by a sweeping majority and in the Senate by a voice vote, there was considerable uncertainty in government circles and among the public as to precisely what the statute meant, what was the "intent of Congress," and how the law would operate in practice.

Many people who had been strong proponents of the original bill felt that the law as finally passed was "watered down," "emasculated," or qualified to the point of futility. Others, who had been unfriendly to or even alarmed by the Murray Full Employment bill felt that, even though the Employment Act might have potentialities of usefulness if wisely administered, it was susceptible to dangerous misuse if members of the Council of Economic Advisers or of the Joint Committee of Congress should show ideological quirks or be technically incompetent. The very generality of the terms in which the act was drawn meant that its actual impact on the economy and on our frame of government would depend to an extraordinary degree on the character of the Council members and the Joint Committee members to whom its administration would be entrusted.

The first roster of membership on the Joint Committee included strong men from both parties and probably somewhat divergent intentions or hopes as to their work on this new committee— whether pushing operations under the statute vigorously forward in

97

particular directions or of preventing its being used to promote dangerous or undesirable activities. Before the Joint Committee was really organized for work, its chairmanship and party control passed from the Democratic to the Republican side and, two years later, back to the party which, in general, was regarded as more aggressive in its interpretation of the law. The Council, on the other hand, has continued with two of its three original members still in office and thus far has served only one Chief Executive—a man who as President signed the act and as Senator had been a supporter of the original bill.

Over a period of a little more than six years there has, therefore, been built up a reasonably coherent and yet somewhat varied administrative experience under this statute. It seems timely now to attempt to write a concurrent history of these administrative developments while events are still fresh in the public mind and while practically all the active participants are still on the scene, available for consultation or for criticism of the analysis which is here presented.

The next ten chapters will be limited in the main to a merely narrative account of events as they have transpired over this six-year period. Naturally my acquaintance is more intimate with the affairs of the Council than with those of the Joint Committee. Likewise my recordings are in the nature of the case more subjective. I have, however, had the helpful co-operation both of members and of staff of the Joint Committee, supplementing my firsthand observations during the period while I was still in office. I have also had the helpful co-operation of many persons connected directly or indirectly with the work of the Council and have endeavored by advance criticism from them to remove as fully as possible any personal bias from the narrative which I present in Part II.

During the five years just before I became a member of the Council of Economic Advisers, I had sat in many deliberations of the Social Science Research Council in which we had discussed the need to "capture and record" social events at the time of their occurrence and in the subjective terms of their participants if later students were to have the basic data for an objective evaluation of the social process. Beginning one month after the passage of the

Agricultural Adjustment Act of 1933, I had directed and participated actively in a "concurrent study" of the new farm price support program—itself a daring experiment in economic stabilization. The Brookings Institution had very shortly instituted a parallel study of the National Recovery Act. From the time I entered the Council, therefore, I felt an interest in studying what was going on in terms of administrative structure and practice no less than economic content. Accordingly, I undertook to keep a personal record from which I might in due time re-examine this episode in the history of our country in its contemporary setting and make this review of the events available to other students who might later wish to assess the causes of success or failure of this political-economic innovation—the Employment Act.

Since I am not by temperament or habit a diarist, this personal record was by no means a daybook. In the weariness and confusion of difficult periods, weeks might sometimes elapse between entries. The most typical kind of memorandum was a fairly long note written just after a talk with the President—nominally at intervals of a month. In this note I would not merely set down the events or comments of the moment but would pick up such matters as had transpired since the last note and which struck me at the time as needed to make a connected account of the Council's life.[1] These current notes are frequently quoted at some length as constituent parts of the narrative of Parts II and III, with citation of source and the date of the original entry. (For brevity, the initials "P. D." have been used to refer to this personal diary.)

In dealing with the Joint Committee I have of course had no such inside knowledge to draw upon. Many phases of its work I followed closely from the vantage point of the Council while I was in that post and later as an interested citizen. I had a previous personal acquaintance with most of the members who have served on the committee's staff, and with several members of the committee itself. The late Dr. Charles O. Hardy, who was the first director of the Joint Committee staff, had been a long-time colleague of mine at the Brookings Institution, and during 1947 and '48 I had numerous frank discussions with him on matters that concerned the commit-

---

[1] These notes, interlarded with some correspondence and documents, are available to any qualified student and, if interest seems to justify it, will eventually be deposited in the National Archives or some university library.

tee's work. I am deeply indebted to members of the present staff for their frank criticisms of my discussion of committee activities and for furnishing me with materials I would otherwise have lacked.

To some readers, Part II may seem to record the words and actions of individuals in needless detail. But in the scientific study of economic and political institutions, these personal details are the basic data which have first to be amassed and organized if we are to make sound inductive conclusions or inferences as to the functioning of an administrative agency. An adequate case history of the first epoch of the Employment Act is necessary before the hypothesis of Part I (the dependence on economic science for the shaping of practical policy) can be re-examined and evaluated in Part III.

Professor Millett has put this issue very well:

Public administration is necessarily personal. The lawyer and the politician may say all they wish about "a government of law." We live in a society of men, and any organization is at best a continuing problem in the adjustment of individual personalities to each other and to a common cause. Much of our writing in public administration has completely ignored this fact. . . . The teaching of what is called public administration in our various universities should be very different in the next few years from what it was before 1939. And much of the writing should take on a personal cast which it has never had in the past.

I suppose there will be some question as to the propriety of those with academic interests writing accounts made possible by their own service within the government. There are a number of dangers. If a person is going to accept government employment only to write about it afterwards, he may be much less welcome in public service than in the past. There is, of course, the further difficulty that any individual who writes about his own experience is almost always convinced that he was right and those who disagreed with him wrong. It is not easy to admit personal mistakes, especially in writing. Yet one may claim that a devotion to the cause of human knowledge transcends ordinary considerations and justifies a reporting of individual experience accurately and honestly.[2]

I had not wanted to exaggerate the public importance of the Council of Economic Advisers or to presume on the degree of interest the reading public might have in my personal interpretation of the Council's role or the significance of day-to-day actions of myself or others. But I decided in the end that the best technique

2 John D. Millett, *The Process and Organization of Government Planning*, p. viii.

was to tell the story with such degree of detail as seemed to me meaningful to "the student," that is the person in or out of academic halls or professional employment who would be concerned with the institutional development of his government or the economy. Personalities and their subjective qualities are dealt with frankly and freely where this seemed useful for illustration, or indeed an indispensable part of the objective analysis. I believe the study would be robbed of essential vital qualities if such personal details were omitted.[3]

In the theater it is only through a troupe of human actors that a drama marches to its tragic ending or a comedy unfolds its happy denouement. These actors through their bearing, their movements, their enunciation, their "stage business" determine whether or how well the message of the piece gets across. But "the play's the thing." The real issue is whether the dramatist has something to say which is important and helpful. Here the question is the social significance of the Employment Act. Is the apparatus of a Council of Economic Advisers and a Joint Economic Committee a practicable means for bringing economic science to bear on the making of practical national policy? This is the question to be examined in Part III, to which the personalities of Part II are merely preliminary.

[3] I have been aware too that to some readers it would be quite meaningless to mention the names of particular members of the Council or committee staffs, whereas to others the mere mention of the name would be highly illuminating as to the professional capacities of the group and the range of its leanings. I have used the names of such individuals where it seemed they would be helpful to even a minority of readers.

CHAPTER SEVEN

Getting the Council Under Way

Late in the evening of July 24, 1946, I received, on my home telephone, a surprise call from the White House.

"This is Charles Ross. I am speaking for the President. He wishes to know whether you would consider a position on the Council of Economic Advisers, which is being set up under the Employment Act. I assume you are familiar with that act."

"Yes, in a general way. But such a job is hardly my dish. And anyway I am in the midst of a heavy work program at the Brookings. . . . Etc. . . . Etc."

"Well, do you mean you won't come in and discuss the matter with the President?"

"Not that, of course. One doesn't send such a message to the President of the United States. . . . Tomorrow? Yes. . . . Ten o'clock? Yes, I'll be there."

I had come to know Ross quite well over the years. Our homes were in the same general neighborhood, and his reporting of economic and governmental matters for the St. Louis Post-Dispatch had caused him to keep in touch with much of the work of the Brookings Institution. I therefore spoke very frankly when I met him next morning. I said that if I were to consider such a move my final decision would be influenced very much by what was expected of the Council, on what plane it was intended that it should function, and who my colleagues would be.

Ross replied by reaching into the top drawer of his desk and handing me two personality sketches. As an old newspaper man,

he might well have said: "Don't you read the papers?" For, two
days earlier, the Washington *Post* had carried front-page pic-
tures of Winfield Riefler and Leon Keyserling over the headline:
"Riefler, Keyserling, and Clark Seen as Economic Council."[1] The
name of Riefler, whose high standing and broad experience
have already been discussed in the preceding chapter, evoked
political opposition and was withdrawn. Thus my number came
up.

The sketches handed me by Ross were those of Keyserling and
Clark, and I was told that both had accepted. Ross said: "I can
assure you there is no politics in Council appointments—except, of
course, that Mr. Keyserling was named in response to Senator
Wagner's wishes."[2]

As to what the President expected of the Council, how he conceived its duties and service, and the conditions under which it
would operate, Ross said: "I am certain you can be satisfied on
these points by talking with the President. I'll see if we can't slip
you in between other appointments." Within ten minutes, I was
seated at the President's desk. He said that he had been a strong
advocate of the passage of the Employment Act and thought that
the Council could render important service in helping to accomplish its purposes. He was not at all specific as to how he expected
to use it, but said it should be "fact-finding" in character. I repeated the remark I had made to Ross about having a full program and no craving for an official position—that I must consider
the matter carefully.

I asked the President how soon he must have a decision. He
said he had hoped to announce the Council appointments at his

[1] At this time also, the name of Oscar Chapman, then Undersecretary of the
Interior, was prominently mentioned in the press. He was in fact offered the chairmanship of the Council some time in June. He demurred on the ground that his
training was in law and his experience exclusively in governmental service. Appointment of both him and Keyserling would not make for a well-balanced Council;
he argued that Clark would supply much needed business experience, along with
his economic training. He also endorsed my appointment.

[2] Some people were not altogether sure that Clark's appointment bore no relationship to his personal friendship for Senator O'Mahoney and his services in
Wyoming politics. "Senator O'Mahoney has known him from the time he was
city attorney at Cheyenne, Wyoming in 1907. This acquaintanceship apparently
explains his emergence as one of the President's principal advisers." *The Nation*,
Aug. 10, 1946.

press conference that afternoon[3] but would give me reasonable time to consider the matter. As I was going to New York within a few hours, it was agreed that I would give him a reply by ten o'clock Monday morning. He strongly urged me to accept as a matter of important public service.

At Ross's tactful suggestion, I left the West Wing by a service entrance, thus avoiding reporters in the lobby.

As soon as I got back from the White House, I sought out two trusted friends, one of whom had been a former academic colleague of John Clark, the other a man who was well acquainted personally with Mr. Keyserling and had had excellent opportunity to observe his governmental career. I also ran on to Albert Goss, Master of the National Grange. This was the first time I had ever talked with him about the Employment Act. The comments of these men were illuminating and, on the whole, reassuring. But for the next three days, I struggled doubtfully with the question to accept or not to accept.

THE DIE IS CAST

I felt that the Employment Act of 1946 contained great possibilities for dealing more soundly with the economic affairs of government or the governmental aspects of business, but also that it could be badly interpreted and gravely misused. I was challenged by the possibility of helping to make objective analysis the basis of government policy-making but questioned whether by temperament or

[3] There had been considerable criticism of delay in setting up the Council. The President was anxious to announce appointments and have them confirmed by the Senate before its adjournment so that work could be organized in time for the Economic Report which he would have to present when Congress reconvened in January. The Washington Post story of July 23 had said: "It [the Council] has never been set up because of President Truman's long-continued failure to obtain acceptances from the individuals whom he considered of proper caliber for the job." The Washington column of Peter Edson commented: "The struggle to get a satisfactory three-man Council of Economic Advisers to administer the full employment act has been one of the longest man-hunts on record. The employment act was signed Feb. 20. In the more than five months since then, over 100 names have been in and out of the White House hat. The three men selected were all last-minute surprise appointments, named to beat the deadline of confirmation by the Senate before adjournment."

The appointments of Keyserling and Clark were announced at the press conference on July 25—along with that of James Webb as Director of the Bureau of the Budget. Both were promptly confirmed by the Senate Banking and Currency Committee.

background I was fitted for the rough-and-tumble of public life. Indeed I seriously questioned whether I would be able to stand for any considerable time the physical and nervous strain which the position, as I envisaged it, would entail. On the other hand, I felt that this was a professional opportunity which should not go by default. Some economists of high qualifications who had been offered the post had felt they had to decline for personal or family reasons. Others had been found politically unacceptable.

What was, I think, the decisive element in my final action was this: It was common knowledge that various interest groups were pushing "their man" for this last place on the Council, and many of the persons being thus sponsored seemed to me quite unfitted for the task described in the act. It was understood that the President was now determined to make an appointment within a few days, before going on a vacation trip. Hence, with some misgivings, I sent the following letter to the White House at ten o'clock on Monday morning:[4]

July 29, 1946

The President
The White House
Washington, D. C.

Dear President Truman:

Last week you did me the honor of inviting me to accept your appointment as chairman of the Council of Economic Advisers created under the Employment Act of 1946. To accept this appointment would completely disrupt the program of professional work which I had laid out for myself for the coming years. However, the importance of the task you propose for me and the possibilities which it offers of rendering public service are so great that I feel I cannot do other than accept.

As you remarked when I talked with you last week, this Act makes a distinct new step in the history of this country. It will be of the utmost importance that the first Council serving under it shall understand its task so wisely and organize its activities so skillfully that all members of the government and of the public alike shall be impressed with the fact that this is a well-conceived agency of democratic government and a great aid

---

[4] The *Washington Post* on July 30, 1946 carried this item: "After a long search for qualified men who would accept the $15,000 a year posts, equal in pay to that of Cabinet members, Mr. Truman last Thursday announced two of them—Leon Keyserling and John Davidson Clark. The Senate Banking Committee yesterday approved their nominations. Nourse, however, did not accept until 11 a. m. yesterday, pending further study of what would be expected of him."

in the promotion of sustained prosperity and economic stability. I should like therefore to state in a few paragraphs my conception of what is properly to be expected of this Council.

In your own words, it is primarily "fact-finding." A great many branches of the Federal Government already operate extensive fact-finding agencies. The first function of the Council will be to piece together a complete and consistent picture of the economic state of the nation from these official sources and from any non-official sources which appear to be useful. The Council must detect errors of method, bias, or inconsistency and, by revealing these shortcomings of the nation's fact-finding machinery, lead to their correction. Quite possibly this might also lead to the elimination of expensive and confusing duplications.

But "facts" do not clearly and unequivocally "speak for themselves." Their meaning has to be brought out by persons professionally trained for reading the record. Anyone can look at an X-ray picture and, with very little training, anyone can take such a picture. But only the skilled specialist can tell what it means. Hence, as I see it, the second function of the Council is to interpret all available literal facts into the soundest possible diagnosis as to the state of the nation's economic health and the causes which explain any evidence of current ill health or which threaten to produce unhealthy conditions in the future. Since even the best of doctors are often in disagreement as to what the picture actually shows is going on in a bodily organism, we must draw many economic specialists into consultation on the special phases of our diagnosis.

All this adds up to saying that the Council of Economic Advisers is conceived as a scientific agency of the Federal Government. Its prime function is to bring the best available methods of social science to the service of the Chief Executive and of the Congress in formulating national policy from year to year and from month to month. There is no occasion for the Council to become involved in any way in the advocacy of particular measures or in the rival beliefs and struggles of the different economic and political interest groups. It should give a clearer and more comprehensive picture than we have ever had as to the economic state of the nation, as to factors which are tending to retard prosperity, and as to the probable effect of various remedial measures which may be under consideration by the Executive or the Congress.

If this statement correctly interprets the act and reflects your hopes and purposes for the Council, I feel that the position you offer me is one of unparalleled opportunity as well as responsibility. To it, if my nomination is confirmed by the Senate, I shall give my most loyal service.

Respectfully yours,

/s./ E. G. Nourse

On July 31, the President wrote me: "I appreciate very much your letter of the 29th. A statement was issued, which I think completely covers the situation. I am looking forward to real results from this setup." The "Statement by the President" given to the press on July 29 read as follows:

I have today nominated Mr. Edwin G. Nourse to be a member of the Council of Economic Advisers, provided for by the Employment Act of 1946, and propose to designate him as chairman.

I consider that this act constitutes a distinct and vitally important new step in the history of this country. It is the function of the Council to formulate and recommend national economic policies to promote employment, production, and purchasing power under free competitive enterprise.

One of its primary functions is "fact-finding."[5] It will piece together a complete and consistent picture of the economic state of the nation. The next function of the Council will be to interpret all available facts and then to present the soundest possible diagnosis as to the state of the nation's economic health.

Our country is capable of maintaining an economy free from the evils of both inflation and deflation. With such an economy, our country can go forward to greater heights of prosperity and full employment than have yet been achieved. This policy must be predicated upon a program of fair dealing and justice to all our people.

The Council will be in a position to present to the nation a clearer and more comprehensive analysis than we have ever had regarding the economic state of the nation and all factors which tend to retard prosperity.

It was suggested to me from the White House that the President wanted to have the Council sworn in as promptly as possible as he was planning to leave on a month's cruise on the Williamsburg. I was in the midst of a busy program at Brookings, and this proposal had come up literally over night. But I dropped everything and, on the morning of August 9, stood with my two colleagues[6] in

[5] Here the President clung to the phrase he had used in my first discussion with him, which I thought reflected a misapprehension of the Council's true role and which I had tried to clarify in the third paragraph of my letter of acceptance. (See also p. 417 f.)

[6] I met John D. Clark for the first time in the office of the President's appointment secretary, Matthew J. Connelly when we assembled just prior to our swearing in. A few days earlier, I had invited Mr. Keyserling to have lunch with me to begin some exploratory talk about the Council's work.

On July 30, Mr. Clark had written me: "I am very happy to learn that you are accepting the appointment to the Council of Economic Advisers. In seeking your services the President has clearly shown how important he considers the post, and

front of the President's desk to take the oath of office. I had been told that the President had hoped to have the Chief Justice administer the oath, as Mr. Vinson (while Director of OWMR and as Secretary of the Treasury) had been Truman's representative in pressing for the passage of the Employment Act. But the Chief Justice was out of town, and I was asked to suggest an Associate Justice. I named Mr. Burton (whose wife was a Wellesley classmate of Mrs. Nourse). He too was out of town, and the oath was administered by Champ Clark of the Court of Claims.[7] After the ceremony, the President gave the Council its "sailing orders." "Now you gentlemen just keep this national income up to 200 billion dollars, and we'll be all right."

PUBLIC REACTION TO COUNCIL APPOINTMENTS

Public interest in the appointment of the Council had been lively, and newspaper, periodical, and radio comment was extensive. Though favorable in the main, it was varied in accordance with the economic alignments of the various individuals and publications. Newspaper stories and editorials and the articles in periodicals sometimes stressed the nature of the Employment Act or the value of the Council's job, and sometimes the suitability of the appointments. Headlines typical of the former class were the following:

NO BOOMS, NO BUSTS IS TRUMAN'S OBJECT
  New Haven (Conn.) *Courier and Times*
TRUMAN IS AN INCORRIGIBLE OPTIMIST
  Troy (N. Y.) *Record*
TO GUARD AGAINST INFLATION NOW, DEFLATION LATER
  Business Week
THE PRESIDENT'S NEW TROUBLE SHOOTERS
  American Metal Market

---

you in turn have assured the validity and the significance of the enterprise." On August 1, I replied: "I am sorry that I have not had the pleasure of knowing you personally in the past, but our mutual friend, Kaplan, has made me feel in some measure acquainted with you. I have great respect for the preparation and talents that you bring to a place on this Council and look forward with keen anticipation to participating with you in its work. It is a tremendous undertaking, but I think also that it presents us with a great opportunity."

[7] From organizations which had been interested in the passage of the Employment Act, the only representative present was William Green, president of the A. F. of L.

EVER-NORMAL ECONOMY BOARD IS COMPLETED
   Phoenix (Arizona) *Republic*
SAYS U. S. CAN BE FREE OF INFLATION;
   TRUMAN AND ECONOMIC CHIEF LOOK FOR MIDDLE ROAD
   Boston *Post*
CHAIRMAN ASSERTS BUSINESS AND LABOR MUST AID
   IN STABILIZING
   New York *Sun*
ANOTHER BUREAU
   Council Bluffs *Nonpareil*
NEW ECONOMIC BOARD SEEN VALUELESS, COSTLY AGENCY
   Frank Kent's column

Several editors expressed the view that the Council would be largely anonymous and its recommendations confidential for the President; "the board does not report to Congress." But one prophesied that "you can just about count on it that before long Mr. O'Mahoney's group [the Joint Economic Committee of Congress] will be summoning the Council members to ask whether they agree with the President." One paper referred to the Council's need for "superhuman powers in forecasting" and another to "initial fanfares heralding an almost omniscient body." At one place we read that, thanks to the Council, "Congress [sic] will be in a far better position to align fiscal policies with broader economic trends"; in another place the Council was seen as "the beginnings of a national economic general staff." One editor said, "The United States is embarked upon a new experiment in government planning," and another dismissed the Council as a costly and useless "fifth wheel." Many suspended judgment. "It remains to be seen what influence the Council may have on eliminating the frequent tendency toward indecision in the White House and how successfully its lantern of economic knowledge can light the way."

As to the President's choice of personnel, suggestive headlines included the following:

IN GOOD HANDS
   Victoria (B.C.) *Daily Times*
RESEARCH ECONOMIST HEADS NEW COUNCIL
   New Haven *Courier and Times*
INDEPENDENCE IS ESSENTIAL
   Wall Street Journal

A REFRESHING APPOINTMENT
  Uniontown (Pa.) *Herald*
GOOD MEN FOR ECONOMIC POSTS
  Indianapolis *Star*
NO POLITICS IN NOURSE COUNCIL DOINGS,
  BUT CAN ITS LUCK HOLD?
  Printer's Ink

Most editors thought that "President Truman made all his appointments to the Council on the basis of merit"—"well balanced from the standpoint of political and economic thinking." But when the first two appointments were announced, a national news letter observed that "they fall far short of the advance hopes. . . . Truman tried to get others, of more ability and reputation, but they wouldn't serve. . . . inauspicious start for the Great Brain Trust." The *Daily Worker* was unhappy. "Nary a trade unionist or well-known advocate of liberal job policies in the lot."

In contrast to this view, Mr. Keyserling was quite generally rated as a stalwart liberal. He "probably would be classed among the economic planners—at least among those who advocate a greater measure of government control and direction over the national economy," said one paper. But another saw him as "a careerist in government service; a sincere New Dealer unconnected with the pre-Truman White House economic planners." A columnist noted that: "New York's Senator Robert F. Wagner is responsible for the rise of Leon H. Keyserling, third and liberal-minority member of the Council. Keyserling was Wagner's legislative secretary. He played an important part in drafting the National Labor Relations Act and Senator Wagner's early housing and slum-clearance acts."

Mr. Clark was often rated the conservative of the group—"Tired of being an 'oil millionaire' and determined to give the rest of his life to study, teaching,[8] and public practice of the economics of government. . . . He should give the Economic Council the balanced view of a progressive hardheaded business man." "Businessman, educator—everyone that knows him says: 'A fine appointment.'" But "people close to Dr. Clark feel he favors more government planning and more government control than do his colleagues." Clark's "one book, *The Federal Trust Policy,* is a glorification of

[8] "He took up teaching not because he failed in business but because he was successful in it."

the Sherman antitrust law. He thinks it is wonderful, which is at least something for a Standard Oil vice president." Elsewhere he was described as "a warm but not emotional supporter of President Roosevelt's policies" or "a real liberal, but not a 'whole-hog' New Dealer." His political connections did not escape notice—"protege of Senator O'Mahoney, a former member of the legislature of Wyoming and very active in state politics."

The chairman was frequently described as a conservative or at most "middle-of-the-road researcher." The *Nation* referred to him as an "economist who represents 'respectable' economic thinking. . . . By numerous writings he had demonstrated a conservative predilection but also openmindedness and fairness in appraising new ideas." Another thought him "somewhat leftish, but not a mere theorist." More specific was the characterization "a highly respected economic analyst who believes profoundly in the free enterprise system and wants the government to help make it work. He recognizes the necessity for government intervention at many points in our economy. His usefulness of course will depend on the degree to which policy-making organs of government seek his advice and act on it, irrespective of purely political considerations." "Nourse considers himself an independent in politics and has not been affiliated with any party."[9]

SETTING UP SHOP

Once appointed and confirmed, the Council's first problem was to find quarters in which to work. Mr. Ross, when I first talked to him, had said: "Of course your offices should be right here in the West Wing where you can have close and frequent contacts. But we are just so crowded that you will have to be in Old State, which is coming to be the Executive Office Building." Mr. Steelman made a similar observation when I talked with him. But action did not match these promises.

I was told that a young man from the administrative staff of the Bureau of the Budget would act temporarily in assisting the Council to make working arrangements. He informed me that a few rooms were available for us at 1712 G Street—a small office building which housed the fiscal division of the Bureau of the Budget. Mr. Keyser-

[9] For further comment, see App. A.

ling and Mr. Clark, with the former's secretary, took up tentative abode there, but I continued to use my Brookings office on Jackson Place.

I felt that it was important—in the protocol-conscious atmosphere of Washington—that we be established at the start in quarters whose character and propinquity to the President's office proclaimed the position that the Council was to occupy in the executive establishment. Congress had set up the Council as an independent agency working directly with and for the President, to perform functions of broad economic analysis, some of which had in recent years been experimentally developed in the fiscal division of the Bureau of the Budget. To move in on the fringe of that Bureau's domain would raise ambiguities in the minds of the sharp-eyed reporters and the public generally and cause embarrassment both to us and to them. In my book, 1712 G Street "was out."

A second suggestion was that we take up certain physically attractive quarters in the North Interior Building. These offices, I learned, had formerly been the domicile of the defunct National Resources Planning Board. In addition to being remote from the White House, this location might link us and our position in the scheme of government with that agency, which was still viewed with suspicion or dislike in certain quarters. I continued to press for space in Old State until the Assistant Secretary who had control of office allotments told me that Secretary Byrnes had cabled from Paris that if he released another square foot of space in that building, the Secretary's resignation would be on the President's desk. The head of the Public Buildings Administration offered us air-conditioned quarters in the building of the Reconstruction Finance Corporation on Vermont Avenue. But I still held out for space in the Executive Office Building, and brought our plight to the President's attention when I made my first progress report to him shortly after his return from his cruise. My memorandum on this occasion reads: "The President stated that he was having a terrible time to get space even for his own executive establishment but would make his best efforts to settle the matter shortly." Nothing transpired in that quarter, and I continued personal efforts to find working space.

Early in October, the Council was assigned half a dozen offices in the basement of Old State, adequate to house the Council members and a few of our top staff. Some additional space was available at 1712 G Street, half a block away. On October 14, we moved into the Executive Office Building and went to work on the first Economic Report of the President to the Congress—with only sixty days before we would have to deliver a product to the President.[10]

ASSEMBLING A STAFF

Our struggle to find quarters had run concurrently with a search for staff. The Employment Act expressly warned against duplication of work and put a ceiling on size by providing that our pay roll (outside Council members' salaries) should not exceed $300,000. In practice, it has been only about two-thirds of that amount. (See pp. 152, 154.)

The plan of staffing on which we worked from the start was clearly set forth in the Council's *First Annual Report to the President* (December 18, 1946). We there said:

It was clearly the intent of the framers of the act that this shall be a small co-ordinating agency immediately adjacent to the President and effecting liaison between him and the vast area of technical services dealing with economic matters already available within the governmental establishment. It is not itself to be a fact-finding agency or one doing original statistical or economic research.[11]

The intent of Congress to keep this new agency within the Executive Office of the President a small top-level consultative organization is evi-

[10] When General Marshall became Secretary of State, he took a quite different position with reference to office space than Secretary Brynes had taken. Also absent from Washington, he cabled officials of the State Department to have quarters ready for him in the New State Department Building (formerly occupied by the Department of the Army) by the time he got back to the United States. When this shift was completed, ample space was available in Old State, not only to the Council and the Bureau of the Budget, but to the newly formed National Security Resources Board. Its chairman moved into the former offices of the Secretary, and we moved from the basement to an adequate set of contiguous offices on the third floor.

[11] This statement was intended to correct any misapprehension growing out of the President's remark when the Council was set up, to the effect that it would be a "fact-finding" body. (See p. 108.) He was doubtless thinking of such things as the "fact-finding" commissions or boards used on questions such as price de-control or labor-management disputes. An "analytical agency" or "interpretative agency" would have been a better description. In the Council's sentence above, the eschewing of any economic research function seems to me now much too sweeping. (See pp. 419–22.)

denced by a statutory limitation on the salaries of members, officers, and employees of the Council to an annual total of $345,000—a limitation which the Council considers very salutary and hopes to see maintained in future. The same intent is manifest in the provision that "The Council shall, to the fullest extent possible, utilize the services, facilities, and information (including statistical information) of other Government agencies as well as of private research agencies, in order that duplication of effort and expense may be avoided."

In conformity with these evident intentions of Congress, the Council has set up a small (not to exceed 10) top staff of broadly trained economists, selected with a view to their competence to analyze the state of the Nation's business as a whole and appraise the functioning of the entire economy. Each, however, has specialized knowledge of the problems, the methods of analysis used, and materials and personnel available in some special area such as labor relations, plant capacity, agricultural problems, consumer demand, price-wage-cost relationships, money and credit factors, taxation, and fiscal problems. Together with a small secondary staff, these "specialized generalists" are utilized under the Council's direction to bring to its deliberations the best thinking of the economic and statistical profession in the Federal Government agencies, in non-Federal governments, and in the private organizations of business, labor, and agriculture. Easy and effective relations were promptly established between the Council's staff and the staffs of these many agencies.

The Employment Act authorized the Council to "fix the compensation of such specialists and other experts as may be necessary for the carrying out of its functions under this Act, without regard to the civil-service laws and the Classification Act of 1923, as amended." We decided, however, as a matter of policy to limit ourselves to the existing ceilings, which then had a maximum for P-8 of $10,000. We also decided to use a number of top-flight specialists on a part-time basis, paying them a per diem rate which would aggregate $10,000 at full time. In practice, some of this time was made available to the Council without any salary cost and, in a few cases, even without travel expense.

Signing up the men we needed was no easy task, in spite of the fact that several large war agencies were in process of liquidation. Scholars no less than soldiers were war-weary. Many wanted to resume their academic careers or to take more lucrative positions in business. Those who had been separated from their families wanted to rejoin them. Those who had brought their families to Washington wanted to get their children into permanent school connections. Some said merely, "I want to digest the experiences of these years, . . . formulate my own economic philosophy, . . . write my book."

Neither of my colleagues had any very intimate or extensive acquaintance with economic personnel and their proficiencies and peculiarities. They were, however, in full accord with my view that we should recruit men in terms of their intellectual ability and their capacity to work with other agencies along problem lines, not be too much concerned about the individual's doctrinal position.[12] They were co-operative to a fault as I dropped our net wherever I thought a good man could be lured into our staff. It did not disqualify a man with them to say frankly, "He is definitely on the conservative side." I had no trouble in getting them to authorize me to invite Professor Leonard Crum of Harvard or Charles Hardy, then vice-president in charge of research at the Federal reserve bank at Kansas City. Unfortunately the conservatives seemed re-

[12] John Corson, then Director of Research for the Washington *Post,* who had found the revisions of the Full Employment bill in the process of its metamorphosis into the Employment Act of 1946 "emasculating" had written, concerning the Council appointments, in *The Nation* of August 10: "There is not a political hack in the trio. Each is a capable professional man. Together they constitute what the President described when announcing Dr. Nourse's appointment, as 'a fact-finding agency.' This choice of words offers an ironical comment on earlier promises that the Full Employment Act was 'an historic Congressional declaration . . . of the Federal government's responsibility . . . to utilize all its resources for the purpose of maintaining employment opportunities for those able, willing, and seeking to work.' Hence, observers suspect the Council may prove no more than a focusing point for the government's fiscal, monetary, labor, wage and social-insurance policies as they affect employment, production, and purchasing power. It will collect reports from various governmental agencies, weigh the trend of events and submit to the President appraisals of economic conditions, which he, in turn, will review with Secretary of the Treasury Snyder. There will be little forecasting of the economic tides and even less in the way of a program to insure that all public administration and legislative policies 'promote employment, production, and purchasing power. . . .'

"The best that can now be anticipated is that the Council will corral a competent and imaginative staff and establish within the federal structure its responsibility for co-ordinating governmental economic policies. Then, when the economic cycle has again run its course, some subsequent president may replace Messrs. Nourse and Clark with men who will constitute the kind of economic general staff which the Federal government certainly requires if the system of free enterprise is to continue without subjecting our society to periodic blights of depression."

luctant to join us even though we were desirous of having them.[13] But Hardy shortly went to the Joint Committee, where he did helpful work.[14]

September came and we still had not a single staff man signed up. Our first acceptance came from Fred Waugh, highly respected as a statistician and market economist. He could be released by OWMR, where he was serving on leave from the Department of Agriculture; Paul Homan, on leave from Cornell, was completing work for the Steel Section of the War Assets Administration and deeply interested in the possibilities of the Council. But he could not renege on his Cornell commitment. He did, however, join us for a few weeks of exploratory work (and returned to us on a full-time basis the following June). I besought Donald Wallace, now Director of the Graduate Program, Woodrow Wilson School of Public and International Affairs at Princeton, to leave OPA and help us get going. He had deep loyalties to his then chief and was in desperate need of a rest. Thereafter he wanted to get back to his academic career. I told him the immediate transition from the high-pressure life of a price controller to the low pressure of Academia would be too severe a shock. He would probably get the intellectual "bends." Our policy-advisory but nonadministrative atmosphere would provide just the right "decompression chamber." He finally agreed to come on October 1 and stay until June 1947.

Gerhard Colm had for several years been one of the top experts in the fiscal division of the Bureau of the Budget and was internationally known in the field of national income accounts, their con-

13 Crum demurred on the grounds of health and rustiness in the field of government statistics (whose reconciliation and improvement I had cited as a responsibility of the Council) but added: "I think you should know that my heart could never be in this work, because I have at all times been emphatically opposed to the philosophy back of the Act. If you can spare the time to read the little pamphlet which I enclose, you will see how violently I objected to S. 380 as it was originally phrased; and although I am aware that the Act as finally passed omits numerous of the difficulties which I found in S. 380, I still remain hostile to the idea. In these circumstances, I am sure you will agree that the kind of job you want done cannot well be done by a fellow who would never really feel any enthusiasm for doing it."

14 Among those to whom invitations were extended were Howard Ellis of the University of California; William Haber of Michigan; Kenneth Galbraith on leave from Harvard; Willard Thorp and Clair Wilcox of the State Department; and Albert Hart, just leaving government service.

struction, and their interpretation for economic policy purposes. His name naturally came under discussion in our Council meetings and I invited him to my office for a frank talk. He indicated that he would be willing to transfer from Budget to the Council and outlined the sort of role he would expect to play. It was clearly that of chief of staff. This precipitated the issue of how the Council's work was to be organized and administered.

This question had been raised by one or two persons who had been invited to join our staff. My answer had been that the peculiar nature of the Council's function and the small number and high attainments of our staff group dictated that the Council should be its own chief of staff. They should be in close and flexible contact with our specialists, each of whom would be peculiarly well informed as to the issues, the methods, and the personnel of his particular problem area and would promote collaboration between us and other economic staffs in or out of government. I believed that the Council and its top staff group should have frequent (say twice a week) seminar sessions as a means of clearing their thinking on questions of fact, interpretation, and policy.

Mr. Colm, in consultation with Director Webb of the Bureau of the Budget, decided that, since the Employment Act assigned intensive study and policy recommendations in the area of national income and fiscal policy definitely to the Council, it was logical for Mr. Colm to transfer to the new agency. This he did early in October, thus becoming one of the charter members of our group of top specialists, bringing to our explorations the momentum of several years of work already done by the Bureau of the Budget. He was best able to make effective liaison of our work with the budget figures as they developed and also gave us a ready-made set of contacts with statistical and analytical agencies throughout the government.

By arrangement with Secretary Schwellenbach, we secured a three-months' interim assignment of Edward Hollander, who was just being called back from service with a war agency to an important post in the Bureau of Labor Statistics. Through the cooperation of Columbia University, the Council secured the part-time services of Carl Shoup, outstanding tax expert and former consultant to the Treasury Department. Wilson Wright, a well-known business economist and statistician with the Armstrong Cork

Company, became a part-time staff member, advising us on general business conditions but with special expertness in the field of construction and construction materials. With the Institute for Advanced Study at Princeton, we made arrangements for part-time service from Robert Warren, a specialist in monetary and banking problems, and formerly on the staff of the Federal Reserve System. A fourth part-time staff member was William Stead, vice-president in charge of economic research in the Federal Reserve Bank of the 8th District (St. Louis). He had formerly been chairman of the Department of Business Administration at Vanderbilt University and before that assistant director of the United States Employment Service. Besides broadening the outlook of our staff work, several of these men contributed a strain of conservatism calculated to improve the balance within our staff.[15]

Staffing the Council called for an administrative officer as well as professional economists. Announcement of the establishment of the agency immediately brought to light a number of people who were interested in the post. We wanted to have someone who was not only familiar with the work of an economic and statistical group but also challenged by the novel or even unique character of the new agency and interested to see how its peculiar administrative problems could most effectively be handled. A former secretary of the National Resources Planning Board seemed to have special claims to consideration but, as in the matter of quarters, we thought it wiser not to take any step which would seem to link us in any line of succession from that agency.

In late August or early September, I was introduced to Bertram Gross. He had played an active part in the drafting of the Murray Bill (S. 380) and in the subsequent struggles in which drastic amendments were accepted and compromises arrived at which produced the Employment Act.[16] Gross had been staff director of Senator Murray's War Contracts Subcommittee, and, later, special

[15] After about a year, Wright withdrew because of a feeling of frustration over making any effective contribution to the material that came to the Council table and unwillingness to be held in any way accountable for some of the conclusions and recommendations contained in the Economic Reports of the President. Robert Warren died in 1950. Stead left the St. Louis Reserve Bank to take a position in the Department of the Interior. By this time, the whole scheme of part-time staff members had been dropped.

[16] See Stephen K. Bailey, *Congress Makes A Law*, particularly Chaps. III, IV, and V.

assistant to Senator Wagner as chairman of the Banking and Currency Committee, to which the Full Employment bill had been referred. "He was the spark plug of enthusiasm which fired the staff [of the War Contracts Subcommittee] with a passionate zeal for the cause of full employment. The productivity of the staff—for good or ill—was the result of that zeal."[17]

I was not familiar with the scope and character of these activities —as anyone can now be through Professor Bailey's book. Mr. Keyserling of course was fully conversant with them[18] though he did not elaborate on the matter when Gross's name came up for discussion by the Council. It seemed obvious, however, that we could not find anyone who was better informed as to the legislative background of the Employment Act and the intentions of its framers and also "on to the ropes" of procurement, appointment, and other administrative procedures in the Federal Government than was Mr. Gross.

I fully recognized that both his temperament and his connections had the "defects of their virtues" and that identities of interest between Gross and Keyserling might tend to give a distinctive quirk to Council development. I said frankly, however, that I did not expect to be unduly conditioned by the forces that claimed priority in the fashioning of the original Full Employment bill or which might press for any particular interpretation of the present act. On the other hand, it was not my purpose to validate the claim that the present statute was a colorless or meaningless law. I would rather "hang on to the coattails" of an administrative officer who was overambitious as to the Council's role and the purposes of the act than to have someone who was inert and had to be prodded into action in the building of the new agency.

The Employment Act did not specify that there should be a Secretary of the Council. My observation and the advice of friends wise in the ways of bureaucracy led me to feel that such a designation generally proves to be a means of facilitating the erection of a

---

[17] Professor Bailey comments (p. 64) on the expanding role of the committee staff man during recent years, concluding: "The increasing importance of these staff assistants in the whole field of policy formulation is one of the most significant developments in Congress in recent years and deserves careful study and analysis." (Compare discussion of staff work in the Joint Committee of Congress, particularly Chap. XII.)

[18] Bailey, *Congress Makes A Law*, pp. 110–11.

self-perpetuating and expanding center of authority which often comes to overshadow or even "contain" the chairman's administrative leadership. This is true also of such titles (and job specifications) as executive director. Gross objected that the title "administrative assistant to the chairman" would imply mere routine functions and no opportunity to help creatively in working out a suitable organization for this new and different agency. We therefore agreed on calling the post merely "Assistant to the Chairman."

Thus, with a three man Council of diverse backgrounds and outlooks, a senior staff of four full-time men and four part-time, and a high-powered executive officer,[19] we commenced our formal labors in the old State Department Building on October 14.

[19] Our administrative set-up was simplified through an arrangement under which we received personnel, procurement, and library services from the staff of the Bureau of the Budget on a reimbursable basis.

CHAPTER EIGHT

The First Reports

The Employment Act (Sec. 3) called upon the President for a new state paper, the Economic Report "to be transmitted to the Congress at the beginning of each regular session (commencing with the year 1947)" and specified four types of material to be included in this report. It provided further "that the President may transmit from time to time to the Congress reports supplementary to the Economic Report." The act also provided (in Section 4, which set up the Council of Economic Advisers) that "the Council shall make an annual report to the President in December of each year."

THE COUNCIL'S REPORT TO THE PRESIDENT

In accordance with this latter provision, we began early to consider the nature of the report that the Council should make annually to the President. On the occasion of my first conference with Mr. Truman (September 18),

I raised the question as to whether it might be desirable to discuss certain broad questions of the Council's approach to our problem of economic stability in a report of an educational character designed for public consumption and given publicity at the time it was submitted in December, somewhat preparing the public mind for the policies which would be stated in his Economic Report [in January] and the specific measures of implementation which he would recommend to the Congress. The President reacted very favorably to this suggestion, and I thereupon indicated that I would proceed to develop this thought and prepare the outline of such a report and draft passages as our work progressed and submit these to him so that he could see how the idea was developing and whether it seemed to him desirable for the Council to proceed, with the expectation of such an informative and orienting public report in December. *(P. D.,* Sept. 18, 1946)

A month later, in my conference with the President, I reported "that we were continuing to work on the possibility of having the preliminary part of our report to him of such a general character that it would serve as an analytical or educational background and give the public something to get their teeth into prior to the appearance of his Budget Message and Economic Report. I said we were tentatively considering this report under three heads as follows: (1) the political philosophy of the act; (2) the economic philosophy of sustained employment; (3) some aspects of the outlook for production and jobs. The President expressed himself as entirely satisfied with such an outline, and I told him that as each portion was drafted, it would be submitted to him so that he could see how the document was developing and make any suggestions he cared to."

In my diary entry covering a conference with the President on November 26, I wrote:

I had hoped to lay before him a draft of the whole of the First Annual Report of the Council—that is the part designed for publication. Owing to last-minute issues raised by Mr. Clark,[1] I had to defer submitting the second and third sections of the report and present only Part I. The President seemed to have very clearly in mind the purpose and character of the Report as I had discussed it with him previously. He leafed through the pages and said this looked like just the sort of thing he thought would be desirable and that he would read it with care as well as the draft of the latter part as soon as it was submitted.

After reworking the draft of the Council's Report to the President in the light of Clark's objections, some additional text prepared by Keyserling, and some comments from the staff, the full text was sub-

[1] At the end of my minute of November 26, I had this explanatory note: "As to J. D. Clark's demurrers concerning the Council Report as I had drafted it, he seemed to have two principal points. One was that it was undesirable to go as far as I had in pointing out shortcomings of the laissez-faire and the fiscal policy schools of thought. He said that no one went to either of these extremes and that to raise the issues in anything more than an incidental way would invite resentment on their part and a claim that we had not clearly or adequately presented their views. He wanted us to center our discussion entirely on the aggressive program which the Council intended to follow in its own area. Here he seems to me to be disposed to advocate a more sweeping and aggressive policy than either Keyserling or I would be likely to follow."

mitted to the President about December 4. After a few days, he returned it to us with his approval, but with two or three minor changes in phraseology. We thereupon proceeded with the printing of this report[2] so that it could be released at a press conference on December 18.

I had had two talks with Charles Ross in arranging for this release, and we had submitted a number of suggestions which Ross said he would use in "briefing" the President for this press release. In fact, however, the President seemed extremely ill at ease at the opening of the press conference and released our report and a statement on the China situation without any comment on either except that the press had already had copies, so they were presumed to know what was in them. On two occasions when questions about the Council report were put to the President, he replied that he had not read it with care, but on one occasion referred to the fact that I was there and might wish to comment—which I did.

We had hoped that the President on this occasion would make a statement to the effect that he attached importance to the work of the Council and expected to make use of its studies and suggestions. He omitted any such comment and indeed professed ignorance of the content of the report although manuscript had been sent to him two weeks before and he had returned it with a few suggestions as to phraseology and the printed report had been sent to him on Saturday of the preceding week. *(P. D.,* Dec. 28, 1946)

Ever since the setting up of the Council, the press had manifested a lively interest in its work and had indulged in recurrent speculations as to its forthcoming report as well as the first Economic Report of the President. It was not strange that they found some difficulty in keeping a clear distinction between the Council's Report to the President and the President's Economic Report to the Congress. In order to clarify this point as much as possible, the opening paragraph of the Council's Report on December 18 stated:

It seems appropriate that, in this first annual report, the Council should clearly set forth its conception of the agency which Congress has established within the executive branch and explain the Council's relation to the administrative departments and independent agencies, to the Congress, and to non-governmental agencies in our economic system. . . . It is the President's Economic Report to the Congress rather than this Council report

[2] Council of Economic Advisers, *First Annual Report to the President,* December 1946.

[to the President and by him released to the public] which will contain specific economic conclusions and recommendations.

Part I of the report outlined the purposes of the act and its machinery of operation. After commenting briefly on the complexity of economic problems engendered by the growth of the country and our deeper involvement in international affairs and on the heavy responsibilities of the Chief Executive, it referred to the legislative history of the Employment Act and the drastic changes made in the Full Employment bill before it was metamorphosed into the Employment Act of 1946.

The measure which finally emerged from this process of legislative coalition was a well-balanced and carefully drawn piece of legislation. Although frequently referred to as a "much watered-down version" of the original proposal, it is in fact a broad enabling act of great flexibility as well as vigor. It is far from being a meaningless verbal compromise. The present act does not make any particular method [of economic stabilization] mandatory. Nor does it legislate any specific remedy into use. Instead, the law states quite fully and clearly the general purpose and intention of the Congress and lays down the principle that the executive and the legislature shall seek diligently for any method which, in the peculiar circumstances of any given situation, appears to them to be sound and to promise helpful results. It is hard to see how a measure can be regarded as "watered down" which so clearly states the "responsibility of the Federal Government to use all practicable means consistent with its needs and obligations and other essential considerations of national policy . . . to co-ordinate and utilize all its plans, functions, and resources"—for the stated purposes of the act— maximum production, employment, and purchasing power. . . .

A mandate is thus laid on the President and the whole executive establishment and upon both Houses of Congress to pursue this goal of promoting maximum productive use of the Nation's resources, natural and human, thereby providing work opportunities as ample as are practicably possible for those who are anxious to apply their labor to the supplying of their wants. . . .

The measure as enacted is fully within the existing frame of government. It does not set up any authoritarian board or official dictator of labor, of plant, or of production. The traditional division of function between the executive and legislative branches of the Government is fully preserved and, as already mentioned, the complementary relation between Federal and State Governments. In the machinery of the act, however, something has been added to our customary equipment for handling matters that concern the Nation's economic life. No longer is the study of the multifarious economic problems of the country and the formulating of Executive programs for dealing with national economic welfare to be merely scattered among the Federal departments and independent commissions or the still more numerous bureaus and divisions within these agencies. Instead, a means is provided for reviewing and synthesizing all these studies, conclusions, and recommendations into a single co-ordinated whole. . . .

. . . although set up as an arm of the Executive Office, the Council as such does not have any administrative powers or responsibilities. It is purely a consultative and advisory agency. . . . it is designed to serve as a continuous agency of counsel to the President on the professional plane in regard to administrative decisions as well as his approval—or even veto—of legislative proposals. . . . Since the President must formulate his policies and shape his program within his own evaluation of the most varied and comprehensive political and social, as well as economic influences and considerations, it is not to be expected that his Report to Congress will merely reflect the conclusions and recommendations of his Economic Council. He will simply use as he deems wise such economic analyses, appraisals, conclusions, and recommendations as they prepare for him. What is said here is intended— as subsequent annual reports and perhaps interim reports will be—to serve as a general explanation of the purposes of the act and the nature of the Council's work.[3]

PUBLIC REACTION TO THE COUNCIL'S REPORT

Press and radio comment on the Council's report was voluminous. Several editorial captions featured the words "sound," "cautious," or "good advisers." Among the more colorful headlines were:

NO BREAD AND CIRCUSES
  New York *Journal of Commerce*
FOR A STABILIZED ECONOMY
  Newark *News*
LONG STEP FORWARD
  Thomas L. Stokes's column
A NEW DEPARTURE IN GOVERNMENT
  Lincoln (Neb.) *State Journal*
THE FIRST BEGINNINGS OF A HISTORIC EXPERIMENT
  P. M. (New York)
UMPIRE'S REPORT
  Detroit *Free Press*
SUPERVISED ECONOMY
  Providence *Journal*

[3] Council of Economic Advisers, *First Annual Report,* pp. 5, 7–8.

EXPERTING THE OBVIOUS
  St. Louis *Globe Democrat*
NEW DEAL SPEND AND OWE CREDO GETS COLD SHOULDER
  N.A.M. *News*
PILLS THAT INCREASE THE ILLS
  Daily Worker

Since many readers were looking for the first indication of what policy line the President would take under the Employment Act, a disproportionate amount of attention was given to the brief Section III of the Report, entitled: "Some Aspects of the Outlook for Production and Jobs." Several papers reprinted this section in full. In it, we said that fundamentally favorable conditions in our country

hold the potential of some years of great activity along lines essentially similar to past periods of prosperity. This much could be accomplished without any material change in traditional patterns of business life. These conditions present the possibility, for a people who know how to use them, of great prosperity in 1947. By foresight and intelligence we believe such prosperity for the Nation could be approximately stabilized and broadly disseminated so long as world peace can be preserved.

On the other hand, even with these favorable conditions, it is easy to visualize such a mishandling of our economic affairs as might make 1947 a year of curtailed production, irregular employment, and unsatisfactory purchasing power. . . . We believe that the outlook for production and jobs in 1947 lies primarily in whether the responsible persons in these groups will show a willingness to face the issues and demands of a free enterprise system realistically and show intelligence and skill or flexible experimentation in arriving at workable formulas of adjustment. . . .

In spite of certain conditions that might make for a dip in 1947,[4] we believe that courageous and sensible action by those responsible for the administration of private business relations (including labor unions) can at least hold such a recession to moderate proportions if not avert it. Thereafter, it would seem that broad basic conditions suggest that it will be easy to have some years of high production, employment, and purchasing power without the display of any extraordinary economic statesmanship by leaders of industry, labor, farming, and finance. In those years, however, we should

[4] In the press conference in which this report was released, the President was asked by a reporter whether he agreed with the Council's suggestion that there might be a dip in 1947. He rather tartly rejected the idea. The New York *Times* of December 22 said: "The President was even more optimistic than his Council on the prospects for 1947. He would not even admit the possibility of a recession. He declared that all strikes which have held up reconversion have been unnecessary. The outlook for next year is good, he said—if everybody stayed on the job."

not be satisfied with a level of production and conditions of use which fail to produce favorable results for all sections of the country and all segments of the population. In those years, also, if foresight is not keen and action vigorous, the stage will be set for serious unemployment, underproduction, and want in the years that follow. It is our belief, however, that enough time is afforded in which wise policy and action on the part of labor, of management, of agriculture, and of finance, with a very carefully considered complementary role by Government, will not only raise the national prosperity to new high levels but will maintain those levels with a degree of stability which has not characterized the earlier exploratory and speculative decades of our industrial life.

Under the caption, "Two Very Big 'Ifs'," the San Francisco *Examiner* (December 30) commented:

The President's Council of Economic Advisers has reported that there is a "favorable" prospect for full employment and production in the country in 1947 if the Government refrains from *undue interference with industry* and if *labor and management compose their differences. These are, of course, two very big "ifs."* . . .

Socialistic experiments by Government meddlers and bunglers and destructive strikes by arrogant and irresponsible labor have already postponed and retarded national prosperity for more than a year. In the light of this experience it is surely axiomatic, as the Council urges, that: "We must recognize the real magnitude of our productive power and *keep it going,* to produce for all the things that only the more favored have enjoyed in the past."

The *United States News* (December 27) reprinted the full text of Section III with the comment:

The President's Council of Economic Advisers places responsibility for maintaining prosperity largely on management, labor, and farm groups operating the U. S. industrial machine. . . . Little reliance is placed on legislation to force "capitalists to invest, employers to hire, or laborers to work," and no need is seen for "heroic measures" of public works, or consumer or producer subsidies.

The New York *Times* on December 22 in its "Review of the Week" reported:

Last week the President called a special press conference to make public the Economic Council's First Annual Report. In the nine months since the Council had been authorized, great changes had taken place in the nation's economic and political affairs. . . . The First Report of the Economic

Council reflected the changed national atmosphere. There was little in it to suggest a planned economy. There was an expression of confidence that the nation, barring great labor-management strife in 1947, would have an unprecedently prosperous year. There was a recommendation that Government's role should be far less active than for many years—probably less active than in any year since the first Roosevelt Administration introduced the National Recovery Act in 1933. . . . Labor leaders who had fought hard for the Full Employment Act declined comment. Industry spokesmen commended the Council.

An editorial in the Scripps-Howard papers concluded:

President Truman's Council of Economic Advisers recently made its first report. Its prescription, in effect, is: Get to work. Adjust labor-management differences without fighting. Be willing to face the issues and demands of a free-enterprise system realistically. If this prescription is followed, we have an excellent chance for full employment and good times in 1947 and for quite a few years more. And meanwhile, we can figure out ways and means of avoiding such great economic sinking spells as we've had in the past.

In other words, if the country will behave itself it will be o. k. But, from the Economic Advisers, no pink pills, no laying on of hands, no magic. So, from some of the New Dealers, outraged protests. The Docs propose that we stop taking economic dope, go on a sensible diet and give our work muscles some exercise.

An editorial in the *State Journal of* Lincoln, Nebraska, on December 21 found the report clarifying as to the role of the Council.

In weighing the Council's report, it is interesting to recall its background, for the council of government economic advisers in a way itself enters the picture of governmental intervention in economics. It is not a legislative nor an executive body, but a group of men charged with the constant study of the economic status and prospects of the country, so as to keep the President fully advised. Their reports are in turn studied by a joint congressional committee, which then makes recommendations to Congress.

This Council, representing a new departure in government, is an outcome of the Employment Act of 1946. While its parent, the "Full Employment bill" was being debated in Congress, there was hue and cry about the hazards in permitting a government agency to prophesy about business conditions. The men appointed by the President have now made their prophecy, and it is for the most part too conservative to carry any hazard.

Its importance, in fact, lies mainly in its definition of its own function. For the first time, the act under which the Council was set up recognizes the government as a permanent factor in the country's business, with a continuing responsibility to plan for its stability with appropriate machinery. There is nothing authoritarian about this policy under which measures will be taken from time to time as they appear advisable and as the traditional democratic instrumentalities assert.

Under the title "Economic Leader Needed," Thomas L. Stokes's column on December 21 noted that:

The first report was not welcomed among New Dealers, as it was in more conservative circles. Their reaction was that it reads like a technical book on economics, cold and dry, or like some of the speeches and forecasts of experts here in the early days of depression in the Hoover Administration. In short, they say, it forgets people, forgets human beings, who, after all, make up our country and our economy. This consideration of people, they explain, is what made the difference in approach of the New Deal from that of some other regimes.

This New Deal criticism has its importance politically, tho it may not seem so now, because this element still represents a good many people in the country and, if economic conditions do take a turn for the worse, probably will represent a lot more. Some went so far as to say the Council seemed to have followed the election returns.

A New York *Times* editorial (December 20) likewise viewed the Council's report in the setting from which the Employment Act emerged. It said:

. . . But for those who recalled the long and bitter legislative controversy over "full employment" and ways of achieving it which at times seemed to imperil the tradition and structure of the American private enterprise system—interest is more likely to center on those portions in which three eminent economist-authors set forth the purposes of the Employment Act of 1946 and the nature of the Council's functions. Here, too, they sketch in for the first time, the general setting of economic philosophy and policy— determining considerations within which their specific conclusions are to be developed. . . .

The Employment Act places a mandate upon the Government to pursue the goal of promoting maximum use of the nation's resources. Thus, while, as its title suggests, it rejects the term "full employment" and the paternalistic philosophy with which that term is popularly associated, it does mark, as the Council observes, "a distinct step in our national life and our frame of democratic government." At the same time, it does not set up any authoritarian board for directing the activities of labor and management. It does not affect the division of functions between the executive and legislative branches of the Government, or the complementary relationship of the Federal and State Governments. And it is to operate at all times "in a manner calculated to foster and promote free competitive enterprise." The basic mechanism of the Act is one through which the multifarious economic problems of the country and the formulation of executive programs for dealing with them, now scattered among the several departments, commissions and bureaus of the Government, would be centrally reviewed and synthesized. . . .

. . . This Act can be the basis for instructive and rewarding adventure in the years ahead, under two conditions, namely: (1) that its basic philosophy be kept intact; and (2) that too much is not expected of it—especially too much too soon.

The Philadelphia *Inquirer* (December 20) contained an editorial "Prosperity in 1947 Must Be Earned." It concluded:

The gist of this generally sensible report is that the Nation's economic welfare is in its own hands, and if we don't make a botch of things we can count on prosperity not only during the new year but for years to come. There is no necessity for a "boom and bust" cycle such as the alarmists are now predicting. Let's get rid of that foolish, dangerous idea for good—for the good of all—and not invite the depression jitters.

The *Daily Worker* (December 20) took a dim view of our efforts:

Since it is made up of capitalist economists, the President's Council of Economic Advisers confines itself in its first annual report to little more than a pious expression of faith in the workings of our capitalist system.

It is forced to recognize that the anarchy of the system is fatal to any extended prosperity. Its remedy is to leave it to the "practical wisdom of management and labor, farmers, and financiers." The cure for capitalist anarchy, apparently, is more of the same.

The Council, set up under the emasculated "Full Employment" law, seems to have no idea of the real facts of our economy and does not even know where to look for them. . . . By urging greater production without backing the fight for higher wages, the President and his Council were actually demanding greater exploitation of the worker and hence more rapid development of economic crisis.

By contrast, the New York *Journal of Commerce* (December 19) thought that

As a statement of basic economic policy, the first report of the Council is sound and constructive. Balance within the economy, adjustments of prices, costs and production in particular industries, are recognized as prime requisites for business stability at a high level of output and employment.

SPADE WORK FOR THE ECONOMIC REPORT OF THE PRESIDENT

The Employment Act in calling upon the President for a new state paper had been fairly explicit as to its character. Section 3 read:

(a) The President shall transmit to the Congress at the beginning of each regular session (commencing with the year 1947) an economic report (hereinafter called the "Economic Report") setting forth (1) the levels of employment, production, and purchasing power obtaining in the United States and such levels needed to carry out the policy declared in section 2; (2) current and foreseeable trends in the levels of employment, production, and purchasing power; (3) a review of the economic program of the Federal Government and a review of economic conditions affecting employment in the United States or any considerable portion thereof during the preceding year and of their effect upon employment, production, and purchasing power; and (4) a program for carrying out the policy declared in section 2, together with such recommendations for legislation as he may deem necessary or desirable.

(b) The President may transmit from time to time to the Congress reports supplementary to the Economic Report, each of which shall include such supplementary or revised recommendations as he may deem necessary or desirable to achieve the policy declared in section 2.

(c) The Economic Report, and all supplementary reports transmitted under subsection (b), shall, when transmitted to Congress, be referred to the joint committee created by section 5.

The role of the Council of Economic Advisers in connection with the Economic Report was set forth in Section 4 (c):

It shall be the duty and function of the Council—

(1) to assist and advise the President in the preparation of the Economic Report;

(2) to gather timely and authoritative information concerning economic developments and economic trends, both current and prospective, to analyze and interpret such information in the light of the policy declared in section 2 for the purpose of determining whether such developments and trends are interfering, or are likely to interfere, with the achievement of such policy, and to compile and submit to the President studies relating to such developments and trends; . . .

(4) to develop and recommend to the President national economic policies to foster and promote free competitive enterprise, to avoid economic

fluctuations or to diminish the effects thereof, and to maintain employment, production, and purchasing power;

(5) to make and furnish such studies, reports thereon, and recommendations with respect to matters of Federal economic policy and legislation as the President may request.

As the Council sat down on October 14, with its handful of staff workers, "to assist and advise the President in the preparation of the Economic Report" to submit to Congress in early January, we had several preliminary questions to face. Would the President expect us to submit topical memoranda for his consideration as our work progressed or should we cover the subject as a whole according to our best judgment and show him a completed draft rather than a series of parts? Should this draft be written by us in the first person so that, with his editing, it might become the President's Economic Report? Or should our document be put in the third person, as a factual and analytical brief which the President and White House staff would then draw upon to prepare the President's own statement of his view of the country's situation and his recommendations of policy? Would the Council members write their own document to submit to the President, or would the staff prepare a document for the Council's consideration, editing, or rewriting?

The President had early—I think at my first conference with him—informed me that he would expect Mr. Steelman to keep close touch with the work of the Council and give us whatever help he could in developing our work. Steelman had been made Director of the Office of War Mobilization and Reconversion in June 1946 and in late July the duties of Economic Stabilizer (following the resignation of Chester Bowles) had been transferred to his office. The OWMR staff published its eighth quarterly report on October 1 and thereafter was passing into liquidation just as we were getting under way.[5] My relations with Mr. Steelman were always cordial and helpful but there seemed no reason to go to his shop for data rather than taking it direct from the various fact-gathering agencies, or to attempt to amalgamate OWMR's interpretation of the current situation and outlook with the analyses of our staff or the views of the three Council members. Time was short, and it seemed

[5] It was formally terminated on Dec. 12, 1946, when Steelman became Assistant to the President.

desirable to simplify as much as possible the task of coming to consensus among ourselves as to the advice we would offer to the
President.

During my second conference with Mr. Truman, I raised the
question of the relationship which the Economic Report would
have to the quarterly reports which OWMR had been issuing, to
the State of the Union Message, and to the Budget Message. I had
talked to Steelman about the first point, and it seemed pretty clear
that the report he had just issued on October 1 would be the last
for that agency, and that the Economic Report would take over
that function in the future.[6] The relationship to the State of the
Union Message was somewhat vague. That message was a matter
of long tradition rather than legal requirement, and in January
1946, it had been consolidated with the Budget Message. The latter
had, under Budget Director Harold Smith, come to include a somewhat extensive analysis of the economic condition of the country
as a background for the President's budget recommendations.[7] It
was clear that in future the President had a statutory mandate to
give separate and fuller treatment to this material in his Economic
Report, relieving the Budget Message of any need to undertake this
service.

Mr. Connelly had informed us that the President had designated Mr.
Clifford, Legal Counsel of the White House staff, Mr. Webb [the Budget
Director], Mr. Steelman, and myself as a co-ordinating committee under
Steelman's chairmanship to see that there was complete harmony among
all three documents.[8] The President stated that it was his preference that
the State of the Union Message, his Economic Report to the Congress under
the Employment Act of 1946, and the Budget Message be prepared as a
three-part document and sent by him to the Congress shortly after its
opening (say, January 5th or 6th). He added, however, that political considerations might make it seem advisable for him to deliver the State of
the Union Message to the Congress in person. The full three-part document would be too long and heavy to be presented orally at one time
and therefore, if he did this, he would send his Report and the Budget to

[6] Though not necessarily with quarterly published statements. (See pp. 178, 213,
237.)

[7] Director Smith's realization of this need led him to strengthen the Bureau's
staff on this side and, to that end, set up a specifically recognized fiscal division.

[8] Nothing came of this arrangement immediately except as I talked with Mr.
Steelman from time to time about the progress of the Council's work.

the Congress as documents at the time of his personal delivery of the State of the Union Message or immediately thereafter. (*P. D.*, Oct. 16, 1946)

In due course, the President did decide to deliver the State of the Union Message in person. This presentation was on Monday, January 6. Allowing two days for Congressional perusal and public discussion of that message, he sent his Economic Report in printed form to Congress on Wednesday, the 8th, and allowed another two days' interval before sending the Budget Message on Friday, the 10th.[9]

"I repeated what I had said at the previous conference about the necessity of our final conclusions and specific recommendations being confidential so that commentators could not discover any discrepancy between our advice and his program." (*P. D.*, Oct. 16, 1946.) On the occasion of my first conference with the President, it had been his "position that much of the material with which we would supply him, as it related to appraisals of current programs and recommendations for future programs, would necessarily be confidential in character." (*P. D.*, Sept. 18, 1946)

As I saw it, the prime task of the Council was to select the salient facts from the great flood of data available in other agencies, streamline this information into a comprehensive and consistent interpretation of the issues confronting the economy, and thereupon give a critique of proposed or possible means of dealing with the problems that would be encountered in the coming year. It seemed to me that the Council should take the lead in shaping up the area of discussion that seemed to its members most pressing and the lines of attack that seemed to them most promising. I thought that the men whom we were assembling on our top staff were fully qualified to be, and should be encouraged to regard themselves as, the full team of economic advisers to the President, of which the Council members would serve as captain and quarterback. I felt too that frequent meetings of staff with Council members to exchange views fully around the table was the most satisfactory way of getting the issues considered from all angles and of

[9] This schedule has been substantially repeated in subsequent years until 1952, when last-minute uncertainty as to how large a budget to recommend resulted in a gap of a week between the State of the Union Message and the Economic Report and another five days before the Budget Message was submitted.

guiding staff specialists in their further collection of materials and their consultation with the professional staffs of other agencies. Between staff meetings these specialists would draft portions of the proposed report for the President but do so with a maximum understanding of the whole situation and policy objective.

This administrative procedure met with only qualified success. My colleagues' attitude to and participation in the meetings ranged from bored indifference to open sabotage. Frequently, if I sought to elicit a Council member's view after canvassing the staff, I would get this reply: "I consider that a matter of policy to be decided in Council meeting, not discussed with the staff." As to the preparation of the finished draft for the President, it would, quite evidently, have been appreciated if I had busied myself with the routine calls made upon the chairman's time and had delegated the task of drafting a Council document from the memoranda secured from staff members in response to topical assignments. This draft could then be dealt with expeditiously in Council meeting. If differences of view were found within the Council, they would be resolved by a majority vote. In spite of the administrative convenience of such a procedure, I could not reconcile myself to accepting it. I thought we should try to educate each other to the maximum degree of honest consensus and frankly inform the President as to differences on which we might divide—as do economists outside the Executive Office—and even the most competent technicians in all lines.

On November 26, "I told the President that I should like, within a short time, to bring all three members of the Council in for a conference at which we would discuss some of the material which would be embodied in our confidential report to him which would be the basis for his Economic Report to the Congress.[10] He agreed to the idea of two such conferences prior to the submitting of our complete draft on December 16. On leaving his office, I made appointments for Tuesday, December 3 and Tuesday, December 10.

Clark Clifford came into the anteroom just as I was waiting to go in. He was very cordial and said he was looking forward to an early meeting of the committee of Steelman, Webb, Nourse, and Clifford, set up to coordinate the three messages—State of the Union, Economic Report, and Budget.

10 As to the form of what we submitted to the President, we had decided to draft our document in a style which, subject to such changes as he might insert, could become his words to the Congress and the country rather than presenting merely our own economic analysis.

He went into the President's office with me, and it was evident that the President had made this arrangement so that Clifford would become fully informed as to the relationships of the Council to the President. It raised the question in my mind whether in future we would find ourselves to any extent dealing with Mr. Clifford rather than Mr. Truman. [This proved to be the case to only a very limited extent.][11]

There was nothing in this half-hour interview which in any way suggested that the President was interested in the content of the work our staff had been doing or in the conclusions toward which we were moving in diagnosing the country's economic situation or the recommendations that we might be offering him on December 16. . . . I left with the feeling that his decisions were already pretty well taken, and this on the basis of information that comes to him casually from a variety of sources, with the final determinant his own political judgment. (*P. D.* Nov. 26.)

. On December 3 and 10, all three members of the Council went to the President's office for discussion of topics which would have a prominent place in the materials which we were to submit for his Economic Report to the Congress. On the first day we discussed briefly the tax and budget situation, indicating that we were in full accord with the emphasis the Administration has recently been placing on reducing government expenditures through economies in operation and the deferring of public works expenditures wherever possible. We indicated our support of the most heroic efforts on the part of the Budget Bureau to get estimates for next year down at least to 37 billion and keep tax rates up so as to have a substantial budget surplus available for debt retirement. The President expressed gratification that we were in full agreement with existing policies but did not really enter into any discussion of the merits of the issue or indicate any interest in our views as to how low an objective should be set for next year's budget or places at which greatest pressure for saving should be exerted.

On December 10, the Council conferred with the President, with emphasis primarily on the labor situation and labor-management recommendations. In general, our Council and staff work has led us to a belief that the greatest possible emphasis must be placed on perfecting the agencies of collective bargaining and that there are relatively few places where legislative curbs on union structure or practice could be clearly and usefully defined and effectively enforced. The President showed no disposition to invite or respond to any analytical points the Council might have to offer. He indicated rather that he had stated a consistent policy in some four or five documents since August 16, 1945 and that he intended to write a

11 Mr. Keyserling was on a basis of personal friendship with Clifford, which gave him a special channel of influence on the thinking embodied in many of the President's messages and speeches.

"strong policy" as to labor matters into his message to the Congress—evidently the State of the Union Message. He apparently entertained the view without question that the Economic Report would be brought into line with those recommendations rather than that they would be held in abeyance pending study of the materials we submitted for the Economic Report and perhaps consultation with us concerning the points raised.

On December 13, we sent to the President a brief special memorandum on the matter of the Budget, copy of which is attached.[12] This memorandum grew out of the fact that it appeared that the Director of the Budget and the President were likely to present a total figure of 38 or even 39 billion dollars of expenditure. We felt that this presented too small a prospect in even a prosperous year of a sufficient surplus for debt retirement of the magnitude which should be made in time of prosperity, and in the event of even a moderate recession in 1947 would create the very real possibility of a deficit. The President made no response to this memorandum or reference to it at the time of our next visit. (*P. D.,* Dec. 28, 1946)

FROM WORKING DRAFT TO STATE PAPER

On December 16 we called on the President and delivered three copies of a draft of "materials for the use of the President in drafting his Economic Report to the Congress." He expressed great interest in it and said he would read it at the first opportunity and make his comments to us by the end of the week if possible. We chatted amiably about several matters, principally the Gridiron dinner and ———'s unfortunate speech. I believe Clark made the remark that our conclusions and recommendations did not mark any departure from existing Administration policy. The President smiled broadly and said that he was increasingly sure that he had appointed the right men on the Council. For myself, I am becoming increasingly sure that he has not thought of the Council as exercising the significant role that I outlined for it in our First Annual Report. (*P. D.,* Dec. 28, 1946)

[12] "We are aware that within the next few days you have to make decisions which will determine the size of your budget recommendation for the next fiscal year. As this budget total will have a very important impact on the economy as a whole, we consider it appropriate for us to express our views to you.

"We believe that the economic outlook for the next fiscal year is such that a budget surplus is urgently called for. If the Government fails to plan for a budget surplus under prosperous conditions it may fail to command support for a wise policy of deficits under adverse business conditions. Economic considerations lead us to the conclusion that it would be most desirable to show a budget surplus of at least $3 to $5 billion for the next fiscal year.

"This view will be expressed also in the draft material we are preparing for your Economic Report, but we thought that you might wish to have our views on this issue even before we submit the material to you."

The material we submitted to the President on December 17 was explained briefly in a covering letter:

Dear Mr. President:

The materials which we are handing you today as the result of Council and staff work since we were organized on October 14 is in the form of a tentative draft of the President's Economic Report to the Congress. We expect to continue our Council deliberations and the work of our staff as the preparation of your Economic Report goes forward. We shall probably wish to make some changes in the form of our statement or possibly additions or deletions. However, we believe that this work can proceed better after we have had the benefit of your reaction to this tentative draft.

Our findings as to the state of the economy at the present indicate high levels of employment; levels of production that, though high, are not fully commensurate with our productive resources in use; and a situation as to purchasing power which presents a serious concern as to the future.

The forecast, so often heard, that a business recession will occur in 1947, is largely based upon the idea that the purchasing power of the mass of the people will be further restricted by rising prices and that before long the consumers will be unable to buy all of the goods produced.

The policy to meet this danger which some people propose would be to encourage the enlargement of the incomes of consumers, already fully employed, by wage advances. We do not recommend this policy. The Council recognizes that many workers have not received increases in wages comparable to those increases obtained in the principal occupations and we believe that their situation must be improved. But for the stability of the economy and for the security of labor it is far more desirable to halt the inflationary spiral than it is to have a general increase in wage rates at this time.

The policy which the Council recommends is to adopt all available policies to restrain further price advances and, where possible, to bring about lowering of prices. Success in this effort would forestall a business recession caused by a collapse in market demand for goods, and it would strike at the very root of the problem responsible for labor unrest and for work stoppages which would seriously interfere with production and employment.

While we propose a modest schedule of Government action, much of it administrative rather than legislative in character, which can be utilized to bring some adjustment of prices, we find that the normal processes of competition do not prevail in many important fields of business and that whether prices are reduced will depend largely upon the deliberate decision of businessmen who realize the importance of halting the price-wage spiral. This leads us to emphasize as a major item among our recommendations, the intensification of the antitrust drive and the study of legislation to stop the further concentration of economic power.

We see the demand for wage increases, and the resulting labor controversies, as an offshoot of mounting prices. Adjustment of prices will restore better labor-management relations, and we propose as the policy relating to labor disputes generally the establishment of a sound process of collective bargaining outside of Government control, but with Government assistance in mediation and conciliation.

We recognize, however, that in the immediate future labor controversies will not be easily settled and there may arise another emergency in which willful men on one side or the other may precipitate a national crisis in which the Government must intervene. We propose that the Congress express now the national will that the President shall act in such a contingency.

A third major proposal is that through affirmative and comprehensive legislation the expansion of house building and especially of rental housing be facilitated. While this is a long-range program, its immediate adoption is important because an increase in investment in housing is necessary in order to furnish the additional demand for goods and services which will be needed to maintain full employment and production in 1947, when the final bottlenecks of the reconversion period will have been cleared away.

Our fourth major recommendation is that taxes be maintained at a level and expenditures held down to a level that will provide a budget surplus for debt retirement of at least $3 to $5 billion annually during these years of great business activity. We endorse the continuance of the Government's policy of low interest rates and point out certain issues for the future with reference to debt management.

Our other recommendations relate to long-term programs, most of which you have already approved.

Respectfully yours,
/s./ Edwin G. Nourse, Chairman

All this past week we have heard nothing from the President's office, although Clifford had indicated on the 20th that he expected to study the materials we submitted to the President and talk to me within a few days. Meanwhile we were busy making changes in the draft which we submitted on December 17. Last night (December 27) I sent three copies of the second draft of these materials to the President's office with a covering letter. This morning I called Clifford and he said that he had been swamped with work on the State of the Union Message but hoped to have a draft in our hands Monday for any comment or suggestions we might have to make with reference to its handling of economic matters.[13] It is our understanding that it will include fiscal and labor matters. He said that the handling of the Economic Report was in Steelman's hands. I therefore called the latter and gathered the impression that he was not personally very familiar with the content of our first draft but expected to get to work on the second draft at once and confer with us next week. I called his attention to the fact that for a printed report to be sent to Congress, presumably on January 8, there would be a printing deadline about the middle of next week. (*P. D.,* Dec. 28, 1946)

Mr. Clifford had told me over the telephone that the President's immediate reaction to the first draft was that it was "too long." We therefore undertook to condense the treatment as much as possible but pointed out that, if the Joint Committee was to review the document fairly, it would need to include a somewhat detailed presentation of data and statement of the reasoning on which the President's conclusions and recommendations were based. We, however, prepared a brief preliminary statement which, in about ten pages, would give the gist of the document for the general reader.

It developed later that President Truman had passed the first draft of material which we had handed him on December 17 over to Mr. Steelman and that he in turn had passed it on to three members of the OWMR staff who were continuing to serve in his new office of Assistant to the President. About December 31, Steelman returned to us a proposed Economic Report of the President which they had prepared from these materials. It had been substantially shortened, drastically changed in order of presentation, and considerably "jazzed up" in style. After this text had been examined by the Council and top staff members, it was the unanimous feeling that many things that were essential to a consistent and workmanlike analysis had been omitted from the draft and that the rearrangement obscured the essential outline of our analysis.

On the afternoon of January 3, "The Council was called by Mr. Steelman to meet in the West Wing with his assistants and Secretaries Snyder, Harriman, and Schwellenbach to consider a plan for

[13] See pp. 175, 374.

the official draft of the President's Economic Report. Prior to this they had discussed with Steelman the much shortened draft of an Economic Report that had been prepared in Steelman's office. It appeared that on this Friday morning the President had taken the matter up with several members of his Cabinet and that, through their assistants, Ewan Clague of BLS, C. C. O'Connell of the Treasury, and Philip Hauser of Commerce, they were to work with Steelman and his assistants in preparing the Economic Report.

Steelman and his three assistants and the three assistants of the Secretaries adjourned at about 4:00 P. M. to work on the Report and completed that evening a draft which went to the Government Printing Office that night and was submitted for our consideration in galley proof the next morning. It was largely the draft prepared by Steelman's assistants, with which we had expressed dissatisfaction, plus a few additions from our third draft of materials.

The Council and staff worked diligently on this draft all that morning and early afternoon, preparing recommendations for revision and particularly proposing the restoration of important things which had been excluded. On Saturday afternoon, at three o'clock the Council met with Steelman, his three assistants, and Philip Hauser from Commerce and worked until after 7:00 P. M. preparing a final revision of the White House draft of the President's report to go to the printer that night for paging. (*P. D.*, Jan. 14, 1947)

The revision was in the main satisfactory to us.

The First Economic Report of the President to the Congress was submitted on January 8, 1947. With text, appendixes, and tables, it ran to a length of fifty-four pages. As to the content and coverage of the report, the phraseology of the Employment Act had furnished the Executive Office a fairly clear guide. The act constantly stressed "maximum employment, production, and purchasing power" as the goals to be attained. Likewise, it called on the President to report to the Congress not only the levels existing in these categories but also the levels of employment, production, and purchasing power "needed to carry out the policy declared" and also "current and foreseeable trends" in these levels.

Thus the body of material we submitted and that was largely incorporated in the President's Economic Report contained, as Part I, a brief statement of the statistics of employment, of production, and of purchasing power. Since any academic statement of purchasing power involved prices paid as well as income received, Section II proceeded to an analysis of the situation as to prices, wages, and profits. Section IV then went on under the title "Goals for 1947" to draw up a sort of statistical model of production and distribution conditions which would fit the objective of prosperity set up in the Employment Act. Section V was entitled "Favorable and Unfavorable Factors in 1947." It undertook to diagnose weak points in the business situation and to identify elements of strength.

The attempt to discuss these complicated economic processes in clear and understandable terms always presents difficulties. It was urged upon us by members of our staff that to this end we should use the statistical device of "The Nation's Economic Budget" as a means of showing the major income flows which need to be maintained at high levels and in good balance if national health is to be preserved. These techniques had been gradually developing since Professor King's pioneer volume *The Wealth and Income of the People of the United States* in 1915, and the study of *Income in the United States* by the National Bureau of Economic Research in 1922. We debated somewhat as to whether the use of this method of presentation could be construed as committing us to theories of compensatory spending which had been deleted from the Full Employment bill in the process of framing the Employment Act of 1946. Eventually we decided that the device in itself was neutral and a useful way of condensing an enormous body of data so as to permit the study of elemental factors in the functioning of the economy.[14] There was also the argument that this method of presentation had already been incorporated in the President's Budget Message of 1945. We therefore made "The Nation's Economic Budget" Section III of the materials we presented to the President. It has continued (with some modification) to be a feature of all Economic Reports since then.

There was also a textual "Summary of Economic Conditions and Trends" as Section VI, followed by the President's "Policy Recommendations" as Section VII. These recommendations were classified as a short-term program and a long-range program. The former urged restraint in policy and practice, both by price makers and by wage bargainers, continuance and strengthening of social security

---

[14] It made more comprehensive the picture of the economic process given by the gross national product figures of the Department of Commerce.

provisions and housing programs, foregoing the reduction of taxes
so that there would be "a surplus in government revenue over
expenditures while employment is high and the total of income is
large," and, finally, improvement in labor relations. The long-
range program "should include policies toward:

    1. Efficient utilization of the labor force;
    2. Maximum utilization of productive resources;
    3. Encouragement of free competitive enterprise;
    4. Promoting welfare, health, and security;
    5. Cooperation in international economic relations;
    6. Combating economic fluctuations."

Since this closing section of the first Economic Report of the
President stated the general philosophy of the government's role of
economic stabilization under the Employment Act, it is worth
quoting:

Only by blending all practicable programs in wise proportions can we
be successful in stabilizing our economy at the highest feasible levels. The
long-range policies I have outlined are designed to strengthen the structure
of the economy and to reinforce its resistance to economic fluctuations.

The greater this power of resistance, the less need there will be for some
of the limited and specialized stabilizing devices which have received much
attention in recent years.

I have directed the Council of Economic Advisers and the other appropriate Government agencies to make a continuing study of the stabilization
devices that may become necessary and to recommend their being placed
in operation in ample time to insure the anticipated effect.

Among these devices are a well-integrated program of employment
stabilization; improvements in the process by which workers find jobs and
employers find workers; improvements in the tax structure; wise management of the public debt; and a flexible credit policy.

Continuing policy cannot be extemporized from month to month or
even from year to year; most policies designed to increase the stability of the
economy are of long-range character. Fortunately, we have time in which
to plan deliberately and wisely, and in which to secure the co-operation
of all our citizens in driving toward our common goal: an expanding economy of maximum production, employment, and purchasing power under a
system of free competitive enterprise, with full recognition of the duties
and responsibilities of forward-looking government.

About noon on January 8, I received a telephone call from the President:

He said he was simply calling to say that he had just finished reading the Economic Report prior to sending it to the Congress. "It's a dandy! I think you have really given us a State document, and it sets a very high standard for us to live up to in the future." I expressed my great gratification and said that I would pass his statement on to the other members of the Council and staff. The President went on to say that he knew how hard we worked within the short time period and wanted us to know of his great appreciation and how highly he regarded the product which we had turned out. (*P. D.,* Jan. 8, 1947)

PUBLIC REACTION TO THE PRESIDENT'S FIRST ECONOMIC REPORT

Newspaper, radio, and periodical comment on the first Economic Report of the President was voluminous and was favorable to a gratifying degree. It reflected a general belief that the Administration was "moving to the right." In a few quarters, this was ascribed to the President's reading of materials furnished by the Council of Economic Advisers. More frequently, it was ascribed to his reading of the election returns. For control of Congress had in the November elections passed to the Republicans, and Senator Taft had displaced Senator O'Mahoney as chairman of the Joint Congressional Committee on the Economic Report of the President. (See Chapter X.)

The St. Louis *Star-Times* called the report a "Blueprint for a Prosperous Economy" and said:

President Truman's economic report to Congress yesterday was something new . . . It marked the beginning of a new approach by the government to the problem of maintaining a healthy economy within the framework of our free-enterprise system. Federal attention to the national economy, of course, is not new. It was there during the New Deal when the country was sick and it brought forth a variety of policies and programs, some of which have become so much a part of our system that they are virtually beyond challenge. But it is an innovation that the government should concern itself so closely with maintaining a healthy economy rather than with the cure of a sick one. . . .

Edward A. Evans of the Scripps-Howard staff suggested that:

President Truman's economic report to Congress merits wider closer reading than it may get. It won't interest folks who think that by some magic formula government can insure full employment and prosperity, now and forever. They're the ones who ought to study it. Its gist is that the country can enjoy fine economic health this year if the people work and act wisely, and that the people, with help from the government, can keep the economy healthy in years to come. . . . This first real attempt by government to look ahead and show a way by which a free people can co-ordinate their own activities to keep American economic life on a steadily rising plane instead of a roller-coaster, is welcome.

"It was Doctor Truman" said the Houston *Post*

rather than President Truman, Wednesday when Congress received a message from the White House giving sage counsel on policies and measures to maintain and promote the economic health of the Nation. . . . Benefiting by the expert advice of an economic council, and a better understanding of the wage-price relationship, the President shied away from blanket increases and proposed, instead, a more sensible policy of a "discriminating regard for the individual situations in revising both wages and prices." He stressed the desirability of pegging changes to the employers' ability to pay.

The President, it appears, has finally come to the realization that there can be no equitable universal or uniform rule to government price reductions or wages. Any business man could have told him that. . . .

The Chicago *Sun* challenged Senator Taft's impression of the Economic Report:

Senator Taft says that the whiskers of the New Deal peek around the corners of the President's Economic Report. But he concedes that it is an interesting and valuable document which deserves the most careful study. If Congress and the country receive it in that spirit, the report and its successors may become landmarks in American history.

No doubt it is the long-range recommendations of the report that arouse Senator Taft's suspicion. In considering them, one should remember that the Council of Economic Advisers, which prepared the report, is a decidedly middle-of-the-road body. . . .

As Congress told it to do, the Council in the long-term section of the report took up the problem of maintaining at high levels of production and employment a national economy that was greatly expanded for purposes of war.

The Christian Science Monitor called the report

"must reading" for a lot of people—including congressmen, labor leaders, and industrialists. Its 54 pages write a lesson in contemporary economics and American prospects for prosperity. But there's some criticism in Washington because the report was not sufficiently outspoken. Perhaps the Council of Economic Advisers wrote in more vigorous tones, and Mr. Truman's advisers applied the soft pedal. Or perhaps Dr. Edwin Nourse and his fellow economists felt the quiet, sweetly reasonable approach would be the most effective with Congress, especially after the class-against-class thunderings of the New Deal years. Certain it is that if you dig down among the mild phraseology, you come close to some startling conclusions, which seem to tell a lot about whether we shall have "maximum employment" in 1947–48 or a recession of mild or less-mild proportions.

Time called the report "Micawber's Masquerade," but the Washington *Post* said:

The Council of Economic Advisers has, we think, proved its worth by helping the President to give Congress and the country at large a better understanding of the relation between specific legislative recommendations and the over-all long-range objective of maintaining a high level of production and employment. Painstaking objective analysis of the factors conditioning economic activity is the best possible safeguard against unpreparedness when depression threatens. It is also a safeguard against undue reliance on mechanistic devices for rescuing the country from depression, such as Government pump priming or attempts to maintain purchasing power by indiscriminate increases in wages and salaries.

In the nature of the case, comment on the Economic Report of the President by economists and political scientists was somewhat slower in making its appearance. A number of such references are to be found in Chapter IX (p. 162) and among the evaluations presented in Part III (pp. 342 n., 400).

THE FIRST MIDYEAR ECONOMIC REPORT

During the spring months of '47 we began to consider the advisability of suggesting to the President that he send a midyear report to the Congress comparable to the annual report specifically required under the Employment Act. We thought it would be desirable for the country to have a statistical and analytical review at shorter intervals than the full year even though, naturally, the midyear report would not present a legislative program such as that which constituted the outstanding feature of the annual report. The suggestion of a midyear report was made to the President in April and met with his immediate approval. We also began a practice of submitting a quarterly memorandum, brief in form and designed only for the President's own information, or such use as he might wish to make of it within his executive family. Later, we developed a practice of monthly memoranda. (See p. 234 f.)[15]

The first midyear Economic Report of the President was transmitted to Congress on July 21, 1947. It was more than half again as long as the President's first annual report. This was due in part to the expansion of statistical appendix material, but also to more detailed analysis of current trends than had been possible in the first report. The analysis in this report was focused around the issues of postwar economic readjustment and the possibility of effecting this adjustment without a depression such as had taken place after World War I. Under the heading "Economic Adjustments for Sustained High Production," somewhat detailed analysis was given of "the process of price adjustment," "the process of wage adjustment," "profits and business finance," and "the responsibility for adjustment by business, labor, and the government." In some quarters, this emphasis on the importance of voluntary business adjustments by management, labor, agriculture, and financial agencies was disparaged as a "jawbone attack" having little promise of efficacy. But the President said:

In a free enterprise system, economic adjustment to changing conditions does not proceed according to any neat plan evolved at the seat of government and promulgated by governmental authority. Belief in the free enterprise system, as expressed in the Employment Act, stems from the conviction that the processes of dynamic economic life are so complicated and conditions change so fast that a multitude of local decisions and flexible revisions are indispensable to economic health and vigorous growth.

The closing section of the midyear economic report dealt with four special factors which appeared to influence importantly the outlook for the remainder of the year. First was the rather unfavorable weather situation, which threatened a somewhat disappointing agricultural output. Second was the threat of wage increases outrunning industrial productivity if the recent settlement between the

15 Beginning in August 1950, the Council has prepared weekly reports for circulation to the White House, the Office of Defense Mobilization, the Bureau of the Budget, and the National Security Resources Board. This report consists of one to three pages of text and three or four tables giving data which have just become available or are particularly pertinent to the moment's economic issues.

soft-coal miners and the mine operators set a general pattern. Third was the unsatisfactory expansion in the construction industry, particularly residential housing. Fourth was the impact of the recently inaugurated foreign aid program. No positive forecast was undertaken, no government program outlined.

The purpose of the midyear report was to bring the statistical picture up to date and explore the significance of what seemed to be "discernible trends." This idea met with a favorable reception from the public.

By October, an inflationary trend was causing considerable concern. Our third-quarter memorandum to the President said:

The present price situation, particularly with respect to rising food prices, creates three dangers which can be characterized as immediate and serious. First, the increasing cost of living threatens to generate another series of wage demands in urban areas, leading either to industrial stoppages and curtailment of production (with a further harmful impact upon prices) or to a wage-price spiral that would introduce new instability and uncertainties throughout the economy. Second, the present high cost of living, even if it does not climb still higher, imposes such discomfort or privation upon millions of families in the lower parts of the income structure that it is a source of nationwide discontent which cannot fail to produce serious economic repercussions. Third, the price situation could jeopardize public acceptance of the foreign aid program and make each dollar of foreign aid worth less to the recipient in terms of buying power.

Though we did not regard the situation as "a cause for immediate alarm or panicky action, it does demand sober consideration of the probable trends during the fourth quarter of 1947." We suggested several steps for dealing with the shortage of food and feed grains and "directed particular attention to the large part played by credit expansion and fiscal action in a situation like the present."

The closing section of the third-quarter memorandum to the President read: "These matters are being given careful attention by the Council and its staff and will be covered in the materials submitted for your use in connection with the preparation of the second annual Economic Report of the President."[16] Mr. Truman, however, did

16 On the Friday following, Mr. Keyserling and I (Clark was out of town) attended the regular Cabinet meeting, and I presented our third-quarter appraisal and had some discussion with the Cabinet. The President stated that since we had presented it on Wednesday, he had read it with great care, found it very helpful to his thinking, and recommended it to the careful attention of Cabinet members.

not wait until the regular session of the next Congress to inaugurate a program of action, but called a special session of the Congress to convene on November 17. At this time, he laid before them a ten-point program on controls which, modified from time to time, has been the backbone of his economic policy. (See pp. 211, 215, 232, 238.)

CHAPTER NINE

Internal and External Relations of the Council

Once the President's first Economic Report was completed and submitted to Congress, the Council could turn its attention to completing its staff, systematizing its permanent working program, and developing more fully its working relations with the appropriate agencies both within and outside the government.

STAFF ORGANIZATION AND PROGRAM OF WORK

We had by this time added an assistant for Dr. Colm, to deal with technical aspects of the national income accounts, and an assistant to Dr. Waugh to have charge of the detailed work of getting such statistics as were needed from other agencies and putting them in tabular or graphic form most useful for Council purposes. The temporary man in the labor area was replaced by a permanent appointee, John C. Davis, and an assistant was added. We appointed Walter S. Salant as specialist in international problems and Edgar M. Hoover in plant capacity and investment. Two second-range men were added, to deal with "stabilization devices" and price relations respectively. In June of 1947, a specialist in natural resources and resource development was added, and a junior man in the field of finance. Paul Homan, having completed his academic year at Cornell, took a permanent place on the staff.

The slow rate of growth in the Council's staff was explained in our Second Annual Report to the President in December 1947 as "due in part to a desire to gain greater familiarity with the precise character of our staff requirements before committing ourselves to a particular range and grouping of specialized jobs. In part it was due to the slowness with which appointees whom we desired to employ could be released from responsible posts in which they were already established. . . .

"The staff included only 5 senior economists full time, and 5 part time, 3 junior economists and statisticians, and 12 secretaries and clerical and administrative assistants on April 24 when we presented our budget justification to the Appropriations Committee of the House. That was a total force—from chairman of the Council to messenger—of 28 persons on full time and 5 part-time employees. The total salaries of the latter were equivalent to the pay of one additional full-time worker."[1] In that budget justification (for the fiscal year 1947–48) we indicated a hope of bringing our staff by the end of June 1947 to a basis of 48 staff employees, with salaries for a full year aggregating $243,000—well under the ceiling of $300,000 set in the Employment Act. We proposed to continue on about that basis thereafter, but in fact the staff never exceeded 42 employees, counting a few part-time workers on the equivalent full-time basis.

"Owing to the deliberation and frugality with which we had proceeded in perfecting appointments and making expenditures during our first year, we indicated in our budget statement of March 1947 that we were quite sure of returning an unexpended balance of at least $77,000 from our first year's appropriation. In fact, we did return over $90,000 on June 30."[2]

The House Appropriations subcommittee took a noticeably cool, if not hostile, attitude in our first budget hearing, particularly R. B. Wigglesworth (R. Mass.) and John Phillips (R. Calif.).[3] Within ten days after the hearing, I received a letter from Chairman Wigglesworth instructing us to make no further commitments pending the committee's action on our budget request. This seemed to be fair warning of a cut in our request. As time passed and no news was forthcoming, I addressed the following letter to the Appropriations Subcommittee on May 21:

[1] Council of Economic Advisers, *Second Annual Report to the President*, December 1947, p. 1.
[2] The same, p. 2.
[3] Phillips was also active in the cutting of the Council's budget in the spring of 1952.

Dear Mr. Wigglesworth:

On receipt of your letter of May 3, I of course immediately issued instructions that all appointments to the staff of this Council should be stopped just where they were, pending action on our budget by your subcommittee. This arrest in the completion of our modest staff has created two serious problems. We earnestly hope that it will be possible for you to authorize us to relieve these difficulties at a not far distant date.

After long and careful search we had selected highly qualified economists for several very important staff positions, and they had made the decision to sever their present connections. We cannot, however, ask them to take such action when we are not in a position to make definite commitments to them.

Our second difficulty arises from the fact that the business and economic situation is now in an extremely active and critical stage of readjustment, with rapid changes, which should be followed with close attention if we are to discharge properly the duties assigned us under the Employment Act. Our success in offering sound advice to the President, the Congress, and the business community will depend very largely upon the adequacy, accuracy, and timeliness of our observations and interpretations of the changing business picture. The members of the Council act as our own supreme professional staff, but we must have a reasonable number of carefully chosen assistants at an early date if we are not to continue to spread ourselves out too thinly over the large area of study which has been assigned to us.

All of the appointments frozen in accordance with your instructions, as well as most of the others provided for in our 1947 appropriation, would have been completed some time ago had it not been for the extreme care with which the Council has moved in selecting and fitting together the members of our highly specialized staff. That careful procedure largely explains the savings that we have been making out of our 1947 appropriation and the relatively large sum which we are expecting to return at the end of the fiscal year.

With appreciation of the careful attention which your subcommittee has given to the work and needs of this agency, I am

Sincerely yours,

/s./ Edwin G. Nourse, Chairman

This letter did not elicit a reply from the House subcommittee, but eventually they recommended a reduction of our budget from the $400,000 we had requested to $350,000.

In the hearing before the Senate subcommittee on the Independent Offices Appropriation bill, we encountered a much more friendly atmosphere, as was indicated by the remark of the chairman, Senator Reed (R. Kan.): "When we set up this Economic Council, Senator McKellar, it was quite an important step as adviser to the President." We stated that we fully concurred in the view of the House sub-committee that no expansion in our plan of work was called for at this time, but explained that "the $400,000 budget did not constitute any request to expand the work of the Council, but that at the end of a partial year of operation, when we have found it very difficult to inaugurate our work, it represented simply a completion of the initial set-up of the Council and its staff."[4]

The Senate committee recommended a restoration of the cut of $50,000, but this was lost in conference. Under an appropriation of $350,000, we continued our policy of having a staff of minimum size but highest quality and economizing through fullest use of materials available to us from other agencies. At the end of the year, we allowed approximately $33,000 of our first full year's appropriation of $350,000 to be returned to the Treasury. For the following year, we requested $350,000, but the Appropriations Committee reduced this to $300,000. This reduction necessitated the dropping of five clerical positions from our staff and the foregoing of some parts of our original plan for professional staffing.[5]

As I entered on the work of the Council, I had one eye cocked over my shoulder for applicants for the well-paid positions on our top staff who might come bearing the recommendation of their senator or representative. These fears proved groundless. In only two instances did anyone seek a position on the basis of political backing. One man, whose training was entirely legal and experience entirely political, was introduced to me by letter from a senator notorious for his use of patronage. He felt that he could render us valuable and efficient service in our public relations, particularly "on the Hill." I explained to him that we did not anticipate having public relations in the accepted sense, that our relations were private with the President or with such persons as we sought for consultation or who spontaneously came to us for such a purpose. I wrote the senator that we were pleased to note his interest in the work of

[4] Senate Hearings on Independent Offices Appropriation Bill, 1948, p. 92.
[5] *Third Annual Report to the President*, p. 10. The same amount was granted for Fiscal 1949, 1950, and 1951. In 1952, it was cut to $225,000 for the period up to March 31, 1953. (See p. 454.)

the Council and that I had been much impressed by the man's qualifications in the line of work for which he was trained but that, unfortunately, our scheme of organization did not contemplate any position calling for that particular training and experience. There the matter ended.

The second case was that of an application from a woman rated under Civil Service as P-6 after a long and varied career on the staffs of numerous government agencies. This application was followed by a letter from a prominent member of the Joint Economic Committee, testifying to his "high opinion of her both as a person and in her professional capacity. [As a statistician], I believe her to be thoroughly equipped for the type of work your staff will be called upon to perform." Examination of her record and interviews with her made it clear that she could perform various chores about the Council but limited largely to the sort of things that were already being done or would be done for us gratis by other agencies who had large staffs. She did not seem to have the standing or the interpretative ability which we required of our staff. Her case could not be dismissed on the score of sheer incompetence, but I felt that we had to hoard our dollars and our supervisory attention for appointments every one of which would advance to the greatest degree possible the delicate and challenging task which was entrusted to this new agency. When I continued to refuse my support to this appointment, I was warned in Council meetings not to blame others "when the heavens fell."

"What heavens?" I asked.

"Well, you can't expect this agency to have the spontaneous and vigorous help on the Hill which we shall need in order to grow and flourish, if we give their recommendations the 'brush-off.' "

"What help do we need from that source in our service to the President?" I asked.

"Well, you'll find you need it when your appropriations come up."

But there was never anything which in the slightest way indicated that the senator linked these two matters, that he questioned our judgment as to the value of this applicant for our particular staff requirements, or that his letter had been anything more than a friendly gesture for a personal acquaintance.

From the start, Mr. Keyserling had expressed a lively concern over matters of agency administration. Early in 1947 he urged that, now

that we had a little time after the scramble of work on the first
Economic Report, we proceed to draw up an outline of specific
duties and responsibilities of each of our staff people or at least of
each one who had a major area in our plan of operation in which
he worked independently or with one or more assistants.

Over a period of some weeks, we labored at this task and eventually produced the chart and job descriptions shown in Appendix B.
After consultation in Council meetings and between Council members and top staff men, we drew up a series of questions on topics
on which each would be expected to keep himself informed and able
to advise the Council when called upon. In my view each of those
specialists was already informed about the definition of problems,
available techniques, personnel, and sources of data in his respective
area far beyond anything sketched in these organizational outlines
and work specifications. I was never able to observe that either we
or the staff subsequently made any practical use of these charts and
outlines.

On the other hand, I was deeply interested in a scheme of committee organization within our staff, focused around four major
problem areas, or fields of concentration. Three of them could be
called research committees; the other was an operative committee.
The latter was the Periodic Reports Committee, which took day-to-
day responsibility for carrying out any instructions of the Council
as to the scope and character of the Economic Reports of the President or any interim reports furnished him for personal use or consideration with his Cabinet.

The Periodic Reports Committee functioned under three "joint
chairmen." Mr. Waugh was, in the main, responsible for statistical
materials used in the President's reports and for the agricultural
area. Mr. Colm, however, had special responsibility for the statistics
of the Nation's Economic Budget, and the analysis that accompanied
it as well as for questions relating specifically to fiscal policy. Mr.
Homan was responsible particularly for bringing together the various phases of the price and distributive analysis and, with his long
editorial experience, in general for the expository quality and internal consistency of the document. The joint chairmen drew upon
all members of the staff group and worked through full or partial
staff conferences as called for.

Mr. Keyserling took responsibility for keeping track of the progress of staff drafts and of condensing and editing them into a form suitable for final consideration by the Council and presentation to the President. He was insistent that he did not go beyond organizational or statistical changes and that he was meticulous in seeing that the factual and analytical picture developed by the staff was transmitted faithfully to the Council. The staff frequently expressed dissent from this view and urged restoration at the Council table of substantive material or shadings of interpretation that had been lost in passage over the editorial desk.

In the last stage of drafting, the Council, the three joint chairmen of the Periodic Reports Committee, and other staff specialists on particular phases of the report sat around the Council table going over the document line by line, endeavoring to reach consensus on the positions taken and on the most effective and appropriate form of statement. Where full agreement was not reached, the Council took complete responsibility and had to face the problem of whether the three of us could arrive at a form of statement that was mutually acceptable. For the first two years, we stayed by the rule of giving the President only one document signed by all three members of the Council, whatever omissions or verbal compromises might be entailed in the process.[6]

It was my desire to conserve as much staff and Council time as possible, between preparation of published reports of the President, which could be devoted to reformulating basic economic problems in the light of the objectives set up in the Employment Act and the growth of our economic institutions and business practices. In view of the character of the statute, it was natural that one of these areas should be designated as "stabilization devices." To one member of the staff was assigned the particular task of reviewing government or private devices that had been developed in the past as means to lessen cyclical swings or secular trends that would impair the economy's ability to operate at continuous high levels of production and employment. This staff member and the Committee on Stabilization Devices reviewed not only those things which had been experimented with or accepted in the past but also whatever proposals for innovations in this direction had been forthcoming, particularly during the period of depression or now as the reconversion process unfolded.

A second research or analytical group was designated as the Wage-

6 For the development of later Council practice on this point, see pp. 234, 281 f.

Price Committee. It was designed to examine the state of professional economic thinking and actual business practice in such fields as wage policy, price policy, collective bargaining, profit margins, and other matters that relate to the possibility of establishing such voluntary bargaining relations in free markets as would sustain employment opportunities and minimize the necessity for rescue or compensatory activities by government.

The third staff committee had as its topic of study the general area of plant capacity and its utilization, investment needs, and capital formation. Obviously, the work of this committee would at many points dovetail into the work of the Wage-Price Committee, and both in turn would be interrelated with studies of the Stabilization Devices Committee.

It was my hope that, as the Council's work proceeded, we could develop a system of problem conferences with economists from the universities, from business and labor union staffs, and from other government agencies. These would take up particular problems on which, in the light of the purposes enunciated in the Employment Act and the development of technological and institutional changes, it appeared to us that new definition of issues, new lines of attack, and further investigational work were required. As matters developed, only one such conference—and that of a rather premature and inadequate sort—was held.

THE COUNCIL AND THE PUBLIC

A second major development in the working organization of the Council turned from the internal relations we have just been discussing to the establishment of external relationship with the business public—and also to some extent with non-Federal government bodies. It was stated in the Employment Act (Sec. 4 [e] [1]) that, "in exercising its powers, functions, and duties under this act, the Council may constitute such advisory committees and may consult such representatives of industry, agriculture, consumers, state and local governments, and other groups as it deems advisable." Even in the absence of this specific mandate, the Council's interpretation of its task was such that, in all probability, it would have sought to establish channels of communication between the world of practical business and the process of government policy-making.

Within a month after the time when we were sworn in, we had extended invitations to the Farmers Union (which claimed parentage of the original Full Employment bill), the American Farm Bureau Federation, the National Grange, and the National Council of Farmer Co-operatives. In the area of business and management we extended a similar invitation to representatives of the Chamber of Commerce of the United States, the National Association of Manufacturers, the National Industrial Conference Board, the Committee for Economic Development, the Conference of American Small Business Organizations, and, a little later, the New Council of American Business—another "small business" organization. When we approached labor organizations, they suggested that, instead of a single labor group, it might prove more fruitful to consult with the representatives of each major part of the labor movement separately. We readily complied with this suggestion and arranged separate conference dates for the AF of L, the CIO, and the Association of Railway Labor Executives.

It was also suggested to us that, under a statute which emphasized the maintenance of "maximum purchasing power," it was peculiarly important that the voice of the consumer should be heard. Since only a few organizations have consumer economics as their exclusive field of work or study, whereas many organizations have this as one part of a broad program of social improvement, we invited some twenty-two organizations that had manifested interest in this phase of the Council's work to set up a standing committee that would select representatives for conference sessions and prepare such material as they thought should be considered by the Council. The arrangement seemed to have real usefulness in promoting better understanding of the nature of the consumer problem in its relation to monetary, fiscal, commercial, and industrial aspects of national economic policy.

The meetings of consultative committees were well attended, and all the groups took an active interest. Agenda were designed to elicit suggestions from the representatives of business, labor, agriculture, and consumers on matters which they thought should be covered in the next Economic Report of the President and their interpretation of difficulties confronting their particular segment of the economy. We likewise invited their criticisms as to the most recent

Economic Report or, in general, of what the President was recommending, or of what the Council was doing or failing to do within its area of responsibility.

On the public side, we made a beginning at establishing relations between ourselves as an agency for the study of national economic policy and the states and municipalities which, in matters of public spending, taxation, and private business legislation or regulation, were themselves actively concerned in local phases of economic policy which had an important impact on national conditions. These included the U. S. Conference of Mayors, the Council of State Governments, and the Association of State Planning and Development Agencies.

Finally, the Council had to consider relations to the general public, which had shown much curiosity about the economic philosophy according to which this professionally constituted staff arm of the presidency would seek to "advise and assist" him in the formulation of policy and particularly about what concept of relations between business and government might emerge from the Employment Act. The desire was frequently expressed to have members of the Council accept speaking dates, write articles, or participate in radio interviews and panel discussions. The President indicated that he was willing to leave this matter to the discretion of the Council, and we in turn were disposed to let it rest on the basis of each individual member's interpretation of what would be discreet and helpful in the particular situations which were presented to him.

Mr. Keyserling and I made numerous public addresses. This seemed to us to afford useful opportunities for discussing with serious business or citizen audiences[7] the broad economic questions of what conditions appeared, in the thinking of the profession, to be necessary to the maintenance of stable high employment and the problems which business, labor, agriculture, or others would need to face if they desired to conduct their own operations in such a way as to contribute to, rather than impede, the effort to maintain high

[7] It was a matter of profound regret to me that I was on only one occasion invited to address a labor union organization—the Brotherhood of Railway and Steamship Clerks. Mr. Keyserling was more in demand at such meetings and also to address the National Farmers' Union. On several occasions Council members appeared before professional gatherings of economists or political scientists to expound the broad economic approach or explain the functional set-up of the Council. (See p. 402 f.)

production and employment. However, question arose as to the propriety of such activities. (See pp. 275 f., 405.)

A distinctive feature of the Council's relation to the business public was a series of roundtable discussions with business (and a few academic) economists conducted by the National Industrial Conference Board. These "economic forums" were held in January shortly after the Economic Report of the President and covered a wide range of discussion relating both to the functioning of the Council and the economics of the President's report. Mr. Keyserling and I both responded to the invitations of the conference to sit in on these forums and participate in the discussion in such way as we saw fit. Economists from our staff and from the staff of the Joint Committee were also invited. A stenographic recording was kept of each of these meetings and, after editing by the participants, was issued in pamphlet form.[8]

It was my intention to keep the participation of the Council representatives on as objective, factual, and analytical a basis as possible so that whatever criticisms the forum members wished to offer could be addressed to actual situations rather than to misconceptions. I thought the value of our presence at these meetings was in getting a fuller and sharper view of the reactions of economists outside the government rather than to defend the policies expressed by the President or reveal any qualifications upon or dissent from these views which we might individually entertain. Forum members, however, were much more eager to get Council representatives involved in various kinds of in-fighting and in successive conferences succeeded in this tactic—as the written record will clearly show.[9]

[8] National Industrial Conference Board, Inc., *An Appraisal of Official Economic Reports* (1948) , *Economics of the President's Economists* (1949) , *Pros and Cons of Council of Economic Advisers' Policies* (1950) , *Defense Economics—CEA Model* (1951) , Studies in Business Economics, Nos. 16, 20, 25, 29.

[9] There were also a series of intimate off-the-record dinner meetings with prominent businessmen in various cities from Boston to San Francisco. The purpose was to give business leaders a clearer understanding of the purposes and possibilities of the Council's work and to give the Council the benefit of the suggestions of businessmen as to how more friendly and helpful relations could be established between business and government to the end of maintaining high-level production. These meetings were under the auspices of Mr. Prentiss Coonley and Mr. Arthur Whiteside. Mr. Coonley was himself a retired business executive who had served as Deputy Code Director and in other posts under the NRA, and he is now a business consultant in Washington. Mr. Whiteside was president of Dun and Brad-

In previous chapters, considerable material has been presented to show newspaper and radio reaction to the Employment Act, the President's appointees, the Economic Reports of the President, and the Council reports. At somewhat more leisurely pace, there appeared important comments from professional economists touching on some or all of these matters. In his presidential address to the American Economic Association in January 1947, Dr. E. A. Goldenweiser said:

The adoption of the Employment Act of 1946 . . . may mark the first step in the process of rationalizing the government on an over-all basis and organizing American democracy to fit modern conditions. . . . The statute is couched in negotiated language, representing compromises between different points of view. Perhaps this should make it easier for its administrators to command broad support. It is beyond doubt that the Act provides a foundation for co-ordinated national economic policy. . . . [It] contains in embryo, what is necessary to start the government on a road to more effective action. It recognizes the unity of the problems handled by the different departments and agencies; it gives the President the kind of help and support that he requires and is entitled to in the discharge of his great responsibilities; and it improves the procedure for co-operation between the executive and the legislative branches of government.[10]

In the June 1947 issue of the *American Economic Review,* Professor Holbrook Working of Stanford University commented on the first Economic Report of the President:

Considered simply by itself as a statement from the President of the United States on the national economy in a critical year, it is a report that merits serious attention; but to the eye of a professional economist it appears much more than an isolated presidential message. It marks the beginning of a great experiment, the success or failure of which might have profound consequences for the economic and possibly even for the political structure of the United States and of other nations. Depending for its success on enlightened public consideration of major economic problems of the nation, the experiment is a venture in economic education on a grand scale, and it presupposes a continuing distillation of critical knowledge and judgment on economic affairs which could significantly affect

street and has served with distinction on numerous occasions as a public representative on various government advisory bodies. Mr. Keyserling was the guest at a number of these meetings, I at somewhat more of them, Mr. Clark at only one or two.

10 E. A. Goldenweiser, "The Economist and the State," *The American Economic Review,* Vol. XXXVII, No. 1, March 1947.

the development of economic science. . . . What are the powers by which the Economic Report may meet the demands laid on it? In a word, they are the powers of education, of economic enlightenment. . . . Many economists may doubt whether the provisions of the Employment Act of 1946 are adequate to its purposes, but few will hesitate to bend their efforts toward its success. Its success would be a triumph of the democratic ideals of individual freedom, enlightenment, and disciplined social action. . . . Every effort must be made to keep the Economic Report above party politics.[11]

In the Harvard *Review of Economic Statistics* for May 1947, Alvin Hansen of Harvard and Jacob Viner of Princeton discussed the early operation of the Employment Act of 1946. Both Viner and Hansen found the Council's warnings against too exclusive reliance on fiscal policy as a stabilizing force misdirected or overdrawn and its emphasis on "the possibility of guiding and educating business to stabilize itself" illusory. Professor Viner concluded that as "to the claim made by the Council of Economic Advisers that 'The Employment Act of 1946 marks a distinct and important step in the evolution of our national life and our frame of democratic government' . . . the only verdict which at this stage seems appropriate is the Scotch verdict: 'Not proven.'" Professor Hansen ended his paper: "Continuous public education is necessary. This should be *one* function of the Economic Report."

In the October 1948 issue of the *Journal of Political Economy*, Professor Bronfenbrenner of the University of Wisconsin published a rather sportive review-article on the volume *The Economic Reports of the President* in which a commercial publisher had assembled the first two annual reports of the President and the first midyear report. He said:

Professional and public interest in the council and its work has tended generally downward since its inception. At the Cleveland and Atlantic City meetings of the American Economic Association in 1946 it was the leading topic of discussion. At the Chicago meeting in 1947 it was barely discussed. Vis-à-vis Congress, the council's standing has fallen to one of "final probation," to borrow a term from deans' offices throughout the land. Its appropriation for the fiscal year 1949 barely escaped excision by the House Appropriations Committee. A one-year reprieve from the Taberian axe was granted as a last chance to reform. The council has lost prestige by yielding alternately to Scylla and Charybdis. One moment it has seemed

[11] Holbrook Working, "Reflections on the President's Economic Report," *American Economic Review*, Vol. XXXVII, No. 3, June 1947, pp. 383, 384, 385.

the "ivory tower" research agency, too remote from reality for meaningful results. And the next, it has sunk to an ideological club for the exclusive use of the President in belaboring his political opponents. It is currently in process of avoiding at least the last-named error by making its services in the study of special issues available to Congress and congressional committees on the same terms as to the President, although its annual reports will continue to be addressed to the President alone. In August, 1948, for example, members of the council testified before the Senate Banking Committee in support of the president's anti-inflation program.[12]

John Maurice Clark of Columbia foresaw a twofold danger in the Council's advisory role.

First, there may be a feeling that if voluntary action fails to stabilize the economy, then, because voluntary action is the thing that has been stressed in these reports, that is all that is to be expected, and we are through. Or, on the other hand, there might be a feeling that, because voluntary measures are sure to fail, the Council must have others up its sleeve, including some that a good many businessmen might regard as having a socialistic character. Either of these feelings could make trouble.

I am very glad that I don't have the responsibility that falls on the members of this Council to steer a course between that Scylla and Charybdis. It is a very difficult course to steer, but if it isn't steered with reasonable success, the consequences could be serious. It is enormously important that the Council should succeed and should be given every fair chance to succeed in its very delicate and difficult assignment.[13]

INTRAGOVERNMENTAL RELATIONS

Coming as a new agency within the structure of the Federal Government, the Council faced two broad types of problems in undertaking to establish smooth and helpful relations with pre-existing agencies. One concerned our staff vis-à-vis other staffs of statisticians and economists. The second involved the acceptance and usefulness of the Council at the policy-making level not merely with the President but with agency heads throughout the executive branch.

The Employment Act (Sec. 4 [e] [2]) provided that ". . . the Council shall to the fullest extent possible, utilize the services, facilities, and information (including statistical information) of other Govern-

12 M. Bronfenbrenner, "Postwar Political Economy: The President's Reports," *The Journal of Political Economy*, Vol. LVI, No. 5, October 1948, p. 375.
13 "The President's Economic Program," *Current Business Studies* (Trade and Industry Law Institute, Inc.) , June 1949, pp. 30–31.

ment agencies as well as of private research agencies, in order that duplication of effort and expense may be avoided." In carrying out this instruction, we had the fullest co-operation of staff workers and administrative officers in all branches of government—in supplying data, exploring techniques, conferring on policy issues, and collaborating on report material.

There is a fine professional camaraderie among the academically trained staffs of the Federal Government agencies which manifests itself, with few exceptions, in a willingness to make their data freely available to their professional brethren and to participate with associates in other agencies in reaching sound interpretation and application of the fact-gathering and analytical work on which they are engaged, wherever it may be needed. In numerous cases, members of the Council staff promoted or participated in interdepartmental committees or informal groups to this end. Most of our people had previously occupied senior positions in other government agencies and were fully acquainted with the problems, techniques, and personnel of all groups working in related fields. Our scheme of organization was designed to provide conduits through which the underlying work of hundreds of government statisticians and economists could be economically and flexibly drawn upon in the prosecution of our top-level syntheses for policy-making purposes.

This arrangement was facilitated by the cordial co-operation of administrative officers right up to Department heads. This was conspicuously true of James E. Webb, Director of the Budget, the agency with which, on the whole, our work was most closely intertwined. Another specific instance of active co-operation by another Department was afforded by the invitation extended the chairman of the Council by Secretary Harriman, to sit in with him and the heads of the extensive statistical and economic groups of the Department of Commerce at times when they were making periodic round-ups of their material in connection with such Department publications as the *Survey of Current Business*. Among other sources on which we drew heavily were the Bureau of Labor Statistics, the Research and Statistical Division of the Federal Reserve Board, and the Bureau of Agricultural Economics.

If we discovered certain gaps in data which needed to be filled if we were to discharge our task most effectively, or discrepancies between ways in which data were gathered or the results presented,

there was great willingness of all staffs to participate in interagency
committees which, with the aid of the Division of Statistical Standards of the Bureau of the Budget, would try to iron out these
difficulties.[14]

As an outgrowth of the work of the fiscal division of the Bureau
of the Budget, there had emerged early in 1946 a small chart book
bearing the title *Economic Indicators*. This publication contained
no text or tabular matter but some half dozen pages of charts covering current developments such as employment, production, and
prices. Only a hundred copies of this small document were multi-
lithed and circulated to the President, agency heads, and administrative officers in various economic and statistical bureaus. Council
members were included in this list as soon as our agency was set up.
I at once took the position that a publication of this sort no longer
fell within the province of the Bureau of the Budget, and Mr. Webb
agreed in principle. Mr. Keyserling was strongly in favor of our
developing a statistical publication along this same line but of a
somewhat more ambitious character. I hesitated to have our small
staff assume the burden of operative functions such as this implied.
The Bureau of the Budget therefore continued and somewhat expanded *Economic Indicators* throughout 1947 and early 1948.

But by April 1948, the Council was ready to take over *Economic
Indicators* and continue it in modified form as a monthly pamphlet
of 32 pages. Each chart and an accompanying table presented the
data of recent years for one of the major aspects of the economy.
Since we believed that this selection of basic statistics would be found
of considerable use by the general public, we desired that it be given
general circulation rather than the limited intragovernment distribution previously made. The cost of publishing such a periodical
would have been quite out of the range of the Council's funds. But
we had learned that certain members of the Joint Committee, particularly Senator Flanders, were impressed with the usefulness of
this up-to-the-minute compilation of basic statistics for their work
and for the use of the general public.

[14] Similarly, a number of outside organizations which had fact-gathering or
analytical services were co-operative, not merely in making their data available to
us, or advancing the date at which it became available, or giving it special manipu-
lations which would give a product most useful for our work. Beyond this, there
were striking instances in which such private agencies did extra work or incurred
extra expense in order to get, through their fact-finding machinery, data which
we believed would complement the statistical services available in government.

Thus an arrangement was made under which, for about a year, *Economic Indicators* came out as a "Joint Committee print." In June 1949, Congress authorized the Joint Committee to continue *Economic Indicators* as a regular monthly publication. (See p. 256.)

The most formal instance of collaboration between the Council and other agencies in the executive branch came in connection with the launching of the Marshall Plan. In June 1947, Secretary Marshall, in a Commencement address at Harvard University, outlined a more comprehensive program of economic aid to Europe, and this promptly became part of "The Truman doctrine" as the European Recovery Program or "Marshall Plan." Since the effectuation of such a policy would involve large expenditure of American funds, the President on June 22 inaugurated a three-part study of this proposal. It was designed to furnish Congress and the country with guidance as to how large a foreign aid program we could "wisely and safely" undertake. The nature of the three-level study was set forth in a White House statement of June 22 as follows:

The impact upon our domestic economy of the assistance we are now furnishing or may furnish to foreign countries is a matter of grave concern to every American. I believe we are generally agreed that the recovery of production abroad is essential both to a vigorous democracy and to a peace founded on democracy and freedom. It is essential also to a world trade in which our businessmen, farmers and workers may benefit from substantial exports and in which their customers may be able to pay for these goods. On the other hand, the extent to which we should continue aiding such recovery is less easy to ascertain, and merits most careful study. . . .

Accordingly, I am creating immediately three committees to study and report to me within the shortest possible time on the relationship between any further aid which may be extended to foreign countries and the interests of our domestic economy. Two of these studies will be conducted within the Government; the third will be conducted by a non-partisan committee of distinguished citizens headed by the Secretary of Commerce.

Of the two studies to be conducted within the Government, one will deal with the state of our national resources, and will be made by a committee of specialists under the direction of the Secretary of the Interior. The other governmental study will deal with the impact on our national economy of aid to other countries, and will be conducted by the Council of Economic Advisers.

The non-partisan committee will be requested to determine the facts with respect to the character and quantities of United States resources available for economic assistance to foreign countries, and to advise me, in the light of these facts, on the limits within which the United States may safely and wisely plan to extend such assistance and on the relation between this assistance and our domestic economy. This committee will be drawn from representatives of American business, finance, labor, agriculture, and educational and research institutions. In carrying out its work this committee will have the benefit of the studies which are to be made within the Government, as well as the materials already prepared by various Government agencies.

In accordance with the President's review plan, the Council set up a special committee consisting of Paul Homan, Gerhard Colm, and Walter Salant to assemble the pertinent facts and develop the analysis necessary to indicate the weight or impact of a foreign aid program of hypothetical size (3 billion dollars) upon the domestic economy. One additional staff member served in a liaison capacity with the Department of the Interior to see that our committee was fully informed as to their evaluation of the technical questions of availability of natural resources. Another member served in a similar capacity with the Department of Commerce to see that the Citizens Committee was kept informed as to the trend and progress of our analysis of the economic impact on domestic business.

On October 28, the Council submitted to the President a report in mimeographed form, embracing eighty pages of text and thirty-two additional pages of statistical appendices. This report considered general effects on the whole economy and specific effects in critical areas, both long-run and short-time consequences. It also dealt with the administrative arrangements and special measures which would be called for to mitigate harmful effects so far as possible if foreign aid expenditures assumed large dimensions. The President's letter of acknowledgment in its first two paragraphs expressed his appreciation of all three reports (Interior, Council, and Citizens' Committee under Secretary Harriman) and his appreciation of the efforts made "on such short notice and brought to conclusion in so brief a period." In the concluding paragraph, he said: "The Council of Economic Advisers played an invaluable role, not only by preparing its own report, but by furnishing staff assistance to the Secretary of the Interior and the Citizens' Committee under the chairmanship of the Secretary of Commerce."

This was the first special or *ad hoc* report which the Council was called upon to make and the most extensive which has thus far been undertaken. We had on our docket another study of the guaranteed annual wage, which had been referred to us by the Advisory Committee of the OWMR when that body was terminated in December 1946. We had the labor specialists on our staff examine the materials collected by the special staff set up by OWMR[15] and begin the preparation of an analytical study of this problem in the light of the policy expressed in the Employment Act. This study was, however, repeatedly pushed into the background by the pressure of other Council work, and no report on this topic has yet been made.

COUNCIL AND AGENCY HEADS

As to intragovernmental relations of the Council at the policy level, it must always be borne in mind that the device of a Council of Economic Advisers in the Executive Office of the President was injected into a long-standing Cabinet system, with largely autonomous Department Secretaries. Furthermore, this system has been expanded by the addition of "independent" commissions whose heads likewise have considerable authority in formulating economic policy within their particular jurisdiction. The Housing and Home Finance Agency, the Federal Security Agency, the Atomic Energy Commission, and the Federal Reserve Board are notable cases. Since the Economic Report of the President was designed particularly to secure an integration of departmental or segmental policies into a truly national and internally consistent policy, it was important that any advisory function that the Council was able to achieve should begin with the separate branches of government and their policy-making heads.

In the very first weeks of the Council's life, we began a series of "courtesy calls" on Cabinet Secretaries and agency heads whose province embraced important economic areas—notably Treasury, Commerce, Labor, Agriculture, Federal Reserve, Social Security, and later, as it got into action, the National Security Resources Board. From the first moment our relationships with the Bureau of the Budget were so cordial and mutually informal that no official approaches were called for. In all cases the Secretary or agency head

[15] *Guaranteed Wages,* Report to the President by the Advisory Board, Office of War Mobilization and Reconversion (Murray W. Latimer, Research Director), Jan. 31, 1947.

expressed accord with the purposes of the Employment Act and a desire to co-operate with the Council both personally and through their staffs in its task of advising the President.

In the hurly-burly of preparing the first report, we did not find ways of keeping those officials fully in touch with the course of our deliberations. I did make a point of sending them the draft of the material which we were preparing for the President forty-eight hours in advance of the time we were to lay it on his desk. In one or two cases, there was a prompt reaction calling attention to slight inaccuracies in our factual statement or recommending a somewhat different form of expression in stating our interpretation. These were quickly worked out in conference to the satisfaction of both parties. In several other cases, however, members of the Cabinet felt that the document submitted by the Council to the President presented them with a *fait accompli* and that they had not had a sufficient opportunity for expressing their views on points which concerned their individual departments. Thus the episode referred to in Chapter VIII (p. 141) in connection with the final draft of the First Economic Report of the President. In the next three reports,[16] this last stage of drafting was accomplished expeditiously and without difficulty by a short series of revisionary conferences between the Council (with the joint chairman of the Periodic Reports Committee) and two or three representatives from Mr. Steelman's office or other representative of the White House staff.

In a very real sense, the Bureau of the Budget and the Council of Economic Advisers constitute twin and complementary agencies for the integration of national economic policy in the Executive Office of the President. The major operative responsibility of the Director of the Budget is to see that the President's policy as to Federal expenditure is faithfully interpreted to all spending agencies and that they prepare their individual budget estimates in strict accordance with this policy. Department and commission estimates of their needs always exceed the total that the President will recommend or Congress authorize so they must be reviewed by the examiners of the Budget Bureau, pared and readjusted by the Estimates Division, and collated by the Director and his aides into a final structure which will meet with the President's approval.

[16] During this period, any sense of frustration or of being bypassed on the part of Cabinet members was absent or quiescent. A subsequent attempt to meet the problem constructively is discussed in Chap. XI.

This is a long and arduous process. It does not have an annual cut-off, but one year's budget is conditioned by projects begun in previous years and continuing into future years or by the need or desire for beginning new government undertakings or of devising the most expedient ways for the government to meet extraordinary demands on military or civilian strains as they arise. The President's policy cannot be set arbitrarily or by divine inspiration at the beginning of a budget-making period but must emerge and finally crystallize in the light of intensive and progressive study of the programs advanced by the several agencies in the light of a continuing analysis of the condition of the economy and probable impact of one or another magnitude and pattern of public activity and spending. There must always be frequent, and over considerable periods, daily, or even several-times-daily, consultation between the President and the Director of the Budget.

As the Council of Economic Advisers took over and expanded the function of broad analysis of the functioning of the economy as it affected and is affected by the Federal budget, it was necessary to develop a procedure between ourselves and the Budget Bureau and between Council and President. Aside from the constant intercommunication between our staff and the Budget staff on factual and detailed analytical matters, there were three major occasions for articulation of the work of the two agencies at the top policy level.

The first occasion comes in May, when the Budget Director consults with the President for the purpose of getting a general benchmark set for the budget which is to be presented to Congress the following January. At this time it is important to get a reconciliation of the basic assumptions as to the state of the economy, the business outlook, the trend of national income, and prospective Federal revenue, as a basis for the President's budget policy. In May 1947, Director Webb invited the Council with such of our staff as we saw fit, to sit in with him and his top aides to clear our views on these matters. This gave us our first formal introduction into this important joint function of the two staff arms of the President's office.

This May meeting was hardly more than exploratory in character but was followed by one in late August or early September for clearing further our analysis of the course of national economic developments before "firming up" the budget total and Departmental breakdown to which agency estimates must be brought into conformity. The third stage of Council–Budget Bureau collaboration comes as the drafts of the Economic Report and the Budget Message take final form. This phase of consultation covers roughly the whole month of December. It involved almost constant interstaff contacts, with clearance between Council and Budget Director as well as our separate contacts with the President—extensive for the Budget Director, fragmentary for the Council. Sometimes these meetings took place around our Council table, sometimes in the Budget Director's office.[17]

Since some estimate of anticipated Federal revenue had to be used both by the Council in its economic analysis and by the Budget Bureau in its budget proposals, it would have been highly desirable if these December conferences had been tripartite, that is, including also the Secretary of the Treasury and his top aides. The Treasury, however, insisted on playing its cards very close to the chest, not basing its revenue estimates on our analysis, but giving us their official figure at the last moment—even when the Economic Report and Budget Message were in page proof.

Not in its first year but later, the Council asked the heads of various agencies which had important economic functions to confer with us around our Council table as the Economic Report was taking shape. Secretary Snyder responded to our invitation, bringing along several of his top aides, but was somewhat reserved in the opening up of vital issues. Secretaries Sawyer, Brannan, Tobin, Krug, Chairman McCabe of the Federal Reserve Board, and Administrators Ewing and Woods likewise came to confer with us at times when an Economic Report was shaping up and we wished to get their views and to have them informed as to considerations we proposed to lay before the President.

[17] There might also be an occasional conference on some special issue. Thus there was a full-dress review of stockpiling needs and strains in the spring of 1949 in which both Budget and Council personnel participated before the Budget Director took a position on this matter in the National Security Council. From mid '49 forward the chairman of the Council became an attendant at staff conferences of the National Security Council, with opportunity to express Council views as to the scale of military expenditures from the standpoint of their impact on the civilian economy.

When Secretary Forrestal initiated (Nov. 10, 1948) a series of Group Orientation Conferences "for the briefing of prominent citizens from all groups, he asked the Chairman of the CEA to make a presentation on "Economic Implications of Military Preparedness." The practice was continued under Secretary Johnson. (See also p. 405.)

In the case of the Department of Commerce there developed a special type of association which partook partly of a Council-Cabinet relation and partly of a Council-business relation. This involved the Business Advisory Council, which has been mentioned in Chapter IV. Its membership embraces a changing but always distinguished group of business executives who meet every two months or so to discuss current business problems among themselves and with the Secretary of Commerce. On occasion they call upon the President to present their views or send him a formal memorandum at the close of their meeting.

Henry Wallace, as Secretary of Commerce, manifested a lively interest in the Council of Economic Advisers and invited me to attend the dinner session of the Business Advisory Council in September 1946 to make such presentation as I thought desirable concerning the Council's prospective role. I found that the BAC had, during the day, been discussing the meaning of the Employment Act and was still echoing with a phrase used by one of their members, Ralph Flanders. He had been an active member of the Committee for Economic Development and was at this time running for a seat in the Senate. His phrase was "This is it" and he told me privately that his first concern if he came to the Senate would be to secure a place on the Joint Committee on the Economic Report.

At this meeting the BAC appointed a special committee to study and report on the forthcoming Economic Report of the President and to effect helpful liaison with the Council. Donald David, dean of the Harvard Graduate School of Business, was made chairman of this committee, but was succeeded shortly by Marion Folsom of the Eastman Kodak Company.

This committee, on frequent occasions when they met in Washington, invited the members of the Council to join with them at luncheon and for an after-lunch discussion meeting. On occasion they would send the Council in advance an agenda of questions that they wished to discuss with us at the time of their next meeting. On at least one occasion they came to our offices and went over these matters with us and a few top staff people at a length of two hours, after which we adjourned to the Mayflower for lunch as their guests and for further discussion until well into the afternoon.

A somewhat different phase of this matter of interagency relationships concerned the Department of Agriculture. Secretary

Brannan had told us in the spring of 1948 that the Department was making a re-examination of farm policy and that, since this was closely related to the stabilization objectives of the Employment Act, he would want to benefit fully from our counsel before deciding on the policy line which he would take. At ten o'clock one morning, I received a telephone call from him saying that he was dispatching to me by messenger a copy of the policy statement which he would be presenting to a Congressional committee at noon that day and that he would be glad to have any suggestions we might wish to offer. This document embodied what has subsequently been known as "The Brannan Plan."

I suggested to the Secretary that the time was rather short for thorough examination by the Council of the nature of his recommendations and the broad economic analysis on which they were based. He hastened to assure me that this was merely an exploratory presentation before the committee, that the plan was not complete as to details or crystallized as to form, and that there would still be ample opportunity for exchange of views between the Council and the Department.

Some days later, in a luncheon conference with the Secretary, I indicated various lines of qualification or dissent as to the economics of the Brannan Plan. With the utmost friendliness and suavity, the Secretary listened to my criticism of the statistical bases and economic premises from which his analysis and recommendations proceeded and of the impact of such a plan on the economy over the long term. There was no indication, however, that he was in any way disturbed by these questionings of the foundations or consequences of his plan. There were no further discussions and no subsequent indication of a desire to test the validity of the criticisms which I advanced. Of course policy-making is the function of executive officers, not of economic advisers. But the potentialities of a system of economic advisership as contemplated in the Employment Act will be achieved only as economic analysis has its day in court before political synthesis takes place. (See Chapter XIX.)

No discussion of the intragovernmental relations of the Council of Economic Advisers would be complete without consideration of the relations between Council and Congress. That story, however, cannot be told except in connection with the role and personnel of the Joint Committee and as part of the relation between the Council and the President. The nature and origin of the issue will begin to emerge in the closing sections of this chapter and will be followed in some detail in later chapters of Part II.

COUNCIL AND PRESIDENT

Chapters VII and VIII have already recounted the President's early expression of interest in the Council and his gratification over the character of the first Economic Report and its generally favorable reception in spite of various specific criticisms.

On January 14, I had an appointment with the President for the purpose of beginning to clarify our Council operations during the coming year. He expressed appreciation of the Council's work in connection with the Economic Report and referred to his telephone call to me the morning it was submitted to the Congress. Nothing was said about the fact that, in spite of our desire—indicated on several occasions—to discuss with him the materials which we had submitted, the Council had not talked with him at any time since December 16, when the first draft of material was submitted.

I myself had seen him on only one occasion since then. That was when a late draft of the State of the Union Message was being read (Mr. Clifford, Judge Rosenman, Charles Ross, Steelman, and I present). At that meeting I had been asked to check those parts of the State of the Union Message which related to economic matters. I had made some suggestions for minor changes but said that in general it accorded with the Council's thinking. To this Clifford rejoined, "it should, since it was largely taken from that source."

As I left this meeting, I expressed to the President the hope of the Council that on the following day, Friday, January 3, we might discuss with him the third draft of the material for use in drawing his Economic Report. No such conference was arranged, but on that afternoon, the Council was called by Mr. Steelman to meet in the West Wing with his assistants and with Secretaries Snyder, Harriman, and Schwellenbach [to work out the final form of the Economic Report (as explained in Chapter VIII, p. 141)]. (*P. D.,* Jan. 14, 1947)

On February 12, I had an interview with the President in which I reported to him how we were getting organized for a full year of work focused on the Council's December 1947 and President's January 1948 reports and raising the possibility that the times might be more disturbed than on the occasion of our first outgivings. We might be in some sort of recession period where we should have to be very sure of our ground as to whether recessionary forces might be in danger of getting out of hand and developing into a real depression.

The President indicated that he was actively concerned about one or two matters, particularly the possibility of dangerous developments in the real estate and housing area. He was pleased when I said that we were focusing our work program on identifying these or other danger spots and preparing special memoranda for him as occasion arose. He said he would be glad to receive them or to talk with us at any time when we were prepared to bring such matters to his attention.[18] He mentioned also the possibility of security prices showing a dangerous rise in response to the present earnings situation.

I took this occasion to set forth my views as to the Council Report as being of a background character designed primarily for public education. I said that as I saw it there was the prospect that under this act the Council might within the next few years be called upon to recommend somewhat vigorous action to check unsound boom developments and should certainly be prepared thereafter to propose perhaps even more aggressive measures to prevent or to check a depression if it should appear to be

[18] I always found it possible to secure an appointment with the President either for myself or for the Council as a body whenever we had matters which we believed should have his attention. Either Mr. Connelly [the President's appointment secretary] had a lively personal sense of the importance of the Council's function or the President had instructed him to facilitate such appointments. But these meetings were uniformly disappointing. Mr. Truman, after a hearty greeting, would launch into casual comment about some incident of his morning walk or other irrelevant matter. When an economic issue was raised, he would toss off an easy generalization about how it should be dealt with or how he "would balance the budget if those fellows on the Hill would do as I tell them."

One or two professional friends of mine, better versed than I in the ways of public administration, had suggested that I should claim a regular frequent consultation time with the President—say, weekly—in order to build up a sense of reliance on the Council for economic advice. The relation of the Director of the Budget was suggested as an example. But the situations seemed to me far from parallel. Budget figures are very concrete and precise matters, and budget problems present a long stream of *ad hoc* issues on which quick and often arbitrary decisions must be reached in the light of information presented to the President by the Budget Director. Frequent and effective conferences thus grow out of the very nature of the work. The President was figure-minded, relished the game, and prided himself on his ability as a budget officer. Economic questions, on the other hand, seem vague, are certainly complex, and cannot be broken down into any such quick and manageable pieces. I did not feel that I could present to the President a convincing picture of the usefulness of a weekly conference to be fitted into his busy program or that I could get such a series established on a satisfactory basis even if he accepted the idea in principle. (See p. 228 f.)

developing. Our first report had given the general background of economic principle which we thought was enunciated in the act and which we expected to put in practice through Council work. I thought that from this beginning we should proceed with other brief pamphlets, taking up specific phases of this general philosophy of stabilized prosperity, each one being dealt with briefly, not to exceed twenty-five pages. I suggested that if we were to develop this additional program adequately, so as to have a proper atmosphere in which his recommendations and program were to be launched, two or three years from now, it might be desirable to have a mid-year report of the Council and not merely the Annual Reports made mandatory by the act. The President said that he agreed absolutely with this view and would be glad to have us proceed along this line and inform him as to the topic chosen and show him the draft of treatment at such times as we saw fit.

This interview was very satisfactory. The President seemed thoroughly pleased with what had been accomplished in our first reports and said: "We want to work right ahead along these same lines." He seemed to indicate also a great willingness to discuss with us at any time any matter which we wished to bring to his attention and was ready to toss off suggestions in the course of an interview but did not suggest or apparently contemplate turning to the Council for advice on matters of taxation, budget, or other subjects on which he is to take policy and action positions right along. For example, he expressed great interest in the matter of resource development and conservation and said: "I am not going to rest until I get a real program of development of Alaska under way." (*P. D.*, Feb. 12, 1947)

On March 7, I sent a note to the President expressing concern over the upturn in prices "advancing the cost of living just at the time when new wage negotiations are being opened, thus making a highly unfavorable situation for the attainment of business stability and full employment in 1947." Mr. Truman made an appreciative reply on March 10, saying "keep your finger on the situation and keep me fully informed on the program."

This was the moment of the enunciation of the "Truman Doctrine" on foreign policy. Since there was little indication of its contemplated size we found the difficulties of the task of advising on domestic policy increased. We therefore inquired in a letter on March 19: "Should we, in the report we expect to make to you covering developments during the first quarter of 1947, leave these probable changes out of consideration? Or could we, in the meantime, be supplied with further information as to the character and magnitude of the activities which are contemplated in connection with the new international policy? We would then be able to consider how far the new program might hold or draw more of the labor force into our military establishment, increase Federal expenditures by amounts large enough to alter the national budget materially and, by diverting productive capacity to military needs or foreign relief and rehabilitation, tighten the demand and supply situation in the domestic market." The President made a completely noncommital reply and subsequent events indicated that the policy was fixed only as to direction and the question of magnitude was deferred (until October, when it was clarified through the report of the Citizen's Committee—see p. 167).

"As the time was short, we decided not to make any special report on the price situation, but to merge it into the regular first-quarter memorandum which had been contemplated in our original working plans. This memorandum was presented to the President at a conference with the three members of the Council on April 7, and at his suggestion was laid before the Cabinet at its meeting on the 9th." (*P. D.*, Feb. 23, 1948.) This was the first of three appearances of the Council at a Cabinet meeting. Discussion of our memorandum was negligible.

An important question as to the relationship of the Council to the President arose at this time. Would we have a special and direct advisory role in the case of legislation of major economic significance? Or would the Office of Legislative Reference of the Budget Bureau simply refer such bills to us in a routine manner along with all other agencies which were invited to comment? Mr. Clark Clifford specifically referred the portal-to-portal pay bill to us, and we responded with a letter addressed to the President.[19] Shortly thereafter the tax reduction bill came to us through the Office of Legislative Reference of the Bureau of the Budget. We informed them that we regarded this area as one on which the Council should advise the President directly rather than indirectly through the

[19] It is interesting to note one feature of this letter (May 8, 1947) which read: "One member of the Council, while recognizing the weight of the views of his colleagues, recommends the disapproval of the bill for the following reasons . . ." This is the only early instance I recall of any differentiation of individual members' views in communications we sent to the President.

Bureau of the Budget. The first paragraph of our letter to the President (June 5, 1947) said:

Our official duty to serve as your economic advisers with respect to government policies that affect production, employment, and purchasing power which the Employment Act of 1946 seeks to maintain at the maximum attainable level, gives us a special concern in the tax measures adopted by the Congress. What fraction of national income is withdrawn as Federal revenue has an important impact on the operation of the economy and the possibility of attaining the economic objectives set forth in the Employment Act. Hence we have been giving close attention to the probable effect of the tax reduction proposed in H. R. 1, now before you for signature or veto. Herewith we submit the conclusions to which this study has brought us.

Neither the Director of the Budget nor the President made any comment on this procedure and we repeated it when the Taft-Hartley bill came up. As to the procedure of the Office of Legislative Reference, we came to agreement with Director Webb that they would refer to us any measures on which they thought we might be interested and that we would reply to them or advise the President direct, depending on the importance of the matter to the purposes of the Employment Act. Or if the measure was of limited importance or technical character, we would inform them that we had no comment to make.

On one matter, not of legislation but of business policy and action, we sent the President at this time the draft of a statement which we believed it might be salutary for him to issue. This concerned the pending rise in coal and steel prices following the settlement of the coal miner's strike. On July 14 he gave this out, with minor changes, as a "Statement of the President."

At about this same time, shortage of steel scrap was becoming acute and the practices of various government agencies were attracting sharp criticism. I raised this matter in Council meeting and suggested that we take the matter up with the President. Mr. Keyserling appeared to be in agreement, but left shortly on a vacation. Mr. Clark participated in one or two discussions with people from the industry that I had brought in but, to my surprise, was unwilling to sign the draft letter to the President which

I had prepared. I thereupon sent it to the President with a covering letter explaining the circumstances and saying:

I am sending it to you as my individual expression because I have such great fear that if nothing is done the Administration might at some later time be subjected to sharp criticism. Mr. Clark's objection was that the Council should not address you on this matter unless we had gone direct to the various agencies involved and satisfied ourselves that they were not taking all the steps that could reasonably be expected of them. It seems to me, however, that such a course could be construed by them as meddlesomeness on our part and would put us into the realm of operative matters instead of considering economic situations and policy on a broad plane.

The letter itself had recommended a Presidential directive to the armed services, the War Assets Administration, and the Maritime Commission,

urging them to leave no stone unturned to secure the maximum flow of scrap metal under their jurisdiction, [and] that full publicity be given to the fact that vigorous steps in this direction were being undertaken. Such a statement would not merely make it clear that the Administration recognizes and is actively discharging its responsibility in this serious situation. It would also serve to warn all parties against attempting to exploit the present shortage by hoarding metal or unduly enhancing its price.

The President made no direct response, but Mr. Steelman telephoned me to say the matter had been put in his charge and he was delegating a young man in his office to follow it closely. While no formal directive was issued from the President's office, Mr. Steelman, as Mr. Truman's personal assistant, put pressure directly upon the agency whose policies or practices had been questioned.

In the fall of 1947, the President became concerned over the inflationary dangers and was contemplating a special message to Congress on the subject. Clark Clifford, who was the President's chief speech writer, requested suggestions from the Council as to the content of such a message, and the Council responded with a nine-page memorandum on November 5. Three weeks later, we sent the President a letter expressing our concern on the question of bank credit restriction. It elicited no response.

When the Council's second report to the President appeared on December 13, 1947 (embodying a discussion of the meaning of "maximum production" and means of attaining it), the President sent the following note: "Thanks a lot for sending me a copy of the Second Annual Report of your Council. I appreciate very much having the printed copy. It is a very interesting document and I think it will be very useful as a preliminary in preparing the report." There was, however, no progressive discussion between Council and President of the analytical points and policy recommendations of his Economic Report of January 1948 or indication of the way in which the Council's report was "useful as a preliminary in preparing the report."

CHAPTER TEN

The Joint Committee on the Economic Report—1946-48

For the carrying out of the national economic policy declared in the Employment Act of 1946, Congress provided a dual implementation. Besides the Council of Economic Advisers, which we have been discussing in the last three chapters, the Act set up in the legislative branch a "Joint Committee on the Economic Report." This body was to make its own continuing study of the problem of national economic stabilization and to review the President's analysis of the country's economic needs and his recommendations for meeting them. It would thereupon express its own judgment as to what measures would promote to the fullest extent or in the best way the Act's declared purpose of high and sustained productivity. Section 5 of the Employment Act provides:

(a) There is hereby established a Joint Committee on the Economic Report, to be composed of seven Members of the Senate, to be appointed by the President of the Senate, and seven Members of the House of Representatives, to be appointed by the Speaker of the House of Representatives. The party representation on the joint committee shall as nearly as may be feasible reflect the relative membership of the majority and minority parties in the Senate and House of Representatives.

(b) It shall be the function of the joint committee—

(1) to make a continuing study of matters relating to the Economic Report;

(2) to study means of co-ordinating programs in order to further the policy of this Act; and

(3) as a guide to the several committees of the Congress dealing with legislation relating to the Economic Report, not later than March 1[1] of each year (beginning with the year 1947) to file a report with the Senate

[1] The Employment Act as originally passed had called for the President to transmit his Economic Report to the Congress "within sixty days after the beginning

and the House of Representatives containing its findings and recommendations with respect to each of the main recommendations made by the President in the Economic Report, and from time to time to make such other reports and recommendations to the Senate and House of Representatives as its deems advisable.

This statement of functions of the committee is, like the parallel statement of the Council's functions, very general. Each of its three directives, however, contains a clearly illuminating word or phrase. The first function is described as "continuing study." While other committees, of course, conduct investigations of problems in their particular areas of responsibility, this committee is designated as a pondering body or is given a research function and an absence of administrative powers or responsibilities which is notable. In the second directive, the word "study" is repeated and joined to the word "co-ordinating." Thus an intention is clearly revealed that the Joint Committee should examine both the President's recommendations and the segmental programs coming up from the various standing committees and the several executive agencies, to see whether they make an integrated or internally consistent national program. A third directive reiterates this same idea by referring to this joint committee "as a *guide* to the several committees of the Congress." While no powers of a steering committee or conference group are conferred, the implication seems clear that, as a result of its continuing study function and its co-ordinating frame of reference, this committee was, in the intention of Congress,[2] designed to attain intellectual leadership in the legislative process wherever matters of national economic policy are involved.

of each regular session" and the Joint Committee to make its report "not later than May 1st of each year." It at once became evident, however, that these dates would make it impossible for either the President or the Committee to exercise any effective leadership in the legislative process. In the Legislative Reorganization Act of 1946 (Public Law 601, 79 Cong. 2 sess.), amendments were made which called for the President to transmit his Economic Report "at the beginning of each regular session" and the Joint Committee to file its report "not later than February 1 of each year." The following year, this date was changed (under S. J. Res. 179, 80 Cong. 2 sess.) to March 1, where it now stands.

[2] Senator Barkley, in presenting the Conference Report on the Employment Act, said: "We felt that there should be a joint committee of the two Houses to function in receiving and appraising the economic reports which, from time to time, the Congress will receive from the President and, through him, from the economic board which will be created." (*Cong. Record*, 79 Cong. 2 sess., Vol. 92, Pt. 1, p. 1138.) For critical discussion of the Joint Committee's role in the light of experience, see Chap. XX.

It thus became a question how this joint committee, as initially constituted and as reconstituted in each new Congress, would interpret these general directives and evolve for itself a significant role in achieving the purposes of the Employment Act.

ORGANIZATION AND PROGRAM OF WORK

Shortly before the adjournment of Congress on August 2, 1946, President *pro tem* McKellar named seven senators who were to serve on the Joint Committee on the Economic Report. Senator Joseph C. O'Mahoney, who had been a leader in getting the Employment Act passed, was ranking majority member and thus presumptive chairman. Speaker Rayburn named the seven House members, of whom Representative Hart was ranking majority member and thus in line for the vice-chairmanship if he wanted it. Senator O'Mahoney shortly returned to Wyoming to conduct his campaign for re-election, but indicated that immediately after election day he expected to return to Washington to initiate a vigorous program of work for the Joint Committee. As a result of the election, majority control in Congress passed to the Republican side, and a change in chairman was in order. Likewise, five members originally named to the committee had been defeated, and considerable reshuffling had to be done when the new Congress convened in January. Senator Taft, who had played an active role in the legislative history of the Employment Act, was a natural choice for the chairmanship of the Joint Committee, and the other six senators were Ball, Flanders, Watkins, O'Mahoney, Myers, and Sparkman. Representative Wolcott was made vice-chairman, with Bender, Rich, Judd (Herter),[3] Hart, Patman, and Huber as the other House members.[4]

[3] Although Representative Judd had been active in House debate on the Employment Act, the press of other work caused him to resign from the Joint Committee on Apr. 17, 1947. His place was taken by Representative Herter of Massachusetts.

[4] The original Murray bill had called for a committee of twenty-eight members, including *ex officio* the chairman of the major Senate and House committees dealing with economic matters. In the Employment Act, the committee was reduced in size by dropping these *ex officio* members. Senator Barkley, in reporting the Conference Committee's action, said: "We did not designate any committees from which he [the presiding officer of each House] would appoint them, so he will be able to make his selections from the entire membership of the House concerned. We did provide that the respective party membership of the committee members from each House should be as nearly as possible in proportion to the

No staff was recruited by the Joint Committee until March, when Fred E. Berquist was appointed, followed in April by Charles O. Hardy, who was designated Staff Director. During the next three months, two more men were added to the permanent staff, both career men in government service, with wide knowledge of sources of material and of personnel in other government staffs. Part-time assistance was available also from the Legislative Reference Service of the Library of Congress. Hardy had for some years been a colleague of mine at the Brookings Institution, whence he went to the Federal Reserve Bank at Kansas City as Vice-President in charge of Economic Research. Our techniques of work and the conclusions at which we arrived often varied widely, but I had tried hard to persuade him to take one of the top posts on the Council's staff. He was an acute analyst and able debater, and I thought his reputed "conservatism" would furnish desirable ballast in a staff that had so high a freeboard as the group we were recruiting—many of them from former New Deal agencies.

Both the initial members of the Joint Committee's staff expressed their desire to function as nonpartisan economists, making analysis of problems on their economic merits and presenting the arguments *pro* and *con* to the committee. Chairman Taft and other members accepted this as a proper interpretation of the role of staff economists and supported it in practice—as was exemplified in the use of staff reports. (See p. 195, also Chapter XII, pp. 259–60.)

REVIEW OF THE PRESIDENT'S ECONOMIC REPORT

The Employment Act had provided (Sec. [5] [d]) that

the joint committee, or any duly authorized subcommittee thereof, is authorized to hold such hearings as it deems advisable, and, within the limitations of its appropriations, the joint committee is empowered to appoint and fix the compensation of such experts, consultants, technicians, and clerical and stenographic assistants, to procure such printing and bind-

---

majority and minority representation in each House. So we have reduced the number of members of the joint committee and we have made provision that the Speaker of the House and the Presiding Officer of the Senate shall have a free hand in making appointments to the joint committee." (*Cong. Record,* 79 Cong. 2 sess., Vol. 92, Pt. 1, p. 1138.)

The managers on the part of the House, in their statement accompanying the Conference Report, stated tersely: "It is believed that the smaller committee would be more efficient." (79 Cong. 2 sess., H. Report No. 1520 [to accompany S. 380], Feb. 5, 1946.)

ing, and to make such expenditures, as it deems necessary and advisable.
. . . The joint committee is authorized to utilize the services, information,
and facilities of the departments and establishments of the Government,
and also of private research agencies.

Since the annual appropriation was initially limited to $50,000, it
would appear that Congress did not expect the Joint Committee
to conduct any very extensive staff work of its own. It could, of
course, go back to Senate or House for additional appropriations
for special studies.

As February 1 drew near, the Joint Committee was still without
any staff, and its members busy with many matters incident to
the problems of economic reconversion and the shift of party
control in the Congress. On January 31, the chairman secured the
signature of all committee members to a two-page mimeographed
statement in lieu of a formal report.[5]

After noting the delay in appointment of both the Council and
the Joint Committee and the need of reconstituting the committee
after the election and the further delay in finding suitable staff,
this statement focused attention on the "short-range" program embodied in the President's recommendations in his Economic Report.
The Joint Committee report then proceeded:

All of these six matters are already under consideration by standing
committees of Congress which will make a detailed study of each one of
them and submit recommendations to the Congress. Most of them are
highly controversial. A recommendation from this Committee at this time
which could only be casual before our studies are made, would not be
helpful to the solution of the problems. The Committee will proceed to
consider these problems with reference to their effect on the maintenance
of a stable economy and continuous employment.

The basic problem which this Committee has to consider is the method
of preventing depressions so that substantially full employment may be
continuously maintained. No problem before the American people is more
vital to our welfare, to the very existence of our way of life, and to the
peace of the world. It is the most complex and difficult of all the long
range domestic problems we have to face. It involves a study of price levels
and wage levels and their relation to each other, a study of methods of

---

[5] This was subsequently printed as S. Doc. No. 11 (80 Cong. 1 sess.) under the
rather pretentious title "Declaring a National Policy of Employment, Production,
and Purchasing Power."

preventing monopoly control in industry and labor from distorting prices and wages, a study of spending for consumption and for capital investment, a study of individual and corporate savings, and a study of many other economic forces bearing on a stable economy.

Until we have further studied and analyzed the basic considerations which underlie this problem, we do not feel we should become involved in controversy on current issues which have many aspects besides their effect on the prosperity of the country.

The committee noted with approval the "special emphasis" the President's Report placed on the preservation of the family-sized farm, on "enlarging opportunities for efficient and enterprising small businesses," and on "free competitive enterprise." The statement concluded: "Regardless of the recommendations of the Report on which there may or may not be controversy, it is our desire to commend the compilation of statistics and economic facts which are contained in the President's report and furnish a substantial basis for further study."

Evidently the President was watching to see what reaction the Joint Committee would have to his first Economic Report, for he sent me on February 1 a preview of the committee's report which Senator O'Mahoney gave him on January 31. Mr. Truman's note said: "I thought you would be interested in reading it."

On February 12, I had an interview with the President, which I opened by inquiring as to how he felt about the committee action on his Economic Report. He said it was "wholly innocuous," that he had urged O'Mahoney to take more vigorous action against that procedure (although he did not say he had endorsed the idea of a minority report). He referred disparagingly to O'Mahoney's having got "one or two sentences into the report" and approvingly mentioned Taylor's protest statement. (*P. D.*, Feb. 12, 1947)

In the Sunday papers of February 2, Senator Glen Taylor of Idaho had issued a statement which sharply criticized the Joint Committee for failing to

comply with its statutory duty. Its chairman, Senator Taft, yesterday offered to the Senate, instead of a report, a series of excuses. He explained that the Joint Committee did not have time to do its job. This excuse is not acceptable. It is the clear intent of the law that the Joint Committee's report should be accomplished within a month—a rapid job with high priority. . . . One of the most shocking excuses advanced by Senator Taft is his statement that the President's recommendations are 'highly controversial.' Surely Mr. Taft does not expect to avoid controversy in the Senate. It is desirable that fundamental differences be aired in public and that the public know exactly where each party stands. If a clear-cut position on so many matters involves personal embarrassment to Mr. Taft's candidacy for other office, he should not have accepted this chairmanship. . . . In years when the President's party is in the minority, an added responsibility falls upon the shoulders of Congressional leaders and it becomes extremely important to have a simple, direct, and comprehensive statement of the plans of the Congressional majority. . . . the public had a right to expect a coherent and consistent enunciation of Republican principles at a time when, in his dual capacity as chairman of the Joint Committee on the Economic Report and chairman of the Republican Senate Steering Committee, his words would be both timely and authoritative. . . . But now the legislative budget will be considered strictly within the cold and detached columns of revenues and expenditures—it will not be considered in relation to employment opportunities, human needs, and the economic cycle.[6]

In mid-April, active work by the committee was initiated through the preparation and circulation of a questionnaire dealing with the general economic situation and price trends and the problem of economic stabilization. This questionnaire approach was not inspired by Hardy, whose leanings were rather toward research by staff members. Senator Flanders was the moving spirit in this initiation of the committee's work. Arthur Whiteside, the president of Dun and Bradstreet, volunteered to use the machinery of his organization in both the preparation and the circulation of this questionnaire. On April 22, at a full meeting of the Joint Committee, a subcommittee was appointed to review the returns from the questionnaire but, as matters developed, the replies never were

[6] In May, a petition signed by 52 "progressive" members of the House called on the Joint Committee to take a more active course toward combating the "old and tragic cycle of boom and bust." This petition echoed the desire for more of an action program which was being expressed by labor unions and Americans for Democratic Action.

On the other hand, Senator O'Mahoney, at the opening of the first public hearings conducted by the Joint Committee (June 24) gave a somewhat detailed statement of the circumstances which had retarded the work of the committee, concluding with this sentence: "In all fairness, I believe that we cannot build a case for cooperation and understanding by opening with an attack upon the lateness of these hearings."

analyzed and used by the committee. Its results were, however, released by Dun and Bradstreet on May 23 under the title "Survey of Business Expectations and Government Policies."[7]

On May 27, the Joint Committee issued a staff questionnaire which was distributed to professional economists outside the government service. It dealt with (a) basic principles of long-run economic stability, and (b) short-run stabilization policy. A second questionnaire was distributed to manufacturers, merchants, construction contractors, financiers, and representatives of labor and agriculture. The material obtained in response to both these questionnaires was used by the committee staff in preparing for a series of hearings on "Current Price Developments and the Problem of Economic Stabilization," which began on June 24.

A copy of the Joint Committee's questionnaire was sent to the Council of Economic Advisers, and Dr. Hardy talked with me about the relationship that this might initiate between Council and Joint Committee. He definitely expected to sit in on Council deliberations for a two-way discussion of economic issues on their merits and of the Council's recommendations and the President's policy. We took the position that it was not possible to make the Council an adjunct of the Joint Committee's staff in this manner, and we made no written response to the questionnaire which had been submitted to us.

On the other hand, we informed Dr. Hardy as Staff Director of the Joint Committee that "the door of our workshop was always open to him and all the workers in his shop." We encouraged them to discuss all pertinent economic issues with our staff so that there should be the most complete two-way cooperation at the staff level. On subsequent occasions, when we were shaping up an annual or a midyear report, I specifically asked our Periodic Reports Committee (see p. 156) : "Have you discussed these matters with the Joint Committee staff?" If not, I urged them to do so, and recall

[7] The questions asked were designed to elicit information as to businessmen's expectations as to market demand, price, and the like, and their "intentions," particularly as to reconversion and expansion activities and investment policies. Dun and Bradstreet were so much impressed with the value of this type of survey that they have made it a continuing part of their program. On subsequent occasions, they worked with the Council of Economic Advisers also in perfecting the technique and made it of substantial service in our work. (See p. 166 n.)

specific occasions when they subsequently said that such discussion
had been held and that they felt both parties had profited from
it.[8]

The series of public hearings on current price developments and
the problem of economic stabilization, begun on June 24, lasted
through July 17 and appeared in published form on October 25.[9]
In opening this hearing, Chairman Taft described the committee's
work and the purpose of the hearing, saying:

. . . our function is to try to develop governmental policies which may
prevent the development of any depression, and consequently at this time
we are interested in hearing from the business, labor, and agricultural interests of the country as to whether they think there is something which
threatens the present condition of full employment, and also whether they
think there is anything the Government can do about it, and, if they do,
what they think the Government should do, what powers might be granted
by Congress, or what general policies might be adopted by the Executive.

The Midyear Economic Report of the President (July 21, 1947)
was given only cursory attention by the Joint Committee. The
staff prepared a preliminary analysis of it and questioned some
aspects of its analysis and of the general economic philosophy
by which it appeared to be animated. This staff memorandum,
however, was never taken up for formal consideration by the committee.

SPECIAL STUDIES BY THE JOINT COMMITTEE

Meanwhile, the staff was preparing an analysis of the current problem of rising living costs. Their findings were issued by the committee in September as a staff report under the title "Food; Prices,
Production, and Consumption."[10] This report consisted of twenty-
five pages of analytical text and forty-three pages of pertinent charts
and tables. Much of its material was available in the preparation
of a series of public hearings on this problem.

[8] It should be mentioned at this point also that the Staff Director of the Joint
Committee was informed of meetings of the Council with its various business,
labor, agricultural, and consumer advisory groups and he was invited to attend
and participate or to send a representative. Members of the Joint Committee staff
did participate frequently in these consultative meetings along with our staff
members. In recent years, they have turned increasingly to the Council staff for
discussion of matters in their common field.

[9] *Current Price Developments and the Problem of Economic Stabilization* (80
Cong. 1 sess.), Hearings before the Joint Committee on the Economic Report.

[10] S. Doc. No. 113. (80 Cong. 1 sess.)

On July 26, 1947, Congress called on the Joint Committee to hold hearings on the cost of living and report back early in 1948.[11] It was not technically necessary to have such a joint resolution inasmuch as the Joint Committee already had power to undertake special studies of this kind. The resolution, however, had a purpose in that it authorized the appointment of additional members of Congress to sit with the committee members in the hearings and preparation of the reports. It also authorized additional funds in the amount of $25,000 to be used by the committee in conducting this study.

The hearings conducted under this resolution partook somewhat of the nature of a British Royal Commission of Inquiry in that the committee went out to the various sections of the country to hear local spokesmen and see local conditions at first hand. Three sets of public hearings were held—one in the East, one in the mid-West, and one in the West. Each was in charge of a subcommittee consisting of several members of the Joint Committee from the given section, together with other local senators and congressmen. Verbatim reports of the hearings were not published, but the results of all three hearings were made the basis of a report by each of the subcommittees, and these were in due time printed as a committee report.[12]

On November 17, 1947, President Truman called a special session of Congress to deal with the problem of inflation and the rising cost of living. The work done by the three subcommittees and by

---

[11] S. Cong. Res. 19 was introduced by Senator Baldwin on June 19, 1947. In its original form the resolution called for a new Joint Committee of five persons from each House and provided a budget of $100,000 " (1) to make a full and complete study and investigation of the present high prices of consumer goods and (2) to report to the Congress not later than February 1, 1948, the results of the study and investigation of its subcommittees together with such recommendations, as to necessary legislation as it may deem desirable . . ." When the resolution was presented, Senator Taft called Senator Baldwin's attention to the fact that the Joint Economic Committee was already proposing to hold hearings which might include this subject. After further discussions off the floor with members of the Joint Economic Committee, Senator Baldwin agreed to an amendment which directed the Joint Economic Committee to make the investigation. This amendment was submitted by the Banking and Currency Committee (of which Taft and Sparkman were members). A further amendment reducing the amount of supplemental funds to $25,000 was made by the Rules Committee and reported out by Senator Brooks on July 24. The resolution, with the two amendments, was then considered and passed on July 26, 1947.

[12] *Senate Report 1565*, June 9, 1948.

the Joint Committee staff during the preceding summer proved of great use in the deliberations of this special session of Congress. The staff analysis under the title "The High Cost of Consumer Goods" and the report of the Eastern Subcommittee (Senator Flanders, chairman) had both been issued as committee prints.

In a special message on the subject of rising prices, the President presented ten specific recommendations for an anti-inflation program. The Joint Committee promptly began a series of public hearings on these recommendations, which lasted eleven days (between November 21 and December 10).[13] On December 19, Mr. Taft submitted an interim report based on these hearings and the committee's study of the problem.[14] It contained six recommendations with reference to the points in the President's anti-inflation message accompanying his call to Congress for a special session. The opening paragraph of the interim report read as follows:

This is only an interim report covering some of the less controversial points in the President's program to deal with the problem of inflation. The committee is still studying the other points, together with the basic causes of inflation, and possible solutions therefor. The fact that this report does not cover all the points in the President's program implies no judgment either way on the points not covered.

1. Credit controls, as recommended in the President's message, approved with qualifications.

2. Congressional study of "measures to regulate improper or excessive speculative trading on the commodity exchanges, with due recognition of maintaining an adequate hedging market."

3. Extension of export controls.

13 *Anti-Inflation Program as Recommended in the President's Message of November 17, 1947* (80 Cong. 1 sess.), Hearings before the Joint Committee on the Economic Report, Nov. 21, 24–26, 28, Dec. 2–5, 9–10, 1947 (published Feb. 27, 1948).

Senator Taft suggested that his committee conduct hearings on the anti-inflation program jointly with the standing committees to which specific proposals might ultimately be referred—particularly with the Banking and Currency Committees. Chairman Wolcott did not feel that the House Committee could participate in a joint hearing and scheduled simultaneous independent hearings on the same problem. The hearings held Nov. 21 to Dec. 10, however, were joint hearings, in which the Senate Banking and Currency Committee sat with the Joint Committee.

14 *The President's Program to Deal with the Problems of Inflation* (80 Cong. 1 sess.), Senate Report No. 809.

4. Extension of authority to allocate transportation facilities and equipment.

5. Approved "the Department of Agriculture's program of encouraging the conservation of grain."

6. Endorsed "the purpose of the program designed to increase the production of food in foreign countries" but only under plans submitted to and approved by Congress.

Thus ended the initial year of the Joint Committee's work.

SECOND YEAR OF THE JOINT COMMITTEE

By the time the second Economic Report of the President appeared, the Joint Committee was a going concern with a small permanent staff and a record of several public hearings and official publications to its credit. But it had not devised an internally acceptable procedure for coping with the "controversial" character of its task. On March 1, the committee was given an extension of time to March 15 to file its report. But March 15 came and went, and no committee report had been agreed to.[15] Rumors of separate majority and minority reports began to circulate, and on May 12, Senator O'Mahoney did in fact release to the press the mimeographed text of a minority report, outspoken in its criticism of the slowness of the committee majority and drawing an unfavorable comparison between the Republican policy of inaction on a legislative program and the President's recommendations—embodied in his Economic Report—of "affirmative action to hold inflation in check, to stabilize the economy, to preserve good business conditions, to stimulate production, and to provide for maximum employment and profitable private competitive enterprise."

The minority report (later printed as Part IV of the "Joint Economic Report")[16] was not geared closely to analysis of the specific appraisals of the economic situation and recommendations for their treatment that had been presented by the President in his Economic Report. There was a good deal of free-wheeling ex-

[15] "This year the date was extended to March 15, but no report has yet been submitted. In part this is due to division within the committee. It appears that Senator O'Mahoney is now the bottleneck, delaying the committee's report while he completes his work on dissenting materials." (*P. D.*, May 10, 1948)

[16] *Report of the Joint Committee on the January 1948 Economic Report of the President* (80 Cong. 2 sess.), (Senate Report No. 1358), p. 48.

hortation for a general policy of "economic preparedness" through "positive, affirmative action by the Government." ●

Those who have urged the policy of inaction have contended that Government controls in time of peace are intolerable, but they overlook the fact that these are not times of peace. It is utterly false assumption to contend that, with the turbulent world discharging economic and political lightning of an intensity scarcely ever seen before and with the peace treaties of World War II still unwritten, the people and the business leaders of the United States can safely close their eyes to realities and pretend that we are living in a normal world.

The minority accepted the President's program without qualification or exception, embracing "ten affirmative measures for combating inflation to be handled at this session of Congress; twenty-two long-range measures designed to reinforce the American economy and strengthen the free, private enterprise system in a postwar world of rival economic ideologies."

The third major plank in the minority's platform for "efficient, free, private, competitive enterprise" was "vigorous support of the United Nations and such economic agencies as the International Monetary Fund, the World Bank, the Food and Agriculture Organization, and the International Trade Organization." The concluding paragraph of the report said:

This is no time of pusillanimous penny-counting, astigmatic nationalism and selfish profiteering. This is no time for a policy of do-nothing and drift. It is a time for faith in our democratic way of life, for courageous pioneering, blazing new trails into new areas of international co-operation. There is a new world to be built, one of full employment and world prosperity. It will be lost by default to totalitarianism unless here and now this Congress backs its protestations of faith in American free enterprise by a vigorous program of action implementing the famous economic bill of rights laid down by Franklin Delano Roosevelt in 1944, carried forward in the Employment Act of 1946 and further developed in the Economic Reports of President Truman in 1947 and again in 1948.

In the Joint Committee report as published on May 12, Part I (99 pages) was labeled "Committee Findings," Part II "Staff Report" (33 pages), Part III "Summary of Recommendations Offered in the Economic Report of the President (5 pages), and Part IV "Minority Views on the President's Report" (26 pages). The division of the committee between Parts I and IV was strictly on the party line. All eight Republicans signed the "Committee Findings"; all six Democrats signed the "Minority Views."

In its introductory section, the Joint Economic Report reiterated the view that the committee had not been able at the time to give sufficiently thorough study to the President's report of 1947, but now

> we have carefully examined and studied the Economic Report of the President of January 1947 and the Economic Report of the President of 1948. We have further examined the reports made by the Council of Economic Advisers to the President of the United States. The economic reports of the President give extremely valuable assistance to all those who are interested in solving the problems of continuous full employment. Necessarily, the President has to enter into more controversial fields than his advisers, and deal with policies which frequently have political implications. We feel, however, that the operations under the act have fully justified its passage and have given us a good start on the national economic policy guided by more information and study than we have ever had before. To the extent that we present any criticism of the reports, we do not intend to reflect in any way on the manner in which this work has been done.

Of Part II of the report of January 1948, the committee observed:

> This is a detailed analysis of the various economic theories and recommendations contained in that report. The committee has gone over the report with the staff and made various suggestions and modifications. We feel that it is a useful commentary on the President's report, but we do not commit ourselves, either individually or as a committee, to all of the points made and arguments developed. We commend the report to those legislative committees which have to deal with specific recommendations.

This public statement of staff views on the economic issues established a precedent that has subsequently been followed.[17]

The report of this committee, that is Part I, signed by the eight Republican members, "attempt[ed] to deal only with certain general observations and a few of the more important recommendations of the President." These points, with the gist of the committee's comment, were as follows:

[17] The explanation of the committee's action in 1948 appears to be this: The staff analysis, written by Hardy, was so technical in character that the committee hardly felt qualified to master its arguments and incorporate them in its report or specifically reject them. On the other hand, they were so much impressed by the document that they thought it should not be ignored. For some comment on later practice, see pp. 259, 321, 443 f.

1. Fiscal policy to combat inflation, including expenditures and taxation.
. . . The inflation condition is due to our attempt to accomplish more than is possible at our present capacity for production. . . . We do not intend to criticize these programs or question their desirability. We merely point out that the attempt to carry them all at once, with very little restraint in the field of spending and liberal credit policies, is the basic reason for inflation, which otherwise could hardly coincide with a large Government surplus. Our first recommendation is that Government expenditures be reduced. . . . This tremendous burden of taxation is a deterrent to hard work and to increased investment in productive enterprise. . . . We disagree with the President's recommendation that a cost of living tax credit of $40 be given for each taxpayer and each dependent, and to offset this decrease in Government revenues corporate taxes be increased sufficiently to yield an equivalent amount on the basis of present figures. . . . This appears to be no time, in any event, to adopt any increase in any form of taxation.

2. The regulation of credit:
This committee considers that the control of credit is a proper government function and one of the most essential if we hope to exercise any control over the forces of expansion and depression. We have already recommended the extension of the power to control consumer credit. . . . Our committee feels that the provisions of Title VI of the National Housing Act extend excessive credit to builders for the construction of houses with practically no capital investment whatever. . . . With regard to the extension of bank credit, our committee is not yet prepared to make a definite recommendation. . . . It is true that the increase in bank credit during the past year has practically nullified the effect of the Government's budget surplus. Much of this expansion undoubtedly is necessary to provide for legitimate purposes of expanding production. We meet again, however, the question whether we can do everything we want to do in the way of current consumption and also expand our capital investments at so rapid a rate. . . .

3. The need for selective controls:
Our committee is very much opposed to the establishment of over-all Government price controls, wage controls, or allocation controls in time of peace. . . . We believe that Government is seldom able to impose an effective control of prices and wages. . . . such controls are impossible to enforce in time of peace. . . . We have recommended a selective control over the distribution of grain for distilling, but only during the present crop year when crops have been short. . . . We have also recommended the continuation of rent control, because we feel that we are still in the midst of a shortage of housing. . . . We recommend further study of the

need for compulsory controls pending the outcome of actions taken under the so-called Anti-Inflation Act. . . . We feel that businessmen making reasonable profits should refrain from and discourage further demands for wage increases.

4. Housing and urban redevelopment:

. . . the social aspects of housing and urban redevelopment are somewhat outside the proper function of this committee. . . . The Federal Government is already committed to a policy of substantial credit aid in the construction of residences. We believe it should assist local governments by grants in urban redevelopment. If a policy of subsidized rents appears wise from a social standpoint, it will undoubtedly require Federal funds for financing. . . . The production of housing as an industry, however, must be of tremendous interest to anyone concerned with a stable economy. It is subject to almost more violent fluctuation than any other major industry. . . . The cost of decent housing is out of proportion to the average income of the American people, with the result that only a limited number are able to buy new houses, and the market for such houses is likely to disappear when demand for commodities and durable goods continues unimpaired. . . . we recommend that Government credit policies be so varied from time to time as to maintain as level a rate of construction as possible.

5. Maintenance of competition:

We agree with the President's report that the long-range increase of production in the United States requires the maintenance of free competitive enterprise and that "to operate effectively without a high degree of Government intervention, a free enterprise economy must adjust itself to changing conditions through appropriate moves of prices, costs, and production." . . . This idea, of course, is seriously interfered with by the manner in which wage rates are practically frozen against reduction. . . . We are also considering the maintenance of farm prices in some relation to industrial prices. Under that program some degree of elasticity will be lost. . . . Nevertheless, the ideal is properly stated and we should not permit it to be impaired by monopoly or private fixing of prices. . . .

6. Agriculture and food policies:

We agree with practically all of the President's report on the subject of agriculture and food policies. . . . We believe Congress should consider a support price program at some relation to the general price level which will carry the farmer through bad times and yet will not maintain a production for which there is no demand. . . . Government action . . . should not be of a character to interfere with a reasonable elasticity in farm prices so that they may be rapidly adjusted to change in supply and demand.

7. International economic relations:

Our committee has not had an opportunity to make any extensive study of [foreign trade, the Reciprocal Trade Agreements and the International Trade Organization]. . . . We therefore reserve our comments for some future report. With regard to foreign loans to pay for exports, we have expressed our general opinion that like all other Government spending programs, this program should be carefully screened, economically administered, and confined to those projects which are of clear value in the promotion of peace and the checking of communism. Without question, the export of a large volume of goods in excess of imports is a serious inflationary element. . . . Financing . . . should be confined to those products in which an excessive draft on our resources will not start a rapid increase in prices.

In more general terms, the "Committee Findings" expressed concern "about the scope of the President's report, covering as it does nearly every domestic policy other than questions of national defense." The committee gave the language of the Employment Act the broad interpretation of having a principal purpose "to maintain full employment in the United States and to avoid the recurrent economic depressions which have brought unemployment, hardship, and suffering to its people." The committee suggested that "work under the Act should not be diverted from this central purpose by the study of all the important and complicated problems of social welfare, health, and education, nor should it be diverted to matters which cannot have an extensive effect on the over-all economy. . . . This does not mean we should concentrate attention exclusively on the short-run business outlook. We are generally concerned with long-range programs directed toward the gradual improvement of the standard of living of the entire country."

The underlying idea seemed in the end to be not so much one of the proper scope of the President's Economic Report as it was a matter of timing. Broad economic reforms or welfare measures should, as I read the majority report, be kept in reserve during periods of prosperity or inflationary tendencies and used in times of slack employment to support weak spots, alleviate want, stimulate recovery, or facilitate expansion.

In February and early March, the Joint Committee gave particular study to the shortage of grain supplies and the propriety of limiting their use for certain types of livestock feeding and industrial processing. Hearings were held (February 5–6) on the allocation of grain for production of ethyl alcohol, and a report on allocation and inventory control of such grain was made on February 11.[18] On March 2, the committee held a brief hearing on increases in steel prices but made no formal report on this subject. Between April 13 and May 27, the committee conducted five days of hearings on credit policies, and these were published on June 21.

On May 1, 1948, the Joint Committee began publication of the monthly statistical pamphlet *Economic Indicators*. This collection of current statistical information had for some months past been prepared by the Council of Economic Advisers and circulated in multigraphed form to a select list of top officials in the executive branch. Senator Flanders felt that these materials would have great usefulness not only to the Joint Committee but to all members of Congress and indeed to the general public if they could be made available in printed form. The pamphlet gave the latest statistics on employment, wages, prices, and other significant factors in the economy, making them available at one place in small compass and more promptly than they could be secured from other government publications. This statistical material is supplied by various government agencies such as the Departments of Labor, Commerce, and Agriculture, the Bureau of the Budget, and the Federal Reserve Board. In a letter to Chairman Taft concerning the origin and purpose of this compilation, the Council commented:

In carrying out its mandate under the Employment Act of 1946, the Council has found it desirable to bring together in concise and graphic form the most important facts showing current trends in the Nation's economy. Thus the Executive Office is in a better position to point up the key problems of national economic policy and to promote the improvement and co-ordination of the Federal Government's widespread statistical services.

We have realized, of course, that this material has a potential usefulness not only to the President, the Council and the executive departments, but

18 *Senate Document No. 188* (80 Cong. 2 sess.). In the special session of November–December 1947, Congress had passed Public Law 395, which had as its general purpose the encouragement of voluntary allocation of critical raw materials and commodities. One section of this law provided that, within fifteen days after a finding by the President that "additional governmental action" was needed to conserve any such scarce item, "the Joint Committee on the Economic Report shall conduct public hearings thereon and shall make such recommendations to the Congress for legislative action as in its judgment the recommendation of the President and any additional information disclosed at the public hearings may require." It was under this law that the above hearings were held and report made.

also to the Congress. Furthermore, its usefulness to the general public has been impressed upon us, particularly by the representatives of business, labor, agriculture, and consumer organizations with whom we regularly consult.

After the Joint Committee took over the publication of *Economic Indicators,* each issue carried a letter of transmittal from the committee to the Congress in which Senator Taft said:

From the time the Joint Committee on the Economic Report was established, its members realized that one of its basic needs was a concise and meaningful picture of current economic trends and developments.

Fortunately, the Joint Committee finds that *Economic Indicators,* a set of basic charts and tables compiled monthly by the Council of Economic Advisers, admirably fills this need. While this material was prepared primarily for the use of the President, the Council and other officials in the executive offices, the Council has made it available to the Joint Committee.

Other members of Congress have also expressed an interest in being able to obtain a quick picture of current economic facts without having to go through voluminous and specialized documents. In addition, businessmen, farm leaders, labor organizations, and representatives of the press and radio have indicated their desire for this information. Since nothing contained in these charts and tables is of a confidential nature, they have urged that the material be made available to the general public.

Accordingly, the Joint Committee has for the past several months provided the Congress and the public with a limited number of copies of *Economic Indicators.* The response to these issues has indicated such widespread interest that the Committee has arranged to release *Economic Indicators* each month as a committee print until action can be taken on authorizing the publication on a more permanent basis.[19]

During the second half of 1948, the committee staff completed a study of "Current Gaps in our Statistical Knowledge," which was issued on July 15 as a committee print and incorporated as a section of the committee's annual report on the *Economic Report of the President* the following January. Largely as an outgrowth of staff work also, there appeared as a committee print on December 30, 1948 a report on the consumer price index.

By this time it was known that the chairmanship and make-up of the committee would again change as a result of the November elections. Likewise other changes were imminent, since Dr. Hardy,

[19] About a year later, *Economic Indicators* was raised from the status of a committee print to that of a regular monthly publication. (See p. 256.)

director of the staff since April 1, 1947, had died on November 15. He had found his task both difficult and at times frustrating, not only because of sharp differences of view within the committee but also because of the impossibility of getting an adequate amount of time for consideration of staff product. It was hard to get enough time with any member to present the staff analysis of any important problem and impossible to get a sufficient number of members together in any one session to have a really satisfactory clearing of issues and registering of such agreements as might have been developed.

The last piece of work completed by the Joint Committee under Republican leadership was an inquiry into corporate profits. In October 1948 authorization was secured from Chairman Taft for the setting up of a subcommittee under Senator Flanders[20] to study the role of profits in the maintenance of employment and production and the current situation as to business profits. "The desirability of holding these hearings was self-evident. Repeated references have been made in the Economic Reports of the President to the unprecedented and rising profits accruing to business in the United States. It was not merely the President's reports and messages which called attention to this matter. It was the subject of extended comment by financial journals, economists, and business writers."[21]

This subcommittee promptly instituted a series of open hearings, which occupied ten days between December 6 and 21. "The plan of the hearings was first to call in expert witnesses of different views, from professions outside of business itself. From them we hoped to receive, and did receive, valuable suggestions as to the line of questioning to be followed. These witnesses included two economists, Dr. Sumner H. Slichter and Dr. Seymour Harris; two accountants, representing different points of view, Prof. William A. Paton and George D. Bailey; and four witnesses from organized labor, Nelson H. Cruikshank, of the AF of L, and Stanley Ruttenberg, of the CIO, Donald Montgomery, economist, of the UAW-CIO, and Russ Nixon, representing the UEW-CIO. The business witnesses were chosen from the industries to which public attention had particularly been drawn." (*Profits*, p. 2.)

[20] The other members were Senators Watkins and O'Mahoney and Representatives Wolcott, Herter, Patman, and Huber.

[21] *Profits* (80 Cong. 2 sess.), Report of a Subcommittee of the Joint Committee on the Economic Report on Profit Hearings (Joint Committee Print), p. 1.

The full hearings were published in due course, but to make their substance more readily available, the committee had a topical summary of the testimony prepared by the Joint Committee staff, assisted by members of the Legislative Reference Service of the Library of Congress. This summary, together with a few pages of explanation by the committee was issued as a committee report (*Profits*, see p. 201 n.). That the inquiry put the profits issue in a broad setting is indicated by the headings in the topical index of this report.[22] These headings were as follows:

The Role of Profits
Profit Levels and Their Evaluation
Inventory Profits and Inventory Reserves
Depreciation on Original versus Replacement Cost Basis
Need for, and Sources of, Investment Funds
Cost-Price-Production and Profit Relationships
Retained Earnings, Dividends, and the Market for Equities
Investment of Profits and Concentration of Enterprise
Price and Pricing Policies
Prices and Profits in Relation to Production and
        Employment Declines
Taxes
Steel Production and Capacity

An interesting commentary on how the Joint Committee was coming to conceive its relation to other Congressional committees was contained in one of the introductory paragraphs of this report. It pointed out that the investigation of business profits "has important relations with the work of the Finance Committee of the Senate and the Ways and Means Committee of the House, the Labor and Public Welfare Committee of the Senate and the Education and Labor Committee of the House, the Banking and Currency Committees, the Interstate and Foreign Commerce Committees, and the Judiciary Committees of both Houses, which we trust they will find useful."

The subcommittee likewise suggested a way in which its intel-

[22] As a result of the party change in the 1948 presidential election, the profits study became something of a "lame duck" enterprise. The report had to be completed by December 31, when the existing Congressional organization would end. Thus it was not carried through on as broad lines as it had been planned.

lectual leadership might be made useful in co-operation with private business agencies. "Several witnesses suggested that a conference between representatives of labor, agriculture, and management should be held, for the purpose of establishing principles of economic statesmanship, to which these great groups in our national economy would subscribe. It is hoped that guidance by these principles might bring inflationary pressure under control, and result in more stable economic conditions. The subcommittee is unanimously in favor of carrying out this suggestion."

RELATIONS BETWEEN THE JOINT COMMITTEE AND THE CEA

As I left the hearings in which the Senate Banking and Currency Committee considered whether to confirm my nomination as a member of the Council of Economic Advisers, Senator Taft remarked to me: "We hope to find your Council of great use to us." I was pleased at the remark as a welcome to a new agency in the structure of the Federal Government. But at the same time I had distinct misgivings as to the purport of these words. Did the Senator conceive of the Council as a staff arm of the legislative, no less than the executive, branch of the Government? Was the antecedent of "we" the Banking and Currency Committee, the Joint Committee, or Congress as a whole and all or any of its committees?

When President Truman nominated me to a place on the Council, I had only a casual acquaintance with the legislative history of the Employment Act. It was, however, my impression that the Council's service was to run exclusively to the President and the executive family. Prior to writing my letter of acceptance to the President (see p. 106), I talked the matter over with Meyer Jacobstein, a former colleague at Brookings and himself a one-time member of the House. When I spoke of the position as having great possibilities of service to the President, he interjected, "and to the Congress." It was that remark, I am sure, that caused me to phrase my letter to the President as I did: "Its prime function [the Council's] is to bring the best available methods of social science to the service of the Chief Executive and of the Congress in formulating national policy." As I became better acquainted with the total situation and acquired experience in the practical operation of the Council, I came increasingly to the feeling that the essential purposes of the

Employment Act would be best served if the activities of the Council were beamed exclusively to the service of the President and the various agencies of the executive branch.

The question of the Council's relation to Congress did not arise in any practical form during the fall months of 1946 while we were busy on preparations for the President's first Economic Report and while work of the Joint Committee was held in abeyance by the distractions of an election and the consequences of a party over-turn. On January 14, 1947, however, in consulting with the President concerning the Council's future organization and activities, I suggested that "an immediate question seemed to be whether the Joint Committee of Congress would expect to have active relations with the Council and what our response should be if they sought to draw us into discussion of the Economic Report. I pointed out that the other members of the Council were inclined to welcome a rather active relationship, whereas I was somewhat apprehensive as to the possibility that the committee might seek to draw us into discussion of policy positions taken by the President in his Economic Report, some of which might not be precisely in line with the views of the individual members of the Council. Little possibility of divergence seemed to be evident in this year's report, but I suggested that we should establish a practice from the beginning which could be followed consistently and with safety in subsequent years when, conceivably, there might be considerable divergence between the Council's recommendations and the President's policy statement to the Congress.

The President immediately agreed that we should protect ourselves against such a situation while at the same time not remaining aloof from the work of the Committee. The formula which seemed to meet his approval was that we should be co-operative in "elucidating" for the committee any points of fact or (with care) of interpretation relative to the President's Economic Report, but that issues of policy were to be left alone and that we should not be drawn into discussion of them. The President thought that it might be well, since it was now known that Senator Taft was to be chairman of the committee, if I called at his office for an informal discussion of relations. He felt sure that the general principles outlined above would be acceptable to Taft and the rest of the Committee.[23] (*P. D.*, Jan. 14, 1947)

[23] This proved to be the case and the issue did not develop an active phase for some two years.

On this occasion, "I also mentioned to the President that I had gone in some detail into my interpretation of the Council's role in a paper presented at the annual meeting of the American Economic Association on January 27, calling his attention particularly to the passage on page 25: 'When we have brought this sort of material [objective economic analysis] to the President's desk, we shall have discharged our responsibilities under the act as I conceive it.' Under date February 13, I received a note from the President, stating that he had read the address 'with a lot of interest' and considered my statements 'perfectly sound.' "

From January to November 1947, the issue of Council-Congressional relations remained quiescent. But as the Senate Foreign Relations Committee progressed with its hearings on the European Recovery Plan, they tentatively scheduled the Council to appear on November 12 for interrogation along the lines of our special report on the impact of the foreign aid program. Such an appearance would seem natural and on its face innocuous. When I got word of this hearing, however, I called the secretary of the Foreign Relations Committee on the telephone

. . . and told him that I would be embarrassed by a formal invitation to testify at these hearings, since it would initiate a precedent of the Council debating issues of Administration economic policy. It would be all the more embarrassing in this case since I had thus far avoided appearing even before the Joint Committee on the Economic Report.

I said that if Senator Vandenberg indicated reluctance to accept this answer, I should be very happy to come to his office and explain the whole situation to him. Mr. Wilcox (chief of staff of the Committee) said that he would transmit this comment to the Senator and if we did not hear further we could assume that it was satisfactory. This ended the matter. (*P. D.*, Nov. 6, 1947)

[The episode, however,] revived an issue which had been smoldering in the Council since the preceding winter. Neither Mr. Keyserling nor Mr. Clark was prepared to accept my interpretation of the Council as a professional agency merely serving the President with factual and analytical material and making confidential recommendations to him, but remaining personally detached from the policies which he subsequently enunciated. They were eager to make themselves influential, particularly on the Hill, in helping to carry out those policies which they had recommended or even some different or more or less modified policy which the President might present in the absence of or contrary to our recommendations.

It had become a matter of comment in the press that Mr. Keyserling, through his personal friend Clark Clifford, had participated actively in the writing of the message which the President presented at the opening of the special session of the Congress. He was particularly eager to appear in behalf of the price control and allocation recommendations, and Clark was more than anxious to break a lance on behalf of credit controls. They both seemed to feel that if we were not prepared to support the President's policies, we should not continue on the Council. (*P. D.*, Feb. 23, 1948)

Senator Flanders of the Joint Committee had expressed a personal opinion on this issue in the autumn (1947) number of the *Public Administration Review*, suggesting that:

. . . from the standpoint of bringing into focus the President's report to the Congress, and particularly before the Joint Committee, much could be gained from a meeting—executive or open—at which members of the Council could present and elaborate on the economic reasoning underlying the President's report. . . . each agency must justify and defend the President's recommendations in respect to itself—even if these recommendations are adverse to its own views and wishes. It is true that embarrassing situations may arise if the President does not take the Council's advice. If there should be consistent major differences on important economic issues the Council naturally would be apt to resign, and should resign.

The senator sent me a copy of this article with a covering letter in which he said: "The first year of operation under the Act has revealed weaknesses in its administration. . . . I have attempted to outline some of the failures and to indicate possible methods of improving the operation of the Act."

After studying the article, I talked the matter over with Senator Flanders and, I thought, convinced him at least in part as to the difficulties entailed by Congressional appearances of Council members. Thereafter I went over the whole situation with Chairman Taft. This interview ended with the Senator saying: "I am not now prepared to take a final position on the question as a matter of principle. However, I am aware of the difficulties that you point out and, since you feel that the matter is important to the proper functioning of the Council, I will not make any call upon you to appear before our Committee."

An illuminating illustration of the sort of embarrassing situation I envisaged came in connection with the Council's budget hearings before the House Subcommittee on the Independent

Offices Appropriation bill. Certain Republican members of this committee sought to confuse the question of what funds the Council needed for efficient operation with issues of whether they agreed with particular aspects of the President's economic policy, and whether the Council as a body or the chairman personally supported these particular recommendations. I tried to show that the Council was not set up by Congress as a policy-making or policy-implementing body but as a factual and interpretative staff for the President. But the committee took a dim view of this kind of service and cut our budget request one-eighth.

In Council discussion Mr. Keyserling said that my tenacity in this matter raised the whole question whether Council matters were to be decided by majority vote or whether one member could block action. I replied that if he and Mr. Clark wished to invoke a majority rule procedure, I would be entirely willing to accept it for the Council but, as a matter of principle, could not accept it for myself in the present instance. I had made it entirely clear to the President in my letter accepting an appointment to the Council that this was on the premise that the Council could and would be kept clear of the political arena. If it were now to be launched into that arena, it would need a chairman of different talents and tastes than mine, and I would gladly step aside so that such an appointment could be made. Both he and Mr. Clark said that this was not an acceptable alternative, and since I was "stubborn" in my position, they would abide by the result. (*P. D.*, Feb. 23, 1948)

On January 22, Mr. Clark in a letter to Mr. Steelman stated his position quite fully in favor of unrestricted activity of members of the Council of Economic Advisers before Congressional committees. Some time later, Mr. Clark told me that he had not received any reply to this letter. However, Mr. Steelman had (whether at the President's suggestion or on his own motion) asked James Webb, Director of the Budget, whether the experience of the Bureau of the Budget would shed any light on the question of the extent to which members of the Council ought to testify before Congressional committees. Mr. Webb had the staff of the bureau prepare a memorandum (Jan. 15, 1948) on this subject in which, after pointing out some of the difficulties entailed by such testimony, they said:

Members of the Council, as spokesmen for the Council, should testify under certain circumstances. The Council should not accept every invitation tendered it to testify, nor should it seek the opportunity to testify. In general the less it presents formal testimony the better, in view of its advisory relation to the President in contrast to a policy-determining or operation role. . . . Even if the type of testimony desired is of a kind which only the Council can present, it can properly refuse to testify in appropriate circumstances. However, it cannot make a practice of refusing to testify without provoking Congressional irritation. . . .

In January 1948, Averell Harriman, Secretary of Commerce, was delegated by the President as field commander to present his economic program before the various Congressional committees and push for its adoption. Harriman took it for granted that, at a designated point, I would appear to argue in support of the President's program. When I demurred (with the support of several Cabinet members), he said he would defer the matter, and he did not raise it again

As the presentation of the President's program was completed and the belated report of the Joint Committee evoked little discussion, this issue again became dormant and remained so until after the outcome of the November elections became known. Since this outcome presaged a change in the chairmanship of the Joint Committee, it was evident that the issue would soon be revived. These later developments are discussed in Chapter XII.

CHAPTER ELEVEN

The Council of Economic Advisers— 1948

During the period from the winter of 1948 to the fall of 1949, there were several important developments in the life of the Council. This period was highlighted by the national conventions of July, the ensuing political campaign, and the Presidential election of November. Inevitably, these events had an important impact on the work of the Council.

Chapter X has already recounted that in April 1948, co-operating with the Joint Committee, we inaugurated the monthly statistical publication *Economic Indicators* (supplementary to the statistical appendixes of the annual and midyear economic reports of the President). Mention has also been made (page 154) of the reduction of our budget request for fiscal 1948 from $400,000 to $350,000 by the House Appropriations Subcommittee on the Independent Offices bill. The same attitude prevailed at the budget hearing in January 1948, and our request for $350,000 for fiscal '49 was reduced to $300,000. This action was linked to the question of what role the Council was to perform. The question had two aspects— one whether the Council as such was an essential or even a useful agency; the other, what should be the scope of its operations.

The view of the House subcommittee was that the Council as a whole was superfluous:

This agency has been the subject of searching inquiry on the part of the committee, many of the members being dubious as to its value. It appears that practically all of the information which the Council has used has been developed by other agencies of the Government and could have been made available in useful form directly to the President by the agency originating it. There is little indication that, to date, the efforts of the Council in endeavoring to co-ordinate and interpret data have produced important results. However, this is a relatively new organization and the committee has made provision for it for another year and expects to follow its activities closely.[1]

"Mr. Keyserling and Mr. Clark attributed the House Appropriation Committee's cut of our budget request to the fact that my presentation did not make a case for an active role on the part of the Council. Personally, I think it is entirely explained in terms of partisan politics and a dislike of the whole concept of the Employment Act." (*P. D.*, Feb. 23, 1947) It seems a strain of logic to argue that by becoming protagonists of Administration programs we would have won the approval of, and a more liberal budget recommendation from, the Republican majority of the Committee on Appropriations. They had us either way. If we were responsible for administrative policies that were personally obnoxious, we should have our power for mischief reduced or removed. If we followed a merely academic line, we were superfluous and should be pruned in the interest of economy.

The issue as to the role of the Council was taken up by various newspaper writers and columnists but, either through deference to, or acceptance of, my view by Senator Taft and several other committee chairmen, the matter was not brought to a head until the following year. (See p. 221.)

The reduction in our budget made it impossible to complete the staffing needed to "co-ordinate and interpret" the data gathered by various specialized agencies. It also precluded our holding topical conferences of academic, business, and labor economists that we had in mind as a means of mobilizing professional thinking on national economic problems, re-defined in the light of the declaration of policy set out in the Employment Act.

THE SECOND ANNUAL ECONOMIC REPORT

Since Mr. Truman had become so much alarmed about rising prices in the fall of 1947 that he had called a special session of Congress to deal with inflation (and European aid), there could be little

[1] *Independent Offices Appropriation Bill, 1949*, p. 5. (House Report No. 1288, 80 Cong. 2 sess.)

suspense in the public mind as to the character of his Economic
Report when Congress met in regular session. The special session
had not grown out of warnings of imminent danger from the Council. Our third-quarter memorandum to the President had stated
that "disturbing price advances have been resumed," but we had
not suggested the need of a special session or participated in any
discussion that led up to it. In response to a request from Clark
Clifford, we had on October 21 supplied for the President's use a
memorandum on "Prices and Wages since 1946," which indicated
that "the rise in the consumers' price index has outstripped the
earnings of wage earners." On November 5, also at Mr. Clifford's
request and after the special session had been decided on, we submitted a nine-page memorandum of "suggestions for a message on
the price situation and measures to deal with it." This statement
stressed a budget surplus and restraints upon credit expansion as
"the policies which should now be adopted," but it also suggested
extension of export controls and selective stand-by price and wage
controls. The President's message to the special session contained
a statement on the latter point which is of peculiar interest in the
light of subsequent events.[2] He said:

> If the Government imposes price ceilings covering a specific area of
> production, it should in all fairness have the authority, in that same area,
> to prevent wage increases which will make it impossible to maintain the
> price ceilings. This authority should be granted, although I believe that
> there would be few occasions for its use.

The January 1948 Economic Report of the President faced
frankly the possibility of price advances getting out of hand and
turning into rampant inflation. Two sections of the report dealt
with "The Nature of Inflationary Pressures" and "Why Inflation
Is Dangerous," and the President resubmitted the ten-point anti-
inflation program which he had recommended to the special session of November 17, 1947, saying:

> The three points . . . which were enacted in the special session of the
> Congress are necessary but insufficient. The other seven points are needed,
> needed badly, and needed promptly. . . . My ten-point program divides
> into three main parts. First, it proposes appropriate restraints upon busi-

[2] It also contained an interesting observation about industrial capacity: "To
expand industrial output, we need a long-range program to overcome basic shortages in capacity and equipment." (Compare p. 240.)

ness credit and consumer credit and commodity speculation. Second, to deal with the scarcities at strategic spots in the economy, it calls for authority to allocate to their most efficient and necessary uses those scarce commodities and services which enter basically into the cost of living or industrial production. And third, it calls for the extension and strengthening of rent control, and for authority to impose rationing and price control on a highly selective basis on items of outstanding importance to industrial production or to the cost of living so that these powers may be used promptly to protect the public if other measures prove inadequate.[3]

In a brief section under the title "Levels of Activity and Adjustments Needed in 1948," the Economic Report analyzed "fiscal policy to combat inflation" and "the regulation of credit." This was followed by a two-and-a-half-page discussion of "the need for selective controls" and "the need for voluntary restraint." A thirty-five page section on "Long-Range Objectives for the American Economy" completed the Economic Report.

This scope and scale of treatment was adversely commented on by the Joint Committee (see pp. 195–98) but in general the President's second annual report met a favorable reception. The New York *Times* (Jan. 18, 1948) called it "a sober and challenging discussion . . . warning of soft spots that could lead to a business recession." The Chamber of Commerce of the U.S.A. said: "For general purposes, no better compendium of timely, factual information is available. In spite of many questions which may be raised about the report, it constitutes a considerable improvement over previous ones and merits wide reading by businessmen and others."[4] According to the Des Moines *Register* of January 16, "President Truman's January economic report to Congress is an admirable statement of current economic conditions, in easy-to-understand language, and well illustrated with charts. We recommend it to businessmen."

On the other hand, the New York *Journal of Commerce* complained that the President offered no concrete or original suggestions as to how the high level of output and consumption was to be stabilized, "and so we are no farther ahead in arriving at a program to solve this problem than we were before the report was

---

[3] *Economic Report of the President,* January 1948, pp. 5, 6.
[4] *Business Action,* Jan. 23, 1948, p. 2.

issued." Peter Edson, Scripps-Howard commentator, opined that the second annual economic report was headed for Congressional oblivion like that under which the first report was buried a year earlier. He noted that the report was referred automatically to the Joint Economic Committee, whose chairman "Senator and GOP Presidential Candidate Taft" had said that Congress had already given the Administration all the controls that are needed to put out the fires of inflation. This columnist thought the stage was all set for Congress to ignore the Economic Report of the President.

On April 7, following the practice established in 1947, the Council submitted to the President a brief quarterly report (fourteen double-spaced typed pages). It was designed to "examine and evaluate certain important new factors that have entered or old factors that have changed since January, and, on this basis, consider what new or modified policies are called for." Among new factors had been the sharp break in prices of agricultural commodities during February and increasing indications that the economy "might be approaching a topping-out area in which the forces of inflation would be abating." On the other hand, attention was called to the mark-up of prices of semifinished steel and a third round of wage increases accompanied by a strike of bituminous coal miners on March 15. Concern was expressed over the fact that Congress had passed a law reducing taxes by an estimated 5 billion dollars annually on the same day that it completed passage of the European Recovery Plan calling for aid in the magnitude of about 6 billion dollars.

In concluding this memorandum, the Council suggested that two points should be clearly recognized and made plain to the public:

1. We are still in a peace economy, not a war economy. The maintenance of an armed force is as much a part of the peacetime system as is the maintenance of a police force by states, counties, and cities, or the employment of railroad detectives and factory guards. The last two years have given us a fuller measure of the productivity of our resources when aggressively used. We were not staggering under the load of $11 billion for our protective forces, and the rise in this item to $14 or $15 billion will not swamp our economy nor require us to pass from free enterprise to regimentation. Some rather systematic and vigorous discipline, however,

must be exercised to redirect our economic effort so as to meet the new goal in an orderly and economical manner.

2. Every citizen must recognize that further diversions of productive effort to military uses inevitably involves some sacrifice of civilian types of consumption. It is our particular application of the old alternative of "guns or butter."

Our people had—and we believe quite properly—looked forward to a postwar period in which larger numbers of people would achieve higher standards of living than had ever been realized before. Those hopes are not nullified by the preparedness program. But they must be in some measure postponed or for the present revised downward. During this period if any group insists that its income shall be advanced in proportion to every advance in prices or that it shall be in a position to pay up to whatever level is needed to bid its accustomed amount of goods away from other users, it is in effect demanding that it be exempted from sharing in the common burden of protecting our country. These economic facts of life should be proclaimed along with every step in working out the practical details of the preparedness program.

In view of the fact that this evaluation, together with the analysis on which it was based, might tend to allay public apprehension over the inauguration of the European Recovery Plan in addition to the military preparedness plan, we suggested to the President that he might wish to release this memorandum to the press. He asked us to attend the Cabinet meeting on April 9 and present this material for Cabinet discussion. After it had been presented, he invited comment from the Cabinet members as to whether it would be wise and helpful to have it given publicity. The unanimous feeling was that this would be desirable, and it was issued from the White House later that day. This was by no means regarded as establishing a precedent and, in fact, there has been no subsequent case in which the Council's quarterly memorandum to the President has been released to the press.

THE SECOND MIDYEAR REPORT

During the spring of 1948, serious attempts were being made by businessmen and by the Administration to "hold the line" on a third round of wage increases and the accompanying price inflation. Several efforts on my part to see if the activities of the President and Mr. Steelman in this direction and the Council's analysis of the evolving situation could not be mutually related came to naught.

(See pp. 175–79.) On May 31, I made an entry: "The President has made no move to discuss [these developments with the Council]. Inasmuch as he leaves in a few days for a rather extended Western trip, the chances of discussion seem remote." After his return, we had no meeting with him to go over the materials in connection with the midyear report, but we made the suggestion that its publication be postponed to a date subsequent to the holding of the Democratic nominating convention. It was obvious that if it appeared just on the eve of this gathering, it would be given all sorts of political treatment. The President immediately approved this postponement. The report was in fact transmitted to Congress on July 30. By that time, its appraisal of the situation and enunciation of a policy had been completely "scooped" by the President's acceptance speech and special message of July 27.

In the small hours of the morning of July 15, President Truman emerged from the wings onto the stage at Convention Hall in Philadelphia for a brief but vigorous acceptance speech. In it he exploded the surprise announcement that he was calling Congress back at once into special session to enact anti-inflation legislation. The Special Message with which he opened this session on July 27 contained a specific eight-point program (essentially "the anti-inflation program I proposed to the Congress eight months ago"— that is, the special session of November 17, 1947). Since all this declaration of Presidential policy was now an accomplished fact, the Midyear Economic Report of the President had little *raison d'être*. The President's report proper consisted merely of a seven-page statement, beginning with an exhortation under the title "A Time for Action"—for passage of the anti-inflation program—and closing with an excerpt from the President's message to the Congress on July 27, setting forth his program under eight points. In between, there was a four-page summary of the accompanying "Economic Situation at Midyear 1948," published in the same document over the names of the Council of Economic Advisers. The Council review was largely statistical and factual and was accompanied by sixty-five pages of statistical and technical appendixes. Its closing section was not a brief for a direct control program, but a *pro* and *con* statement of "the issue between inflation and stabilization." Back of this separation of the Economic Report into two distinct parts lay some significant developments.

CHANGED FORM OF THE MIDYEAR REPORT

It will be remembered that, while the Employment Act was under consideration in Congress, various proposals were made for a national economic commission which would make public reports of its findings. When this idea was rejected by Congress and the Council of Economic Advisers was established in the Executive Office of the President, the suggestion kept appearing from time to time that the Council should make an independent report accompanying, or at least simultaneous with, the Economic Report of the President. Different people held different views as to the scope and purpose of such a Council report. Those who still wanted to see a National Economic Advisory Council established would not have this public report of the Council a mere statistical presentation of measurable facts and an interpretation of trends discernible in these statistical time series. They wanted it to include an outline of recommended policy on a presumably "objective" economic plane, free of any "political" distortion that was to be expected or that would be suspected in the reports submitted by any President.

The other concept of an independent economic report, to appear over the Council's own names, was that it should be a purely "factual" statement or statistical array which could be used by the public as background in appraising the economic diagnosis and prescription that are the essential features of the Economic Report of the President. There was in some quarters a lurking suspicion that data were, in some devious ways, manipulated so as to appear to support whatever policy the President decided to recommend.

A formal expression of the desire for a change in the form of the Economic Reports came to the Council on May 14, 1948. On that day, Charles Sawyer, Secretary of Commerce, transmitted to us a formal recommendation for change in the form of the Economic Reports of the President which had been adopted by the Business Advisory Council (see p. 173) at a previous meeting.

This memorandum, after reciting the terms of the Employment Act as to the Council's report to the President and the President's Economic Report to the Congress, proceeded as follows:

It is respectfully recommended that changes be made in the forms of the two previously mentioned reports from the form in which they have been submitted on the past two year ends. This would be in order that they may better serve the purposes of the Employment Act of 1946 for the uses of the Congress, the public, and the business community of the United States in general.

The first report, that of the Council of Economic Advisers, would contain all of the statistical data pertinent to the economic situation existing in the United States. It would incorporate a review of the economic trends during the year just passed and a survey of the economic situation existing at the end of the year. This would be a purely factual report, with no statements of policy. It would be a comprehensive summary of the princi-pal factors in the current economic situation which would, over the years, be accepted as an unbiased report by all groups. This report, with its related statistics, charts, and other pertinent data, would be available to the Cabinet and other concerned governmental agencies several weeks in advance of the preparation of the President's Economic Report to the Congress and would be made public at the time of submission to the President.

The President's Economic Report to the Congress, based upon the facts presented in the Council's report, would be confined, as far as possible, to such policy recommendations as he decided were necessary. It is recognized that his report would necessarily take into account political, national, and international considerations not primarily related to the fields of economics and business. In the preparation of this report, the President would get the views of the Cabinet and other agencies, and the Council of Economic Advisers and its staff could be used to assist in its preparation.

This recommendation was discussed orally with the Economic Policy Committee of the BAC when they met with the Council on June 9. We made no commitments but took the matter under advisement in subsequent Council meetings.

It continued to be my view that if we made this sort of separation it would be practically impossible to keep from revealing differences between our conclusions and the President's policy decisions. Both my colleagues, however, were eager to have the Council's report cover not merely factual but considerable interpretative material. Clark argued that the President had always followed our advice so that there was no issue anyway, whereas Keyserling's position seemed to amount to saying that we could always phrase our analysis and recommendations in such a way that there would not appear to be any conflict between our views and those of the President.

This of course went to a very fundamental issue. What are "our" views? We had always sought to speak as a Council with one voice, and to this end, I had participated in partial and ambiguous treatments of various matters and acquiesced in the complete omission of others. Mr. Keyserling seemed to feel that on all matters of Council operations and apparently even on economic positions we should speak in one voice by following a majority rule. I had refused this and frequently urged that we plainly disclose to the President such differences of view on economic matters as were important but irreconcilable.

At this juncture, the President advised me through Mr. Steelman that he would very much appreciate it if I were willing to have the Council's report differentiated from the Economic Report of the President in the midyear document since there had been so much talk of the White House injecting politics into the Economic Reports. He wanted at this time (at the threshold of the campaign period) to show the world that his reports were straight economics and that the White House did not inject any politics into them.[5]

I pointed out the long-range difficulties of this procedure and he said that he was asking it only in the case of this particular report and did not regard it as a precedent. There were extended exchanges (a sort of arm's length bargaining) at the end of which I agreed to the separation, recommending to the Council that we limit our report to merely factual and technical matters and that interpretation as well as recommendation be left to the President's report. My colleagues wanted the interpretation of the inflation situation to be ours, but I insisted that if this were done, it would have to be a much more reserved statement [than the then current draft] of both *pro* and *con*. We finally agreed on the draft that appeared as Section III ("The Issue between Inflation and Stabilization") in the Midyear Economic Report of the President. (*P. D.*, Nov. 27, 1948)

Advance copies of this midyear report were sent to all members of the Economic Policy Committee of the BAC and also to several other persons who had expressed active interest in the work of the Council. We received a number of replies indicating that the separation of the semiannual document into the form of an Economic Report of the President and an Economic Review by the Council met with a good deal of approval. Two replies were especially sig-

[5] This becomes more than a little amusing as one contemplates the way economic policy was handled by the President in the ensuing weeks. (See p. 215.) On the one occasion when I discussed this matter with Mr. Truman he was quite frank to say that it was political considerations that moved him to urge the change—that is, it was politically necessary to use the professional standing of the Council to blunt the charge that there was politics in his program.

nificant. Earl Bunting, managing director of the National Association of Manufacturers, wrote:

I congratulate you and the Council for your current midyear report. You have, for the first time, made a clear-cut distinction between the economic findings of the Council and the interpretation and suggested policies of the administration. In my judgment this will materially increase the usefulness of the work of the Council. We all recognize, of course, that the President and the Congress have to consider more than cold, economic facts in the determination of policy. This is both necessary and desirable in a system of political freedom. But it still remains true that each of us needs to be able to look at the bare facts themselves without having them overlaid with political consideration. . . . [I approve] your stopping short, in the report, of carrying your analysis to specific recommendations of policy. I assume that the Council does make these recommendations to the President and the Cabinet, and that certainly is proper. But since final determination of policy is the responsibility of the President and his Cabinet, publication of the Council's recommendations as such could not help but create confusion and difficulty because it is inevitable that they would not always agree with the policies decided upon at the political level.

Enders Voorhees, chairman of the Finance Committee of the United States Steel Corporation, on the other hand, commended the initiation of a separate document over the signature of the Council as a first step toward an independent interpretation and policy statement by the Council of the kind contemplated by those who wanted to set up a National Economic Advisory Council outside the Executive Office. I showed both these letters to the President as evidence that there were real grounds for my fear that a separate document over the Council's signature might make it easier for critics to point to real or imagined discrepancies between our factual and analytical presentation and his policy recommendations. He said he realized that some people wanted a separate Council report as a means to embarrass him, but on the whole he thought it most helpful to have separate reports at this time.

That there was such a danger was further evidenced in comments from a number of the more acute editorial writers. The Philadelphia *Bulletin* (Aug. 4, 1948) commented: "Reading of the report will not promote the crisis atmosphere with which the President in his Friday message to Congress seemed to surround it. The Council sees danger ahead and is in favor of some Government action to ward off future trouble. But it doesn't think we are about to go over Niagara. . . . The Report gives some reasonable basis for Congressional unwillingness to be rushed into re-establishing rationing and Government controls in an 'emergency' session."

The San Diego *Union* (Aug. 19, 1948) began its editorial: "While inflation and high prices insist on becoming entangled in politics as a national election approaches, a temperate and well-considered statement on the two subjects comes from President Truman's own Council of Economic Advisers. . . . Nothing is suggested, it may be observed, about reimposition of price controls and rationing. (As a matter of fact, it is reported from reliable Washington sources, the Economic Advisory Board had prepared a statement against such action, but withheld it in the face of the President's message asking for controls.) "

The New York *Sun* (July 31, 1948) editorialized: "Members of Congress . . . have cause to be grateful for the report of the Council of Economic Advisers which the President sent to Congress yesterday, along with an inadequate abstract. What the Council has to say about the country's economic situation at mid-year is longer and more difficult reading than what the President has had to say, but it is also more fundamental, less alarming, and more rewarding." And the New York *Post* added: "The Council's report is important to the very extent that it, perhaps unwittingly, highlights the contradictions in Mr. Truman's double play."

And from a lengthy editorial in the Charlotte, North Carolina, *Observer* we excerpt a few lines: "When the midyear report of the Council of Economic Advisers was finally sent to Congress . . . it could be seen at once how the economists . . . squirmed out of the bad spot in which the President had put them by simply passing the buck to Mr. Truman. . . . Without actually contradicting the President's demands, the report is deadpan and noncommittal. With tongue in cheek it merely quotes the President's message and lets it go at that. . . . The statistical appendices of the report are a mine of information on the economic condition of the country, its generalized findings are in the main correct, but its caginess about contradicting the President's message betrays a political influence that has no place in a report that should be objective and scientific."

At this time also there developed another stage in the problem of Council appearance in the Congressional arena in support of Administration policies. For the special session the President turned to an outsider as field commander for his legislative program—to Paul Porter, a prominent lawyer who had been the last Administrator of the wartime Office of Price Administration. Porter was not disposed to view my scruples on this matter as tolerantly as had the chairmen of various Congressional committees, members of the Cabinet, and the President himself. As he was mapping the strategy of his campaign for the President's 8-point "emergency" program, he came to my office to explain the part he wished to assign to the Chairman of the Council of Economic Advisers. When I said that this was not a part that, in the best interests of the Council and the President, I could play, he suggested that a subpoena from the appropriate committee might bring me into action. I replied that it would probably not be a course that a committee chairman would think it altogether wise to take, but that, if he should do so, I felt sure Mr. Truman would challenge his right to summon one of the President's personal aides.

Mr. Porter did not accept this answer very cheerfully. He seemed more impressed when I pointed out some difficulties that I might encounter in answering, to his complete satisfaction, certain enquiries as to strictly economic issues that congressmen might raise as to the proposed program. The issue brought sharp division in the Executive Office. "After numerous telephone conversations with Mr. Steelman, Mr. Clifford, Mr. Porter, and Mr. Turner, and with lengthy conferences on the Williamsburg between the President, the White House aides, and Mr. Porter, and after positions had been taken and reversed, as I recall it, four times within the week, the President's final decision was given me in his letter of August 3: (*P. D.*, Nov. 27, 1948)

Dear Dr. Nourse:

Mr. Paul Porter has raised with me the question of whether I would regard it as appropriate for members of the Council of Economic Advisers to testify before Congressional committees concerning the anti-inflation program I have recommended to the Congress.

As you know, I have considered from time to time in the past the question whether members of the Council should testify before Congressional committees. I am aware of the difference between your views on this subject and the views held by your colleagues on the Council. I respect these varying views, which I am sure all of you hold most conscientiously.

Under these circumstances, it seems that the wisest course in the present instance is to permit the members of the Council to be guided by their own convictions. Accordingly, I do not wish to induce any member of the Council to testify if he feels it inappropriate for him to do so; nor do I wish to restrain any member from testifying if he feels that to be an appropriate part of his duties.

I am informing Mr. Porter of this letter, with the expectation that he will make arrangements for testimony by the members of the Council if any testimony is to be presented by them.

Sincerely,

/s./ Harry S. Truman

Mr. Keyserling had already been diligently preparing material to present in support of the control program if he could get the "go" signal from the White House. On August 4, he made this presentation before the Senate Banking and Currency Committee and was warmly praised by Senator Tobey. I had been invited to appear but was excused by the chairman of the committee.

AD HOC ACTIVITIES OF THE COUNCIL

In addition to its work on the January and midyear economic reports of the President and its quarterly (and some monthly) memoranda to him on current developments, the Council during 1948 extended itself, or was drawn, into more active participation in several current situations. First was the wage, price, and inflation issue as it was related to the objectives of the Employment Act.

On February 12, the Council sent to Mr. Clifford, in response to his request, a two-page draft of a statement on the current drop in commodity prices, which had caused alarm in some quarters. He said the White House was thinking that perhaps a frank, analytical statement by the President would have a reassuring effect. Shortly after this memorandum was submitted, Mr. Clifford telephoned us that "after consultation with Cabinet members, it was decided that it would be unwise to give the attached statement to the press."

During February also, there arose concern about a series of advances in the prices of various classes of steel products. The President instructed the Department of Justice, through the FBI, to investigate evidences of collusion in these mark ups, the Department of Commerce to prepare a factual statement as to the steel price situation, and the Council of Economic Advisers to analyze the economic impact of the price increases. Our report was submitted on March 10 as a seven-page memorandum, and it was released to the press along with the reports of the Department of Justice and the Department of Commerce. No specific action was taken by the government.

A third development in Council relations grew out of the first moves in the rearmament program. On March 24, the Council wrote to the President:

Following our report to you on the steel price advance, we have been carefully reviewing the industrial and financial situation. . . . The new preparedness program which has been taking shape since your address to the Congress on March 17 greatly complicates the picture. We are studying this new factor in conjunction with the National Security Resources Board and the Bureau of the Budget. . . . The additional pressures coming from the expenditure, the appropriation, or even the consideration of some additional billions of government money must inevitably aggravate this danger.

The President replied (March 25):

I read your letter of the twenty-fourth with a great deal of interest and I think you are working in the right direction.

We must be very careful that the military does not overstep the bounds from an economic standpoint domestically. Most of them would like to go back to a war footing—that is not what we want.

This was the beginning of the widely ramifying issue of the size of the military budget which the economy can stand and of the feasibility and necessity of economic controls under given conditions of military preparedness. It became a pivotal matter in the Presidential campaign of 1948 and has dominated Mr. Truman's second administration. The Council's relationship with this issue included the statement of the Chairman of the Council at the first Group Orientation Conference arranged by Secretary Forrestal and our special report on the budget ceiling in July–August 1949. (See pp. 172 n., 281.)

It has been noted that the rise in steel prices evoked considerable unfavorable reaction. At about this time also, a demand was made by the United Steel Workers for an increase in wages. Their contract had another year to run, and the union announced that it would honor the no-strike pledge contained in that contract. On April 22, Benjamin Fairless replied for the United States Steel Corporation that no wage increase would be granted; such increase would start a "third round" of inflationary wage increases whereas, in the interest of the country and of union people generally, everything possible should be done to check inflation. He promised, in this connection that on May 1 a schedule of price decreases would be announced on products of his company, amounting to an estimated 25 million dollars, or more than twice the amount realized by the advance in semifinished prices made in the preceding February. If the whole industry followed the example of United States Steel, total savings would amount to 75 million dollars annually.

In view of the Administration's outspoken criticism of the steel price advances in February, I wrote the following letter to the President on May 3:

I am deeply troubled over the absence of any statement with reference to the steel wage-price move. It was for the purpose of presenting some phases of this matter that I sought an appointment last week.

The announcement of the United States Steel Corporation was put specifically in terms of a willingness to participate in a general effort to stem inflation. If there is no word of approval from the White House, I fear that the spirit of co-operation may be chilled.

As to the labor aspect, I understand that Mr. Murray's broadcast this evening will be quite critical in tone. It had seemed to me that a statement from you recognizing the sacrifice necessarily made by these unions that bear the brunt of any effective anti-inflationary move might moderate the character of his comment.

Finally, might not a reiteration of the Administration's position on the wage-price spiral do something significant toward bettering the tactical position in dealing with Mr. Lewis and the new coal strike threat?

On May 18, Mr. Truman replied:

I have been holding your letter of May third hoping that an opportunity would come along so that I could give you an answer to it. The situation, however, has not turned out as anticipated and, therefore, I am not ready yet to make any statements on the conditions which are developing in the third round of wage demands. You and I will discuss it later.

No such discussion in fact developed, but the note illustrates the complexity of considerations which inevitably condition a President's

action in economic affairs. At this time, a considerable effort was
being made both in business and in government circles to stem
the tide of inflation which grew rather naturally out of the conditions of World War II financing and postwar reconversion. The
difficulties of such a struggle were being further illustrated at this
time by the wage demands of several railroad brotherhoods. In the
hope of keeping economic considerations as much to the fore as
possible in these politically-conditioned negotiations, I ventured to
raise my voice in that matter also. This interposition took the form
of a letter (May 7) to the President's assistant, Dr. Steelman:

> I note by the papers that the President has delegated to you the task
> of "settling" the rail strike. This carries the suggestion that you may be
> seeking the best compromise which will avoid a strike. As a matter both of
> economics and of political science, I believe that to compromise this issue
> at this juncture would be so unfortunate as to be little short of disastrous.
>
> I am aware that this is not a situation in which you or the President
> conceive that my duties need concern me or that the services of the
> Council are called for. However, I hope that as an older man I may be
> indulged in stating my views in a matter that challenges us both simply as
> social scientists and as citizens.
>
> As I understand the purposes of the Employment Act, we are trying to
> substitute methods of reason and social engineering for resort to force, to
> the end that we may effect better stabilization of our economy. Under the
> Railway Labor Act, we have one of the most advanced pieces of adjust-
> ment machinery thus far made available. It used a professionally compe-
> tent fact-finding body to study the railway wage issue, and this Board made
> an award which was accepted by a preponderant part of the railway labor
> group. If an intransigent minority is to be allowed to set aside such orderly
> procedures and is to have the support of the government in doing so, I do
> not see how we are ever going to make much progress toward establishing
> sound economic stabilization devices.
>
> Besides condoning the use of monopoly power, I believe that any dif-
> ferential increase given the three brotherhoods under present circum-
> stances would have serious inflationary repercussions. The actual monetary
> sums involved in the rail controversy are relatively small, but concession in
> this case would probably "pull the plug" for the large and strategic areas
> of automotive and coal wages. Thus the effort to hold the line against the
> wage-price spiral would practically be lost. Fairless gave clear intimation
> that steel will have to follow coal, even though the steelworkers them-
> selves cannot reopen the issue.
>
> For the government to be a party to this new inflationary break would

seem to me utterly inconsistent with its announced position. Of course a firm stand against it carries the threat of strike and thus challenges the government's ability to deal with the power of small monopolistic groups to paralyze the civilian economy and defense effort. I do not see that that challenge can safely be evaded. The situation confronting our democratic government today is quite similar to that which France was faced by—and failed to meet effectively—between the World Wars and since. It is the danger that follows the growth of strong factions and the revelation of weak government. I believe our government has the inherent strength to meet this danger. But the present manifestation of factional power is very real and will have to be met most decisively if our future is not to be clouded by the way responsibilities are met in the next few weeks.

While this is my own purely personal communication to you, I have shown it to Mr. Keyserling and understand that, in general outline at least, he shares by views. Mr. Clark is out of the city.

On May 11, Mr. Steelman telephoned me, saying that he had been so swamped with conferences with the three striking railroad brotherhoods that he had not been able to make an earlier response to my letter of May 7. He called now "to thank me heartily for having sent it and giving him the benefit of my views on the situation. He had taken my letter at once to the President and they agreed that the positions were sound and that they were in full accord with them."

Steelman went on to say that the officers of the brotherhoods had not felt that, in terms of union politics, they could afford to accept concessions. Other men were clamoring for their executive positions in the unions and would claim that it was a sign of weakness on their part if they bowed to anything short of Presidential action and a court restraining order. He said he had argued with them that, in following the course it did, the government had not merely protected the process of collective bargaining but had protected them against legislation that Congress would probably have passed by Monday night in a spirit of resentment at any interruption of transportation service. (*P. D.,* May 11, 1948)

At this time, a new question as to the distribution of tasks and responsibilities in the Executive Office arose. The newspapers carried announcement that Mr. Steelman had set up a special committee in his office for studying the need for further economic controls. All members of the Council were concerned as to the precise scope of this study and its implications. I therefore promptly arranged a conference with Mr. Steelman to canvass the matter.

After a friendly and helpful discussion, I undertook to analyze the situation in the following letter (May 18, 1948):

I was glad to have an opportunity to discuss with you the work of the *ad hoc* committee on the need for further economic controls which you have set up under the direction of Mr. Robert Turner. As I understand the purposes of this undertaking, it is primarily to get a comprehensive picture of the requirements of ECA and the armed services for certain critical materials during the next year and of the availability of supplies to meet these requirements. I understood you to say that the purpose of setting this up as an *ad hoc* committee in your office was to collate at one point all the materials on these subjects which are available from existing executive departments such as Commerce, Agriculture, and Interior, and from special agencies such as ECA and NSRB. I assume that after this first roundup of preliminary evidence is made by this committee that the continuing function of gathering, checking, and refining these estimates will need to be carried on in some central workshop, and that in all probability this will be done by the staff of NSRB as the basis of their advising the President as to security needs and resources under the defense program . . .

As I told you, we had been somewhat concerned owing to the fact that the committee is designated in the memorandum of May 11 as a "committee on the need for further economic controls" and to the fact that it is stated in the second paragraph of the text that it is the function of the committee to prepare a statement of "the possibility of meeting these requirements without controls and the type of controls needed, if any, beyond those presently authorized or in effect." Several memoranda prepared by subcommittees seem to go beyond the factual area into the realm of policy recommendation. . . . This raises the question whether any device was contemplated for securing consistency between the two reports or what would be the effect if they should not be in complete harmony. . . .

We feel that our participation at this juncture is called for under the responsibilities laid upon us by the Employment Act. We feel also that a rather delicate problem is created for the President if steps are to be taken or recommendations made with sufficient promptness to be effective and at the same time to present a desirable consistency and continuity of policy from the Interior-Council-Commerce reports on ERP last fall, the President's message opening the special session, the Economic Report of the President in January, to the Midyear Report to be presented this coming July.

We shall look forward with very great interest therefore to the foundational material which we hope to receive from this *ad hoc* committee and shall give it most careful consideration in the light of consultative meetings that we will hold from time to time with the heads of NSRB, ECA, and the Bureau of the Budget. We believe that in this manner a well-informed and well-co-ordinated body of analysis and suggestions for policy may be made available to the President from the Council as well as from these other arms of the executive office.

As matters developed, the work program of the National Security Resources Board was arrested by organizational difficulties. (See p. 252.) The Economic Co-operation Administration pursued its own operational course without any policy articulation with the Council of Economic Advisers; and the work of the Steelman-Turner committee virtually ceased with the latter's return to an academic post. The incident, however, illustrates the American tendency to set up a new committee for each new problem or different turn in an old problem and the difficulty of securing administrative integration within the executive branch.

THE CABINET COMMITTEE FOR AN ANTI-INFLATION PROGRAM

A development of considerable importance for the evolution of the Council took place in the closing months of 1948, when the President suggested a somewhat more definite procedure for integrating the advisory service of Cabinet officers and executive heads with that of the Council in developing the content and text of his Economic Report.[6] Mr. Truman, with a group of his aides, had gone to Key West, for a period of recuperation right after his election triumph. But he was considerably concerned about inflationary dangers and how they should be dealt with in his forthcoming economic report. On November 15, I received a telephone call from Mr. Steelman from Key West, saying:

the President wished me "personally" to take over the task of co-ordinating the anti-inflation program. I would, of course, use the Council in such way as I saw fit, but the purpose was to secure continuous discussion of policy matters with the Cabinet members or other agency heads particularly concerned, so that they would be in touch with developments and that we would promote as much agreement as possible on all features of the program. . . .

[6] It will be noted that the letter of transmittal covering the Economic Report of the President to the Congress states: "In preparing this report, I have had the advice and assistance of the Council of Economic Advisers, members of the Cabinet, and heads of independent agencies."

When I passed on this information to my colleagues, Mr. Clark accepted it with apparent satisfaction, whereas Mr. Keyserling appeared to be considerably less than elated at the development. I interpret it as meaning an important recognition of the work of the Council and as affording an opportunity to have our materials and views fully considered throughout the executive branch before policy decisions are arrived at. Secretary Sawyer and Secretary Snyder called me even before I had an opportunity to call them, expressing their gratification at this development, together with proper pride that they had helped to bring it about.

As soon as the Presidential party got back from Key West, I had an extended discussion with Mr. Steelman (Monday, November 22) and with the President for half an hour on Tuesday, November 23. . . . and another discussion of an hour and ten minutes with Mr. Steelman this morning. He was immensely gratified with the newspaper and radio reception of this move and said the President was also much pleased and had felt that we had a very satisfactory discussion last Tuesday. (*P. D.*, Nov. 27, 1948)[7]

In pursuance of the President's request, I at once invited five Cabinet members (Treasury, Commerce, Labor, Agriculture, and Interior) and the chairman of the Board of Governors of the Federal Reserve System to constitute the nuclear committee. As particular problems arose, we asked other agency heads to sit with us to discuss the Council's analyses and the Cabinet's views. Meetings were held, generally twice a week, in the conference room of the west wing of the White House. In the last few meetings, all members of the Council were present, and the draft of its "materials for the use of the President in the preparation of his Economic Report" was in the hands of the members of the Cabinet committee.

I made the President a progress report on the work of this group just before he left for Independence for the Christmas holidays, and again on his return. Finally, an appointment was made for him to meet with the committee in its closing session. On December 31 he stepped across the hall from his office and sat down with the Council and full committee to consider our finished draft. I called his attention to salient points in the draft and noted that on certain of them there was not complete agreement within the Council or among

[7] With newspaper men and others, I made every effort to get away from the title "anti-inflation committee" and to stress the purpose of having a clearing house of thinking in the executive branch, focused broadly upon economic stabilization rather than narrowly on a current and exclusive inflationary threat.

members of the Cabinet committee. The form of statement in the draft was that which was in accord with his policy as we understood it, but if he wished to have members of the group state and explain their qualifications or dissents, we would be happy to do so. After reading the controverted passages, he said, "No, that's the way I want it to stand." The session lasted about an hour. After a final conference between the Council and members of the White House staff on minor editorial matters, the Economic Report of the President went to the Government Printing Office.

CHAPTER TWELVE

Economic Reports and Council Relations—1949

The year 1949 presented increased difficulties for the Council in analyzing the economic situation. It also brought internal relations to the breaking point. Before the year was out, the chairman had resigned.

THE ECONOMIC REPORTS OF THE PRESIDENT

By January 1949, the Economic Report of the President, which in 1947 had been limited to 33 pages of text and 20 pages of technical appendixes, had expanded to a total of more than 160 pages. It continued in the dual authorship form inaugurated in the midyear report of 1948. Although Mr. Truman had said that the separation of the Council's analysis from the President's recommendations introduced at that time did not constitute a precedent, many people, for various reasons, had expressed approval of the change. I therefore did not even raise the question of going back to the earlier form.

The President's Economic Report proper ran to a length of only seventeen pages under the topics: "Sources of Our Economic Strength," "High Points in the Economic Situation," "Guides to Economic Policy," and "Legislative Recommendations." Congratulating the country on "another year of bountiful prosperity," the President proceeded: "Let us all remember that our unparalleled prosperity has not been maintained by chance, and that we can lose it if we leave the future to chance. Courageous and positive action has contributed to our progress, and some of the most serious difficulties still confronting us exist because our thought and action have not been sufficiently clear and vigorous."

"Legislative recommendations" included a "sound fiscal policy to have a budget surplus now. . . . I recommend legislation to increase the Government revenue from taxation by 4 billion dollars a year. The principal source of additional revenue should be additional taxes upon corporate profits. . . . Another source of additional revenue should be the tax upon estates and gifts. . . . I also recommend an increase in social security contributions under existing and extended social insurance programs . . . recommended above."

On debt management, the President proposed continuing "the policy of supporting the price of long-term Government bonds at the 2½ per cent yield level [which] has been eminently successful" but urged that "adequate means be provided in order that monetary authorities may at all times be in a position to carry out their traditional function of exerting effective restraint upon excessive credit expansion," with extension of some powers of the Federal Reserve System made applicable to all banks insured by the Federal Deposit Insurance Corporation.

The President further recommended continuation of rent control, selective price and wage controls, export controls, and "mandatory controls over key materials in short supply."

Under the heading "Promotion of Supply and Production," the Economic Report said: "There are shortages of supply in certain critical areas which are so serious as to impede maximum production in an expanding economy and to limit programs related to national security" and recommended careful surveys of future supply needs and productive capacity.[1]

To "protect the victims of inflation," the President recommended substantially raising benefits under old-age and survivors insurance, increasing the minimum wage from 40 cents an hour to at least 75 cents, and expanding the public assistance and housing programs.

To "promote balanced economic growth," the Economic Report advocated a vigorous long-time program for development of natural resources; support of agriculture; improvement of international economic relations; aid to housing, urban development, education, and health; and old-age, disability, and employment insurance. "Abundant resources and rapidly advancing technology are both a blessing and a responsibility. Our strength lies, however, less in these resources themselves than in our will to use them effectively.

[1] See p. 240 f. for further developments on this point.

This task requires adapting our private and Government institutions to changing circumstances."

The Annual Economic Review presented by the Council in the January 1949 report kept pretty well to the factual level. It did not get over the line into policy recommendations of its own or argument in support of policies enunciated in the Economic Report of the President. It did, however, open the door to the staff to develop a rationale of long-run economic planning and "targets" for future development of the economy. In fact a major explanation of the greater length of the 1949 Economic Report is to be found in Section III of the Council's Review. This was entitled "Basic Objectives for Balanced Economic Growth." It covered nearly twenty-eight printed pages but that was only about half of the material which had come to the Council in the form of a staff draft.

The technique used in making the elaborate projections of the "basic objective" was that of the Nation's Economic Budget, broken down not merely by categories but by industries on the production side and classes of expenditure on the consumption side. Daring use was made also of the newly developed input-output technique to project quantitatively the investment needed over a ten-year period in the various categories of industrial and commercial plant and public facilities. "Objectives for consumption and living standards" were projected in similar detail.

Mr. Clark and I both felt that the statistical figures from which the projections were derived were of a very inadequate character and the judgments which guided the hand of the projector relied on subjective rather than objective standards to an extent that left the projections on too highly speculative a basis to justify their presentation as a part—even a separately signed part—of the Economic Report of the President. In fact, we thought that the Council itself would be subject to criticism on professional grounds for releasing such a long-range outline. Whatever its exploratory value for scholars, we thought that giving it the dignity of either a Presidential or Council report at this time was premature.

Our reaction to these labors of the staff produced such a sense of frustration and of tension within the Council organization that, with many misgivings, this section was included in the Council's review but in a more tentative and sketchy form than that in which it had first been submitted. Even so, it revived adverse criticism on the ground that the President's report was intended as a one-year program and that the Council's analysis should limit itself to materials strictly pertinent to such a short-run program. The reader will recall the Joint Committee's criticism of earlier reports. (See pp. 195–98.) The issue of how far even a short-run program can be adequately developed outside the context of long-run economic evolution is not a simple one. The Joint Committee has subsequently published staff projections of a more daring character than those. Further comment appears on page 322.

The regular monthly memorandum presented by the Council to President Truman on February 4, 1949 had special significance in that it completely abandoned the attempt to have the Council speak with a unanimous voice in their appraisals and recommendations rather than revealing frankly to the President such real differences of view as might exist. This memorandum opened by quoting two paragraphs from the Council memorandum of December 7, 1948 in which we said:

> In the opinion of the Council, the economic situation in the coming months will be inflationary unless action is taken by the government to halt price advances. Price increases might become really threatening if wage increases were large and produced the price reflexes customary in a boom economy, or if the expenditures by the governmnnt were expanded greatly.

Recognizing that the President's Economic Report of January had continued to stress inflationary dangers, this memorandum raised the question whether there had been a subsequent change in the economic signs. After quoting various price, employment, and production indexes, it concluded: "This is not the performance of a softening economy. The situation is strong, and there will now come into it the demands of labor for wage increases."

Following the citation of the latest available statistics in this memorandum, there was inserted a paragraph which was differentiated from the body of the text by indentation and double-spacing. It read:

> Mr. Nourse believes that there are other facts than those cited above, additional developments not yet reducible to a statistical basis, and questions of business attitudes which lead him to an interpretation materially different from that contained in the remaining paragraphs of this memorandum. In a word, he does not believe there are clear indications that

inflationary pressures are increasing or unabated, although developments are conceivable which might renew the process of inflation.

Shortly after this February memorandum, I departed for a somewhat extended trip to the Pacific Coast but, before leaving, had responded to some questions of reporters in the foyer of the West Wing by saying that I viewed the current softening of prices as a sign of "healthy disinflation." On March 18, I addressed the Executives' Club of Chicago under the title, "The Gentle Art of Disinflation." The gist of my message was as follows:

The broad objective of disinflation through true economic adjustment has been stated several times in Economic Reports of the President as seeking to find—to work out among ourselves—after the sharp disturbances of depression, war, and reconversion, a "new set of workable price and income relations" on which American business can go forward at sustained high levels of production. How this is to be accomplished is to be discovered by the managerial skill and ingenuity, by the courage and the moderation, of many men in the myriad operational posts of America's gigantic business system. There has been an easy and I think naïve assumption in many quarters that the prolongation of prosperity was to be accomplished by some force of monetary or fiscal magic engineered from Washington and indeed inspired by the Council of Economic Advisers. I for one do not believe in fairies or conceive myself as an economic magician. I firmly believe that governmental policy is one important constituent of any dependable condition of national prosperity. But correct private policy and individual action are also indispensable and are needed to tailor action down to varied and fast-changing local situations. . . .

This [present situation] is not, to my mind, a picture of unforeseen or uncontrollable disaster. It marks the abatement of pressure of monetary purchasing power on scarce goods, and the transition from sellers' markets to buyers' markets—which are the normal estate of a productive and competitive economy. Now the fundamental question is: Are we going to show the ability of free business enterprise to meet the challenge of real competition, or can American businessmen make the grade only when we have the external stimulus of government orders and a deficit economy and its brief aftermath? I suggest that disinflation is a rational and guided action by responsible and economically sophisticated persons. It is capable of warding off the unforeseen and catastrophic deflation and depression that would result from blind and impersonal forces. I have called this speech "The Gentle Art of Disinflation" to express my belief that we may, through the process of intelligent diagnosis of business conditions and economic needs, formulate and execute policies and programs to prolong

our period of economic health. We may take off some fat, but we shall not
die and need not really suffer.

Meanwhile Mr. Keyserling and Mr. Clark, in response to Senator
O'Mahoney's invitation, had testified before the Joint Committee
on the analysis and recommendations contained in the President's
Economic Report of January 1948. The lengthy prepared statement
of Mr. Keyserling included a comprehensive discussion of all factors
in the current situation, deflationary—or disinflationary—as well as
inflationary. The exposition was too detailed and subtle for the
ordinary listener to follow readily and, since the whole tone was
that of complete support of the President's Economic Report of
January, with its inflationary emphasis, the public gained the impression that Mr. Keyserling was fighting inflation amidst the facts
of deflation.

Mr. Clark's statement was short and forthright: "The program
now proposed by the President in his annual Economic Report,
which you are studying, is based upon the judgment that the postwar inflationary forces are still strong and will probably become
more active in the near future, requiring the provision of measures
now to curb spiraling prices. . . . The administration should have
the anti-inflationary measures the President has requested without
delay, for the risk in delaying action until spiraling prices are more
actively at work and are establishing the base for the ultimate crash
is too great." At a time when businessmen and the public were fearful about current price weakness in both agricultural and business
lines, this emphasis on inflation dangers in the first forensic appearance of Council representatives evoked a great deal of comment
about the practical value of the Council's work. The comment was
often disparaging—but sometimes amused.

On March 8, while I was still out of the city, Mr. Keyserling and
Mr. Clark sent the President a memorandum reviewing the preceding month's developments. It began: "The following highlights indicate that the pulse of the economy is still strong." The key to this
interpretation is to be found in two of the concluding paragraphs,
which read:

The fundamental conditions for very high-level employment and production in 1949 are all present. The only condition in sight which could
materially alter the optimistic outlook would be if business on a large
scale seriously reduced its investment plans. This could happen only if

business listens to some of the trade journals which seem to have a perverse desire to create the impression that the Government wants economic conditions to get worse, instead of realizing that the Government has the greatest interest in maintaining prosperity because it represents the people and is therefore determined to take every necessary step toward that end. . . .

If there should unexpectedly be a substantial downturn in business, there are elements in your proposed program designed to combat it just as there are elements in your program designed to combat the remaining inflationary forces which are still present. In an economic situation as complicated as the present one, the Government should have both types of weapons available so that they can be used promptly in the right combination.

In our quarterly report to the President on April 1, we tried to get the whole picture in fuller perspective by stating frankly that "The first quarter of 1949 contained a mixture of trends which makes it hard to characterize the quarter by a simple label or to discern the immediate outlook with clarity" and suggested that three possible lines of development need to be considered.

First, there is the possibility of another spurt of inflation. This seems least likely unless the Congress votes large appropriations not offset by new taxes. Consumers have recently shown a disposition to save more and to spend less, and if this mood changes there could be a marked increase in market demand because personal incomes remain very high. Businessmen, while talking in terms of uncertainty and hesitation, have thus far continued to make investments at a high rate. Government expenditures will increase, and without increased taxes the surplus will be reduced to negligible proportions or become a deficit. Wage increases, if moving beyond increases in productivity, might be inflationary. The crop outlook is always uncertain although it now looks promising. These factors do not permit us to rule out the possibility, although there is decreasing likelihood, of another spurt of inflation.

Second, there is the possibility that the substantial downturn in business activity predicted or feared for several years may develop within 1949. Much depends upon attitudes which have not yet crystallized fully. The uncertainty of businessmen could lead to substantial contraction of investment and production. The more extensive price readjustments that will be necessary as more and more markets become buyers' markets may be harder to execute skillfully and may cause more repercussions in employment and production than those which have thus far taken place. The future character of consumer responses is still hard to appraise. Because of the more ambiguous economic situation, we feel that the magnitude of tax increases proposed at the beginning of the year should be reconsidered.

Third is the hoped for further process of price adjustment in a manner to facilitate the clearing of markets with only moderate temporary departure from maximum levels of employment and production. Thus far, this process of healthy adjustment has taken place in a more orderly and constructive fashion than many people anticipated and we may find ourselves hanging up an unparalleled record of transition from a postwar boom to a period of stable prosperity without intervening hard times. The Government by word and deed should extend every feasible encouragement to this process of adjustment.

The President's Midyear Economic Report was tuned to the "Abatement of Postwar Inflationary Forces" since "a moderate downward trend [had] characterized most phases of economic activity in the first half of 1949. . . . Prices generally decreased, reflecting the shift from a sellers' to a buyers' market." The President said: "The fundamental task facing us all—businessmen, workers, farmers, Government—is to apply positive policies with confidence and courage in order to achieve a sounder price structure and the restoration of maximum production and employment. . . . Over the course of the last sixteen years, many steps have been taken by the Government to bulwark our economy against the forces of recession. The way to check a decline in business investment or production is to take affirmative action that will lead to more investment and more production. The way to check an increase in unemployment is to take affirmative action that will provide more jobs. The way to prevent our economy from shrinking is to take affirmative action that will help it to expand."

The legislative recommendations contained in the Midyear Economic Report covered eleven points:

1. Repeal the tax on the transportation of goods, liberalize the provisions for carry-over of losses by corporations, and raise estate and gift taxes. No major increase in taxes should be undertaken at this time. [This in effect withdrew the recommendation of the January Economic Report for a $4 billion tax increase.]

2. Extend the maximum time limit now fixed by law on the maturity of loans to business made by the Reconstruction Finance Corporation.

3. Provide for a broad study of investment and development needs and market opportunities in an expanding economy.

4. Adopt an improved program of farm income supports.

5. Increase the minimum wage to at least 75 cents an hour and broaden its coverage.

6. Strengthen the unemployment compensation system by increasing the amount and duration of benefits and extending coverage.

7. Extend to July 25, 1950, the availability of readjustment allowances for veterans not protected by State unemployment compensation laws.

8. Raise benefits and extend coverage under the old-age and survivors insurance system and improve the public assistance program.

9. Enact legislation to permit Federal agencies, and assist States and localities, to intensify their advance planning and to acquire sites for useful projects.

10. Enact legislation to provide technical assistance to underdeveloped areas abroad and to encourage investment in such areas.

11. Restore the Reciprocal Trade Agreements Act.

In some quarters where fear still lurked that the dip of the spring months was only the beginning of a real recession, this report was regarded as "whistling in the dark," and deficient in that it proposed no vigorous antirecession program. In less jittery quarters, it was regarded as a sober appraisal of the current situation and as breathing a reasoned optimism as to the future. Within a few weeks a brisk autumn recovery was under way and the lack of panic in the Midyear Report was seen to be justified.

The Council's review of the economic situation at midyear 1949 elaborated the factual details of the situation and analyzed "the course of economic adjustment and its problems. The economy in transition [had] factors of underlying strength, but also [elements of uncertainty]." The Council examined the nature of "the process of price and income adjustment" and laid emphasis on "the need for maintaining the rate of investment." Finally, the Council presented its view of "public and private responsibilities" needed to effectuate the purposes of the Employment Act. It indulged in some frank justification of Administration policies and practices of preceding years, but did not outline a future program or present a brief for it.[2]

---

[2] The difficulty the Council encountered in getting together on a draft of this report is recounted in Chap. XIV (p. 278).

THE SPENCE AND MURRAY BILLS

Largely obscured by the generalities of the 1949 Midyear Economic
Report and Council review was an issue which had been assuming
new prominence in public policy and in the affairs of the Council.
This was the issue of government responsibility for the maintenance
of capital formation or industrial investment as a means of stabilizing the economy. To get it in perspective, we must go back at least
a year.

In the Economic Report of the President in January 1948, there
had been a quite detailed and objective analysis of productive capacity and business investment. The President said:

> In some industries present capacity appears adequate for the near
> future. In others, such as electric power and petroleum refining, expan-
> sion of capacity is substantial and is likely to continue for a considerable
> period until a better balance between demands and capacity has been
> reached. In a few industries, net capacity expansion during 1947 was less
> than that required annually to sustain maximum production and employ-
> ment. . . . There is a serious question, in particular, whether our capacity
> to produce fuels and energy, is being expanded fast enough to meet fuel
> and energy demands indicated by expansion in other lines. If the whole
> level of output is to rise steadily and rapidly with minimum waste of
> capacity, the balancing of expansion in different industries calls for con-
> siderably more thorough study than it has been given in the past.[3]

There was no intimation of a policy of government intervention
other than what could be read into this sentence from the President's
statement of long-range objectives (p. 8): "Government has the
responsibility of providing favorable conditions for adequate and
well-balanced private investments in productive facilities, with prudent use of Government initiative when private resources lag." In
fact the government's role was at that time apparently envisaged as
that of a brake rather than an accelerator. The next sentence read:
"Both private and public policy must, however, impose restraints
on boom-time overdevelopment and overcapitalization."[4]

The Economic Report of the President in January 1949 (p. xxvi)
again referred to the problem of industrial capacity in more exigent
terms but still guardedly as to government's role. Under the heading,
"Promotion of Supply and Production," the President said:

[3] *The Economic Report of the President,* January 1948, pp. 59–61.
[4] The same, p. 8.

I *recommend immediate legislation* to deal with this problem of capacity and supply. It should impose upon the Government the specific responsibility and provide the funds to make careful surveys of future supply needs and productive capacity. It should further require that these specific studies be correlated with the general requirements of an economy operating at maximum employment, production, and purchasing power. To the extent that facts reveal the need, it should provide additional authority *to deal more effectively with inadequacy of capacity and supply.* [Italics added]

The Council's annual Economic Review (p. 18) displayed somewhat more restraint. The Council said:

Plant and equipment outlays during and since the war have greatly expanded productive capacity in many industries. A survey by a private agency indicates that manufacturing industry as a whole has increased its capacity by more than one-half since 1939 and by perhaps as much as a quarter since the end of 1945. To keep pace with a normal growth trend in total demand, as will be indicated in Part III, the recent over-all rate of increase in manufacturing capacity would not need to be maintained indefinitely. However, in connection with two prominent areas of current shortage, it should be noted that electric utility generating capacity has increased only about 45 per cent since 1939 and 12 per cent in the past three years, and steel furnace capacity about 16 per cent since 1939 and about 3½ per cent in the past three years.

While there is some indication of prospective softening of investment in manufacturing lines, plans for expansion and modernization are still strong in chemicals, petroleum, and metals. In some major non-manufacturing lines also—particularly utilities and transportation—the program of expansion and improvement is still active, and the outlook is for continued high expenditure.

And later (p. 46):

There is need to determine the extent to which serious shortages will persist for essential products and to determine what special measures may be needed to stimulate the increase of capacity and production.

The Midyear Economic Report of the President (1949) "kept the record straight" by re-emphasizing inflationary dangers and reminding that he had "recommended repeatedly for private and public action an anti-inflation program to curb these dangers before we suffered the consequences. . . . The dangers that are latent in inflation, of which I repeatedly warned, are now being revealed"—in the recession of the spring months.

The President, however, immediately turned to a new theme—leadership for recovery.

The 1949 decline has been moderate, and the opportunity is now ours to reverse the trend and achieve maximum production and consumption of goods and services without the evils of inflation. . . . Many of the price adjustments that have taken place have been healthy, and afford ground for expectation that our economy will work its way successfully through a difficult period of transition. But there is nothing healthy about more unemployment or less production. Such trends can and must be reversed by positive action, private and public. The way to check a decline in business investment or production is to take affirmative action that will lead to more investment and more production. The way to check an increase in unemployment is to take affirmative action that will provide more jobs. The way to prevent our economy from shrinking is to take affirmative action that will help it to expand.

Under the heading, "Business Investment," the President said:

Businessmen should lift their sights to the need of an economy that grows and prospers from year to year. I have previously recommended, and I again recommend, that the Congress provide for a broad study of potential business investment, expansion, and market opportunities under conditions of maximum use of our productive resources in a growing economy—conditions which the Employment Act of 1946 contemplates and which can be achieved if we have the confidence and determination to achieve them. This study should be designed especially to discover inadequacies in capacity in basic industries which may serve as limiting factors to expansion when the upward movement of business is resumed.

Here one finds no suggestion from the President that expansion of industrial capacity would be regarded as a direct responsibility of government. This neutralism is the more notable in view of the fact that a vigorous campaign had been under way during the preceding months to secure legislation of this very character. Between the annual and midyear Economic Reports of 1949, the episodes of the Spence Stabilization Bill and the Murray Economic Expansion Bill evoked no small measure of controversy, in which the Council had become an inadvertent participant.

It had been the philosophy of the Murray "full employment" bill of 1945 that when the Federal Government detected, through the projection of investment trends, a scale of private spending for business expansion and technological improvement inadequate to keep total spending up to the full employment level, it should itself embark on a spending-investment program sufficient to close this gap. This would call primarily for a shelf of public works but, since a stabilized economy calls for the maintenance of private enterprise in the major productive areas, it was recognized that, if the government undertook to bring spending-investment up to a full employment level, it would have to look to mining, manufacturing, and power industries, not merely the building of highways, reclamation works, and slum clearance projects.

Any specific espousal of such a range of government activities in the private investment area had been talked down in Congressional debate and hearings on the "full employment" bill and had been kept from specific inclusion in the Employment Act of 1946. The act did, however, pledge the government to "utilize all its plans, functions, and resources for the purpose of creating and maintaining . . . useful employment opportunities . . . for those able, willing, and seeking to work." Those who had sponsored the more aggressive type of statute hoped to see this general declaration of policy followed by one or more supplementary statutes as occasion might arise for government support to declining industrial activity. Such a need, according to thinkers of this school, might emerge in either of two ways. The advent of recession might call for prompt activity on the part of the government in construction of large public works or stimulation of the construction of private works in volume sufficient to offset any sag in private capital formation. On the other hand, as the inflation movement persisted and accelerated through 1947 and 1948, the argument was advanced that these price rises were due to, or aggravated by, the inability or unwillingness of private business, but particularly industrialists, to expand productive facilities fast enough. Thus the flow of goods was not proportionate to the flow of money, and market scarcity led to price inflation.

Numerous attempts had been made to have this view expounded in the Economic Report of the President or, after the dual form of document was adopted, in the Council's economic review. The President himself did not at this time manifest any desire to espouse the policy of having government supersede private enterprise in this manner, and he declined to lend his support to various senators and representatives who wished to introduce legislation of this character. They were of course free to proceed without active Administration sponsorship, and this led in late 1948 and 1949 to the drafting of the so-called Spence bill.

Its proponents, both in Congress and in the executive agencies sought a rendezvous in the headquarters of the Council of Economic Advisers. They had spiritual support from some staff members and from at least one member of the Council, and it was rather hard as a matter of principle to take the position that our good offices should not be available to the drafters of a law, helping them to bring its terms into conformity with the general policies of the President and the purposes of the statute under which our agency has been created. It could plausibly be argued that such co-operation would serve as a safeguard against the economically more exuberant or politically more interventionist types of thinking among the drafters.

At all events, H. R. 2756, introduced by Representative Spence of Kentucky on February 15, 1949 did have what amounted to a legislative drafting bureau in the Executive Office but was presented as a private rather than an Administration measure. It was to be cited as "The Economic Stability Act of 1949" and was described as "a bill to implement the established national policy of promoting maximum production, employment, and purchasing power and for other purposes." It was an expression of a philosophy of implemented Federal economic planning. Title IV embodied the continuous "standby" price and wage controls which had been sponsored by the President since the special session of November 1947. Title III set up a system of "voluntary" priority and allocation plans, with provision for making them mandatory upon a finding of necessity by the President. But it was Title II of the Spence bill which departed most from traditional concepts of the role of government and which aroused a veritable storm of opposition.

This title provided that, upon a finding by the President that a shortage of given materials or facilities "is affecting adversely or threatens to affect adversely the domestic economy (including the maintenance of maximum production and employment), free competitive enterprise and particularly small business, the general welfare, the national security, or the carrying out of the foreign policy of the United States . . . he shall

(1) determine approximately the quantity goals to which it is necessary and feasible to increase the supply within a specified reasonable period of time;

(2) explore fully the extent to which these goals can be attained through the efforts of private enterprise, and toward this end promote consultation between Government and industry, labor and agriculture;

(3) develop and administer within the limits of existing statutory authorization, including the authorization contained in this Act, such Federal programs at home and abroad as may be needed to supplement the efforts of private enterprise in achieving the quantity goals for such materials and facilities.

To this end, the Government might purchase at home or abroad essential materials "either for Government use or for resale in the United States (particularly to small or independent enterprises)"— at a loss if deemed necessary to meet the quantity goals.[5]

Besides these procurement activities, the President was authorized to stimulate production by making loans "to private business (particularly small or independent enterprises) or to State governments or subdivisions or instrumentalities thereof, for the expansion of capacity and production." Finally the bill authorized outright construction of additional industrial capacity. Section 205 (b) provided:

Whenever the President determines that it is necessary in order to help achieve the quantity goals established under section 201 (b) for designated essential materials or facilities, he may, by or under contract with private enterprise, construct new plant facilities, or expand or rehabilitate existing plant facilities, including Government-built war plants, for the expansion of capacity and production. Such contracts may be made without regard to the limitations of existing law, and on such terms and conditions as the President deems necessary, except that such construction, expansion, and rehabilitation of plant facilities shall not be undertaken if the President finds that private enterprise is willing to undertake such construction, expansion, and rehabilitation with the assistance of Government loans on terms and conditions deemed by him to be reasonable. The President may enter into contracts with any responsible person or persons for the private operation of plants constructed, expanded, or rehabilitated under this section. For the purposes of this section, the President is authorized to acquire real property and any right, title, or interest therein by purchase, lease, or otherwise, as he deems necessary in carrying out the purposes of this section; and assume the obligation to pay rentals in advance on real property.

The titles of the act dealing with price and wage control and with priorities and allocations were to terminate on June 30, 1951,

[5] Materials bought in the United States could be sold only to producers who would use them on defense orders.

but Title II had no termination date except that any corporation created under it "shall not have succession beyond June 30, 1954 except for purposes of liquidation unless its life is extended beyond such date pursuant to act of Congress."

Administration of this act was left to the discretion of the President, using whatever agencies of the Federal government he saw fit. He might appoint an assistant to aid him "in the co-ordination of activities of departments, agencies, and officials of the government under this act." It might be inferred that such a functionary would greatly circumscribe, if he did not actually supersede, the Council of Economic Advisers. It is notable that the President was called upon to make a quarterly report to Congress of the operations under this act, and that "all such reports shall be referred to the Joint Committee on the Economic Report, which shall study such reports and from time to time transmit to the Senate and the House of Representatives the results of its studies."

Even before the Spence bill was introduced in the House, Senator Murray introduced a bill of somewhat similar character, known as the Economic Expansion Act of 1949 (S. 281). The bill underwent extensive reconsideration by its framers, with amendments registered in a succession of committee prints up to the number of eleven. Though given slight attention at first, it began by May to attract some public support. Americans for Democratic Action held a meeting in New York at which Mr. Keyserling was scheduled to appear as an exponent of the bill. On the morning of the meeting, Mr. Truman sent word to him that such an appearance "would be regarded as an unfriendly act," and the appointment was canceled. In June, Senator Murray, with five colleagues from the Senate and House had an appointment with the President in which they urged him to take this over as an Administration measure. The President cordially assured them that "they were his kind of folks" but was definite in withholding his name from support of the bill.

In presenting the final amended version as a substitute measure on July 15, Senator Murray said:

> The bill is designed by the sponsors to carry out the recommendations in President Truman's economic program. While the bill is not being introduced at the request of the Administration, and while its sponsors take full responsibility for it, we feel that a careful study of the bill will reveal the

point-by-point similarity in form and substance to the analysis and recommendations contained in the President's midyear Economic Report.

The programs contained in the five main titles of the bill deal with the five main problems that the President identified in his Economic Report. They deal with these problems along the general lines that the President has recommended. Being legislation, the bill is more specific and detailed than the President's message, and in a few points the proposals in the bill reflect the decision of the sponsors to carry the program a little further than the President has specifically recommended. This was necessary to meet all the problems involved. There are, however, no inconsistencies between the bill and the President's program, and the bill is as close to the President's program as it could be while retaining the independence of action of the President in presenting the problem to be considered.

Senator Murray went on to explain that the bill

has deliberately omitted certain measures which, whether rightly or wrongly, some groups have come to regard with concern. For example, it makes no provision for controls or for construction of plants by the Government. It follows the logic of the President's Economic Report, in relying primarily upon the stimulation and encouragement of voluntary investment by private business and voluntary price and wage adjustments. The supplementary Government programs which it proposes, such as advance planning of resource development and public works and the improvement of social security, are in accord with the best business thinking of how to prepare ourselves against the possibility of a further economic downturn.

Earlier drafts of the Economic Expansion Act of 1949 centered the national planning function in a National Economic Co-operation Board which would "include representatives of industry, labor, agriculture, and consumers and, in so far as feasible, State and local governments and regional developmental organizations." This board was to "meet to advise and consult with the President from time to time at his request [and] meet regularly to advise and consult with the Council of Economic Advisers . . . and representatives of other departments and agencies of the Government may be invited from time to time to attend such meetings. The board shall be consulted by the Council of Economic Advisers during the course of the Council's assistance to the President in the preparation of his Economic Reports to the Congress." In the final draft, this National Economic Co-operation Board became merely an "economic co-operation committee," one among the several advisory committees that the Council had already established.

This bill undertook to implement the national policy of maximum employment, production, and purchasing power by various forms of incentives and assistance to private enterprise, including accelerated amortization, guaranteed loans, measures to combat monopoly, and to provide for a large-scale expansion in foreign investments. The bill provided for price, wage, and profits studies under conditions of maximum employment and production as guides for voluntary adjustments of prices, wages, and profits. It proposed minimum standards for unemployment compensation and extended unemployed veterans benefits under the G. I. Bill of Rights. Title III sought economic expansion through sound budgetary policies with an orderly reduction of the national debt under conditions of maximum employment and production. Title IV sought economic expansion through public works activities and large-scale advance planning of local, state, and Federal projects. To deal with areas of serious unemployment, the bill provided government contracts or loans in such areas and for the retraining of workers and assistance in moving from one area to another. Financial operations up to 15 billion dollars were authorized, no more than 4 billion dollars of which would be appropriations and not more than 11 billion dollars would consist of public debt transactions.

In seeking public support for this measure, Senator Murray addressed a meeting of Americans for Democratic Action in Washington on July 19, following a discussion of the current economic situation by Mr. Keyserling. After these two presentations, there was general discussion under the chairmanship of Governor Chester Bowles. This bill, however, like the Spence bill, died on the calendar when the Congress adjourned.

RELATIONS WITH THE SECURITY RESOURCES BOARD AND THE NATIONAL
SECURITY COUNCIL

One development that began in late 1948 and continued in '49 seemed to me to have great potential usefulness toward enabling the Council of Economic Advisers to make a significant contribution to the economic basis of national policy-making. This concerned the activities of the National Security Resources Board and the National Security Council. Through them it involved our relations with the Department of Defense insofar as the military program is a major determinant of the national budget.

Under the National Security Act of 1947 there was established in the Executive Office of the President a National Security Council whose membership consisted of the President, the Secretaries of State, Defense, the, Army, the Navy, and the Air Force, and the chairman of the National Security Resources Board. Upon designation by the President, it may include also the secretaries of the executive departments, the chairman of the Munitions Board, and the chairman of the Research and Development Board.

Since national security in any fundamental sense involves also the functioning of the economy under strain of war or preparedness and its ability to bear a given financial strain, it would seem that the deliberations of the National Security Council should include advice from the Bureau of the Budget and the Council of Economic Advisers even if the heads of these agencies were not included in the official make-up of the Security Council proper. The Director of the Budget was, by virtue of his review of the military component of the budget, drawn into active discussion of military policies. He, in turn, wished to base his judgments on adequate consideration of broad economic issues. Thus, for example, in the spring of 1949 when the issue of the size and timing of a stockpiling program was under consideration, he invited members of the Council and its staff to sit with him and his staff in attempting to formulate a recommendation for the forthcoming budget.

I suspect it was at the suggestion of the Director of the Budget, after discussing the matter with the President, that Admiral Souers, Executive Secretary of the National Security Council, invited the chairman of the Council of Economic Advisers to participate in staff meetings of the National Security Council during the spring and summer of 1949. This promised to be the beginning of a very useful kind of relationship for the Council. It was accompanied by a rather striking gesture on the part of the President toward integrating economic analysis from the Council into the setting of a ceiling on defense appropriations at the time when budget total and subtotals were being decided upon.

On July 1, 1949, the President called a meeting in the Cabinet Room, attended by the Secretary and Undersecretary of Defense, Secretaries of the Army, Navy, and Air Force, the Secretary of State,

the Chiefs of Staff, the Executive Secretary of the National Security
Council, the Director and Assistant Director of the Budget, and the
chairman of the Council of Economic Advisers. The purpose of this
meeting was to apprise the military people that the President intended to limit the defense budget to $13 billion in a total budget of
$41.8 billion. (The preliminary defense budget estimates had been
$30 billion and the Department was currently insisting on $23
billion.)

In opening the meeting, the President passed across the table to me
the following letter, which he read to the group:

My dear Mr. Chairman:

I have today sent the attached document to the National Security Council requesting their advice on a number of important matters affecting our
national security. The response of the Council will be of assistance to me
in firming up the program of this Government to be reflected in the 1951
Budget.

The budget policy on which my ceiling determinations for 1951 are
based is that of (a) holding governmental expenditures as closely as possible to present levels and, in particular, (b) preventing the prospective
large rise in the military area by adjustments in present plans. Even under
this stringent policy the outlook is for sizeable deficits, at least in the next
two years, under present tax rates.

I recognize that proper budget policies cannot be determined without
recognition of the requirements for maintaining a healthy and secure
economy. Therefore, I feel that it is necessary to re-evaluate the character
and size of our major governmental programs before making final decisions
with respect to the 1951 Budget.

The same financial problems which prompt the memorandum to the
National Security Council thus bear a direct relation to the responsibilities
of the Council of Economic Advisers to advise me concerning the effect of
our fiscal policies upon the maintenance of high employment and a sound
domestic economy. I am requesting you to furnish me by September 1
your advice on the following matters:

1. The probable effect upon our economy of the governmental programs contemplated under the tentative ceiling determinations, and of the
general budget policy on which they are based, which will be furnished you
by the Director of the Bureau of the Budget.

2. The relative effect upon our economy of a substantial deficit which
may continue for a period of years, as contrasted with (a) a lower level of
governmental activity during the years immediately ahead, or (b) higher
tax rates.

3. The economic consequences of the proposed resource diversion to military and foreign aid programs. In this connection I should specifically like to obtain your advice with respect to the relative economic impact of moderate changes upward or downward in the level of military and foreign aid programs from that proposed in the ceiling determination programs.

/s./ Harry S. Truman

The Council at once prepared to make the analysis requested in the President's letter. In doing this, we encountered considerable difficulties, but they are so much involved with the step of my final withdrawal from the Council that this discussion is deferred to Chapter XIV. (See p. 279.)

In discussing our relations with the National Security Council, casual reference has been made to the National Security Resources Board. This agency was established under the National Security Act of 1947 "to advise the President concerning the co-ordination of military, industrial, and civilian mobilization" and to recommend policies for unifying the activities of Federal agencies and departments in time of war, securing maximum utilization of the nation's manpower and natural and industrial resources, establishing adequate reserves of strategic and critical materials and promoting the strategic location of industrial and governmental agencies so as to insure continuous operation in the event of war. This board went into actual operation in the early part of 1948 and, with an appropriation of 3 million dollars, rapidly burgeoned into a staff development approaching and promising to exceed that of the Bureau of the Budget.

The first task of the National Security Resources Board was to prepare a plan for industrial and civilian mobilization which would define the board's role as well as analyze the nature of the mobilization problem. A number of conferences were held by the chairman of the National Security Resources Board (Mr. Arthur Hill, formerly chairman of the Greyhound Corporation), the Director of the Budget, several persons who had served on World War II defense agencies, and the chairman of the Council of Economic Advisers. There was a marked desire on the part of the Security Resources Board to outline a scheme of mobilization in which the board itself would become the operating agency in the event of war. To others in the Executive Office, it seemed that this was not the intent of the law, nor did it embody a correct concept of the Executive Office. The

President likewise held the view that the National Security Resources Board should be an advisory agency, studying problems and progressively perfecting plans for wartime mobilization, including an outline of structure and functions for the kind of operating agency which should be promptly established as an emergency body in the event of war.

Since the first chairman of the board could not accept this view, he resigned; the President's nomination of a successor met senatorial opposition; and the board lapsed into a state of suspended animation under the nominal direction of the President's assistant, John Steelman. There did seem, however, to be a potentially admirable complementary relationship between the Defense Department and Munitions Board, the National Security Resources Board, the Council of Economic Advisers, and the Bureau of the Budget. The staff of the National Security Resources Board would embrace a corps of technicians who would develop and keep up to date a detailed picture of our natural resources, industrial capacities and manpower which would constitute one of the most important factual resources for the successive analyses prepared by the Council of Economic Advisers for any periodic or special economic report of the President. The Board would advise the President as to the peculiar strains or difficulties involved in partial or complete mobilization, whereas the Council would advise him as to the policies and programs for promoting the welfare of the economy under conditions of peace or the nearest approach thereto that we might be vouchsafed.

CHAPTER THIRTEEN

The Joint Committee—
Second Phase

In the national election of November 1948, both houses of Congress swung back from a Republican to a Democratic majority. The way was thus open for Senator O'Mahoney to regain chairmanship of the Joint Committee on the Economic Report. Representative Edward J. Hart of New Jersey became vice-chairman.

There had been, before this time, some discussion of the desirability or propriety of having the chairmanship of the committee alternate between Senate and House, thus avoiding a sense of Senate domination which is somewhat prone to develop in joint committee relationships. When it came to actual organization of the committee, however, the intense interest of Senator O'Mahoney in its work, and the fact that Mr. Hart's health was not such that he could easily add the leadership of this committee to his other duties resulted in the chairmanship remaining in Senate hands. Hart was shortly succeeded by Representative Jesse Wolcott as vice-chairman.

As to membership, Senator Ball of Minnesota had been defeated, and his place was taken by Senator Paul H. Douglas, the newly elected Democrat from Illinois. Douglas had for years been a professor of economics at the University of Chicago and other institutions and was a past president of the American Economic Association. On the House side, Representative Bender of Ohio was replaced by Frank Buchanan of Pennsylvania.

STAFF AND PROGRAM CHANGES

Dr. Charles O. Hardy, who had been made staff director early in 1947, had died in November 1948. Professor Theodore J. Kreps of the faculty of Stanford University, who had been economic adviser to the TNEC and was now a member of the staff of the Legislative Reference Service of the Library of Congress,[1] was designated "economic consultant" to the committee. He, however, divided his time between the work of the Joint Committee and teaching at Stanford, and Frederick Berquist, who had been assistant staff director under Hardy, was listed as acting staff director. In August, Dr. Kreps was designated staff director and Berquist was thereafter designated "minority economist."[2] Dr. Grover Ensley, who had been economic assistant in Senator Flander's office had become associate staff director on June 15. The committee's clerk and one other economist completed the regular staff. All four members of the secretarial and clerical staff which had been recruited by Dr. Hardy were retained and are still with the Joint Committee.

As soon as the new committee organization had been completed (or before), Chairman O'Mahoney began organizing the work of the committee. No formal program was drawn up, discussed, and approved by the committee. But it soon became evident that Senator

[1] That Dr. Kreps had from an even earlier date participated actively in the work of the Joint Committee is indicated by a list of studies of the Advanced Research Section of the Legislative Reference Service in the Library of Congress for the fiscal year ending June 30, 1948 (p. 143). Credited to him were: Report on Affirmative Measures to be Handled by this Session of Congress bearing on Major Recommendations made by the President in his Economic Report to the Congress on January 13, 1948 (Jan. 16, 1948, 9 pp.); Analysis of Pending Legislation on Recommendations Listed in the President's Economic Report for 1948 (Mar. 11, 1948, 13 pp.) ; Minority Report for the Joint Committee on the Economic Report Appraising the Major Recommendations made by the President in the Economic Report (Mar. 13, 1948, 38 pp.).

[2] When Senator Taft took over the chairmanship of the Joint Committee in January 1947, he suggested that they have a professional staff of two full-time men, one to be designated by the majority members of the Joint Committee, the other by the minority. In early March, Senator O'Mahoney made a recommendation that Mr. Berquist, who had worked with him while he was chairman of the TNEC, be given a staff appointment. At the end of the month, Chairman Taft, in formally announcing the appointments of Hardy and Berquist, stated that neither was to be regarded as representative of either majority or minority members of the committee. By the time that Dr. Kreps was advanced from economic consultant to staff director of the committee, Berquist openly expressed his dissatisfaction with the trend of staff work and suggested that he himself be designated "minority economist." By this time also, Senator Taft seemed to entertain a somewhat different view of staff functioning than he had expressed at the beginning, and wrote a letter to Chairman O'Mahoney asking to have Mr. Berquist in the future report direct to him. The division within the staff organization, thus formalized, has continued down to the present.

O'Mahoney's administration of its work would be strongly influenced by his experience in the Temporary National Economic Committee, which had conducted a broad study of the functioning of the national economy from 1938 to 1941. O'Mahoney had been chairman of that investigating committee and, apparently, conceived the Joint Committee set-up under the Employment Act as a permanent national economic committee, taking up about where the TNEC left off.

That committee had been notable for the extent to which administrative officers, technical experts, and representatives of all major public interests had been organized into a working team.[3] The TNEC held extensive public hearings and published a series of forty-three monographs, prepared by members of its own staff and by the staffs of participating agencies on the basis of hearings and of studies made by statisticians and economists in or outside of government service. Although the resolution under which it was set up (Public Res. No. 113, 75 Cong.) described the purpose of this *ad hoc* committee as an "investigation of the concentration of economic power," the phrase was interpreted broadly by the committee. Its studies were directed toward specific analysis of various segments of the economy and of various functional problems but also attempted to synthesize these topical studies into a somewhat comprehensive explanation of how the economy as a whole operated and the places at which changes in structure or practice were needed.[4]

The work of the Joint Committee as it has developed during the last four years can conveniently be considered from two general approaches. The first is featured by the review of the Economic Report of the President, conducted during January and February

[3] The membership of the TNEC consisted of three senators, three representatives, and six administrative officers—members of the "little Cabinet" or commissioners from independent executive agencies. Each of the latter had an alternate designated from the top staff of his agency. An Economic Co-ordinator, an Executive Secretary, and an Economic Adviser completed the set-up.

[4] "Dr. Dewey Anderson, Executive Secretary of the TNEC, in his final report of March 31, 1941, declared that the monographs (together with the TNEC reports and hearings) 'constitute the basis for a modern education in economics, the formulation of a philosophy for economic and political behavior.' " The National Association of Manufacturers was so much disturbed at the prospect that the general public might accept this evaluation of the material that it had a critique prepared by John Scoville, chief statistician of the Chrysler Corporation and Noel Sargent, Secretary of the NAM. It was published as an 800-page book under the title *Fact and Fancy in the T.N.E.C. Monographs*. The quotation at the beginning of this footnote is taken from p. v of the foreword to that volume.

each year and resulting in the formal report by the Joint Committee to Congress, as the broad outline of a legislative program for the session—either reinforcing or revising the program to effectuate the purposes of the Employment Act suggested by the President in his Economic Report.

The second line of approach followed in the work of the Joint Committee consists in a series of studies of problems, either of continuing importance or of current acuteness, conducted by various subcommittees using their own staff resources and those of the Legislative Reference Service of the Library of Congress under the direction of subcommittees set up for the purpose. For the work of these subcommittees, various members of the Joint Committee have themselves considerable technical competence as well as practical experience and several of them have devoted an amazing amount of time to these studies and the preparation of reports and recommendations growing out of them.

Besides its committee reports, staff studies, and hearings, the Joint Committee continues to publish the monthly pamphlet *Economic Indicators* whose origin was discussed in Chapter X. By joint resolution on June 23, 1949 (S.J.Res. 55, 81 Cong. 1 sess.), the committee is authorized to continue as a regular monthly publication what had, for the preceding year, appeared as a committee print. The resolution provided

that a sufficient quantity be printed to furnish one copy to each member of Congress; the Secretary and the Sergeant at Arms of the Senate; the Clerk, Sergeant at Arms, and Doorkeeper of the House of Representatives; two copies to the libraries of the Senate and House, and the Congressional Library, seven hundred copies to the Joint Committee on the Economic Report; and the required number of copies to the Superintendent of Documents for distribution to depository libraries; and that the Superintendent of Documents be authorized to have copies printed for sale to the public.

There is now a complimentary distribution of more than 1200 copies of *Economic Indicators* and a subscription list of more than 3,000.

COMMITTEE REVIEW OF THE PRESIDENT'S ECONOMIC REPORT

Early in January 1949, a formal schedule of public hearings was arranged to examine the major topics covered in the Economic Report of the President submitted to Congress on January 7 and referred to the Joint Committee for review and report. These hearings occupied nine days—from February 8 to February 18—and included statements by thirteen Cabinet officers and executive agency heads (or their deputies) and by Mr. Keyserling and Mr. Clark of the Council of Economic Advisers. Their testimony was followed by two round-table discussions. The first of these was participated in by fifteen "economic and fiscal experts" and the second by ten agricultural, business, and labor representatives, with supplementary statements by two others. The printed hearings covered 684 pages.[5]

On March 1, the Joint Committee filed its report on the Economic Report of the President in a document of ninety-one printed pages (including statistical appendix and excerpts from the committee hearings). The report proper began with consideration of the economic responsibility of government under three heads: (1) the problem of debt management; (2) the problem of economic preparedness; (3) the problem of protecting the victims of inflation. The report thereupon proceeded to discuss further "the problem of promoting balanced economic growth" through development of natural resources, promoting capital investment, housing and other grants-in-aid, and the improvement of human productivity. The closing section was entitled "Freeing the Economy from Restrictive Policies." This stressed the need of combating monopoly and of providing more adequate statistical information.

In general the report was a blanket endorsement of the policies recommended in the Economic Report of the President, although the committee's discussion was not so closely geared to specific points as the committee report of the previous year had been. This report was signed by seven "majority members approving the report," with a footnote statement that Representative Huber (the other Democratic member) did not vote on the adoption of the report.

Republican Senator Flanders and Representative Herter appended a one-page statement of "Objections to Majority Report of the Joint Committee on the Economic Report," saying: "Aside from questions of tone and viewpoint which are to be expected, we find much in the report with which we can agree and a few important points on which we must register dissent." They found that "the insistence on the danger of inflation and the assumption that we are having or may

[5] *January 1949 Economic Report of the President,* Hearings before the Joint Committee on the Economic Report, 81 Cong. 1 sess., Feb. 8–18, 1949.

have both inflation and deflation simultaneously seems a bit in-
genuous . . . [perhaps] a rationalization of the desire to have the
powers of allocation and price control granted the administration
even though they may not be necessary at the moment or at any
immediate time in the future." These members of the committee
could not take the view that the granting of these powers of control
is "routine and unimportant." They recommended voluntary rather
than administrative allocation of scarce materials and expenditure
reduction rather than tax increases alone as a means of balancing
the budget.

On April 28, Senator Taft submitted from the committee to the
Congress a twenty-two-page statement of "Minority Views," which
opened as follows:

> We reject the basic philosophy of the President's Economic Report
> which, in effect, recommends that we set up in this country a planned and
> controlled economy and increase taxation for that purpose. The Presi-
> dent's report ignores the broad powers already existing in the hands of the
> President, particularly in the control of credit and the determination of
> fiscal policy, and carries on a crusade for more executive power, which we
> consider unjustified and dangerous. The report of the majority of this
> committee accepts without criticism or reservation the philosophy of the
> President's report and his legislative proposals. We feel that under the
> Employment Act of 1946, our committee should have subjected the Presi-
> dent's report to a detailed and discriminating criticism.

The minority suggested that "The President's Economic Reports
threaten to become political propaganda rather than a scientific
analysis . . . without recognizing the possibility of sincere differences
of opinion." They proposed that the Joint Committee's report should
be "confined to economic discussions without entering into controversial political fields . . . The principal attention of this
particular committee should be devoted primarily to solving the
problem of full and continuous employment and not be diverted too
much by social and political issues."

The report ended with eight specific recommendations:

1. The reduction of Government expenditures to avoid increase
in taxation.

2. Continued control of general banking and credit policies
through the Federal Reserve Board.

3. The public-works program to be varied in relationship to the general economic situation.

4. No further selective controls but specific action by Congress if need arises.

5. Additional antimonopoly measures if a careful study shows them to be necessary.

6. A support program for farm prices on a sliding-scale basis.

7. Active interest by the Government in the development of housing.

8. A comprehensive study by this committee of the subject of foreign trade.

This minority report was signed by all six Republican members, but Senator Flanders appended the statement:

> In general this minority report and the earlier one by Congressman Herter and myself will be found to be in agreement. I am therefore glad to add my signature. In so doing I would make clear, however, that I do not desire to be put in the position of having prejudged the results of the investigation of investment practices which is to be undertaken shortly by the joint committee.

Four appendixes constituted the staff's contribution to the committee's report. Appendix A presented two tables supplementary to those contained in the Economic Report of the President. Appendix B consisted of a list of witnesses at the committee's hearings on the President's Economic Report and of participants in the round-table discussions and excerpts from the statements of both groups. Appendix C summarized the work of the Joint Committee during 1948, and Appendix D was a staff statement on statistical gaps supplementary to the report on that topic which had been published by the Joint Committee during 1948. The co-operative character of this project was indicated by its opening statement:

> At the initiative of the members of the staff of the Joint Committee on the Economic Report, staff of the Division of Statistical Standards of the Bureau of the Budget and staff of the Council of Economic Advisers prepared the following statement as a supplement to the statistical programs outlined in the joint committee's report on current gaps. This statement shows rather concisely the present work being done and the plans for the immediate future.

In January 1950, the Joint Committee's report on *The Economic Report of the President* followed much the same lines as that of January 1949. Two days had been devoted to public hearings, at which various government representatives had presented statements and been interrogated. Two additional days had been devoted to round-table discussions, first with a panel of economic and fiscal experts and then with a panel representing agricultural, business, consumer, and labor organizations. This material was extensively used by both staff and committee members in the preparation of the committee's report, but excerpts were not included in the document as had been done the previous year.

On the other hand, more prominence was given to "Supplementary Staff Materials," which constituted Part III of the Joint Committee Report and had attached to it an appendix which included technical memoranda by the Council of Economic Advisers, the Machinery and Allied Products Institute, and the Bureau of Labor Statistics, several statistical tables, a memorandum on major federal loan programs, and recommendations from four subcommittees of the Joint Committee which had made studies during the preceding year. There was also a series of legislative recommendations which had been made by business, farm, and labor organizations. The report closed with a summary of the Joint Committee's work during the previous year and a list of its publications.

The text of the Joint Committee report of January 1950 began with a general discussion of the current economic situation and policy for dealing with it. The picture was drawn on a big canvas with broad brush strokes:

Wisdom and integrity in the policies of government, and responsibility and courage in the conduct of industry are the fundamental requirements. To sustain an increasing level of production, employment, and income to meet the needs of a growing population, and to enable this country to provide the broad economic base for a leading position in the world economy—these are the primary responsibility of industry under free competitive enterprise. To guide so that maximum benefits may be obtained for the Nation as a whole is the task of government. . . . The fiscal and other economic policies of the Government must be designed to promote growth. Government must deal with trouble spots in the economy."

"The fundamental problem" was to make sure that there be an adequate market "for the products of field and factory in the years following 1950 to supplement the market created by the extraordinary Federal outlay for war and the extraordinary private outlay to satisfy the accumulated demand for civilian goods." In a section headed "The Basic Solution: Private Capital Investment" the committee said:

The guiding principle throughout is simple. The field of private capital investment should be encouraged, fostered, and promoted to the maximum extent for those projects which it can adequately serve. The Joint Economic Subcommittee on Investment made several highly useful recommendations for the establishment by Government of mechanisms through which private capital might more easily be channelled and made more productive in aid of independent, competitive, private, local enterprise.

As to the government aspects of the problem,

A critical examination of the present level of government expenditures is imperative. In years of such booming business as currently is causing prices to boil up in inflationary manner throughout the economy, this Government should not be incurring deficits. It should put its financial house in order. Inability to vote against appropriations or vote for increased taxes needed to foot the bills this Government now incurs, is a sign of weakness that enemies of free enterprise are gleefully exploiting throughout the world. It presents the greatest single danger to freedom and national security. . . . Having fixed what the government has to do, we must decide whether we are willing to pay for it, and how. If the cost seems excessive, we must be prepared to abandon those objects of Government expenditure for which we are unwilling to impose taxes upon ourselves sufficient to foot the bill. There are many programs that obviously cannot be abandoned. National defense comes first. . . . to finance essential national defense and international peace programs, we cannot afford to abandon those government expenditures which promote and sustain a sound and expanding economy. It would be short-sighted to cancel the Government's policy, for example, of sustaining a developing aviation industry, just because thereby some measure of curtailment might be effected in Government outlays. It might help to balance the budget so far as Government expenditures are concerned, but on the revenue side it would make such a balance more difficult to attain because it would cut down the amounts the Government receives from all the business, industrial, and commercial activities that revolve about the aviation industry.

Recommendations which expand and sustain the domestic economy obviously likewise broaden the tax base. By promoting industrial and commercial activity, they encourage the increased formation of real purchasing power without which neither business nor Government can succeed.

Pages 15–17 of the report were devoted to "Comments on the President's Legislative Recommendations." The committee's comment on the President's legislative recommendations covered twelve points: revision of the tax structure, middle income housing, maximum maturity for RFC loans, farm income production, Columbia Valley Administration, Federal aid for education, expansion of social security, extension of rent control, the foreign recovery program, ratification of the charter for an International Trade Organization, technical assistance for underdeveloped areas, and the scope of Federal Reserve authority. While this section contained no explicit criticism of the President's recommendations, endorsement was also qualified or ambiguous. Typical is the following:

> Federal aid for education, Federal co-operation to improve local health services, and Federal grants to the States for surveys of needed school construction are all designed to increase human productivity, improve human resources, and thereby promote business expansion. The spurt in our population since the war will increase the number of children in elementary schools by over 30 per cent during the next five years. In many States the provision of additional facilities ought no longer to be delayed. In other areas the need for a program of Federal aid can await the final decision of Congress with respect to revenue.

Senator Douglas, though signing this report with the other seven Democratic members of the committee appended a personal statement, putting greater stress on reduction in government expenditures and expressing regret that the report did not contain more forthright endorsement of "the principles of monetary and debt management policies recommended by the subcommittee on Monetary, Credit, and Fiscal Policies last January."

The majority report was followed by eleven pages stating the "Views of the Minority." As in the previous year, the minority objected to the wide scope and very general character of the majority report. After a six-point "appraisal of the philosophy of the President's report," the committee observed:

> . . . whether the growth envisioned in the goals of the report will or indeed can, develop under the recommendations of the President is subject to very serious doubt. In fact, such a program will eventually frustrate the

basic processes through which growth has been or can be achieved. It threatens to cripple the ability to carry out existing programs affecting general welfare, or probably even worse, achieve mere dollar goals through further inflationary effects upon the economy.

The President, on the opening page of his report, summarizes what a good job was done of adjusting the inflationary boom to "firmer ground" and that "by no accident," for which businessmen, workers, farmers, and Government should congratulate themselves for their "judgment and restraint" and "understanding." It is noteworthy that the transition from inflation to greater stability, however, does not appear to have resulted from recommendations of the 1949 President's report. Many of those regarded as essential by the President were not accepted or enacted into legislation by the Congress.

The minority expressed definite objection to reliance upon

detailed controls, a "planned" economy, and a detailed attack upon prices, bottlenecks, and "needs." . . . Opposed to this type of approach, we believe that the tremendous power which the Government holds over credit, monetary and fiscal policy offers the best method of preventing depression and instability. We believe that they are infinitely preferable to plans for controlling details and closely regulating individuals in their economic choices. . . . We are urged to spend money and create greater and continuing deficits for new projects, extended social services, and more benefits during a time of high national production to generate greater income to wipe out the deficits created through the programs. . . . With this bootstrap argumentation of the President's report the minority strongly dissents.

All six Republican members of the Joint Committee subscribed to these "Views of the Minority."

SUBCOMMITTEES AND SPECIAL STUDIES

As soon as the Joint Committee had completed its review of the Economic Report of the President, it held an executive meeting (February 28, 1949) to lay out a program of work in discharge of the responsibility laid upon this committee in the Employment Act "to make a continuing study of matters relating to the Economic Report." Following this meeting and after further deliberation on which topics were most in need of study by the committee, Chairman O'Mahoney introduced in the Senate (March 26) a concurrent resolution providing for a series of four special investigations. Each was to be in charge of a subcommittee, and a supplemental appropriation of $30,000 was made. The problems were described in the resolution as follows:

1. The problem of investment, including but not limited to: the role of investment institutions in the investment marks in industry and in the economy generally; changes in sources of investment funds and the reason therefor; availability and character of investment funds for national, local, and independent enterprise and the effect of such investment or lack of investment on different classes or size groups in industry; and needs, by industry, for various types of capital.

2. The problem of the effectiveness and co-ordination of monetary, credit, and fiscal policies dealing with general economic policy.

3. The problem of low-income families in relation to economic instability.

4. The problem of unemployment trends and their significance in current economic analysis.

This resolution was agreed to on May 24 and, during the following month, the subcommittees were set up as follows:

Investment Subcommittee (Senator Joseph C. O'Mahoney, Chairman)

Monetary, Credit, and Fiscal Policies Subcommittee (Senator Paul H. Douglas, Chairman)

Low-Income Families Subcommittee (Senator John Sparkman, Chairman)

Unemployment Subcommittee (Representative Edward J. Hart, Chairman)

Public hearings were held by the Investment Subcommittee on September 27–29, participated in by representatives of small business, large business, and the Brookings Institution. Meanwhile, the committee staff had done research work on this problem. On October 11, materials prepared by it were issued as a committee print under the title "Factors Affecting Volume and Stability of Private Investment." Further hearings by this subcommittee began on December 6 with a round-table conference whose members were drawn from the Small Business Advisory Committee of the Department of Commerce. On the three following days and all the following week, witnesses were heard from insurance companies and investment banking groups. Several representatives of labor unions and manufacturing industries also presented testimony. The final report of the

Investment Subcommittee was issued as a Senate Document on March 20, 1950.[6]

The Subcommittee on Monetary, Credit, and Fiscal Policies under the chairmanship of Senator Paul Douglas in opening its work (August 1949) did not turn first to the method of public hearings. Instead, it issued a rather elaborate questionnaire, copies of which were sent to economists and bankers and to agricultural, labor, and industrial organizations. This general questionnaire was supplemented by a series of specialized questionnaires dealing with particular phases of the problem and sent to those government agencies especially concerned with the respective issues. The committee also utilized the good offices of the National Planning Association to assemble a conference of fourteen prominent university economists to try to arrive at a "consensus" statement on principles of fiscal policy. This conference resulted in unanimous agreement within the group as to the principles of Federal expenditure and revenue policy which would promote economic stability and as to a fiscal policy for the future based on these principles. On September 23, this subcommittee conducted a hearing in which they discussed these reports with three representatives of the university group. Testimony presented at all the hearings of the subcommittee and replies to its several questionnaires were issued on November 7 as a Joint Committee print, and two weeks of final hearings were held during late November and early December, with representatives not only from banking and business but also from farm and labor groups. A final report was submitted to the full committee early in January 1950.[7]

The Subcommittee on Low Income Families began its work at the staff level. Two studies prepared in co-operation with various government agencies were released as committee prints in November 1949. The first was entitled "Low-Income Families and Economic Stability" and the second "Selected Government Programs which Aid the Unemployed and Low-Income Families." The latter study was done in collaboration with the Unemployment Subcommittee. Hearings for the low-income subcommittee were conducted during December 1949, and expert testimony was heard from representatives of various government agencies and from private organizations,

---

[6] *Volume and Stability of Private Investment* (Final Report of the Subcommittee on Investment) S. Doc. No. 149, 81 Cong. 2 sess.

[7] *Monetary, Credit, and Fiscal Policies* (Report of the Subcommittee on Monetary, Credit, and Fiscal Policies) S. Doc. No. 129, 81 Cong. 2 sess.

including college and other research groups. The subcommittee's final report was transmitted to the full committee in February 1950.[8]

The Subcommittee on Unemployment began its work early because of the sense of emergency that surrounded this problem. Since employment conditions improved rapidly during the fall, no public hearings were held, but an initial report on employment and unemployment was issued as a committee print on July 11, 1949 and a final report on February 3, 1950. This included considerable staff material on employment conditions in five problem industries, employment trends between 1929 and 1949, and a methodological discussion of the problem of measuring the labor force and unemployment and what would be regarded as a critical ratio of employment to concepts of "maximum employment" pertinent to the Employment Act of 1946. The final report also included staff summaries of replies received to a questionnaire sent to the Department of Labor, the Department of Commerce, and leading labor unions, and statements prepared by other government agencies.

Interest was taken by the Joint Committee also in a study on "The Impact of Federal Policies on the Economy of the South," conducted under the auspices of the National Planning Association's Committee of the South and supported in part by funds from the Council of Economic Advisers. The report thus developed through the collaboration of private agencies and public agencies—Federal, state, and local—was published as a committee print by the Joint Committee in July 1949.

While the Joint Economic Committee did not act upon the report, and hence could not assume responsibility for the ideas expressed by the authors, they did recognize it as a significant work, representing a systematic effort to define, analyze and appraise the complexity of Federal policies which handicap or facilitate the economic development of the South. Members of the committee have explored with leading citizens of New England and the Rocky Mountain States the desirability of developing similar studies in those regions. On December 12, 1949, the National Planning Association announced that in response to the Joint Economic Committee's interest a special committee of New England was being organized and would start its work early in 1950.[9]

[8] *Low-Income Families and Economic Stability*, S. Doc. 146, 81 Cong. 2 sess.

[9] *Report of the Joint Committee on the Economic Report*, Senate Report 1843, 81 Cong. 2 sess., p. 111.

This interest in promoting regional studies was also furthered by publication of a "Handbook of Regional Statistics" as a committee print.[10]

The Joint Committee continued its interest in the problem of improving government statistics needed in carrying out the purpose of the Employment Act, and incorporated a statement of progress in their report of January 1950.

RELATIONS WITH OTHER COMMITTEES AND WITH EXECUTIVE DEPARTMENTS

The foregoing discussion of the developing work of the Joint Committee has made numerous references to their collaboration with other agencies of the government. The committee commented explicitly on this development in its annual report of March 1, 1950. Noting that the law under which it was established authorized the Joint Committee to "utilize the services, information, and facilities of the departments and establishments of the Government" it added:

The necessity for this arrangement has been demonstrated many times over during the past year. Hardly a single report of the committee was issued without the aid of one or more of the executive agencies in the development of the basic economic facts. Special studies of mutual interest to the agency and the joint committee have been made at the committee's request and several agencies have made highly trained personnel available to the committee on a reimbursable loan basis to assist in the technical work on various economic problems.[11]

At this time also, the committee took occasion to comment quite pointedly on a change of relations with the Council of Economic Advisers:

[10] By this time the Joint Economic Committee had developed a practice of borrowing highly trained technical staff for its various subcommittee investigations. For example: Harris P. Dawson, Jr., an economist with the Bureau of Labor Statistics and formerly their regional director in Atlanta, was borrowed to assist the Unemployment Subcommittee; Lester V. Chandler, at that time Professor of Money and Banking at Amherst and now at Princeton, was the staff man for the Subcommittee on Monetary, Credit, and Fiscal Policies; and Samuel L. Brown, who was on the faculty at Georgetown University, worked with the Low-Income Families Subcommittee. Both Mr. Brown and Mr. Chandler spent the entire summer as full-time employees and worked through the fall months on a part-time basis as their academic schedules permitted.

[11] *Report of the Joint Committee on the January 1950 Economic Report of the President,* Senate Report 1843, 81 Cong. 2 sess., pp. 111–12.

The committee is glad to report the development of an increasingly constructive relationship between the Council of Economic Advisers and the Joint Committee. Full and free discussion of economic problems with those who have the statutory responsibility to advise the President on economic policy is essential to a complete understanding of the President's Economic Report by the committee and, therefore, to the committee's fulfillment of its responsibilities under the Employment Act.[12]

This reference to "the development of more constructive relations between the Council of Economic Advisers and the Joint Committee" requires a word of explanation.

I called at Senator O'Mahoney's office in the Senate Office Building some time about the middle of November and chatted with him in connection with the work of the Joint Committee, which presumably would fall under his chairmanship in the future. He immediately made some comment about how now we would get the Council and the Joint Committee together in active co-operation. To this I responded that of course we wanted to co-operate in every proper way, but that in my judgment they should not expect active participation in the legislative process and that I would not feel free to appear on the Hill to discuss the President's policies. At this he quickly changed the subject.[13] (*P. D.*, Jan. 11, 1949)

On January 26, an Associated Press news release, in announcing the election of Senator O'Mahoney as chairman of the Joint Economic Committee had said:

O'Mahoney tentatively scheduled hearings for Feb. 8 on Mr. Truman's eight-point program. He said the first witnesses will include Secretary of Agriculture Charles Brannan and the three-man presidential Economic Advisory Council, headed by Edwin G. Nourse. Brannan and Nourse will amplify Mr. Truman's program, O'Mahoney said. The Senator added that his committee faces an "extensive job" in preparing its report which must be submitted to Congress by March 1. Mr. Truman's eight-point program, which O'Mahoney termed the "core" of Administration efforts to curb high prices, includes standby authority to impose price ceilings and limit "unjustified" wage increases, strengthen federal rent controls, and last

---

[12] The same, p. 21. The committee staff made a somewhat more detailed statement of relations between committee and Council in their summary of the year's work on p. 112 of the report.

[13] Mr. Keyserling had testified on the President's anti-inflation program at hearings of the Senate Banking and Currency Committee on Aug. 4, 1948 (see pp. 221–22) and Mr. Clark at hearings of this same committee in January 1948 (on extension of RFC) and two months later before the House Committee on the Judiciary (on antitrust matters).

resort authority to construct plants for production of such scarce materials as steel.

On February 1, a press release from the offices of the Joint Committee outlined the strategy to be followed in presenting the President's economic program to the Congress: "Secretary Brannan, acting as co-ordinator in the presentation of the President's legislative program, will be the first witness, and will be accompanied by members of the Council of Economic Advisers." In the preceding year, the role of co-ordinator had been assigned to Secretary Harriman. When I demurred at appearing as a chief witness in support of the program (in which I had the backing of several Cabinet members), Harriman dropped the matter of Council participation. (See p. 208.) Brannan made no formal request to me to appear but mentioned to me casually when he ran into me at a dinner party that he assumed that I would not wish to appear and he would therefore ask Mr. Keyserling and Mr. Clark "to carry the ball."

As February 8, the date set for the opening of the hearings drew near, and I had heard nothing direct from the committee, I was naturally curious. On February 4, shortly after my departure on a trip to New York, a lengthy telegram from Chairman O'Mahoney was received at my office, inviting the Council to appear at the Joint Committee's hearings on the Economic Report of the President.

. . . Secretary of Agriculture Brannan as opening witness will outline and discuss in broad terms the President's legislative recommendations as contained in his Economic Report, followed by members of the Council of Economic Advisers, who are requested to develop and amplify those major analyses and findings in the Annual Economic Review of Current Economic Problems and prospective trends and developments which accompanied the President's Report and to which consideration should be directed by the committee in accordance with the terms and purposes and objectives of the Employment Act. . . . I am wiring you because time is pressing and the law requires the Committee to file its report on March 1.

On my return from New York, I at once wrote Chairman O'Mahoney, saying:

Your telegram of February 4, inviting the members of the Council to appear at hearings of the Joint Committee yesterday has only now reached me. I was out of town attending several meetings important to the work of the Council on Saturday, Monday, and yesterday. I understand that Mr. Keyserling and Mr. Clark freely and gladly accepted your invitation to appear before the Committee. If I had been here, I would have had, in good conscience, to ask that I be excused.

After restating my position on this matter in some detail,[14] I concluded:

I am confident that there will be active and useful developments in the work of the Joint Committee under your chairmanship. We desire to have our staff co-operate in every possible way with your staff. Committee members also may wish to discuss various economic issues with Council members in private. I shall be happy to participate in this way and believe that in time we may develop a practice which you and your Committee will find eminently satisfactory.

Copies of this letter were sent to all members of the Joint Committee. On February 17, Senator Flanders replied, saying: " . . . after sitting in at various sessions of the Joint Committee I concluded that the position you have taken is the only one it is proper for you to take." (See his earlier position, p. 206.)

The President never mentioned this episode. Nor did I feel called upon to raise the issue since the Council's actions were in conformity with the latest instructions received from him.[15] (See p. 222.)

Mr. Keyserling prepared a 25,000-word brief in support of the President's economic program, supplemented by numerous large charts. He was interrupted before completion of his presentation, but it was highly praised by some attendants at the hearing. Mr.

[14] For full text of the letter, see App. C.

[15] Two months later, I was invited by Senator Pepper to have the Council testify on pending fair labor standards legislation. I thereupon wrote the President expressing "my hope that we may have a clear-cut statement from you that it is your wish that in future no member of the Council shall appear before a Congressional committee to discuss specific legislative proposals dealing with issues of economic policy. . . . I have a strong feeling that the participation [of Mr. Keyserling and Mr. Clark] in Congressional hearings a few weeks back was seriously harmful to the position and future usefulness of the Council, and I have heard this view expressed by many people, both privately and publicly. They, I think, both still very strongly hold the opposite view."

On April 8 (1949) the President wrote me: "Replying to yours of April sixth, it has been my policy to allow the Council of Economic Advisers to follow their own viewpoint with regard to appearances before Committees. If you do not desire to appear it is perfectly all right with me. If the other gentlemen feel that they should appear, I would not interfere with that procedure. Other members of the President's staff, however, do not appear before Congressional Committees."

Something new had been added in the closing sentence.

Clark was assigned by Secretary Brannan the task of "summarizing the views and recommendations of the Administration offered in the Economic Report of the President and in the statements in these hearings by Department Chiefs and by members of the Council of Economic Advisers." His presentation was relatively brief and was designed to show consensus of thinking in the executive branch.

Besides its reference to co-operation with the Council, the Joint Committee report of March 1, 1950, in its summary of the committee's work during the preceding year, made somewhat encouraging reference (p. 112) to relations of this new committee with the other committees of Congress: "The standing committees of the Congress have made use of committee reports and hearings in connection with the consideration of specific legislation and arrangements have been made to supply these committees with all materials of special interest to them." In a few cases, other committees had joined with the Joint Committee in hearings on a topic in which they were particularly interested.

With the expanding work of the Joint Committee, there was evident a need for funds larger than those authorized in the Employment Act as passed in 1946. Of course funds for studies needed in connection with the work of the committee could be and were at times secured through special resolutions, but on June 15, 1949, a bill was introduced (S. 2085) calling for increase of the Joint Committee's basic annual authorization from $50,000 to $150,000. This was later reduced by request of the chairman to $125,000 and was approved in this form on October 6, 1949.[16] In its favorable report on the bill, the Senate Committee on Banking and Currency referred to the "tremendous responsibility" vested in the Joint Committee and said that it "should be properly provided with research and statistical technicians to summarize and present the economic information to members of the joint committee and the Congress in the most useful and objective form."

[16] Public Law 330, 81 Cong. Ch. 627.

CHAPTER FOURTEEN

The Chairman Steps Aside

Mr. Truman's amazing victory at the polls on November 2, 1948 caused all members of the Council of Economic Advisers to take a new look at its probable future. During the campaign, there had been a widespread expectation that there would shortly be a new chief executive in the White House, and changes in the personnel and activities of the Council would surely have resulted. When Mr. Truman became the choice of the country for the next four years, our thinking naturally was given a substantially different turn. As for myself, I came rather promptly to the conclusion that the difficulties and burdens of further service would be quite disproportionate to any possibility of accomplishing helpful results.

TWO STEPS TOWARD RESIGNATION

On November 12, I drafted a letter to Mr. Truman at Key West suggesting that he might "want an entirely different kind of chairman" for the Council. Before this letter was put in final form to go to the President, I had received the call from Steelman transmitting the President's request that I set up an intra-Cabinet committee on stabilization policy. Since this looked like a promising development, with which I should co-operate to the fullest extent, I withheld the letter I had drafted. It read:

November 12, 1948

Dear Mr. President:

I know that you have been communing with yourself these days as to the enormous opportunity and the terrific responsibilities of national and world leadership that have been laid on your shoulders as the outcome of the recent election. I think you know that all of us who are agency heads in this great national establishment are giving our best thought to the question of how we can most fully serve you in our respective corners.

It is important not merely that every horse in this "big horse team" be strong and ready to throw himself into the collar, but also that there be a properly constructed harness so that his pull may be effectively added to that of others in moving the load forward. As chairman of the Council of Economic Advisers, I am especially desirous that this agency play its part toward the accomplishment of this desirable condition. I have labored hard in the past two and a half years to lay a solid foundation for the Council as a permanent feature of the Executive Office, to establish effective relations inside and outside of Government, and to get systematic studies under way on problems that emerge from the declaration of policy of the Employment Act of 1946. Upon this foundation it should be increasingly possible to bring the product of the best thinking of professional economists and of experienced business and labor leaders to your desk. All this preparation, however, will be relatively useless unless the Council has opportunity to be heard before final policies are determined and decisions for action made. Certain issues will have to be faced and appropriate adjustments made with reasonable promptness.

Your decision as to the role you wish the Council to play in future and the way in which it can most helpfully serve you will be interrelated with the question of its chairmanship. I have indicated clearly in the past that I am suited to my present position only if it is intended to make the Council a strictly professional agency and to give it a really effective position as a channel for "economics in the public service." If it is in any way to be assigned a political role or to be allowed to stray over into political activities or lay itself open to political influences, you would want an entirely different kind of chairman, and I would want to be relieved of the position at once because I feel that it would be impossible to accomplish results proportionate to the labor and strain involved.

I have talked some of these matters over with Dr. Steelman in the past, and he has shown a lively understanding of the difficulties and possibilities. He would give you wise counsel as to how they will eventually have to be met. I shall hope to talk to him at some length and to you yourself in so far as your crowded schedule permits.

I hope you are having a wonderful rest and building up a big stockpile of strength for the trials ahead.

Sincerely yours,

About a month after the above letter was drafted, a friend of mine who was well informed as to what was going on behind the scenes at the White House told me that persons somewhat unfriendly to me had been repeatedly telling the President that during the campaign I had been "trading with the enemy." Thereupon, I rewrote my letter of November 12 and sent it to the President on December 15 in the following form:

December 15, 1948

Dear Mr. President:

I have reason to believe that you have been told that for some weeks or months prior to November 2, I devoted a major part of my time and effort to "saving my skin" in the event that there were a change in Administration. This is absolutely untrue.

I have been deeply concerned that the Council of Economic Advisers should become established on a high professional plane, with its members not subject to the vicissitudes of politics but retained or replaced solely on the grounds of their qualifications as objective economists.

In the nature of the case, various people interested in the work of the Council asked me what would be my attitude in the event of a change of Administration. I always replied that I hoped replacements would be made solely with a view to strengthening the ability of the Council to serve the President as contemplated in the Employment Act, and that there should not be a merely political housecleaning. I said that if there were a new President, and he wished me to remain for a time in order to give a new chairman or members the benefit of our initial two and a half years' experience, or because he thought my competence and standing were as good as those of other persons who might be available, I should be glad to remain and serve to the best of my ability for a reasonable time. In view of my age and the hard work and tensions involved in the job, it was—and still is—my hope that I can be relieved at a not too distant date.

On only two occasions, to the best of my recollection, did I myself make any move to make my views known to persons who might be consulted as to how the Council of Economic Advisers should be dealt with in the event of a change of Administration.

In view of this and other considerations, I think it appropriate at this time to hand you my formal resignation. Of course, I am not backing away from any duties or responsibilities in connection with your forthcoming Economic Report or the co-ordination of anti-inflation policy among the several agency heads in the Executive Branch. However, I hope you will regard this resignation as being on your desk any morning after these immediate responsibilities have been fulfilled to the best of my ability and that you will pick it up and inform me of your acceptance on the first day when you feel that the service of this agency to you would be bettered by such a change in personnel.

Sincerely yours,

This letter received no acknowledgment from the President. Nor did he allude to the matter subsequently at any time when I saw him personally.

When discussion got rather acrimonious in a Council meeting several days ago [early January], I told Mr. Keyserling and Mr. Clark that I had presented my resignation and that therefore they might entertain some hope that they would be relieved of my incubus on the Council in the not too distant future.

In talking with Webb on one or two occasions, I referred to my connection with the Council as probably not being very extended. This led him to ask what I meant, and I therefore told him that my resignation was on the President's desk. Both before and since he was named Undersecretary of State, he has expressed the hope that I would continue so that the several phases of staffing in the President's office could be worked out satisfactorily. He told me in this connection that both the Hoover draft and the Acheson draft of the Hoover Commission report recommended an "economic adviser with staff" rather than a Council. I said to him that I would be glad to continue helping on this plan of perfecting a good staff organization for the Executive Office under any reasonable terms, but that I simply will not undertake to go through another annual or midyear report struggle with the present set-up. After two years and a half experience, I regard it as impossible both internally and externally. We cannot organize and operate our staff satisfactorily or produce a product which will stand the time test of any reasonably professional standards. Nor can we maintain proper external relationships. (*P. D.*, Jan. 11, 1949)

During the first half of 1949, I was deeply engrossed with the work of the Cabinet stabilization committee, the President's annual Economic Report, repercussions to my Pentagon speech of November 15 (see p. 485), issues connected with the Spence and Murray bills, and the preparation of the Midyear Report. Since the President manifested no desire to pick up the resignation which I had laid on his desk in December, I thought it no time to press the matter. The difficulties of the situation were, however, growing apace.

ACCUMULATING STRAINS

In an informal talk and question period at the Harmonie Club of New York on January 15 (supposed to be "off the record"), I had indicated, incidentally but less guardedly than I should, my dissociation from proposals to have the government construct or operate industrial facilities. This was currently a hot issue in connection with steel capacity. The New York *Herald-Tribune,* the Philadelphia *Inquirer,* and some other papers played up this episode as revealing "sharp disagreement within the official White House family." The *Inquirer* added: "Leon H. Keyserling, vice chairman of the Economic Council, said today that his position in favor of the Presidential request had not changed. Keyserling is reputedly the author of the proposal. He declined to comment on Nourse's views."

References began to be made to the possibility that I would be "squeezed out of my position as chairman of the Council." In March, J. A. Livingston captioned his financial column: "Truman's Economists Split; Nourse Threatens to Resign," saying: "What began as a difference over procedure has widened into a rift over philosophy, purpose and economic outlook of the Council. . . . How the President resolves the conflict will determine—in large part—the future vitality and usefulness not only of the council but also of the entire Employment Act of 1946." Livingston developed this theme further in his column on April 7. In May, one of Drew Pearson's "predictions of things to come" was that I would soon be out—"probably within two months."

I did all I could to quiet these rumors, but I could not deny any basis for the reports, since my resignation had for several months been lying on the President's desk. On the other hand, the formula "no comment" merely tended to confirm the idea that something was in the wind. In mid-February I steadfastly declined an invitation to appear on the radio program "Meet the Press." Mr. Keyserling took my place. "About the third question related to rumored differences of view between him and the Chairman of the Council. He replied that the Council had always got on with remarkable harmony. Pressed harder as to whether there really was no difference of view, he said: 'No, absolutely none.' They gave him a fairly rough time on the question why he and Clark were plugging for controls and arguing that we are still in the grip of strong inflation in spite of present declines in prices. . . . " (*P. D.,* Feb. 21, 1949)

Mr. Keyserling expressed deep concern about public impressions of a lack of complete unanimity in the Council. In a memorandum of January 19 in reference to the Harmonie Club incident, he said:

I do not think that we, as Economic Advisers to the President and in confidential relationship to him, should criticize at a public meeting and in

the presence of the press proposals which the President has already made
. . . [or] use a public meeting or the public press as a forum for expressing
favor or disfavor of important proposals which the President currently has
before him for decision. . . .

You know that my action has always been consistent with the foregoing
principles which seem to me incontestably sound. Despite the many talks
that I have made, and despite the dangers of press misquotation, there
has never yet appeared any story attributing to me either a disagreement
with my colleagues or a disagreement with the President. This has resulted from following the simple rule that the rare disagreements among
ourselves are not public property, and that further, as Economic Advisers to the President, we should not take a public position on vital and
immediate issues until we have first conveyed our views to the President
and know what his policies are. This does not mean that we should
stultify ourselves by supporting policies of the President with which we
might be in disagreement, but that question is not involved here.

I feel very sincerely that this is the only kind of procedure which can
prove workable for an institution such as the Council, and I want to urge
it upon you for careful consideration.

In a reply directed to Mr. Keyserling and Mr. Clark (copies of
which were given to Clifford and Murphy of the White House staff),
I corrected some misapprehensions as to the actual circumstances
of the Harmonie Club speech and called attention to the different
ways in which it was reported by different papers. The New York
Times ran this story on an inside page under the headline "Year
of Decision in Economy Seen." The Philadelphia story was front-
page under the headline, "U. S. Economic Aides Split on Truman
Plan to Build Steel Plants," with emphasis on the personal issues.
I concluded my memorandum:

The episode is of course most regrettable from the standpoint of the
Council and not only distressing, but humiliating, to me. If either of you
wishes to discuss it further by memorandum or in Council meeting, I shall
be happy to do so. All of us have been around Washington long enough
to know that sooner or later every one makes a mistake or gets a "raw
deal." On several occasions in the past, I have been deeply concerned at
positions taken by other Council members in radio speeches or public
forum debates which seemed to me to put the Council on record on issues on which we had not taken a position or done the Council and staff
work which would justify us in taking a position. I have not, however,
been too seriously concerned about some individual departures of this
sort, and up to the present we have fortunately escaped headline treat-

ment on revealed divergences. I hope that we shall be quite free of it in the future.

Developments in connection with the Midyear Report were very interesting and significant, even though wearing to a high degree. It had become evident during the later spring months that Mr. Keyserling was much disturbed at so much prominence being given to conflicts within the Council and was determined to have a Report and so far as possible an entire Council program on which we were in explicit public agreement.

This I discovered later was particularly for the purpose of claiming that ambitious proposals for extension of government power, such as the new Spence and Murray bills, derived from Council analysis and had Council support. Even before I sensed all this, I had, just as a matter of professional self-respect, stated flatly at one of the first Council meetings in which plans for the Midyear Report were discussed that I positively would not sign a review of the situation at midyear which included policy recommendations or whose analytical findings did not seem to me to be objective, consistent with, and securely based on, our factual data.

As draft of text began moving forward, Mr. Keyserling was very active both in needling the staff and in redrafting the text which came to the Council. On Saturday and Sunday, June 25 and 26, we worked till 10 or 10:30 each night, I trying to get back to a draft which I could feel was satisfactory in the important situation presented by this Report—with its modification of the President's former position. Sunday evening I gave Keyserling my draft (Clark having quit in irritation over the delays and gone home). Mr. Keyserling took about fifteen minutes to glance over it and then returned to my office to say that this changed all sorts of things on which he thought we would agree and had made such additions and deletions that he just couldn't accept it. We had a brief though turbulent session in which I said it was his privilege to make his personal views known in any way he thought appropriate, but that I would submit material of the general sort embodied in my draft, subject to further discussion with Council and staff. I left a copy of my draft in Clark's desk with a covering note, saying that Mr. Keyserling found it wholly unacceptable and assured me that he (Clark) would find it no less so. "Thus," I concluded, "it appears that we have come to the ultimate parting of the ways."

This apparently was good strategy for dealing with the impasse because the next morning both Clark and Keyserling were ready to proceed with the work of completing our review on the basis of the Nourse-Homan [staff] draft rather than the Keyserling draft. Of course many changes were made during the next few days. But we secured a final draft from which

I thought the really untenable positions or objectionable kind of exposition had been eliminated, and most of the needed defining of issues and
cause-and-effect reasoning had been included. Subsequently, I have found
at least two passages in which the highly generalized and apparently innocuous language of the Report is being quoted in support of specific
action which we refrained from accepting in the draft. One is the passage
calling on the Congress

"to provide for a broad study of potential business investment, expansion
and market opportunities under conditions of maximum use of our productive resources in a growing economy—conditions which the Employment Act of 1946 contemplates and which can be achieved if we have
the confidence and determination to achieve them. This study should be
designed especially to discover inadequacies in capacity in basic industries
which may serve as limiting factors to expansion when the upward movement of business is resumed."

Of course I find no difficulty in subscribing to the desirability of having
this issue probed deeply and competently. That would be no more than
quickening and correlating the studies now being made by various agencies
of Government and by outside agencies, the Council participating actively
in raising questions, guiding study programs, and making application of
findings. But now I find that this is conceived to imply the setting up of
some new *ad hoc* body using perhaps as much as $6 million for what seems
to be a precommitted study—this possibly attached to the Council. But
beyond this, the passage cited and others of the Report are being represented as intended to support the Murray bill (S. 281). Mr. Keyserling
is quoted as saying that the Report was being so drawn as to support the
pending Murray bill. The introduction of that bill was held up till after
the Midyear Report was in. Then it was given a final redrafting and was
offered as an implementation of the Employment Act of 1946 and of the
President's Economic Report. Mr. Keyserling claims not to have participated in the drafting of this bill. (See p. 244.) (*P. D.*, Aug. 9, 1949)

Another cause of sharp disagreement within the Council arose
during the summer of 1949 over the nature of our response to the
President's request for comment on the impact of a 1951 budget of
$41.8 billion. The first draft materials for our reply seemed to me
to give an unduly complacent picture of the budget coming into
balance in 1952 and thereafter rolling up large surpluses. I doubted
that "we would be giving the President (and Pace) proper staff help
if we give him only this kind of analysis."

The events of recent weeks have confirmed my belief that it is useless to try to go on in my post under present conditions. The physical and nervous strain is so great that several times I have seen my breaking point just around the corner. Further, the President's handling of the Midyear Report shows how little real opportunity there is for having our work adequately considered in actual policy making. Although the President said when we submitted our draft materials, "I want to study these very carefully and discuss them fully when I get back [from a week-end on the Williamsburg]," he never consulted with us thereafter, nor did he sit in with the Cabinet-Council group as he did last December. It was a couple of young assistants of Steelman's—not the Council—who had the chance to talk to him.

RESIGNATION PRESSED

I had intended to write a note to the President before I left Washington a week ago, urging that he hasten the selection of my successor as requested on December 15, 1948. Now I shall do this on Tuesday, August 9, the third anniversary of the swearing in of the Council. It may seem that I would not be justified in refusing to continue in case the President should ask me to do so. But I think such a compromise would be completely futile. It would make necessary another garbled and compromised report in January, which will probably be a pretty critical time, and would lead to a still more difficult situation a year or so later, when I would certainly have to be relieved. The issue must be faced now—either make possible a truly professional and non-political Council or let it be known for the political agency it so largely is. (*P. D.*, Aug. 9, 1949)

Hence I wrote:

August 9, 1949

Dear Mr. President:

On December 15 last, I tendered to you my resignation, to be effective as soon as tasks to which I was then committed could be completed. I asked you to "regard this resignation as being on your desk any morning after these immediate responsibilities have been fulfilled. . . . In view of my age and the hard work and tensions involved in the job, it . . . is my hope that I can be relieved at a not too distant date."

I have not pressed for the acceptance of my resignation during the busy and troubled conditions of this spring, as I felt that I should serve through the completion of the Midyear Economic Report if you desired me to do so. That report has now been presented and appears to have been, on the whole, very well received both by the Congress and by the public. I passed my 66th birthday on May 20 and during the past year have become convinced that I no longer have the physical resources to carry the responsibilities of this post. As today is the third anniversary of the swearing-in of the Council, it seems an appropriate moment to urge as much speed as possible in the selection of my successor. Considerations of efficiency suggest that he should be installed at least a couple of months before the time when the next annual Economic Report of the President is due.

I believe deeply in the soundness and value of the Employment Act and in the great possibilities of usefulness for the Council. I trust that these will be fully realized under the new Chairman.

Sincerely yours,

This letter, like the previous letter of resignation met with no direct response from the President. I had an appointment with Mr. Steelman to discuss another matter, and he invited me to lunch with him on August 10.

He immediately launched into a discussion of my letter of August 9, though he did not express for the President or for himself any regret that I felt this to be necessary or any feeling that my services thus far had been useful to the Executive Branch. He said: "Of course this had to come sooner or later. The only question is about timing in naming the new man. The President says we must have this all fixed up and ready to send his name to the Senate the very minute your resignation is announced, because, of course, all sorts of people will be moving in, pressing to get their man appointed." . . . Steelman indicated that they wanted a man who has standing as an economist and would be well received by the public. (*P. D.*, Aug. 12, 1949)

The Council's report on the impact of proposed budget ceilings for Fiscal Year 1951 has [August 13] not made great tangible progress, but it appears that we are quite far apart in our approaches and conclusions. . . . Clark seemed genuinely anxious to see just what my reasoning was. But he ended up by taking a very narrow view of what our task should be—merely answer the questions in the President's letter on the assumption of full employment, present prices, and present tax rates. But as we got into discussion of the economics of the matter, it became apparent that he takes this complacent view because he accepts a return to inflation as the real *modus operandi* of a full employment economy. It goes back to his oft-repeated proposition that an economy can't keep on an even keel. If you aren't headed for recession, you must have prices, wages, profits rising and in general be promoting inflationary boom conditions. . . .

I had at first intended to write a brief but vigorous statement of my quite different approach and submit it regardless of what the others do and also present the matter orally to the President. But if he makes no response to my letter of resignation, I shall hardly have the heart to seek to see him. (*P. D.,* Aug. 13, 1949)

We have just ended a Council meeting [August 22] at which Mr. Clark reported that he had had to give up his effort to draft a response to the President's request for our views as to the impact on the economy of $41.8 billion for fiscal year 1951, which would reconcile the views expressed in the three memoranda drafted independently. I said I had been doubtful of his success in that effort because the views of himself and Keyserling were essentially at variance with mine. They would leave the President with a sense that all would be well under the proposed budget of $41.8; the purport of my memorandum is that a budget of that size in the present situation would give ground for great uneasiness as to the ultimate outcome of economic and fiscal adjustment.

Mr. Keyserling made a case of this being a repudiation of the President's policy stated at midyear under our guidance. Clark joined in to say that we had then said that domestic expenditures had been "held to a minimum consistent with their basic needs in view of the inflationary strain upon materials and manpower then prevailing." This was actually in the President's Report, not our review. I said that I was by no means free of apprehension at that time about going into deficit financing, but in any event did not believe that such a statement in the President's report should estop us now from analyzing present and prospective conditions to give the President a frank view of the economic impact of a possibly increasing deficit under assumed conditions that would be much above depression level.

This brought out clearly the view of Keyserling and Clark that when the President has decided that he cannot hold expenditures below a certain figure we should not presume to say that they should be lower. I said I thought it to be our function to tell him of any unfavorable repercussion on the economy that that expenditure and deficit level would have, no matter how hard he had worked to keep it down to that level. I am constantly being accused of "running out on the President" because I fail to join in briefs in support of policies or actions he has felt constrained to follow. It is frequently argued that I have helped lead him into them because I have participated in the preparation of reports whose labored ambiguities mean one thing (or various things) to them and something quite different to me. A notable case was the Brannan Plan. Keyserling insisted that this was Administration policy (even though it went to the Hill without Budget Bureau clearance) and that therefore nothing we might do should in any way reveal its economic shortcomings. He specifically criticized me for my Kentucky and Cornell speech—even though it was based on the statements in the annal Economic Report of the President and I had talked it over in advance with Brannan and sent copies to him and to the President.

Well, we ended up by agreeing that Keyserling and Clark would complete their document and I would do the same for mine. Keyserling is very unhappy as to how we will operate with the Budget Bureau over the next few months while the separate items of the Budget are being worked out. At the Council meeting this morning he expressed a hope that we should keep it from leaking out that there was a difference of view among us. But Clark said: "My view is just the opposite. I want it to be known that I do not share Mr. Nourse's position." (*P. D.*, Aug. 22, 1949)

With great reluctance Mr. Keyserling accepted the procedure of two separate memoranda, and he and Mr. Clark agreed on a final text for their draft. We had an appointment with the President at 12:15 today, at which time both documents were laid before him. I stated that we had two different evaluations. Theirs seemed to me unduly complacent as to the outcome of a budget of the proposed size, quoting their own phrase that it led to "conclusions clearly favorable to your proposed expenditures and tax policies." I said that I was more impressed with the danger that we might not under those conditions return to a balanced budget in calendar '51 but get into continued and growing deficits, with mounting problems of debt management, strains due to rising taxes, and complications of price and wage adjustment. It seemed to me that they were accepting a generally inflationary solution of our problem and that such a solution caused me grave concern.

After these comments, I said that Mr. Keyserling had the majority document and that the President would probably want to have him and Mr. Clark present it. Keyserling made a brief statement which was practically limited to the assertion that there was really no significant difference between our two interpretations but that they thought the economy could stand the burden of such budget as he in his wisdom found necessary after examining all the conditions. This seems to me to reflect the general tone of their memorandum and to be deeply symptomatic of their attitude toward the whole role of the Council. It seems to me completely to negate any proper function of objective professional advice for a Council of Economic Advisers. . . .

I thought it bootless to raise any of the issues in my memorandum. The President is a better reader than listener, and he said he would read both documents with care. I think the major product of this needlessly laborious procedure is to get the issues more sharply defined for Mr. Pace and the Bureau of the Budget. He seems quite sympathetic to the points of view which I have expressed. (*P. D.*, Aug. 26, 1949)

As soon as we had completed our reports to the President on budget ceilings, both Keyserling and Clark were eager to take up in detail the consideration of our staff arrangements and working program in accordance with our final budget figure of $300,000. I said that Gross reports that with shifts in clerical personnel already completed we would be saving one job there and that by holding down on travel and getting Commerce to do our chart work gratis, we would just live within our income. Both Keyserling and Clark, however, expressed great dissatisfaction with the work of practically everyone on the staff, and Keyserling said that the Council itself could in two months' time do the Economic Report without any help from the staff, and that they had done little of value on any of the special job assignments outside the Economic Reports.

Clark said he had been in complete disagreement with me at the time of the last Economic Report when I had said that I hoped they would leave major responsibility for the staff draft of the Economic Report to the Periodic Reports Committee and continue with their basic studies with as little interruption as possible. Clark had protested such a view in that meeting and now went on to elaborate his position as follows: The writing of the annual and midyear reports is our main job. Two years and a half of experience have given him no evidence that we are capable of getting answers to the problems (such as income-price relations, investment needs and sources of capital, stabilization devices, and nation's economic budget) that I have regarded as "basic" staff work. If we are to learn how to write the proper kind of annual and midyear reports we should practice by having a full-dress report each month. This seems to me utterly stupid and wasteful as a theory of Council and staff work.

Mr. Keyserling would, I think, have the Council itself draft each of the Economic Reports and not begin with a staff draft as has been my procedure. He would have each Council member call on the staff for data or assistance on his particular aspect but would expect them to validate the Council member's view rather than make an independent appraisal. As to reconcilement of Council members' positions, he has always argued that the majority view should prevail and that the minority member should concur rather than dissent or dissociate himself from a majority view. I have said I cannot operate on this basis. I think differences should be made explicit, with the reason therefor rather than devising slippery ambiguities which obfuscate the issues and can later be interpreted by any member according to his own liking.

Keyserling and Clark were quite impatient with my idea that, since we have to do a great deal of re-thinking of economic theory and business practices, the staff work is heavily weighted with refinement of issues and statement of *pros* and *cons* rather than setting forth dogmatic answers. Keyserling said that he knew it was quite possible to get prompt and definitive answers to the problems. When he was in the Housing Administration he had in two and a half months prepared a report that was a perfect example of the succinct laying out of a major economic problem with its proper solution. . . .

Some good is emerging from these discussions because we are shaping plans for lessening emphasis on some of the fields set up in our original organization chart, expanding at other points, and planning to redefine staff assignments along the lines of questions on which experience shows we need more light. Personally, I should like to keep a fair slice of our funds uncommitted to regular staff salaries and be able to finance conference sessions of the best men on particular topics which had been formulated for study by Council and staff. But with the present personnel of the Council, we could not agree on how the questions were to be formulated and then conduct the conference in such a way as to be really fruitful.

In the present Council discussion I always speak as though I were continuing as chairman even though I am fully decided to step out not later than early November. I have never heard a word from the President nor anything from Steelman since my luncheon conversation with Steelman on August 11. (*P. D.*, Sept. 2, 1949)

I therefore sent the following letter to the President on September 9:

Dear Mr. President:

On August 9, I wrote you urging early action on my resignation, submitted on December 15, 1948. I have not had any direct response from you to this letter, but Mr. Steelman informed me on August 10 that the only question which would be involved was that of timing of the announcement of my retirement. He said you desired to name my successor at the same time that you announced my resignation. You could thus avoid pressure on behalf of persons whom you would not care to consider for appointment.

In accordance with this suggestion, I have not mentioned my pending retirement even to my colleagues on the Council. This has caused some delay in organizing our program of work and our staff arrangements between now and the Economic Report in January. My relations are rendered ambiguous and awkward also with reference to Mr. Pace and Budget discussions, and Mr. Souers and the deliberations of the National Security Council. I feel that I should not appear before these other agencies as spokesman for the Council of Economic Advisers without their knowing that I am retiring within the next few weeks.

If the work of the Council is to be kept from serious demoralization,

I feel that I shall need to inform Mr. Keyserling, Mr. Clark, Mr. Pace, and Mr. Souers by Wednesday or Thursday of next week that I shall be leaving not later than November 1. I shall of course emphasize that this information is confidential, and I trust there will be no leak before you are ready to make your announcement of my successor.

Sincerely yours,

The President did not respond directly to this letter, but on September 12, Mr. Steelman telephoned, saying:

"It looks like we'll have to be getting together soon on the matter we spoke about at lunch the other day. The Boss has your letter. He doesn't like to cross this particular bridge just now. But, of course, he can't ask the man who is in to go on and on. It's quite a problem. Of course, your successor will have to be someone of considerable prominence. I asked you for suggestions of names, and I confess I haven't been able to come up with any names that are worth a nickel. I hope you have some, and I will give you a ring in a day or so, so we can discuss it." (*P. D.*, Sept. 12, 1949)

On September 26, I had another luncheon conference with Steelman in which he alluded to my having "stayed longer than I had originally committed myself to the President," and that they "could not expect me to go on indefinitely." This seemed to have the quality of a face-saving formula inasmuch as no period had been mentioned at the time I accepted the post. The White House staff had now assembled a list of names of prominent economists who had been mentioned in connection with various government posts. It included a number of the most eminent men in the profession. I added three or four other names, and discussed also the possibility raised by Steelman of promoting one of the outstanding members of the Council's staff. This seemed impracticable, and I was skeptical also that any of the thirteen on Steelman's list who clearly were competent would be willing to accept under all the circumstances. The post was in fact offered to quite a number of them and declined—sometimes pretty brusquely. Thus when I left the Council offices on November 1, no appointment had been made, and the vice-chairman automatically became acting chairman.

CHAPTER FIFTEEN

The Council "Under New Management"

When the first chairman of the Council withdrew, there was naturally much speculation as to who would be his successor and whether this would make a difference in economic thinking within the Executive Office or in the role of the Council. As the weeks passed and no new chairman was named, interest centered on the intentions of the acting chairman. The first important clue as to the line he would take came when the Council made its next annual report to the President.

RECHARTING THE COURSE

The Fourth Annual Report to the President by the Council of Economic Advisers (December 27, 1949) followed the general character of the three preceding reports. Its "philosophical essay" was keyed to the theme Business and Government. It contained much sound and salutary discussion under such headings as "From 'more for some' to 'progress for all,'" "From social theory to economic 'balance,'" and "Toward mutuality of interests." Even on controversial issues its language was most disarming: "It is our earnest desire that this report will have some influence upon attitudes both in business and in government, and that it may uncover the solid ground on which they can deal with each other in ever-increasing harmony and trust."

In general the document was hailed as conciliatory toward "business." The New York *Times* (December 29) under the headline "Truman's Advisers Push Free Economy to Cheer Business" reported:

The Truman Administration offered a friendly hand to business today
in a report of its Council of Economic Advisers which strongly urged the
desirability of an ever-expanding, free, American economy in a divided
world. . . . the Council enunciated a new policy line to the effect that
Government and business were far from incompatible, and that, in fact,
they were friends.

Merryle S. Rukeyser, Hearst columnist, suggested that "The Truman
Administration in this congressional election year is trying to make
a trend toward statism acceptable to businessmen as well as to
workers and farmers." And the *Wall Street Journal* (December 30)
said: "President Truman's economic counselors are holding out a
year-end olive branch to businessmen. But they make it plain that
business will have to come over to government's side of the fence
to pluck the symbol of peace." Alfred Friendly commented in the
Washington *Post* (December 30):

The Administration gave assurance yesterday that the business community and the system of free enterprise have nothing to fear from the
Fair Deal. The pledge of amity came in the 11,000-word fourth annual
report of the President's Council of Economic Advisers. . . . The document,
known to have been carefully cleared by the White House, amounted to
a statement of the philosophy underlying the Fair Deal's principles. . . .
The report points out, there should be more consistency of various Federal economic policies, by appraising each in some "unifying framework."
This would not be "central planning" or "blue-printing the economy,"
but simply good management practice.

Following the pattern of previous reports, this document had a
section dealing with "Recent Developments in Council Operations."
This was a forthright declaration of a new policy as to relations with
Congress and an intention to improve the working program of the
Council. Under the first point the report said:

The signatories of this report have never found any reason to believe
that our special service to the President under the Employment Act could
be inconsistent with that degree of co-operative servicing of Congressional
Committees—particularly the Joint Committee on the Economic Report—
which has become the traditional practice of policy advisers to the President who are set up under law, entrusted by law with a specific field of
study and advice, and responsible under law for explicit participation
in reports and recommendations transmitted to the Congress. The "problems" which such advisers face in occupying a confidential relationship to

the President while co-operating with the Congress have been exaggerated, and in any event are not peculiar to economists; and it is less important that the Council be spared these "problems" than that the Congress, at least as much as the economic groups with whom we deal, have access to our open and full discussion of economic fact, outlook, and policy.

Our most recent discussions with members of the Joint Committee on the Economic Report have strengthened our belief in this principle and practice. We look forward to exerting every effort toward making our best contribution to the furtherance of one of the most important objectives of a free government—mutual respect and common purposes between those who serve in the executive and those who serve in the legislative branch. The only way to further these ends is to work together on problems confronting both.

Under the caption, "Work with Private Economic Groupings," we read:

The Council has continued during the year its frequent meetings with representatives of business, labor, agriculture, and consumers. During our first years, these meetings were devoted mostly to general discussion of the economic outlook, supplemented by somewhat random consideration of specific problems which our visitors might raise with us around the conference table. But beginning with the last quarter of this year, we have instituted a new idea for which we have high hope. We have suggested to our conferees that together we undertake to designate one or two special problems for consideration at our next succeeding quarterly meeting, and that in the interval their staff resources as well as ours undertake to work up specific studies which might be circulated in advance of discussion. In addition to the manifest merit of this pooling of resources, we hope that the psychological advantage of *working together* as well as *talking together* will intensify the realization that the purposes of the Employment Act involve the whole nation and certainly cannot be furthered in an ivory tower.

The high hope entertained for this new idea of Council-business relations was not fully realized. The "private economic groupings" felt that their own work programs were already too full for them to accept extensive assignments from the Council. Some of them even entertained a suspicion as to the purposes of this intellectual leadership.

The Council report proceeded:

In the course of our development of this plan, some of our conferring groups have suggested that, instead of meeting separately with representatives of various sectors of the economy, we should undertake joint meetings and perhaps joint studies with representatives of industry, agriculture, labor, and consumers functioning as a single team. There are some practical difficulties involved in this method of approach, but the Council does not deem them insurmountable. Certainly the argument that such meetings lead to hot disputation instead of calm analysis can carry little weight among those who realize—as this report has sought to stress—that the reconciliation of conflicting views and seemingly conflicting interests is the hallmark of free enterprise and free government. We hope that procedures along these lines may be perfected, and that one of the most important collateral benefits will be the encouragement of mutual efforts along the same pattern but on a more decentralized basis throughout the nation. In such efforts the Council will not generally be able to join because of limitations of time and staff, but it is encouraging to note that already in some states agencies somewhat similar to the Council are being considered or have already been established.

This was an idea that had for some time been proposed by certain labor organizations, but when we came to set up our advisory committees, the union representatives had not even been willing to meet with us as a single labor group but came on three separate days. (See p. 159.)

As to work with other governmental agencies:

The Council should not be simply a reviewing body which looks over the proposals made by operating agencies and recommends to the President how these proposals may be fused into a consistent and sound economic policy. Our work to be effective must commence at a much earlier stage in the process. It should include participation in the developmental thinking about those policies and programs which are of central concern to the whole economy. Only thus can other agencies receive our assistance at an early enough stage for it to be fully effective; and only thus can we be brought in contact with their work at an early enough stage for us to comprehend it fully and be benefited fully by their thinking and experience. We feel that during the course of the coming year, encouraged by the splendid co-operation thus far received, we shall be able to move toward the fuller professional service which the reading of the Employment Act and of its legislative history shows so clearly to have been the expectation of the Congress.

This prospectus of the Council's future program implied not only enlargement of activities but a considerable change in their character. If carried out, it would transform the Council from an analytical staff of technicians serving the President into a wide-ranging agency for the formulation and prosecution of economic policies. This new interpretation of the Employment Act was noted by some of the commentators. Under the title "Policy-Making Advisers?" Peter Edson, Scripps-Howard columnist, pointed out:

The "Business and Government" report of the President's Council of Economic Advisers is turning out to be not so much of a peace message as it was at first cracked up to be.

Business representatives here in Washington, after reading it the second and third time to figure out some of the bigger words and the more obscure passages, have been coming up with some new answers. One is that this is no olive branch and kiss on the brow from Truman's fair dealing economic planners to the fair-haired captains of industry. . . .

In other words, some business representatives here in Washington view this as a declaration by the council that it intends to have a hand in the making of Government economic policies from here on out. That means the Council of Economic Advisers will now have to be watched for possible new policies affecting business, as well as the White House and the various administrative agencies.

Nor does the council, apparently, intend to stop at giving the executive branch of the Government the benefit of its advice. It makes a pass at offering to tell Congress what it should do about things. . . .

As for the type of policy on which the council seems willing to give its advice, the report offers several hints. In a section on "Policy Making" near the end of the report, it mentions the size of the defense program required for national security, and the question of how many houses should be built in an inflationary period.

On the controversial questions of pensions, unemployment insurance and other Social Security measures, the council's report is bold enough to state a policy, without even being asked for it: "We also believe that as (Social Security) coverage becomes more general, a larger part of Social Security receipts should be obtained thru general revenues rather than payroll taxes."

A VOICE FROM THE COUNCIL IS HEARD AT PARTY GATHERINGS

Besides the intention expressed in the Council's Fourth Annual Report to the President that in future the Council would have more direct and active participation in the deliberations of Congressional committees—particularly the Joint Economic Committee—the acting chairman became increasingly conspicuous in party affairs. This emancipation began even during the last months of his tenure as vice-chairman.

In September 1949 there was held in San Francisco the second of a series of Democratic party pow-wows. It was known as the Western States Democratic Conference, but in effect it swallowed up a Conference on Land, Water, and Jobs that had been projected as an eleven-state nonpolitical conference for economic discussion of these problems. A press photograph under the caption "Three of the Democratic Party's Big Guns" showed Mr. Keyserling arriving in company with Secretaries Tobin and Brannan. Mr. Keyserling's address, "Prospects for American Economic Growth" was in the main an expression of his familiar doctrine of "economic expansion." In mentioning the agricultural problem, he said: "Personally, I believe that the Brannan Plan is the best yet proposed." His opening paragraphs presented a clarification of his views of the proper role of Council members. He said:

A few days ago, someone asked me what an economist was going to do at a conference having some political overtones. I happen to be a member of a political party because I believe that every citizen should; and it happens to be the Democratic Party primarily because its philosophy in the main has conformed to my philosophy of life, and secondarily because I was born in South Carolina. But that is not why I am here. It is rather because of a profound conviction that the problems of the American economy are sufficiently vital to merit the attention of any group which gathers in the American spirit to consider what policies they believe merit the popular support which alone can make policy effective in a free country. If any other group operating in the American tradition asked me to talk with it about economic conditions and policies, the invitation would receive a most cordial reception.

Those who look down their noses at the political process are in fact looking down their noses at the institutions of democracy. And any economist who believes that his "objectivity" depends upon isolating himself from all the main streams of American life has lost contact with the world of today—a world in which mankind's economic and social and political problems are inseparably intertwined and depend for their solution upon the good conscience, full co-operation and highest attributes of human beings everywhere.

This episode was commented on in the press as foreshadowing greater political activity by at least some of the Council members.

The acting chairman did in fact participate in the Southern Regional Conference of the Democratic Party at Raleigh on January 30, 1950. This was referred to in the press as "The Truman-program thought-control clinic." Commentator Frank R. Kent linked this episode with the President's inability to find a new appointee for the Council. "Mr. Keyserling," he added, "not only attended the 'pep' rally of Democrats in Raleigh, North Carolina, engineered by Jonathan Daniels with a view to allaying opposition to Mr. Truman and promoting Democratic unity. But along with such detached and nonpolitical fellows as Chairman Boyle of the Democratic National Committee, Vice-President Barkley, Secretary of Agriculture Brannan, and others he made a speech. It just does not seem the place where a Presidential economic adviser ought to have been or a speech that should have been made—that is if it is expected that the reports of the President's Economic Advisers are to carry weight in Congress and in the country."

On May 10, President Truman designated Mr. Keyserling chairman of the Council of Economic Advisers and nominated Professor Roy Blough of the University of Chicago as the third member. The latter was promptly confirmed by the Senate Banking and Currency Committee but did not take up active work until after the end of the academic year.

The newly named chairman participated in the "Jefferson Jubilee" of the Democratic party in Chicago on May 15, where he made two speeches—"Toward an Expanding American Economy" and "The Federal Budget and the National Economy." In the latter, he said: "I do not intend to be placed on the defensive, or to apologize for policies which in my judgment have been sound. These policies have raised us to new pinnacles of economic strength and prosperity . . . I believe profoundly that the budgetary policies of the Federal Government since the first administration of Franklin D. Roosevelt until the present moment have been basically right. And because they have been subjected to misrepresentation and sophistry, we must continue to fight for them to assure their maintenance." This address evoked so much criticism that the mimeographed text of the speech which had been prepared for distribution from the chairman's office was withheld and it was practically impossible to secure a copy.[1]

[1] Mr. Keyserling participated in a similar manner in the Midwest and Western States Conference at Denver, Colorado, on May 23, 1951.

The impression among the public that the Council was moving into a more active policy-making and political role was enhanced when the Economic Report of the President was issued in January 1950. This report was optimistic as to the economic situation and outlook and complacent as to the part which government policy had played in producing this condition. Many commentators picked up a paragraph which read:

> The relatively safe passage from inflation to greater stability was no accident. Businessmen, workers, and farmers demonstrated much greater judgment and restraint than in earlier similar periods. Their actions showed that they had gained understanding of the causes of our economic situation and what should be done to improve it. Their efforts were aided by public policies which had been developed over the years and had been improved by experience. Government measures in such fields as credit banking, social insurance, and agricultural price supports, proved their worth in cushioning the downswing and lending strong support to the recovery movement.

Some reviewers expressed doubts as to the validity of the suggested cause-and-result relationship. The New York *Times* (January 7, 1950) editorialized:

> The public policies to which Mr. Truman is apparently alluding do not represent anything new in Government. They were simply a reversion to, or a continuance of, the pump-priming of the Thirties, with this main difference: The general policies of deficit financing and wholesale encouragement of public and private borrowing (as in residential building) were introduced originally when the national income was badly shrunken, industrial activity was at low ebb, and unemployment had reached historic proportions. In 1949 they were superimposed upon the economy at a time when the latter was close to its record peacetime level.
>
> It is not possible to say to what degree, if at all, these policies contributed to the 1949 readjustment. Considered in terms of the long-run situation, however, they must be viewed with misgivings. If we are going to resort to inflationary stimulants every time production slackens slightly as a result of an overdue adjustment in the price structure, what are we going to turn to when the need arises for combating a recession of serious proportions? And what becomes of Mr. Truman's observation that "federal receipts should be sufficient over a period of years to balance the budget and provide a surplus for debt reduction"?

The editor of the Washington *Post* observed:

The President's Economic Report is in large part a repetitive appeal for enactment of the legislative program outlined in his state-of-the-union message. . . . The President quite properly underlines the importance of effective teamwork between free enterprise and the Government. But his conclusion that the "relatively safe passage from inflation to greater (economic) stability" shows that businessmen, workers, and farmers "exercised much greater judgment and restraint than in earlier similar periods" is certainly open to challenge. It ignores the fact that 1949 was a year of serious labor disturbances and that the coal industry is still in a state of turmoil. The President also declares that we have regained stability, although there is no assurance that a further round of wage increases and subsequent price advances can be avoided. . . . Despite the restrained tone of the report, there is no indication that the President is prepared to curtail his welfare program. Moreover, he insists that the anti-inflation controls for which he vainly appealed would if applied in time, have prevented the 1949 business recession. "We must not again make the mistake," he warns, "of failing to adopt affirmative policies necessary for continued economic stability and growth."

The Baltimore *Sun* added:

Mr. Truman did not stipulate which branch of our tri-partite Government it was whose wisdom helped most in the transition. He does not say, what is true, that the transition was aided if not insured outright by Congress' stout refusal to pass the semi-screwball economic legislation which Mr. Truman recommended at the time and which Messrs. Keyserling and Clark obediently defended before the appropriate congressional committees.

The President's Economic Report is in tone serene, complacent, and friendly, like its predecessors, the annual report of the economic council and the annual presidential message. But like those earlier documents, the economic report is suffused with the gentle sap of politics. This leads to some paradoxes which are, naturally enough, at no point resolved by the annual economic review of the economic council which accompanies this particular message.

The Council's Economic Review, which accompanied the Economic Report of the President, had the customary elaboration of statistical and analytical material, but in its concluding section launched boldly out into the enunciation of "Needed Policies." These included fiscal policy, farm policy, policies for the development of physical and human resources, social security, and international policies. This section bore out the indications contained in the Council's December report to the President that in future the Council would deal affirmatively with policy questions over its own name. At this time, Marquis Childs in a column headed "Politics in the Council" observed:

A great deal of wrangling has gone on backstage over the series of reports which the President's Council of Economic Advisers is issuing on the state of the Nation's economy and the prospects for 1950. Directly at stake is the willingness of the public, on the one hand, and the professional economists and business analysts on the other hand, to continue to put credence in the council's reports.

From professional economists on the council's staff came most of the criticism. They are fearful that the original purpose in creating the council, which was to establish a group of experts who could objectively and dispassionately appraise the Nation's economic balance sheet, is being perverted. . . . In general, members of the council's staff are in agreement with the hopeful outlook for 1950. But they felt that the all-important report to Congress should say more than, in the refrain of the popular song, "It's a Big, Wide, Wonderful World." They were arguing through long sessions with the Council that there are elements that may dim the optimistic perspective of the present. . . .

In this political year the reaction to the newest report is likely to be tinged with politics. . . . far more is at stake than the future of any one individual. The whole concept of the Council—a body of expert appraisers—may be lost sight of, and that will be a serious loss to the Government.

The Midyear Economic Report of the President continued to stress the notes of national productivity and national unity, but with specific programs adapted to the new situation growing out of the Korean invasion.

Viewed in its entirety, the economy at midyear 1950 had made a remarkable recovery from the moderate recession of 1949. New records of peacetime production, employment, and real incomes were reached. Reasonable balance of prices had been achieved. The outlook in mid-June was for stability and new growth on a sound basis. Toward the end of June, however, the Korean outbreak brought rapid changes. The necessity for large new public outlays began to have both economic and psychological impacts. Many important prices commenced to rise rapidly. New private and public policies are needed quickly to deal with these new developments.

We have gathered a wealth of practical experience about how our economy works, and about what promotes its strength and progress. Five years after the greatest of all wars, and even before the events of last month, we had reached the highest levels of peacetime production and employment ever known. We had passed through a period of inflation and conquered a postwar recession without permitting it to deepen into a depression. Based upon this record, those who work in private enterprise and those who work in Government—of both political parties—have reached agreement upon many national economic policies. (p. 2)

Four legislative recommendations were offered:

1. On account of the cost of expanding our military strength, and to help contain inflationary pressures, an interim revenue measure should be enacted immediately to yield substantial additional revenue in the current fiscal year. . . .

2. As a safeguard against inflationary buying, and to reduce the demand for scarce materials, authority should be granted to regulate consumer credit, to restrain mortgage credit, particularly for housing, and to limit speculation in commodities.

3. In view of the mounting shortage of some commodities required for the national defense, authority should be granted for priorities and allocations of these commodities, for the limitation of nonessential uses, for the prevention of inventory hoarding, and for the requisitioning of supplies.

4. To expedite the production of certain commodities needed for the military and for adequate stockpiling, and to guard against a dangerous shortage of these materials in the event of any emergency calling for further expansion of our military efforts, a program should be adopted which provides loans and incentives for the expansion of capacity, for technological developments, and for the production of essential supplies. (pp. 14, 15)

Examination of our expanding material and human resources indicates that the substantial increases in our military forces and in supporting activities now under way do not call for a complete set of economic controls now—if business, labor, and consumers practice moderation, and if adequate steps are taken at once to adjust private and public policies and programs to our supply needs and to the curbing of inflation. (pp. 9, 10)

This report did not attract very lively public attention. Like the Midyear Report of 1949, it had been "scooped" by previous action of the President—a special message to the Congress calling for prompt and substantial tax increase and the setting up of a defense mobilization agency. In the state of alarm created by the Korean

advance, there was general approval of the President's call for increased taxes and accelerated production effort. In the matter of
controls, the President was criticized somewhat widely for not
recommending all-out controls even though up to this time, he had
been criticized for every recommendation of even "selective" and
"standby" controls.

The report to the President by the Council of Economic Advisers
which accompanied his Economic Report was divided into three
parts: "(1) A general interpretation of the economic events of the
past five years and of their current significance; (2) an analysis of
problems ahead and of desirable policies; and (3) a detailed description of economic trends during the first half of 1950." (p. 25)
This "description of economic trends" was purely factual; the interpretation of "Five Years in Retrospect" culminated in the general
conclusion that the country was better prepared to deal both with
inflation and deflation dangers than ever before. Such built-in stability had become "just as integral a part of our economy today as
the conditions which made for greater instability were an integral
part of the economy of 30 years ago." (p. 37) With confidence in
this institutional strength should go confidence in our powers of
economic expansion. While "confidence is no substitute for sound
policy, sound policy must rest upon confidence commensurate with
our natural resources, our business equipment and skills, and our
uniquely proficient working population." (p. 39)

Accompanying its analysis of problems ahead, there were several Council recommendations of "desirable policies" for meeting
them. In general, however, these were economic policies rather than
specifically governmental policies. They were keyed to the general
belief that even at current levels we were still below maximum production and that closing up this slack would enable us to carry the
burden of partial mobilization without trenching on standards of
civilian consumption and without danger of inflation. Urging "that
businessmen expand plant capacity and investment to meet the constantly expanding requirements of an economy operating at maximum production and employment," the Council proceeded, "There
need be no fear that this enlarged productive capacity would become unusable if and when international tensions subside. With
enlarged capacity available, the great and growing domestic market

for goods and services of all kinds should never reach the end of the road." (p. 43)

The Council ended with a list of seven recommendations:

On the fiscal side, we should seek to reduce the size of the cash deficit substantially or, better still, to remove it entirely. . . . The economy is strong enough to bear the burden of financing the needs which have now been outlined, without deficit financing and extensive increases in the money supply. . . .

In our judgment, the economy is now strong enough to bear the burden of substantial increases in tax rates in accord with this principle and to do this without endangering the maintenance of maximum production. . . .

Further restraint upon civilian demand for goods should now be imposed through the control of consumer credit, and through the tightening of credit for building construction.

Shortages with respect to some of the essential elements of a military program require a compulsory allocation program, not only to assure adequate military supply, but also to prevent price and cost increases in these limited areas from spreading outward through the whole economy. The program should therefore provide for limitation of nonessential use. . . .

Careful analysis of available material requirements for the expanding defense effort indicates that some specific measures should now be taken to expand capacity and accelerate production, as a supplement to allocation. . . .

We do not recommend the employment of general controls over prices and wages at this time. . . .

Action is needed this year to improve the Federal-State unemployment insurance system along the lines recommended by the President. Without such action, many of the State legislatures will probably not act in 1951, and considerable delay would then result in achieving these necessary improvements. (pp. 47, 48–49)

The extent to which the Council had moved into the area of policy statement in their own right may be noted in their closing paragraph:

The Council of Economic Advisers has confined its proposals at this midyear to a relatively short list. We are mindful of the crowding of the congressional calendar with transcendently important issues of international policy. We have therefore thought it best at this stage to identify only those matters which appear to us to be of greatest urgency in the current situation. Our views on a broader range of programs, inseparably connected with the stability and growth of the American economy, have frequently been stated. (p. 49)

The Council's Fifth Annual Report to the President (December 1950) was written to the theme "The Economics of National Defense." It examined the possibilities of increasing national production and how large a proportion of our resources we can afford for defense. "Clearly," said the Council, "no military build-up now in contemplation is of a size or speed to justify objection by the economist on this ground"—that is, "the strain and burden upon the economy and the people" and "inflationary pressures". . . . "The concentration of our productive efforts upon defense objectives could rise far above this point [7–8½%] and we could still maintain a vigorous national economy capable of meeting additional demands upon it." The report discussed broad principles of efficient production effort, wage and price policy, taxation, and the use and limits of controls, but pointed out that specific recommendations would be found only in the Economic Report of the President in January.

The concluding section of the Council's Fifth Annual Report related to its own work program. Here the Council reiterated the proposition that

It must furnish, upon request, information and advice to members of the Congress who are concerned with economic policy. In these respects, the members of the Council are not dissimilar to some other officers of government, although the fact that the members of the Council are called "advisers" has led to some misinterpretation. For while officers in other fields may, unlike the members of the Council, operate specific programs, yet these officers are also advisers to the President on major matters of policy. He alone, to the extent that he accepts their advice, transmits it to the Congress for action where legislation is requisite. Or, in matters of major policy, it is only with his consent that recommendations are transmitted by others.

The Council is nonetheless distinguishable from most other agencies of government. It does not operate programs nor carry out policies. To this extent, it is not an executive agency. Nor is the Council in conflict with those agencies which develop policies in specific areas; its task is rather to evaluate specific policies in terms of the over-all economic situation.

Here the Council was apparently calling attention to the duty laid upon it in Section 4 (c) of the Employment Act:

(3) to appraise the various programs and activities of the Federal Government in the light of the policy declared in section 2 for the purpose of determining the extent to which such programs and activities are contributing, and the extent to which they are not contributing, to the achievement of such policy, and to make recommendations to the President with respect thereto.

This is a very important and sweeping power which had never been exercised in any systematic way by the Council during its earlier years. The possibility of its development in future is discussed in Chapter XVII.

Finally, the Council called attention to the fact that the character of its work was somewhat modified by the setting up of the Office of Defense Mobilization. "The work of the Council in recent months has been meshed with that of other agencies whose attentions have been directed mainly to the problems of a defense economy," with members of the Council sitting in at various policy conferences or members of the staff being designated as observers at staff meetings of the principal mobilization and control agencies.

In December 1951, it was decided that there was undue duplication between this separate agency report and the discussion of principles which had come to be included in the Council's part of the President's Economic Report to the Congress (since the change in form requested by the President at midyear 1948). On the other hand, administrative questions connected with the operation of the Council were not matters that concerned the public and could better be discussed in a personal document to the President. Such a "housekeeping report" dealing primarily with staff and operating problems was sent to the President, as was also their report to him on the economic situation, which in January appeared as part of his Economic Report to Congress. The same procedure was followed in 1952.

The economic reports of the President in January and at midyear 1951 and in January 1952 followed familiar patterns in the main as to both form and substance. They stressed the great inherent strength of the economy and the country's powers of economic expansion, the need for co-operation, the soundness of past policies, and our ability to carry the load of both defense and welfare. Somewhat typical is the statement from the Midyear Economic Report of 1951:

The magnitude of the proposed security program, including foreign assistance, is well within the capacity of our productive resources. Proposed outlays for assistance to the other free nations over the next year comes to less than 15 per cent of our total security program, and to only about 2 per cent of our estimated total output during this period. We can carry forward both the domestic and the foreign aspects of our total security program, and still maintain domestic consumption and business investment at high levels. . . . We are now in a position where, if the Congress enacts adequate legislation, we can continue to enlarge our defense efforts, to expand our productive capacity, and to hold inflation in check. (pp. 10, 11)

The President continued to urge further tax increases of at least $5 billion a year. In his Economic Report of January 16, 1952 (p. 21) he said:

Early last year, I asked for a minimum tax program to yield 10 billion dollars or more. The bill enacted by the Congress came late in the calendar year, added only about one-half of this amount, and included a number of provisions which lost the Government revenue and reduced the equity of the tax system. . . . In view of this fiscal outlook, I urgently recommend that the Congress, as a minimum provide additional revenues in the amount by which last year's legislation fell short of my recommendations. This can be achieved by eliminating loopholes and special privileges, and by some tax rate increases. While new tax legislation along these lines could scarcely affect the deficit for the current fiscal year, and would not restore a balanced budget in the fiscal year 1953, it would make a major contribution to the Government's budgetary position and to the stabilization program.

The President's legislative recommendations at this time (p. 25), besides military defense and economic aid to free nations, included "certain urgently needed development projects, particularly the St. Lawrence seaway and power project," provision for "the construction of needed housing and community facilities in defense areas," raising the level of benefit payments and making other improvements in our system of old age and survivors' insurance, and strengthening of the Federal-state unemployment insurance system; Federal aid to help meet school operating costs and increased aid to school construction and operation in critical defense areas, and Federal aid to assist medical education and provide for strengthening local public health services. The President also recommended revision of

"the basic legislation concerning labor management relations"—
that is, repeal of the Taft-Hartley Act and also repeal of the "sliding-scale provision in existing agricultural support legislation" and
the inclusion of perishable commodities under farm price supports.

The Midyear 1952 Economic Report of the President, unlike the
report at midyear 1948, was not deferred until after the party conventions had been adjourned, but was released just on the eve of
the Democratic party convention. Somewhat shortened and fresh-
ened in style, it continued to stress the note of national strength and
our "common aspirations for the domestic economy—stability,
justice, and advancing prosperity. . . . [Since] the Congress may not
again be in session until January 1953, the Report does not contain
specific legislative recommendations. It is limited to a broad view
of the Nation's economy, its current condition of strength, and its
prospects and problems for the future." (p. 1)

Addressing himself to those who express the opinion that "our
security efforts are weakening us at home, and that we must reduce
them in order to save ourselves," the President explained that "The
facts reveal beyond question that the security programs now being
undertaken are not even threatening—much less depleting or
impairing—the strength of our domestic economy. Despite the
burden of these programs—and they are a real burden—our business
system has been doing better and our people have been living better
than ever before." (pp. 1–2)

On the broad fiscal issue, he said:

> It was my view at the commencement of the defense emergency that, in a
> period of full prosperity and partial mobilization, enough taxes should be
> collected to balance the Budget. By January of this year, it was clear that
> this principle had been departed from by the Congress to a degree which
> made it impossible to avoid a deficit. . . . During the current fiscal year
> 1953, the Government is likely to run a budget deficit in the neighborhood
> of 10 billion dollars, according to tentative calculations by the Council of
> Economic Advisers. . . . But the prospective deficit is not sufficiently
> threatening to our economy to justify reducing it by gambling with our
> national safety. (p. 12)

Whether because of preoccupation with the Democratic party
convention, because the reports of the Defense Mobilizer now caught
the limelight, or for other reasons, the public gave scant attention
to this Economic Report of the President; in fact, the report

marked a new low in this regard. Such comment as there was seemed inclined to be somewhat skeptical of the confidence expressed in the report that the nation was not only prosperous at the moment but assured of continuing prosperity during the ensuing years. Editorial comments in the New York *Journal of Commerce* raised the question of the political coloration of the President's Report and detected a contradiction or divergence in the position taken by the Council of Economic Advisers in their report. The editorial (July 21, 1952) said:

The Midyear Economic Report of the President to Congress is a political rather than an economic document. Was it a coincidence that it was published on the eve of the Democratic Convention and that, point by point, it takes issue with the economic conclusions of the recent Republican Convention? Publication of the report was delayed just long enough to make us strongly suspect it was not.

Moreover, significantly enough, there is a noticeable cleavage this time between the President's report to Congress and the Midyear Economic Review by the Council of Economic Advisers which accompanies the President's report, and on which the President's report usually is based. This time, it seems to us, the Council's review is less arbitrary than the President's report. While both the President and the Council believe in the possibility of an uninterrupted economic growth, the Council members now admit that the economy "seems by no means invulnerable" to recessionary forces. But they, too, still believe that "intelligent" private and public policies can "circumvent initial downward movements before they gain cumulative force." In contrast, the President's report is completely arbitrary in asserting that "we have come to recognize that depressions are avoidable; and that a steadily expanding economy is attainable."

For this, Mr. Truman—the politician—takes full credit. But he also boasts that the economic progress under the Democratic regime has been accomplished "not by any ventures that would be strange to our economic or social institutes, but by conserving what is best in responsible free enterprise and responsible free government." The trouble with this statement is that Mr. Truman, apparently, has ideas as to what constitutes such "strange ventures" away from the path of free enterprise quite different from those of his political opponents and, we believe, the vast majority of American business men.

In the economic reports of the President for the last two years, that portion which appears over the names of the Council has contained a broad analytical discussion of national policies focused both to the defense period and to longer range conditions thereafter. In the report of January 1951, the Council observed:

> In early 1950 the Council sought to outline profit, price, and wage policies for peacetime stability and growth. We found the key to stability and growth in continuing "balance" between investment and consumption. . . . The Council feels it can be most helpful by outlining policy guides, rather than by treating those detailed questions of formulae, timing, and application which must necessarily rest with specialized agencies charged with segments of the stabilization effort. (p. 113)

The Council's report at midyear 1951 devoted more than 100 pages to discussion of the "shaping of the defense economy [objectives and required adjustments] and economic policies for defense."

In the annual Economic Report of the President of January 1952, the Council organized its discussion of policy under the title "Central Problems for 1952." In a section on "Increasing Production," passages dealing with "guiding investment," "programmed expansion of productive capacity," "public investment," and "increasing agricultural production" set forth particularly significant phases of the Council's views on national economic policy:

> The necessary shifts in resource use outlined above will involve some further major changes in the pattern of private and public investment. To meet war preparedness objectives, and to work toward the substantial elimination of basic shortages by 1954—when, so far as can now be judged, military production will have passed its peak and be on the way toward a substantially lower maintenance level—investment in Government-aided industrial expansion programs will have to increase further. . . .

> The basic expansion programs are an important part of an economic strategy for a long period of partial mobilization. They contemplate, in addition to meeting the top priority needs of the military, the provision of an enlarged base of additional capacity—not only as a reservoir of quick strength in the event of war, but also as the long-range solution to the problem of adequate supply in all major sectors of the economy while maintaining a large security program. The bulk of the investment in such programs is private, though publicly-owned facilities constitute a major share of the program for expansion of munitions facilities, and a quarter to a third of the electric power program. (p. 108)

In view of the increased pressure on scarce materials in 1952, stemming from the build-up of the security program and defense-related industrial expansion, many lines of public investment need to be curtailed still further. But this curtailment is highly selective. (p. 109)

Under existing legislation, if farmers succeed in increasing production sufficiently to build up reserves to safe or desirable levels, they could be penalized by having their support prices reduced from 90 per cent to as low as 75 per cent of the effective parity. This possibility may act as a deterrent to maximum production of basic commodities by raising concern in the minds of many farmers lest the Government, after enlisting them in an all-out production drive, might leave them worse off as a result of their patriotism and hard work. Support prices for corn, wheat, cotton, and dairy products at 90 per cent of parity have already been announced.[2] (p. 112)

Another striking feature of the Council's report to the President in January 1952 was the "separate note by Mr. Clark upon monetary and credit policy" (pp. 142–44). Mr. Clark could not concur in his colleagues' statement of credit policy, which seemed to him to ascribe too great efficacy to monetary policy in accomplishing the stabilization purposes of the Employment Act of 1946, "the usefulness whereof in a strong inflationary movement has been challenged in former reports of the Council of Economic Advisers." This is the unique instance of a published dissent by a Council member.

Besides the passage already noted from the Council's report of July 1952, one other passage from the discussion of the longer-range prospects for stability and growth seems to epitomize their thinking.

The economy of today may be said to have "grown up" to its defense burden. Productive power has been enlarged to an extent enabling us, without excessive strain, to carry the defense burden while maintaining a high and advancing level of business investment and consumer supplies. . . .

The longer-range outlook which here concerns us looks to the time when defense outlays are stabilized—under current plans, sometime during 1953 —and later begin to decline. When they stabilize, the issue of maintaining maximum employment and production will depend upon whether the private demand of business and consumers and the nondefense expenditures of Federal, State, and local governments maintain in the aggregate

[2] In Public Law 585, signed by the President on July 18, 1952, the "flexible support" provisions of the 1949 Agricultural Act were deferred for another two years and likewise the use of the modernized parity criterion was made optional. Either the old or the new standard can be used, "whichever is higher."

a rate of expansion consistent with improvements in productivity and a growing labor force. . . . The decline in defense outlays during the period under consideration will, in any event, be a relatively small factor compared with others operating in so vast and varied an economy. . . .

Given an intelligent and confident approach by businessmen, investors, and consumers to the problems of the period under consideration, the prospect is bright that adjustment policies within the enterprise system can largely, perhaps fully, meet those problems. Public policies, however, can be helpful, and they may be needed since the prospect, although bright, is by no means certain.

The Council . . . has said a good deal about the importance of confidence in future growth. It is not easy to overestimate its importance as a necessary condition for prosperity. Confidence without a reasonable basis may result in destroying the very prosperity it produces. . . . The Council believes that, assuming peace is maintained, the factors necessary for the development of a sound confidence in the future of the economy exists today. . . .

First the economy has great possibilities of growth and expansion. . . .

Second is the characteristic of our economic system that, for the most part, when downward fluctuations occur in any sector, the forces of the private economy will react to correct them if the total economic environment is favorable . . . like a well-constructed ship which rights itself after rolling from the impact of the waves. . . .

Third, if downward forces should at any time become too pronounced for the private economy assisted by the built-in stabilizers to compensate for them automatically, the Government has the ability and the will to take those measures which may be necessary to end and reverse the downward movement.

Fourth, we now have time in which to apply private and public policies geared to the longer-range maintenance of prosperity, which are easier to formulate and easier to apply than policies which stand ready only with plans to reverse the course of a depression after it is well under way. . . .

The Council believes that it is safe for business and consumers to rest on these foundations of confidence, and, more importantly, to act accordingly.[3]

CHANGES IN PERSONNEL

Dr. Roy Blough, who had become a member of the Council of Economic Advisers in May 1950, resigned the post in July 1952 to accept a position with the United Nations Organization as Princi-

[3] *The Midyear Economic Report of the President,* July 1952, pp. 112, 118, 120–22.

pal Director of its Department of Economic Affairs. On July 23, the White House announced the appointment of Professor Robert C. Turner of Indiana University as Blough's successor. Dr. Turner had served as director of the Foreign Division of the War Production Board during World War II, as staff member of the Office of War Mobilization and Reconversion, and as assistant to John R. Steelman since the termination of OWMR. He had extensive contacts with the work of the National Security Resources Board and the Office of Defense Mobilization, during periods when Steelman was acting director of these organizations, and had served as liaison man between the White House staff and the Council of Economic Advisers. After his return to teaching in 1948, he had continued his White House connection during vacation periods.

Beginning in 1950, the staff of the Council underwent extensive change. All but two of the men who made up the top staff during the initial years returned to teaching or research positions outside the Government or transferred to other government agencies. Bertram Gross, initially assistant to the Chairman of the Council and thereafter its executive secretary, resigned in January to become research director for the Democratic National Committee.

The new executive secretary had his assignment limited to administrative functions without the concern for substantive matters that Mr. Gross had manifested. A new assistant to the chairman was chosen with a view to lightening the chairman's load by doing certain research and drafting tasks under his direction. Mr. Clark had already had a staff appointee designated as his assistant, and Blough soon followed suit. Staff positions have been filled in general by men of less age and reputation than the first incumbents but of high professional quality.

CHAPTER SIXTEEN

The Joint Economic Committee, 1950–52

The scope and methods of the Joint Committee's work program initiated under Senator Taft and Staff Director Hardy and further developed under Senator O'Mahoney and Director Kreps, which Chapter XIII has traced to about the middle of 1950, have followed essentially similar lines down to the present, but with some new developments which will be noted presently.

The personnel of the committee was necessarily altered by the Congressional elections of November 1950. On the Senate side, William Benton of Connecticut took the place of Francis Myers of Pennsylvania and, on the House side, Representatives Buchanan of Pennsylvania and Boggs of Delaware took the places of Walter Huber of Ohio and Robert F. Rich of Pennsylvania. The outcome of the election of November 1952 will now call for sweeping changes in the committee.

The committee staff has also undergone some changes. On January 16, 1950, there was added to the staff a specialist on the "aggregate" method of drawing up a periodic "nation's economic budget" and preparing the economic outlook reports, which are becoming an increasingly important part of the staff's work. In October 1951, another staff appointment was made—a man capable of assisting in the work of preparing the nation's economic budget, but also a specialist in agricultural economics. On April 1, 1951, the title of Theodore Kreps was changed from Director to "consultant" to the Joint Committee, and Grover Ensley, who had been Associate Director of Staff, became Staff Director. Dr. Kreps continues his part-time connection with the Legislative Reference Service at the Library of Congress and comes to Washington from time to time to work on special problems for the Joint Committee or its chairman as such problems arise and as his teaching program permits.

Mr. Berquist continued as a full-time employee of the Joint Committee and was referred to even in published documents as "minority economist." He has not participated in the initial preparation of what are called staff materials, and has had the opportunity of commenting on them only when they were circulated in draft form to committee members. He has done research for Senator Taft or other members of the minority group and participated in the preparation of such separate statements as they put out from time to time.

HEARINGS AND COMMITTEE REPORT ON THE
PRESIDENT'S ECONOMIC REPORT

Public hearings on the 1951 Economic Report of the President were begun on January 22 and lasted seven days. First to testify were Chairman Keyserling and Dr. Clark of the Council of Economic Advisers. They were followed by Budget Director Lawton; Cyrus Ching, Chairman of the Wage Stabilization Board; Michael DiSalle, Director of the Office of Price Stabilization; Marriner Eccles of the Board of Governors of the Federal Reserve System; Eric Johnston, Administrator of the Economic Stabilization Agency; and Charles E. Wilson, Director of the Office of Defense Mobilization. The testimony of these government officials was followed by four days of roundtable discussion by twenty-four nongovernment economists. This part of the hearings was divided under four topics: direct controls; fiscal policy; the inflation problem; and monetary, credit, and debt management problems. Letters expressing views on the economic situation were also received from "various institutions and organizations"—business, labor, agriculture, and so forth —in reply to a letter of inquiry from Senator O'Mahoney.

The committee report in 1951 was filed on "legislative day" March 26 (April 2 on the calendar). It departed from the precedent of the preceding years in that it took the form of a single committee report rather than separate majority and minority reports. Some amusement was expressed over the presentation of this as a consensus report in spite of the fact that a lengthy "supplementary view" was appended by Senator Benton and a shorter one in which Representatives Wolcott and Herter joined, while there were footnote qualifications or additions by Senator Douglas (9), Senator Sparkman (5), Senator Benton (9), Senator Taft (2), Senator O'Mahoney (1); Representative Bolling (8), Representative Hart (3), Representative Herter (2), and Representative Patman (1). Representative Boggs made the following supplementary statement:

> I wish to make it clear that I was not appointed to committee membership in time to participate in any of the committee hearings or deliberations, except three brief executive sessions called after this report had been drafted. Therefore, it would seem improper and misleading for me to join in this report.
>
> I would like to observe, however, that I have noted the marked shift in position of the majority views as compared with previous reports. This is good, especially in regard to Government spending programs and the recognition of the dangers of inflation.

In fact, it was apparently this modification of view on spending programs and inflation dangers on the part of majority members which led to the decision to present this as a full-committee report. Chairman O'Mahoney undertook to reconcile this difference by remarking in his note:

> The "shift of position and emphasis" seen by our three colleagues is no shift at all; it is merely a recognition of the fact that when the Government, under the necessary impetus of an expanded preparedness program, is forced to incur unusual expenditures for national defense, no logical basis remains to continue expenditures which were wholly justified at a time when the objective of government, largely supported without partisan division, was to expand employment, production, and business enterprise. The simple theory of this report is that the Government, when fighting inflation, must necessarily adopt an economic policy different from that which is wholly justifiable when it is endeavoring to fight deflation [i. e., in 1948 and 1949].

In spite of this explanation, the Joint Committee's report on the President's Economic Report of January 1951—perhaps because of its bipartisan character—reads much less like a brief in support of the President's report than previous reports had. It, with its footnotes and explanatory statements, presented a quite independent and stimulating discussion of the major economic issues before the country. Its opening paragraphs read:

With a national debt hovering at a pinnacle of $257 billion since 1946, and the cost of living still rising above the all-time peak reached in December 1950, the people and the Government of the United States are face to face with the imperative necessity of stopping inflation and turning it backward if the national hope for the winning of the peace is to be achieved. . . . Milk and munitions are both mounting in cost and, as a result, the problem which every householder faces in providing for his family is faced by the President and the Congress in providing the necessary military power by which freedom is to be defended.

When it is realized that the national debt, which was less than $50 billion at the beginning of 1941, had risen to $277 billion by the time Japan surrendered, it is clear that deficit spending cannot be contemplated even for the current defense program, unless we are willing to invite the crack-up of the American system. We cannot permit the cost of living to continue to rise, nor can we pile a new national defense debt on top of the unpaid debt of World War II without creating the very conditions upon which the dictators of the Kremlin are relying to destroy the economic basis of this Government and thereby the hope of a free world. (p. 1)

Passing to the discussion of "the paramount need for government economy," the committee said:

. . . we must be prudent, frugal, even parsimonious. We must avoid duplication, swollen inventories and extravagant construction—in short, all unnecessary military expenditures. This is no time for luxury, waste, or extravagance anywhere, not even in the armed services. . . .

It will be necessary also to economize in the civilian branch of the Federal budget. Stimulated by the Congress, the Bureau of the Budget last summer at the direction of the President made an auspicious beginning in cutting back public works, reclamation and other expenditures more than $580,000,000 in accordance with the principle that programs which are not essential to the defense effort, or to maximum civilian productivity (without which the civilian economy will be unable to produce the revenue on which the defense program rests) should be rigorously cut, if not eliminated. Such co-operative economy efforts must be greatly expanded. . . .

This committee is making an intensive study of the 1952 budget, some results of which are to be found in the staff materials and in appendix 3 of this report. There it is noted that existing laws may have to be altered or repealed if major economies are to be effected in nondefense spending. The appropriate legislative committees of the Congress should study and recommend what changes shall be made. In fact, economy is a vital responsibility of every Member of Congress and every citizen. (pp. 3–4)

Under the heading "reducing the cost of living," the committee's report was quite specific:

One cannot quarrel with the principle of the price-support law, the purpose of which is to maintain general parity between agricultural and industrial prices. It is an altogether different problem, however, to what extent the price-stabilization law should prevent price-control officials from holding the line on agricultural prices. . . . The provision in the Defense Production Act therefore tends to gear agricultural prices to the highest level of industrial prices. The advisability of a re-examination of the provision of the Defense Production Act, from the point of view of its effect upon the fight against inflation, is clearly indicated.

Likewise when in certain industries, such as the motor car industry, the compensation of labor was based upon the cost of living, another escalator was brought into existence. However desirable such co-operative arrangements between management and labor may be in ordinary times— and on that point no reflection of any kind is intended—one of the effects important for these times is that it serves as a basis to push up prices. Congress itself has long used the same principle. Government pay has in recent years likewise been increased upon the justification that the Government worker, like the farmer and the industrial worker, was entitled to larger compensation because of the rising cost of living.

Thus a challenge is presented to the Congress to modify, by legislative enactment, this engine of inflation which will continue to press constantly upward on prices unless we find the way to stop the inflationary spiral so that a just stabilization ratio may be attained between agricultural prices, wages, industrial prices, and profits. All must be stabilized on a just basis by the removal of every factor contributing to the inflationary spiral.

To permit administered prices to be maintained in some important industries with undiminished force, to allow the resultant corporate profits to continue at present extraordinary levels, to try to keep farm prices by Government price-support programs on a parity calculated from such industrial prices, to allow escalator clauses to continue in force in wage contracts tying wages to the cost of living, to make price-ceiling adjustments on the basis of increases in materials and labor costs and thereby to raise further the cost of living—is merely to set up an unbeatable mechanism of built-in inflation that, however endurable for a short war, could prove disastrous during a long preparedness period. (pp. 8–9)

After noting that economic statesmanship must seek "solutions for a long period of watchful peace," the Committee Report proceeded to comment on the President's recommendation in his Economic Report under twenty-one points. It endorsed the effort to expand production, both to fulfill defense needs and to check inflation. It recommended against the President's proposal to authorize direct government construction of government facilities "except in limited fields where clearly demonstrated to be necessary." It dealt very gingerly with the St. Lawrence seaway and power project and a variety of welfare measures, but went farther than the President in recommending "additional tax measures to finance the cost of national defense on a pay-as-we-go basis. . . . It feels that the defense garment should be cut to the revenue cloth."[1] (pp. 12–17) It supported the strengthening of rent control and credit control on purchase of existing homes.

In January 1952 the hearings of the Joint Committee followed almost identically the pattern of the preceding year except that there were three panel discussions by the economists instead of four and a somewhat less voluminous series of replies from business, labor, and other organizations and institutions to questions submitted by the chairman of the Joint Committee.

The Joint Committee's report on the President's policy recommendations was not in final form for submitting on March 1 as required by the law, but on February 29, Senator O'Mahoney released to the press a "proposed draft of a committee report of the 1952 Economic Report of the President as submitted to the members of the Joint Committee on the Economic Report by Chairman Joseph C. O'Mahoney in executive session, Thursday, February 28. The proposed report was not acted upon by the committee, but the Chairman was authorized to release these draft materials to the press." On March 7, Senator Douglas released a supplementary statement of almost equal length, with Senator Benton concurring. On March 12, these two documents, with slight additions and changes, a page and a half of "minority views," and 104 pages of staff materials were transmitted to Congress and printed as Senate

---

[1] At this point (p. 15), however, there was a footnote signed by Senators Douglas and Benton and Representative Bolling. They said: "We are opposed to this recommendation. It states that 'the defense garment should be cut to the revenue cloth.' In our judgment, the revenue garment should be cut to fit the defense cloth. Furthermore, we oppose the level of defense spending in the President's budget as an absolute minimum. We may need more. We may even need to build up our defense to a greater degree than present plans call for. Freedom is more important than opulence and without freedom opulence will disappear." This position of Senator Douglas may be compared with his stand a year later. (See p. 315.)

Report No. 1295. For the first time the staff section of the Joint Committee report was given a separate formal title page under the caption "National Defense and the Economic Outlook for the Fiscal Year 1953."

A striking feature of the 1952 committee report was that, even more explicitly than in the preceding year, it enunciated a major policy not in full accord with that recommended by the President in his Economic Report. After noting that, even after some adjustment to the idea that World War III can be avoided and the program for the military build-up prolonged to a peak date two or three years later than originally planned,

> The preparedness program is nevertheless . . . so expensive that it cannot be financed within the limits of the revenues estimated to be derived from present tax laws. Assuming these expenditures to be necessary, a pay-as-we-go program would require an increase in taxes greater than that recommended by the President. There being no possibility that this Congress will increase taxes as requested, the pay-as-we-go anti-inflationary program can be preserved only by a reduction of expenditures to eliminate the cash deficit. A reduction of approximately $10 billion would seem to be necessary to accomplish this purpose. (pp. 1, 2)

The Douglas supplemental statement began: "The committee report is generally acceptable. But in my opinion, it is not specific enough and lacks proper emphasis. In support of this conclusion, I submit the following statement of supplemental views. Senator Benton joins with me in this statement." The pages that followed spelled out chapter and verse of a program of specific savings and expenditure reductions amounting to $7.6 billion and proposals for increasing tax revenues without increasing general tax rates which Senator Douglas calculated would yield $2.4 billion, thus reducing the prospective deficit by a total of $10 billion.

The minority views were similar but sharper in tone. "We feel that the report sets forth many of these high purposes [adequate national security without deficits and inflation] but appears to lack both conviction and method as to their accomplishment."

> Thus the suggested $10 billion reduction in expenditures, to avoid the "luxury" of a deficit, is finally termed "unrealistic" and a smaller figure of reduction is probably expected. Perhaps that accounts for the omission of any schedule of expenditure cuts, but instead a considerable analysis

is given of the nature of various expenditure items, which emphasizes the difficulty of cutting them. . . . (p. 27)

Although the absence of signatures to what was offered as a report of the Joint Committee implied that it was endorsed by all members unless otherwise specified, the minority view said: "Accordingly, we do not join in approving the report as a whole and briefly state our position below, reserving the privilege to comment in greater length and detail at a later date." They continued:

The majority report rejects the two major recommendations made by the President and his economic advisers: (a) the high level of expenditures proposed, and (b) an increase in taxes.

We welcome this position. It recognizes as unrealistic further increases in taxes, which have already reached the point of diminishing returns, only to fall short of ever-growing expenditures. Under existing law only by reducing expenditures in every possible area can we counteract the inevitable inflation resulting from deficits. We are convinced the cuts can be made and must be made if we are to maintain our basic economic strength, the prerequisite to our whole defense program. (p. 27)

The minority likewise took the position that

the report fails to recognize the importance of monetary and credit policy and its role as an anti-inflationary force. In this we concur with the views as set forth by Senator Douglas. These restate the position taken by the minority in its three previous annual dissents with the President's and the majority's reports. We believe that much, if not most, of the anti-inflationary effect that might have been expected from the imposition of taxes since Korea has been dissipated by the delay in freeing the Federal Reserve Board's monetary and credit functions from Treasury domination. (p. 28)

The minority views were signed by Senators Taft and Watkins and by Representatives Wolcott, Herter, and Boggs. Senator Flanders did not join in the minority views, but appended three footnotes over his own signature to the committee report proper.

SPECIAL COMMITTEE REPORTS AND STAFF WORK

The major investigational enterprise undertaken by the Joint Committee during the last two years was its study of monetary policy and the management of the public debt. This study was initiated by the appointment of a Subcommittee on General Credit Control and Debt Management in the spring of 1951 under the chairmanship of Representative Wright Patman. The project was somewhat in the nature of an extension of the study conducted during the latter part of 1949 and early 1950 by the Douglas Subcommittee on Monetary, Credit, and Fiscal Policies. Said Mr. Patman:

> The two years which have passed since that time have been packed with events. The international situation has deteriorated markedly, and the United States Government has embarked on a vast program of military preparedness with its inevitable corollary of increased inflationary pressure. . . . There has been much disagreement, both inside and outside the Government, with respect to the proper steps to be taken in the present emergency in the fields of credit policy and debt management; and, notwithstanding the "accord" announced by the Treasury and the Federal Reserve System in March of this year, much of the course to be followed remains to be charted. The policy disputes of the past year have also brought into sharp focus the question of whether our machinery for the determination of monetary policy—set up, for the most part, many years ago—is appropriate to cope with the problems of the present day and to carry into effect the policy of the Congress with respect to economic stability as set forth in the Employment Act of 1946.[2]

The new subcommittee undertook to investigate these questions very broadly, beginning with a carefully prepared set of questionnaires which were sent to thirteen government agencies and private groups and organizations as follows: the Secretary of the Treasury, Chairman of the Board of Governors of the Federal Reserve System, Chairman of the Open Market Committee, the presidents of the Federal Reserve banks, the Council of Economic Advisers, the Comptroller of the Currency, Chairman of the Federal Deposit Insurance Corporation, Administrator of the Reconstruction Finance Corporation, state bank supervisors, economists, bankers, life insurance company executives, and United States government security dealers.

This inquiry was taken very seriously by the recipients of the subcommittee's questionnaires, and replies were prepared in great detail and with careful consideration.[3] They were published (Feb-

[2] *Questions on General Credit Control and Debt Management* (Joint Committee Print) 82 Cong. 1 sess., October 1951, p. 1.

[3] The reply of the Council of Economic Advisers covered 47 pages. Mr. Clark did not participate in the development of the answers to the questions submitted to the Council by the subcommittee. But, for the convenience of members of the subcommittee and the public generally, the "Separate Note by Mr. Clark upon Monetary and Credit Policy" which appeared on pp. 142–44 of the Annual Eco-

ruary 1952) in two volumes totaling 1300 pages and constitute the most authoritative and comprehensive body of material on this whole subject. The questionnaire procedure was supplemented by a series of public hearings covering sixteen days between March 10 and 31, inclusive, which also were made available in published form. The committee's report was published on June 26, 1952.[4]

In his letter of transmittal, Representative Patman observed:

> The report covers a wide variety of subject matter, and, dealing as it does with material which has so often been treated more in the heat of the emotions than in the light of the intellect, shows a surprisingly large area of agreement. We believe that this widening of the area of agreement on matters of monetary policy and debt management, both among the members of the Subcommittee and among students of the subject generally, represents the principal accomplishment of our inquiry. The extension of areas of agreement by patient discussion represents the democratic process at its best; the persistence of residual areas of disagreement shows that the process is the democratic process indeed, for complete agreement can seldom be attained this side of either Utopia or Tyranny. (p. iii)

This view as to the value of the study is fully shared by the financial community and by professional students of the problem. As in the case of other subcommittee reports, an economist not on the regular staff of the Joint Committee was retained as economist for the subcommittee and took a large part in synthesizing the materials which it gathered.

Since mid-1950, the activities of the Joint Committee have quite naturally focused on defense needs and their impact on the longerrun economic stabilization problem. Within a month after the Korean outbreak, Chairman O'Mahoney directed a memorandum to the members of the Joint Committee on the subject: "Has the Joint Committee a Function to Perform in the Present Economic Crisis?"[5] After commenting on the nature and scope of the military

---

nomic Review by the Council of Economic Advisers (January 1952) was appended to the Council's reply.

[4] *Monetary Policy and the Management of the Public Debt* (Report of the Subcommittee on General Credit Control and Debt Management of the Joint Committee on the Economic Report) 82 Cong. 2 sess.

[5] The full text of this memorandum appears as Appendix 2 in the *Report of the Joint Committee on the Economic Report of the President* of April 2, 1951 (Senate Report No. 210), p. 82 under the title "Economic Preparedness Requires Higher Taxes."

threat, Senator O'Mahoney said: "Congress is ready now to approve increased military expenditures. Such appropriations should be accompanied by a tax bill which will finance the expense without increasing the debt."

At my request the staff has made a review of the present economic situation involving recommendations as follows:

(1) Balance the cash budget. Federal expenditures should be held to the minimum, particularly those not directly connected with military requirements and vital economic expansion. Once the expenditure program for the next fiscal year has been enacted, the Congress, after conservatively estimating the increased yield in taxes likely to result from increased levels of business activity, should increase governmental revenues by enough to balance the cash budget.

(2) Restore consumer credit control.

(3) Authorize allocation machinery for critically scarce materials.

(4) Implement through the United Nations the point 4 program and other measures, providing not only for expanded technical, education, and economic assistance, but for freer flow of goods, services, and capital, to every member of the family of nations seeking peace and freedom.

Furthermore, immediate administrative action should be taken (1) to contract credit for all activities that unduly compete with expanded armament effort; (2) to impound, insofar as possible, funds appropriated for nonvital postponable objectives; (3) to develop a program for private expansion of productive capacity of critical items such as steel; and (4) to encourage increased private savings, via sale of savings bonds.

I venture to suggest that this committee, with its background of economic information, can and should make its contribution to public understanding of the profound effects of the present acute situation. (p. 83)

Following up this memorandum, the chairman called the committee together in executive session three days later—July 21, 1950. This was the beginning of Joint Committee leadership in Congress toward something approximating a pay-as-you-go defense program and toward credit and other controls that would help reduce inflation pressures. This trend of the committee's activities has already been noted in connection with its two subsequent reports on the Economic Report of the President.

Besides the analysis referred to in Senator O'Mahoney's memorandum, the staff in early 1951 prepared a study of *General Credit Control, Debt Management, and Economic Mobilization* at the suggestion of Representative Patman and Senator Flanders. This was published as a committee print in January 1951 and was a factual review (98 pages) designed to "supplement and expand, in the light of current developments, information made available in 1950 by our Subcommittee on Monetary, Credit and Fiscal Policies under the chairmanship of Senator Paul H. Douglas."

On February 23, the staff furnished the committee further materials for its study of national policy under the title *The Economic and Political Hazards of an Inflationary Defense Economy* (committee print). This report introduced a technique of economic "projections" which has since been continued. (See p. 322.)

On June 13, they transmitted a report on "the importance of industrial development from the point of view of security in the event of war emergency and, second, from the point of view of strengthening the domestic economy."[6] This was followed in early August by a midyear review which was published as a committee print under the title *National Defense and the Economic Outlook*. This memorandum illustrates the way in which staff work was designed to keep members of the Joint Committee supplied with the latest figures and other information as to most recent economic developments as the legislative session progressed. It began:

> This report presents economic data intended to be helpful to the Congress in considering legislation in two major areas in which action is scheduled before the congressional recess: (1) the 1952 appropriation and foreign-aid bills which, allowing for prospective lags in deliveries of military goods, may result in a level of Federal expenditures in fiscal year 1952 of $68.4 billion according to latest estimates of the Bureau of the Budget, and (2) the proposed increase in taxes with the hope of closing the consumer inflationary gap, estimated at $5 billion for the fiscal year 1952, and of balancing the administrative budget. (p. 1)

The report then proceeded to review the first year of the defense economy as it had actually worked out, prospects for the second year under stated assumptions as to revenue and expenditure, and the consequences in subsequent years if a deficit were permitted. Thus this report marked the third use[7] by the Joint Committee staff of its projections technique on the Nation's Economic Budget.

The implications of the figures and the analysis presented were so

6 *The Need for Industrial Dispersal* (S. Doc. 155, 82 Cong. 1 sess.)

7 The second was in the staff materials included in the *Joint Committee's Report on the Economic Report of the President* (April 2, 1951).

convincing to the Joint Committee that they converted this staff memorandum into a committee report by prefacing it with a one-page statement of their conclusions and recommendations. This report appeared under the title *Inflation Still A Danger*.[8] The key statements of the Committee were as follows:

The committee believes that fundamental inflationary pressures will continue to mount in the months to come as the presently scheduled defense effort diverts larger portions of national production from civilian use. . . .

Doubts as to the efficacy of direct controls, including selective credit controls, under the Defense Production Act as amended make it all the more important that the expected inflationary gap be closed by rigorous Government economy and increased taxes. (p. 1)

This report was signed by all fourteen members of the Joint Committee and reaffirmed its position on sound fiscal policy, initiated by the Korean outbreak.

In February 1952, the staff of the Joint Committee completed a quite detailed study of the current situation and outlook, designed for the use of the committee in considering the nature of its report on the President's Economic Report. This study, under the title *National Defense and the Economic Outlook for the Fiscal Year 1953*, appeared as a committee print on February 21 and was subsequently incorporated as the staff materials section of the Joint Committee report on the Economic Report.

Thus there appears to have become established a practice on the part of the staff of the Joint Committee of presenting a detailed independent appraisal of the economic situation and trends for the use of the committee in preparation of their report on the Economic Report of the President and for its inclusion as a part of that document. The staff also prepares briefer and less formal interim reports on the economic situation and outlook. Events were moving so fast in the spring of 1952 that the chairman of the Joint Committee requested the staff to bring their figures and analyses up to date after the first quarter "to keep the members of the committee informed as to the current economic situation." In response to this request, the staff presented a five-page mimeographed memorandum under the title "Economic Outlook as of April 1, 1952." Later, as soon as figures for the end of the fiscal year (June 30) were avail-

[8] *S. Rept. No. 644*, 81 Cong. 1 sess.

able, the staff prepared a summary of "The Economic Outlook as of July 5, 1952." This was a nine-page memorandum transmitted to members of the committee and made available to other interested persons.

All these analyses are based on, and the annual outlook statement presents in detail, the "aggregate" method of analyzing economic trends and of making projections as to what may be expected to happen under each of perhaps three sets of reasonable assumptions.[9] Here the staff of the Joint Committee is making application of some of the newer statistical and analytical techniques being developed by the economics profession. It does this parallel to, but independent of, the analysis used by the staff of the Council of Economic Advisers. While these methods are somewhat technical in character, their presentation is reduced to terms readily understandable by the layman in the staff materials prepared for the use of members of the Joint Committee, other Congressional committees, government agencies, and the public.

In an introductory paragraph to the Review and Outlook statement of the staff in the Joint Economic Report for 1951, Senator O'Mahoney (as the chairman had whenever staff materials were prepared in the past) noted that: "Neither the committee nor the individual members are in any way committed to any of the views expressed or to any of the conclusions that may seem to follow, directly or indirectly, from any of the analyses or statistical data selected for presentation." To this Senator Taft added a note:

In signing the foregoing report, I wish to make it clear that I do not approve many of the conclusions reached by the committee staff and printed at the end of this report under the caption "Supplemental staff material."

The matter relating to the distribution of incomes, the burden of taxa-

[9] A fairly detailed discussion of this method of projection is printed as Appendix A in the Joint Committee's Report of March 12, 1952. Dr. Ensley describes the method briefly as follows: "An economic budget for the Nation is a tool for synthesizing data and for providing a methodology for seeing in perspective the operation of all segments of the economy—consumer, business, and Government. . . . use of the Nation's economic budget procedures in no way implies or justifies a 'planned economy' in the sense usually associated with the term—an economy directed by central authority, either democratic or autocratic. Rather, the procedure provides a method or a tool whereby economic data may be made available and used by individuals, businesses, and governments in improving their own programs, and thus the general welfare." (p. 99)

tion, the analysis of corporate profits, is interesting and provocative, but the conclusions particularly as to the proper method of taxation to finance the mobilization effort are certainly open to question.

As a member of the Finance Committee, I will be required to pass on these questions at a later time, and I do not desire, therefore, at this time to state specifically my differences with the staff report.

On December 11, 1952, Senator O'Mahoney transmitted to members of the Joint Committee "an analysis by the committee staff of some of the major sustaining forces which are likely to influence the Nation's economy in the future." This appeared shortly as a Joint Committee print under the title *The Sustaining Forces Ahead* (70 pp.).

From this account of the extensive use of staff studies, it must be evident that in this way and also through the selection of participants in the committee's hearings and the drafting of letters of inquiry or questionnaires sent out in connection with these studies, the staff of the Joint Committee has gradually become a very influential factor in the actual functioning of the committee. The work of the "minority economist" is not integrated with that of the staff as a whole but he performs a special staff function for the former chairman of the Joint Committee and other minority members when they wish to make an independent audit of general staff materials, prepare dissenting statements, or make their own inquiries on topics related to the Joint Committee's work.

OUTSIDE CONTACTS OF THE JOINT COMMITTEE

It may be recalled that in the committee's annual report of March 1, 1950, gratification was expressed at the more active and helpful relations that had been established between the Joint Committee and other Congressional committees and between the committee and the various executive departments and agencies. Further evidence of this development has accumulated during the last two years.

Not only have various administrative officers of government participated in the hearings on the Economic Report of the President which are conducted by the Joint Committee or in connection with the questionnaires and hearings on such special studies as that on *Monetary Policy and Management of the Public Debt.* Their agencies have also collaborated directly on Joint Committee studies on several occasions. In the case of a Joint Committee study of *Constitutional Limitations on Federal Income, Estate and Gift*

Taxes (February 1952), the staffs of the Treasury Department and the Legislative Reference Service of the Library of Congress operated in full collaboration with the committee staff. There was also a novel instance of collaboration with a nongovernment organization in the case of the Conference Group on Low-Income Families. This group, in response to a request by Senator Sparkman as chairman of the Joint Committee Subcommittee on Low-Income Families, prepared case studies of 100 low-income families, which were presented as a Joint Committee print under the title *Making Ends Meet on Less than $2,000 a Year.*

Likewise, the Joint Committee's continuing study of problems of national economic stability is gradually leading them into more active co-operation with and service to other committees of the Congress. For example, Senator Sparkman, besides being a member of the Joint Committee was chairman of the Senate Select Committee on Small Business. This committee was interested from the standpoint of the small businessman in the problem of price cutting and "fair trade" laws. This was a problem of interest also to the Joint Committee in its broad concern in the problems of monopoly and competition. A study to ascertain the effects of a recent Supreme Court decision in this area was conducted over a one-month period through the facilities of Dun and Bradstreet and published as a committee print for the Joint Committee and the Committee on Small Business under the title *Prevalence of Price Cutting of Merchandise Marketed under Price Maintenance Laws (May 28 through June 25, 1951).*

Two other instances of collaboration of the Joint Committee with outside agencies concern the National Planning Association. While the work of the Subcommittee on Monetary, Credit, and Fiscal Policies was under way, Chairman Douglas and Senator Flanders invited the National Planning Association to sponsor and arrange a conference of outstanding economists not in government employment, to see how large an area of agreement existed among them as to the role of fiscal and monetary policy in the stabilization efforts of government. The National Planning Association decided to confine its first conference to fiscal policy since the inclusion of monetary and credit issues would make the problem too complicated. At their invitation, fourteen outstanding economists from universities widely scattered over the country—all specialists in fiscal and taxation problems—were assembled at Princeton University for a three-day session. During this conference, they developed a succinct statement under the title *Federal Expenditure and Revenue Policy for Economic Stability*. To this statement all fourteen agreed without reservation.

The central principle of the document was that the national budget should be balanced over a period of years, with surpluses accumulated and debt curtailed in periods of prosperity and especially of inflationary boom so that support could be given to the economy when recession threatens or that extraordinary war strains may be met. They raised, but did not attempt to answer, the question whether the necessary flexibility could be obtained "without granting to the Executive wider discretionary authority than it now possesses to initiate changes in the timing or extent of the fiscal program." The second part of the committee's report outlined a number of suggestions for fiscal policy in the near future.

This group recommended that the National Planning Association call a similar conference to discuss questions of monetary policy, which were suggested by the Joint Committee but which the conference group did not think it possible for them to deal with during the limited time of their meeting. The second economist group was somewhat larger than the first—twenty-three as against fourteen. Nineteen members of the group signed a set of ten recommendations on "Monetary Policy to Combat Inflation" with a footnote qualification to the statement as a whole by two of the signers and to seven of the separate recommendations by eight of the signers. Four members of the group declined to sign but appended explanatory footnotes. Professor Alvin Hansen said: "The statement implies that monetary policy is more potent than it actually is," whereas Professor Jacob Viner of Princeton declared that "the support here given to vigorous use of monetary policy is too weak and excessively qualified."

It remains to be seen whether or not this experiment in trying to get economists to define their areas of agreement on problems being dealt with by the Joint Committee proves sufficiently fruitful so that it will be repeated in future. At all events, it seems likely that the practice of using panels of nongovernment economists for discussing questions as part of the hearings procedure on the Economic Report of the President will be continued.

On December 19, 1952, Senator O'Mahoney transmitted to members of the Joint Committee a rather lengthy report prepared under the auspices of the National Planning Association, entitled *Pensions in the United States.* "This report was prepared at my invitation to the Association to sponsor a study of the effects of public and private pension programs on the national economy as recommended in the final report of the Subcommittee on Low-Income Families. . . . We are grateful to the National Planning Association and its board of trustees for arranging for the conduct of this study with the help of a special grant from the John Hay Whitney Foundation of New York City." This study was published shortly as a Joint Committee print. Appendix B presented a list and brief description of "research in progress" on the pension problem.

The Joint Economic Committee is in a state of somewhat reduced activity at the present moment (December 1952). Members naturally were, in varying degrees, preoccupied with the Presidential election and various state campaigns.[10] It would hardly have been appropriate to initiate large subcommittee studies which could not have been completed before the end of the present calendar year. As a result of the November election the make-up of the committee in the 83rd Congress will differ materially from that of the previous session. Meanwhile, basic staff work on the study of current trends and the checking of their past projections against actual developments continues. Of particular interest is the expressed intention of the staff to focus attention on a study of "Long-Term Economic Adjustments."

This study will attempt to provide materials on the needs and opportunities to which the Nation can devote itself once the defense buildup is completed. The analysis will center upon the role to be played by business, consumers and Government in the period of readjustment [and] . . . will undertake to answer such questions as:

What will private investment requirements be after the period of major defense expenditures?

How is such private investment stimulated?

What will the demand for housing be?

---

[10] In fact, of the seven Senate members, three ran for re-election (two of them being defeated) and a fourth was a candidate for the Vice Presidency. Two of the House members were nominees for Governor of their state and both were elected.

Will there be a sufficient supply of industrial raw materials to enable the economy to operate at high levels?

Will the labor force grow faster than economic expansion can provide jobs?

Will research, technology, new industries and new enterprises go forward at the pace necessary for a stable economy at maximum employment?

What will be the nature and size of accumulated public needs?[11]

Here as elsewhere the Joint Committee staff will not undertake original fact-gathering or duplicating analyses but rather the collation of such materials from the full range of Government agencies. "This approach has served to minimize the duplication of work but has in no way affected the independence of operation and thinking of the Joint Economic Committee staff."[12]

[11] *Report of the Joint Committee on the January 1952 Economic Report of the President*, 82 Cong. 2 sess., Senate Report No. 1295, p. 128.

[12] The same, p. 132.

PART
III

First Tries and Second Reflections

INTRODUCTION

In Part I there was presented a conceptual picture of our representative system of government reaching forward to the conscious expression of a national philosophy of economic life. It challenged our power to construct a scheme of business organization in which men, risen above the life of the cave and the jungle, could associate peacefully and productively under a self-imposed system of property rights and voluntary bargains, individual and group, so as to apply their labor in the satisfaction of their wants and those of their families up to the point where they value leisure more than additional goods or services.

Those opening chapters started from the premise that, at an accelerating rate in recent years, we have developed means of visualizing the economic process as a totality of infinitely numerous constituent parts, of analyzing cause and effect relations within that process, and of devising means of measuring the forces involved and guiding their action to our purpose. The last three chapters of Part I noted a number of recent steps toward national economic policy-making and the growing use of professionally trained economists to give technical advice to those executives of the political state who are the authorized makers of government policy.

The Employment Act of 1946 was seen as the latest explicit effort to set national economic policy-making on a higher plane of performance and to use the tools of formal economics and the personnel of the craft more effectively to that end.

In Part II there was unfolded a personalized record of the first phase—or two phases—of operation under this new statute. Every effort was made to limit the narrative to facts and to defer judgments. "These persons did these things in these successive situations." Several professional friends who have read parts of the manuscript while it was in process have suggested that this section should have been preceded by a chapter analyzing the Employment Act or at least giving a systematic account of its legislative history. Some were inclined to feel also that Part II should have opened with a "scholarly" presentation of the assumptions from which we began the administration of the act and the criteria we sought to apply or that should have guided our actions.

Perhaps I am carrying inductive empiricism too far, but it seemed to me more realistic to let the narrative of actual events unfold with no more of an "apperceptive mass" in the mind of the reader than there was in the mind of the writer when he entered this field of action. I had only a sketchy knowledge of the history of the act and the intent of Congress in passing it. It would be presumptuous and probably misleading for me to attempt to say what assumptions, intentions, or criteria were in the minds of my colleagues, the President, and others in the executive branch of government, or the members and staff of the Joint Economic Committee of Congress. The Employment Act was a unique venture in our government annals and no other government had pioneered before us with similar machinery for implementing stabilization policy. Events crowded upon us, and we all had to improvise from such varied trainings and experiences as we then possessed.

But now that some of us have had time to reflect upon matters of which we were a part and the reader has—if his patience has not deserted him—followed a streamlined record of these events, it is well to turn back to the origin of the act, do a little "homework" on the intent of Congress—the plural intents of various elements in Congress more or less responsive to their constituents or to others who participated in the framing of the act. Such is the purpose of Chapter XVII. It will show that the members of Congress, while actively, sometimes even violently, concerned about the economic features proposed in their respective bills, were hardly less insistent on certain administrative aspects. While they battled some points out to solution or compromise in the bill, they completely overlooked other administrative issues, some of which in practice have assumed crucial importance.

In Chapters XVIII, XIX, and XX, we will look back over the

record sketched in Part II to consider how well the administrative provisions made by Congress have worked in practice, how some ambiguous mandates have been interpreted by the various parties, and how unforeseen problems have been dealt with as they arose. These chapters undertake some retrospective analysis of major mistakes and misadventures of the several parties to the administrative process. The final chapter will try to peer ahead a bit to estimate the probable permanence and degree of success of this new venture in Federal economic policy-making and consider modifications that might be introduced in the light of six years of experience.

CHAPTER SEVENTEEN

What Was the Intent of Congress?

Seeking to discern the intent of Congress in passing the Employment Act, one naturally turns first to the text of the statute itself. It is very brief, and the legislative history of the act shows that many expressions or provisions contained in early bills were discarded in the final drafting because they became involved in controversy. In other cases a final text was arrived at only by having an idea clothed in vague or very general terms. Some further insights can, therefore, be gained by going back to examine the two bills that were the parents of the Employment Act.

The outstanding feature of S. 380 was the application of compensatory fiscal policy to the attack on business depressions.[1] It called on the President to present a National Production and Employment Budget (abbreviated to National Budget), but the preparation of this document was conceived as a function which could be discharged by the President through existing agencies, notably the Bureau of the Budget. This bill contained no suggestion of a Council of Economic Advisers or any new administrative machinery in the executive branch. In the legislative branch, it proposed a

[1] "Mr. Whittington: The Senate bill declared that it is the responsibility of the Federal Government to assure at all times sufficient opportunities for employment to enable all Americans able and willing to work to exercise their right to continued full employment. The declaration was implemented by Federal expenditures and investments to attain the policy of full employment. . . . Without question there was emphasis in the Senate bill on spending, expenditures and disbursements. Deficit spending would have obtained." *Cong. Record* (79 Cong. 2 sess.) , Vol. 92, Pt. 1, pp. 984–85.

Joint Committee on the National Budget, but this was largely an *ex officio* conference group of the ranking members of the Senate and House committees particularly concerned with economic matters. While this committee, like other Congressional committees, was authorized "to employ such experts, consultants, technicians, and clerical and stenographic assistants as it deemed necessary and advisable," there was no hint of any elaborate or permanent committee staff. The Senate, in its discussion of this bill, tended to be preoccupied with its economic proposals and had very little administrative subject matter to consider.

The first draft of H. R. 2202 proposed only a flexible public works program, adjusted to conditions of employment. But the House subsequently dropped even this vestige of compensatory spending in favor of a comprehensive analytical approach to the whole problem of economic stabilization. By the time the bill was passed by the House, public works were reduced to a subordinate position as one item in an eclectic program for attacking the broad program of national economic welfare. This change in economic philosophy was naturally accompanied by a shift to greater emphasis on administrative aspects of the whole problem of policy-making. Instead of a National Budget to be submitted by the President in rather bare financial terms, the bill finally passed by the House called for a detailed factual and interpretative report of the President "on economic conditions affecting employment in the United States or any considerable portion thereof, on the extent to which the policies declared in section 2 are or are not being achieved, and on the extent to which the various programs and activities of the Federal Government are, and the extent to which they are not, contributing to the achievement of such policies."

The Economic Report, moreover, was to include the President's explanation of the causes of economic instability (whether of a deflationary or an inflationary character), the adequacy of existing legislation, plans for dealing with unsatisfactory conditions, and means of financing such plans. These features of the Economic Report were spelled out separately for each of three contingencies: "if at the time of submitting the Economic Report (a) high levels of employment, production, and purchasing power are not being maintained or are threatening to decline; . . . (b) widespread unemployment exists in the United States or in any substantial portion thereof; . . . or (c) inflationary conditions exist or threaten."[2]

The larger and more exacting character of the task thus imposed on the President led the House members to propose the setting up of a professionally trained Council of Economic Advisers in the Executive Office and to include specific provisions as to the character of its staffing and activities.

The Senate eventually concurred both in the more generalized interpretation of the economic attack to be followed under the Employment Act and in the House proposal for establishing a Council of Economic Advisers in the Executive Office of the President. But the final act was brief in form and did not specify in any great detail the functions of the Council as they were understood in either house of Congress, and it was no more explicit as to the functions and organization of the Joint Committee. Whereas S. 380 and H. R. 2202 had both had rather lengthy declarations of policy, the conference bill and final act reduced this section to a single sentence, albeit a lengthy and rhetorically atrocious one.

For this reason and because no statute can reveal in any full sense the intent of a legislative body of more than 500 members, we shall need to go back to the hearings, debates, and committee reports to piece together as clear a picture as possible of the actual intent of the Congress. This review can perhaps best be organized in terms of the intent of Congress as to each of the parties involved in the functioning of this quite novel statute: namely, the central government, the Chief Executive, the Council of Economic Advisers, and the Joint Congressional Committee on the Economic Report. It will focus upon some dozen or more specific questions which have arisen during the first six years of operation under the Employment

[2] This feature of the House bill is worthy of particular attention in that it specifically recognized inflation as a threat to the stability of the economy which should be dealt with in policy analyses and recommendations. The Senate bill had been focused exclusively on dangers of recession and need for government support measures, and it was concern over deflationary dangers that was strongly to the fore in the final passage of the Employment Act. Since inflation rather than recession has been the danger which has confronted the Administration in these first six years under the act (and not been met or faced) it seems unfortunate that the references of the House bill to inflationary dangers disappeared in conference committee. This omission leaves the door open to interpretation of "maximum employment, production and purchasing power" as being synonymous with inflation as a way of life.

Act and on which there has repeatedly been uncertainty and on
several occasions considerable controversy. These questions will be
analyzed in subsequent chapters.

FOR THE GOVERNMENT

In the Declaration of Policy in the Employment Act of 1946 one
reads that "the Congress hereby declares that it is the continuing
responsibility of the Federal Government . . . to co-ordinate and
utilize all its plans, functions, and resources for the purpose of
creating and maintaining . . . maximum employment, production,
and purchasing power." There are several qualifying clauses, and
to the most important of them we shall return presently. But there
can be little question that this sentence enunciated a more positive
policy on the part of the Federal Government to accept responsibility
for activating the economy than had ever previously had statutory
expression.

The nature and scope of the responsibility thus assumed for
stabilization of the economy was the major issue between House and
Senate while the bill was under debate, and there were many individual differences of intention and interpretation in both bodies
—though not along any discernible party line. While many words
and phrases were inserted to express or to mask these divergences,
the exact meaning of the commitment finally made was not clearly
defined in the act. Nor has such clarification been undertaken subsequently by the Joint Committee which Congress set up to aid
in the implementation of the act, by the President, or by the Council
of Economic Advisers. Its actual meaning will have to be derived
from events subsequent to February 20, 1946.

There was a keen sense of urgency in Congress for prompt passage of a bill that would give some feeling of security against
postwar depression.[3]

[3] "It was our conviction . . . Mr. President, that the welfare of American business,
American farmers, American workers, and American veterans depends more than
anything else upon whether or not the Federal Government shall assume the
responsibility of maintaining a balanced economy and conditions of full employment in our country. Every practical business man knows that unless the Government develops a positive and far-sighted economic program, business operating as
in the past cannot by itself maintain continuous employment opportunities for
workers. During the 1920's the Government had failed to recognize its responsibilities in this respect, [made] . . . no attempt to maintain a general purchasing
power in the hands of the people. The inevitable result was the great depression

There were manifestations also that broad segments of public opinion would support or indeed were demanding that the Federal Government take a more active role with reference to depression dangers and stabilization possibilities. The extent and range of this sentiment is impressively revealed in a letter dated February 11, 1946, addressed to the President and signed by forty national, civic, labor, and veteran groups.[4] It read, in part:

Dear Mr. President:

The undersigned organizations have, for a period of many months, been actively engaged in mobilizing support for a full employment program of which the full employment bills (S. 380; H. R. 2202) were the first essential step.

We are completely convinced, and our opinion is substantiated by all public-opinion polls, that the overwhelming majority of the American people are prepared to support the strongest possible legislation designed to assure the objective of full emloyment and to avoid the periods of boom and bust which have heretofore marked the course of American history and which, if continued in the postwar period, can lead only to national and international disaster.

Despite this overwhelming support for effective legislation, and despite your vigorous efforts in its behalf, a small but powerful minority has steadfastly opposed any and all efforts to obtain its enactment. Indeed, this articulate minority, by virtue of its strategic representation in certain committees of the Congress and its disproportionately powerful control of the organs of public opinion, almost succeeded in preventing passage of the necessary basic legislation.

While the bill which has been reported out by the Senate-House conference committee does not contain the language and provisions that we believe the over-riding significance of the issue demands, it is nevertheless with a sense of real satisfaction that we note that the conference bill makes a distinct contribution to the solution of the basic problem. The contribution is made along the following lines.

1. The bill establishes the responsibility of the Federal Government to "utilize all its resources" for the purpose of "creating and maintaining . . .

---

starting in 1929, which created widespread bankruptcy and destitution—all but wrecking the capitalistic system. . . . We could not agree with those who maintained that depressions were inevitable in a free society, and that without regimentation and loss of our freedoms nothing could be done to maintain continuing employment opportunities for our growing population." Senator James E. Murray, *Congressional Record,* 79 Cong. 2 sess., Vol. 92, Pt. 1, p. 1139.

[4] Known as "the Continuations Group." See Bailey, *Congress Makes A Law,* p. 75.

useful employment opportunities . . . for those able, willing, and seeking
to work, and to promote maximum employment, production, and purchasing power."

While the conference bill does not use the term "full employment," nor
does it measure up to our concept—and your concept—of what an ideal bill
should contain, we feel called upon to insist, despite the contrary insinua-
tions of some of the opponents of adequate legislation, that we have not
been fighting a battle of catch phrases or of slogans. We have been fighting
for a congressional statement of policy which would recognize that it is the
responsibility of the Federal Government to use all its vast resources to
assure employment opportunities to all of our citizens able to work and
seeking work. This is accomplished by the conference bill.

2. The bill calls for an annual Presidential report to the Congress on
the national employment situation, and specifies that the report should
include the basic analyses included in the national employment and production budget proposed in the original legislation.

3. The bill establishes a Council of Economic Advisers to assist the
President in this undertaking.

4. Finally, the bill establishes a joint committee of the Congress to receive and analyze the President's report, and to transmit it to the Congress
with recommendations.

Thus the conference bill provides you and the Congress with a clear
declaration of national policy of full employment and with machinery for
discharging the Federal Government's responsibility for full employment.
Again, we may not think it is the most perfect machinery—and you may
not—but we are satisfied that, in conjunction with all of the agencies in the
executive departments, this machinery will work if a genuine and sincere
effort is made to make it work.

We, therefore, believe that the Congress should approve the conference
bill, and we trust that you will sign it. . . .

The passage of the Employment Act of 1946, if adequately implemented
in terms of personnel and program, can mark the beginning of an American crusade for economic security, stability, and justice, and consequently
a contribution of enormous significance to the cause of international peace.
Unless, however, the act is adequately implemented, history will record it
as a mockery and an affront to the millions of Americans who are determined that our free institutions shall not again be threatened by the curse
of unemployment.

Most respectfully yours,

(The signatories included the American Federation of Labor, the
Congress of Industrial Organizations, and five other union groups,

eight church organizations, the National Farmers Union, half a dozen women's organizations, six that were educational, four professional, three veteran, and three business groups.)

The basic conflict that showed up in Congressional debate and that had finally to be resolved in conference committee concerned the double-barreled question of whether the government proposed to guarantee full employment and whether deficit spending was a resource or power with which such an obligation could safely be undertaken and successfully discharged. Drafters and supporters of the House bill and Republican senators, notably Taft and Buck, were irrevocably opposed to the provision in S. 380 that Congress should, "to the extent that continuing full employment cannot otherwise be attained, provide . . . such volume of Federal investment and expenditure as may be needed . . . to achieve the objective of continuing full employment." The conference committee, after bitter struggle, accepted as a substitute the declaration of "continuing policy and responsibility of the Federal Government . . . to co-ordinate and utilize all its plans, functions, and resources for the purpose of maintaining conditions under which there will be afforded useful employment opportunities for those able, willing, and seeking to work."

While this verbal subterfuge was found acceptable by the conference committee and stands in the act as passed, its precise meaning is uncertain, and many critics have pointed out that if the Government is in fact to use "all its resources" for the maintenance of business activity and employment, this would prove to be a more sweeping declaration of intent to use Federal spending to prevent or to check business recession than that contained in the Murray bill. "The Senate sponsors felt, not without reason, that the Conference phraseology was stronger than that in the original bill or in the Senate version. The House managers felt equally certain that dropping the specific mention of Federal spending was a victory for their side."[5]

Peter Edson's column in the Scripps-Howard papers informed his public that:

Opponents of the full employment theory think they scored a great victory in knocking out all the objectionable experimental economics stuff. Senator Taft, of Ohio, went so far as to say that the act passed is definitely

[5] Stephen K. Bailey, *Congress Makes A Law*, p. 255.

not a victory for Truman. If Taft, Congressman Carter Manasco of Ala-
bama, and Will Whittington, of Mississippi, want to think they scored a
great victory by watering down the original draft of the bill, they can. But
if anyone will sit down and read the full—pardon—the Employment Act as
passed, he will see for himself that it accomplishes nearly everything the
original bill set out to do. That makes it definitely a victory for Truman
and for Senator Jim Murray, of Montana.

The way this job was done is one for the book. It took six meetings of
the conference committee of Senators and Congressmen to iron out differences between the Senate and House versions. Manasco and Whittington
sat tight on their watered-down version. They were supported by Senators
Taft, Buck of Delaware, Radcliffe of Maryland. It looked like a deadlock.
So the other Senators, Barkley of Kentucky, Murdock of Utah, Taylor of
Idaho, and Tobey of New Hampshire—suggested changes in language.

The significant point for our purpose is that, although the Conference bill was passed in the Senate on February 8, 1946 by unanimous voice vote, and in the House on February 6 by a sweeping
majority vote (322–84), it does not specifically register an intention
on the part of Congress either to affirm or to repudiate Federal
spending (and particularly deficit spending) as a means of creating
employment or preventing unemployment.

This, as an outcome of the legislative process, is not as silly as
it sounds. Whatever expenditure the Government undertakes to this
end, would have to be in conformity with a specific piece of legislation, under particular circumstances, authorizing and appropriating
definite sums to be directed to certain activities. The inclusion of
the more explicit spending clauses of the original bill in the final act
could not bind future Congresses to take such action under unfore-
seeable future circumstances. Nor did the deletion of the expression in any way cramp the style of any future Congress in taking
such steps if recommendations to that effect were made by the
President and if they commended themselves to the judgment of
Congress in those circumstances. I myself lean to the view that
there is more political and economic dynamite in the phrase that
was finally accepted than in the one which was rejected.[6] This was

[6] Professor Viner takes a quite different view: "Many persons attribute great
importance to this declaration of itself. They regard it as a definite repudiation
of the laissez-faire doctrine and as the heralding of a new age in which Government will recognize its responsibilities to promote economic stability. The Act
originated, however, in a bill which went beyond the recognition of governmental

apparently the view of Senator Murray, for he said, in urging acceptance of the Conference Report:

On the day the conference bill was made public I expressed my great disappointment that the basic concepts of the bill were not set forth in more clear-cut and vigorous language. However, it seemed to me that the conference measure, as explained by the distinguished leader of the majority [Senator Barkley] in submitting the conference report, contained all the essentials of a full employment program, which, if properly and firmly administered, would constitute a real contribution to the successful operation of our economic system.

First of all, the conference bill declares a full employment policy. The House conferees succeeded in eliminating from the bill the words "full employment," and other forthright language. They did not succeed in eliminating the fundamental concept that the Federal Government has the ultimate responsibility for creating and maintaining conditions of full employment.

Second, the bill provides an employment, production, and consumption budget. The term "national production and employment budget" was eliminated and the term "economic report" used instead. However, the content of the national production and employment budget has not been changed in any material fashion. . . .

The original bill and the Senate bill committed the Federal Government, with certain qualifications, to provide whatever Federal investment and expenditure might be needed, as a last resort, to maintain full employment. But the conference bill does not refer to specific methods of affecting the level of employment. It makes no mention of Federal investment and expenditure, public works, loans, monopoly and competition, taxation, or other specific function of the Federal Government. Instead it calls upon the Federal Government to "co-ordinate and utilize all its plans, functions, and resources" to achieve the desired objective. This concept of utilizing all the vast resources of the Federal Government for the purpose of maintaining conditions of full employment appeared in none of the previous versions of this measure. It is a constructive and statesmanlike

---

responsibility, and the opposition to the bill centered on this phase of it. In recent decades at least, Congress has usually been willing upon request to acknowledge its obligations to promote national prosperity 'consistent with . . . other considerations of national policy.' Herbert Hoover himself would have subscribed to this, and to more than this. The preambles to hundreds of Acts of the last generation say as much. The fact that no Senator felt hostile enough to the Act to vote against it at least suggests that it would be a mistake to read too much into the declaration of policy as marking a change of economic philosophy." Jacob Viner, "The Employment Act of 1946 in Operation," *The Review of Economic Statistics*, Vol. XXIX, No. 2, May 1947, p. 76.

method of defining the Government's obligation to its citizens. I regard it as an improvement in the bill.

On the other hand, Senator Taft, in a speech of hardly less vigorous support of the Employment Act, said:

The original bill contained one thing about which I was most concerned, the provision embodying the so-called compensatory spending theory, by which we would figure up the number of jobs there should be—60,000,000 jobs—and how much income would be required to provide for them—$20,000,000,000. Then, if we found we were not going to get the money, a program was provided to make up the difference, the so-called compensatory spending theory. To some extent, the Senate modified that provision by adopting my amendment proposing that if a spending plan were presented, a tax plan should be presented along with it to take care of it. It was not in very satisfactory language, but no one need be concerned any longer, because there is no provision for the compensatory spending theory, no suggestion in the bill anywhere that the Federal Government has to unbalance its budget to cover the difference caused by spending anywhere from five, to ten, to twenty billion dollars, as might be necessary to meet the calculations which were required by the original bill.

A national-budget idea suggested the same thought, and while I voted for the bill with the national-budget provision in it, I have some doubt as to the wisdom of the suggestion of a spending program to make up the so-called deficit in the Budget. Anyone who is concerned about that can be completely at ease, because the words "national budget" are completely eliminated from the bill, and all that is provided for in the bill is an economic report. . . .

I do not think any Republican need fear voting for the bill because of any apprehension that there is a victory in the passage of the full employment bill, because there is no full employment bill anymore. The bill is one which I would have supported from the beginning. It is a bill which provides in effect that the Government shall take thought and shall provide the machinery for eliminating economic depression.

We create a Commission of three, who will have the duty of studying economics, determining how the law can be carried out, and making their report, and we declare a general policy of the Government to use all its means to bring about a prosperous condition so that people looking for work may expect to find work.

Thus it seems clear that it was the intention of Congress at this time to express a general responsibility of Government to do something positive about the maintenance of high-level business activity and employment opportunities. But it made it clear also that, in so doing, it did not intend to make any basic change in our form of government. This brings us back to brief examination of three qualifying clauses that were inserted in the Declaration of Policy, to guard it against interpretation by administrative officers or by subsequent Congresses in such ways as to lead to too ambitious undertakings or to invite departure from the basic character of our economic system. First there was the qualification that, in using "all its plans, functions, and resources for the purpose of creating and maintaining" high-level employment, the government was to proceed "in a manner calculated to foster and promote free competitive enterprise." This proviso appeared in even the first drafts of the bill and tended to disarm the fears of many in both Houses who were suspicious of the measure as something intended to open the door to socialistic schemes of "economic planning" in some authoritarian sense.

The bare phrase, "free competitive enterprise," of course, does nothing to specify the essential conditions of freedom, of competition, or of economic enterprise in a democracy. But it is patently anticommunist and antisocialist. Illuminating in this connection is the question raised by Senator Saltonstall and the response of Senator Barkley, who had been chairman of the conference committee.

Mr. Saltonstall: "May I ask if there was any discussion in the conference committee as to the interpretation to be placed upon the words 'economic program of the Federal Government'? I have in mind the question of a public works program, and I have also in mind that during the war the Federal Government really went into industry and competed with industry. I take it that the words 'economic program' could not be interpreted to mean or to imply in the future, possibly, that the Federal Government would go into business and compete with industry, and that sort of thing. I judge, rather, that the activities of the Federal Government under the authority granted would be confined to public works."

Mr. Barkley: ". . . it was the theory of the Senate bill, which the House conferees accepted, that beyond the mere expenditure of money from the Treasury, there is a field which envisages a greater obligation on the part of the Federal Government in co-ordinating its policies, performing its functions, and carrying out its plans. . . . For instance, in connection with the policy of the Government, toward trade matters, and in co-operation with labor and with agriculture, with industry, and with State and local governments, there is a responsibility more or less of a moral nature which goes beyond the mere expenditure of money out of the Treasury. . . . But it was at no time understood that the Government of the United States, as a matter of policy under the section declaring our purpose, was to embark upon enterprises competitive with private factories, and so forth.

"Of course, that could not be done anyway, unless Congress authorized it. If there should occur, as there did in 1932 and 1933, and the following years, an acute depression accompanied by widespread unemployment, Congress then would have to determine what its policy would be with respect to the expenditure of money. But I do not think the Senator from Massachusetts or the Senate or the country should consider the war period as an analogy to be used and considered in connection with our effort to bring about economic conditions which will foster and promote employment to the fullest possible extent and production and purchasing power to the fullest possible extent, which is the goal of this legislation."

Second, instead of guaranteeing jobs, there was an intention to create "conditions under which there will be afforded useful employment opportunities (including self-employment) for those able, willing, and seeking to work." This was intended to lay the ghost of "leaf-raking," of forced labor, and of "pork barrel" public works. It would also, logically, exclude militarism as a remedy for depression.

A third qualification inserted in the Declaration of Policy stipulated that the Government's efforts to maintain maximum production and employment should be limited to "all practicable means consistent with its needs and obligations and other essential considerations of national policy." The latter part of the clause was a contribution of the Senate drafters and the first part was supplied by the conference committee. Aside from being a rhetorical foil to the ambitious phrase "all its plans, functions, and resources," the precise meaning of this limitation is not clear. Probably it was a warning to future dreamers to get their feet on the ground and, pretty clearly, it sounded a warning against preoccupation with the reduction of even moderate unemployment at all costs—such as "exporting unemployment" by policies that would make business conditions harder for other free nations or by impairing the domestic financial structure.[7]

[7] Thus Representative Rich cautioned: "We can go too far in trying to create full employment. . . . I do not want to create jobs to the detriment of sound economy and of good common sense." *Cong. Record* (79 Cong. 2 sess.) , Vol. 92, Pt. 1, p. 978.

One line of opposition to the systematic and analytical approach to national economic policy which characterized the Employment Act was that it implied regimentation or "plan economy." The final form of the act was obviously free of this charge but Senator Murray made an important point as to the relationship of public action to private business planning when he said:

I should like to point out that [the Full Employment] bill aims at eliminating business uncertainty over the Government's fiscal policies. Business cannot plan effectively for full employment without knowing the Government's plans, and reasonable consistency and stability in the administration of the Government's program.

For example, revenue measures are often enacted only a few weeks before they are to become effective. This, I submit, does not give the businessman sufficient time to consider the Government's tax policy in relation to his own plans for future investment. Under this bill it would be easier for Congress to develop its fiscal policies in a unified manner, and to enact both revenue and appropriation measures before the beginning of each fiscal year.[8]

To sum up, we see a basic intent of Congress to have the Government take a positive role of economic stabilization without impairing free competitive enterprise—indeed conceivably improving its functioning—and a correlative intention to supplement or buttress the political apparatus of policy-making with more systematic use of a professional economic apparatus. This intent was expressed in the dual implementation of the Employment Act by setting up, in the Executive Office of the President and in the Congress respectively, two continuing agencies (a) for the study of the national stabilization problem and the devising of economic programs suitable to changing conditions and expanding knowledge; (b) for correlating the several strands of the policy-making process both in the executive branch of the Federal Government and in its legislative branch; and (c) for bringing the professional training of the economist and statistician more effectively to the staffing of both these implementing agencies.

FOR THE PRESIDENT

As to the President's relation to the Employment Act, the intent of Congress seems to have been: (a) to furnish him special assistance

[8] James E. Murray, "A National Policy and Program for Continuing Full Employment," *Cong. Record,* Appendix (79 Cong. 1 sess.) , Jan. 22, 1945.

in dealing with the increasingly complex economic problems that had emerged along with our industrial growth and military involvement; (b) to call upon him for a more comprehensive and better integrated formulation of his economic statesmanship annually or oftener for consideration by Congress and by the country; and (c) to set up certain criteria for his guidance in selecting a Council of Economic Advisers and using them as a staff aid.

The first of these purposes was visible only dimly, if at all, in the early draft of the "full employment" bill. Under that bill Congress itself identified the supposedly major cause of depressionary breaks and prescribed a means for dealing with it. All that the President was called upon to do was to forward the chart readings of the patient's condition (furnished by the Budget Bureau and other existing statistical agencies), and Congress would then prescribe a recommended dose and instruct suitable agencies to administer it. With the shift from this theory of specific treatment to one requiring the executive branch to make comprehensive studies of the problem of economic stabilization, broadly conceived and uncommitted to any particular theory of causation or of treatment, it was obvious that a large additional duty was laid upon a President already busy with foreign policy and military problems as well as other matters of domestic civilian administration.

In the words of Senator Murray: "The provisions on the economic report should be of incalculable value in giving the entire country an annual appraisal of how our economy is operating. The provisions for a Council of Economic Advisers should be of great help to the President and the Executive Office in co-ordinating the vastly expanded operation of the executive branch."[9]

It seems self-evident, however, that the Employment Act did not reflect an intent on the part of Congress to "strengthen the Presidency"—a move that had been going on in the executive branch under F.D.R., Hoover, Wilson, and Theodore Roosevelt. On the other hand, the Congressional debates do not manifest fear on the part of either senators or representatives that any of the proposals of the Employment Act would enlarge the powers of the President or encroach on the prerogatives of Congress.

Whether so intended or not, the requirement of an Economic Report and the setting up of a Council of Economic Advisers would

[9] *Cong. Record* (79 Cong. 2 sess.) , Vol. 92, Pt. 1, p. 1142.

tend to improve the administration of the executive branch by calling on the President to co-ordinate the activities of the several departments and independent agencies. In Section 4 of the original Murray bill, it was provided that "(a) The National Budget shall be prepared in the Executive Office of the President under the general direction and supervision of the President and in consultation with the members of his Cabinet and other heads of departments and establishments; (b) the President shall transmit to the several departments and establishments such preliminary estimates and other information as will enable them to prepare such plans and programs as may be needed during the ensuing or subsequent fiscal years to help achieve a full employment volume of production." These provisions had the intent or at least would have the effect of tightening up the policy-making relations within the Executive Office, welding the Cabinet Secretaries and other agency heads into a more closely knit team under the direction of the President, and helping to integrate the segmental policies into an internally consistent national economic policy.

In the Employment Act, with its creation of a Council of Economic Advisers, these provisions had disappeared, and it was simply said that "It shall be the duty and function of the Council to assist and advise the President in the preparation of the Economic Report; . . . to appraise the various programs and activities of the Federal Government in the light of the policy declared in section 2; . . . to develop and recommend to the President national economic policies to foster and promote free competitive enterprise, to avoid economic fluctuations or to diminish the effects thereof, and to maintain employment, production, and purchasing power."

This issue did not escape attention in the course of the Congressional debates. Representative Church expressed a "wonder if the Cabinet members are going to quit advising the President." To this query, Mr. Cochran of the joint conference committee responded:

Naturally the Cabinet is not going to be able to take on additional duties. The purpose in setting up the Council of Economic Advisers is to meet the situation that the Secretary of Commerce, Mr. Wallace, and other members of the Cabinet explained to the committee, and that was that one of the reasons President Hoover failed to meet the crisis confronting him was that he did not have the proper advice, and it was also stated that had President Roosevelt been properly advised in reference to the situation he might have done a better job in meeting the deplorable conditions that existed at the time. Therefore we are setting up this Council of Economic Advisers because we feel that the men who are to canvass the situation should have nothing else to do. Naturally when the Council makes its report to the President, he will discuss the report and the conditions with his Cabinet before sending the message to Congress.[10]

The President's letter of transmittal accompanying his annual and midyear Economic Reports has always stated, "In preparing this report, I have had the advice and assistance of the Council of Economic Advisers, members of the Cabinet, and heads of independent agencies." Some incidents relating to these several advisory relations have been noted in Part II (pp. 170, 228 f.), and the issue will be examined further in Chapter XIX.

As to the intent of Congress that the President should provide them with a fuller and better co-ordinated statement of economic policy, the act imposed upon him a mandate to send an annual Economic Report to the Congress at the opening of its session and to supplement this with interim reports as occasion might require. It specified four features to be covered in this report: "(1) the levels of employment, production, and purchasing power obtaining in the United States and such levels needed to carry out the policy declared in section 2; (2) current and foreseeable trends in the levels of employment, production, and purchasing power; (3) a review of the economic program of the Federal Government and a review of economic conditions affecting employment in the United States or any considerable portion thereof during the preceding year and of their effect upon employment, production, and purchasing power; and (4) a program for carrying out the policy declared in section 2, together with such recommendations for legislation as he may deem necessary or desirable."

The language of this section (particularly (1)) still bears strong marks of the emphasis on compensatory spending which had animated the earlier Murray bill. Undoubtedly, this intent still remained in the minds of Senator Murray and other senators and representatives who were in accord with him in their basic economic philosophy. At the same time, debates and hearings on the bill make it clear that members of Congress quite generally hoped that the

[10] *Cong. Record* (79 Cong. 2 sess.) , Vol. 92, Pt. 1, Feb. 6, 1946, p. 980.

statute would evoke a thoroughly objective analysis of all aspects of ever-changing economic situations, not prejudged in favor of any particular theory of treatment. Items (2), (3), and (4) of this section support this interpretation of the Congressional intent. It was expressed by Congressman Whittington, in discussing differences between the Senate and House bills. He said:

We substitute for the so-called national budget a provision for a report by the President of the United States, give him an entire year to study the matter and we say to him without having made any commitment for the expenditure of a single dollar that we want him to ascertain what added legislation is necessary. We say to the President that if there is unemployment or if it is anticipated we invite him to submit his suggestions for any additional outlay or expenditures and for any other measures; and we say to him: "Mr. President, we invite you to submit with them a sound fiscal program to protect the credit of the United States."[11]

Various members stressed the point that the President must be left free in making his appointments and the Council left free for making its studies. Representative Manasco said: "Unless the most able men in the United States are appointed on this Advisory Council and unless they are given the opportunity to freely study the economic fluctuations and financial conditions of our government and the needs of our people, it will be a complete failure."[12] This point was also made by Senator Barkley:

We left the President's hands free in looking over the country and in selecting men of experience and vision when making such appointments. The idea of the conferees was that in making these appointments without designating the appointees as representatives of groups, the President would choose men who would be able to speak in a broad way for all the people, and at the same time have adequate knowledge with reference to any particular segment of the population.

Taft: And while they might tend to represent one or another of the groups I should hope that they would be of such broad experience and knowledge that they would not be merely representatives of any particular group.

Barkley: The Senator is correct, and what he has stated was the feeling of the conferees. It was hoped that the appointees would be men of such

[11] Rep. William M. Whittington, *Cong. Record* (79 Cong. 1 sess.) , Vol. 91, Pt. 9, p. 11982.

[12] *Cong. Record* (79 Cong. 2 sess.) , Vol. 92, Pt. 1, p. 977.

outstanding ability and experience that they would be representing the whole country, and at the same time bring to the service of the council whatever experience they may have had in their respective callings.[13]

In the House also, Representative Robsion observed: "If the President appoints a board or council made up of incompetent persons who are bent on serving one particular group in the country, this plan will prove to be harmful rather than helpful."[14] Earlier, in discussion of the House bill, Representative Judd suggested that "No one could properly object to the President's appointing to the Council one member who had a particular economic theory, such as deficit spending. But certainly we should put in every possible safeguard to make sure that not all three members of the Council are of one particular economic political philosophy."[15]

As to the President, then, there appears to have been essential agreement in Congress that he should present an Economic Report that would be thorough, competent, and not biased by particular economic theories or special economic interests, and that he should avail himself of the best professional assistance in its preparation.

FOR THE COUNCIL

As to the character of the Council which was intended to aid the President in preparing his Economic Report, the act laid down the general criteria according to which the President was to make appointments to the Council of Economic Advisers in the following terms:

> The Council shall be composed of three members who shall be appointed by the President, by and with the advice and consent of the Senate, and each of whom shall be a person who, as a result of his training, experience, and attainments, is exceptionally qualified to analyze and interpret economic developments, to appraise programs and activities of the Government in the light of the policy declared in section 2, and to formulate and recommend national economic policy to promote employment, production, and purchasing power under free competitive enterprise.

This is reasonably explicit so far as it goes, but leaves uncovered a number of points which were raised during Congressional debate.

13 *Cong. Record* (79 Cong. 2 sess.) , Vol. 92, Pt. 1, p. 1138.
14 The same, p. 979.
15 The same, Vol. 91, Pt. 9, p. 12074.

From these discussions, some further light can be secured as to the intent of Congress.

Representative Whittington, who may properly be called the father of the Council proposal, described the purpose quite fully:

We provide here not for a committee of the Cabinet, the members of which are thinking about political questions and are engaged in administration; we provide here for an advisory commission of three of the outstanding men of the United States, representing all segments of our population, familiar with our economic conditions, familiar with our industrial, our agricultural and our labor problems. We say to them: "We are placing you at the disposal of the President of the United States. We invite you to discuss the causes of these depressions, or of these inflations and give us the remedy, if it may need legislation. You submit your report to the President so that he will have the benefit of it." We will then profit by the experiences of the thirties when the President had to rely on the members of his busy Cabinet. We provide that those men shall be on a par with the Cabinet. They shall receive a salary of $15,000 a year, the same amount paid members of the Cabinet.

We provide further that when they submit a report to the President of the United States they shall not merely be a planning board. Now I know something about planning boards and I know about their defects. The defects in planning boards, whether State or Federal, are that they plan and plan for nothing except spending and at no time were they required to submit measures by which to finance the plan. Whatever may be said about these economic advisers, we require in their report to the President that they shall submit a sound fiscal program and policy of financing any outlays for any works, or other programs.[16]

Senator Cordon raised the question "if perhaps the conference committee had in mind the three great divisions of effort in this country, namely, agriculture, management or industry, and labor, and that perhaps it had thought that in selecting the members of the Council the President might be able to place upon it men each of whom would be well versed in one of the great divisions of effort to which I have referred. It would appear that if that were done, it would be a consummation devoutly to be wished." To this query, Senator Barkley replied that this very question had been discussed but that

Inasmuch as the council was to be within the executive department for the purpose of assisting the President in arriving at conclusions, after all

16 *Cong. Record* (79 Cong. 1 sess.), Vol. 91, Pt. 9, p. 11982.

the facts had been assembled on which he would base his report, it was felt that: a council consisting of three members would be sufficient. We also discussed whether we should set out in the statute a provision that the President should make the appointments from three groups. We decided that if the law were to make it mandatory for the President to appoint a representative of each of the three groups, the appointees would automatically consider themselves as spokesmen and representatives of their respective groups, and that it would be more difficult for them to arrive at a consensus of opinion if they were made to believe they were acting merely as representatives of their respective groups. . . .

Cordon: Mr. President, I am in entire accord with the Senator's view that the President should not be limited in his selections. I hope, however, that the President will have in mind the three great economic divisions when he makes his selections.[17]

Elsewhere, there was a tendency to urge that the President should select "practical business men." Representative Rich stressed the President's responsibility to appoint "good sound business men with a desire to work out the problem and an ability to analyze the conditions of the country and make their recommendations to the Congress. Then we should be able to meet the problem of unemployment at all times." To this statement, Representative Smith responded: "Does the gentleman have full confidence that the President will appoint the type of men to serve on this Council that he describes? And will the gentleman tell the House the basis of his answer?" Rich replied: "The President should appoint competent men, men of business ability, men well versed in economics, men familiar with the economic conditions of the country. That is the most important part of this bill; and these three men should be good, honest, conscientious, sound Americans who will not be influenced by a lot of radical people." But Representative Fred Crawford lamented:

The bill prohibits the appointment of practical businessmen on the committee because the language is—"who as the result of his training, experience, and attainments is exceptionally qualified to analyze and interpret economic developments." One type of man reaches out and grabs

17 *Cong. Record* (79 Cong. 2 sess.) , Vol. 92, Pt. 1, p. 1138.

Comment on the initial Council set-up was inclined to note Clark's previous connections with business, Keyserling's friendly relations with labor organizations (as Senator Wagner's assistant and otherwise) and my previous identification with agricultural economics and agricultural colleges. (See pp. 111, 467.)

the economic forces of the world, puts them together and brings forth goods. The analyst sits down and analyzes economic facts, figures, and statistics. I think that language prohibits the appointment of practical men.[18]

Besides its statement covering qualifications of members of the Council, the Employment Act provided that

(c) It shall be the duty and function of the Council—

(1) to assist and advise the President in the preparation of the Economic Report;

(2) to gather timely and authoritative information concerning economic developments and economic trends, both current and prospective, to analyze and interpret such information in the light of the policy declared in section 2 for the purpose of determining whether such developments and trends are interfering, or are likely to interfere, with the achievement of such policy, and to compile and submit to the President studies relating to such developments and trends;

(3) to appraise the various programs and activities of the Federal Government in the light of the policy declared in section 2 for the purpose of determining the extent to which such programs and activities are contributing, and the extent to which they are not contributing, to the achievement of such policy, and to make recommendations to the President with respect thereto;

(4) to develop and recommend to the President national economic policies to foster and promote free competitive enterprise, to avoid economic fluctuations or to diminish the effects thereof, and to maintain employment, production, and purchasing power;

(5) to make and furnish such studies, reports thereon, and recommendations with respect to matters of Federal economic policy and legislation as the President may request.

With all this explanatory matter before us, however, several points require further clarification. These concern confirmation and tenure, position in the executive branch, and relations to the Congress as well as to the President

Concerning tenure of Council members, the act was completely silent. No term of office was mentioned. This might suggest either of two interpretations of the intent of Congress. They might have intended that the Council be established as a body of professionally trained technicians at the service of the Presidency, undisturbed by a change of incumbent as a result of political vicissitudes. Under

[18] *Cong. Record* (79 Cong. 2 sess.) , Vol. 92, Pt. 1, p. 978.

such an interpretation members would not serve strictly "during good behavior"—like the Supreme Court—but so long as the President felt that, in discharging his staff service, a member was at least as satisfactory as any other person who might be brought in. The other interpretation would be that Council members would expect to serve to the end of the Presidential term in which they had been chosen, but would automatically pass out with the departure of the President who had selected them.

Up to the end of 1952, this question has not become a practical issue. It was not raised in the presentation of the conference report to the Senate by Mr. Barkley or to the House by Mr. Manasco and Mr. Whittington. We have only the tangential comment made by Senator Murray: "The Council set up in this bill is entirely subordinate to the President. It has no independent nor autonomous authority. Its members, like other officials in the Executive Office, can be removed by the President at any time and for any cause."[19]

The Employment Act specified that members should be confirmed by the Senate. This raises a similar question as to the personal quality of their relation to the President. The House bill as originally drafted did not contain this provision. Representative Judd introduced it in the committee, apparently as a safeguard against the appointment by the President of incompetent, partisan, or political members to the Council. It was defeated by one vote. He thereupon presented his amendment on the floor of the House but failed to secure its adoption. The highlight of the debate was as follows:

Personally, I wanted the Council of Economic Advisers to be an independent agency, not in the Executive Office of the President, and I tried to get that done. . . . I had hoped that the Council of Economic Advisers might be something like the National Research Council, an independent establishment not immediately under the Congress, not immediately under the President; that it would be a group of economic and financial experts, sort of elder statesmen, who would be able to stand aloof from the general political struggle and perhaps be able to see in better perspective than we in the Congress can, or the President and his Cabinet members and their subordinates can, because the latter and we are so overwhelmed every day with other duties. However, that proposal was rejected in the committee.

It seems to me that the very least we can do is to provide that these men who are to have such influence, in the sense of their reports carrying

[19] *Cong. Record* (79 Cong. 2 sess.), Vol. 92, Pt. 1, p. 1142.

great weight with the country, should be scrutinized carefully by the Senate and receive their appointment only if the Senate consents. . . .

Mr. Whittington: Mr. Chairman, it is not correct to say that all of the President's advisers are approved with the consent of the Senate. These officers are to aid and assist the President in drafting his economic plans and presenting them to Congress, just as the Director of the Budget aids and assists the President in submitting his budget. Let me remind you that the Director of the Budget is appointed by the President and holds office at his pleasure, and he does not have to be confirmed by the Senate. We think that in all fairness to the Chief Executive whether he be the present occupant of the White House or someone who may occupy the White House in the future, that these men who are his close advisers, these men who are to aid and assist him in the preparation of his report should be on a par with the Director of the Budget who is not confirmed by the Senate. . . . They hold office during the pleasure of the President. . . . If we mean to enable the President to submit a constructive proposal for the solution of the problems of unemployment, it does strike me that we can do nothing more or less than to give him the men of his choice to aid him and assist him in preparing his budget [Economic Report].[20]

When the House and Senate bills came to conference, the Senate managers secured the insertion of the requirement for confirmation. Only once was this point questioned in either house when the conference bill was reported and adopted. Representative Cochran simply observed: "In my opinion, this provision is to be regretted."[21] He did not elaborate. In practice, however, Senate confirmation does raise problems. (See p. 397.)

As to the position of the Council, the intent of Congress is clear in the act itself in so far as it establishes the Council as a distinct entity in the Executive Office, charged with specific functions as a staff aide to the President. It is clear, also, that it has no executive duties or responsibilities but a purely intellectual and advisory function. This character was alluded to at numerous points in the debates, and Representative Whittington's comment, quoted above (p. 351), emphasizes the intent here of preserving the Council's independence of the political influences which inevitably and quite properly play upon the President, Cabinet officers, and all executive heads. It seems clear also that making the economic advisers on stabilization policy a separate Council with considerable prestige

20 *Cong. Record* (79 Cong. 1 sess.) , Vol. 91, Pt. 9, pp. 12074–5.
21 *Cong. Record* (79 Cong. 2 sess.) , Vol. 92, p. 980.

clearly differentiated them from such White House aides as the President already had and who are available to him for spot advice on the whole range of economic questions and the political context in which they have to be decided. Several quotations have emphasized this characteristic of independence contemplated for the members of the Council.

It was clearly also the intent that the Council should remain a small agency and should not duplicate the fact-finding or interpretative work of existing departments and agencies. This intention was expressed in the act by a limitation of $300,000 on what the Council could spend for staff salaries and by the proviso that it should, "to the fullest extent possible, utilize the services, facilities, and information (including statistical information) of other Government agencies as well as of private research agencies, in order that duplication of effort and expense may be avoided."

There was here a subtle issue in the intent of Congress (a) that the Council should supplement the role of Cabinet officers in advising the President and (b) that the Cabinet officers should co-operate in this co-ordinated study function by making the statistical and economic resources of their agencies available to the Council. Since the Council, in advising the President, would perform a function that ran parallel to that of Cabinet officers but was also expected to speak for a national interest that transcended that of any segmental agency, it was the intent of Congress to give them a position of great prestige in the executive branch. In quotations already presented, there have been incidental references to the fact that Council members in rank as well as salary were to be equal to Cabinet members. Besides these citations and one or two others, we note that Representative Whittington in making the closing speech in support of the conference bill in the House said:

The agreement authorizes the President to obtain the best talent in the Nation to aid him in formulating, developing, and recommending a national economic policy to provide for employment and production under the system of free competitive enterprise. Three members are to be appointed, their offices being of equal dignity with that of the Cabinet. . . .

This conference agreement authorizes the President of the United States to appoint statesmen of the very highest caliber, on a par with the members of the Cabinet, three of them, not one as is the case with the Director of War Mobilization and Reconversion, to advise the President, to survey conditions, and to recommend a program and policies for the solution of, I repeat, one of the most important problems confronting our Government.[22]

In the Senate, while Chairman Barkley was presenting the Conference Report, Senator Taft got the floor to observe: "Of course, practically, these appointees would have the rank of Cabinet officers." Barkley simply replied "yes" and the point was not elaborated further. This idea of the Council of Economic Advisers being "of Cabinet rank" was eagerly seized upon by the press and became an important element of the atmosphere within which the work of the Council was launched. Its significance will be discussed in Chapter XIX.

Section 4 of the Employment Act describes the Council of Economic Advisers entirely in terms of its position in the Executive Office of the President and as serving him exclusively. As the House bill was passed and sent to the Conference Committee, it contained a subsection which read: "The President is requested to make available to the Joint Committee on the Economic Report, if it desires, the various studies, reports, and recommendations of the Council which have been submitted to the President." This clause was dropped by the conferees.

In presenting the conference report in the Senate, Chairman Barkley was apparently under the impression that the conference bill retained the provision of H. R. 2202 that Council materials would be made available to Congress. He said: "We also have provided that the reports as well as the recommendations made to the President [by the Council] may become available to the Joint Committee for its information and benefit in determining both the facts relative to and the wisdom of any legislation on any policy which might be brought before it for consideration."[23] Senator Murray, following him almost immediately in the discussion, corrected this misapprehension when he said:

The House version of this section provided that all of the studies, reports, and recommendations of these three advisers to the President be available for use by the joint committee. If this provision had been maintained it would have given the three economic advisers an independent status apart from the Presidency. Conference bill eliminates this provision,

22 *Cong. Record* (79 Cong. 2 sess.) , Vol. 92, Pt. 1, p. 985.
23 The same, p. 1137.

thereby emphasizing the fact that their function is to assist the President in discharging his responsibilities under the act.[24]

Other members did not pick up the point for discussion.

In the House, Representative Manasco had his facts about the conference bill straight but gave the point a dubious interpretation. "The provision in the House substitute [H. R. 2202] that the report[25] should be made available on request to the joint committee is eliminated. The Congress or the joint committee without the provision has all the powers that the provision would have given to secure the studies, reports, and recommendations of the Council."[26] That Mr. Manasco thought that the Congress had inherent powers to get these materials direct from the Council is suggested by his remark a few moments later: "I am sure that unless this Council does its duty and makes recommendations to the Congress that are practicable and worth while, the Congress in due time will repeal this act."[27]

This leaves the question of the intent of Congress confused. At many points, we have noted an intention to give the President the best of assistance in arriving at wise economic policy but to leave him free to use the services of this agency in whatever way he saw fit.[28] Even taking Mr. Manasco's words as reflecting an intent to look

[24] *Cong. Record* (79 Cong. 2 sess.) , Vol. 92, Pt. 1, p. 1142.

[25] This use of the expression "the report" is an obvious slip. The Economic Report of the President is of course sent to Congress and referred to the Joint Committee as are any other special or interim reports he cares to make and on which the assistance of the Council would be used in such ways as the President sees fit. The only issue is whether studies and analyses prepared by the Council for the President's use or any recommendations which they make and which he is free to modify or disregard shall be made available to the Joint Committee or other Congressional committees. This is correctly stated at the end of the quotation from Mr. Manasco.

[26] The same, p. 976.

[27] The same, p. 977.

[28] In urging acceptance of the conference report, Representative Cochran said: "Section 4 sets up a council of economic advisers in order to give the President the personal assistance of three outstanding experts on economic problems. . . . The conference bill drops the provision that the reports, studies, and recommendations of the President's economic advisers should be made available to the joint committee. This is a distinct improvement, because it emphasizes the fact that the council is not an autonomous agency, but that its sole purpose is to provide the President with essential assistance and information on economic matters." *Cong. Record* (79 Cong. 2 sess.) , Vol. 92, Pt. 1, p. 980.

behind the President's Economic Report and to give the Council's views an independent status, it has never been established that Congress has the right or power to requisition such materials from the Executive Office of the President. And should that issue be resolved in the affirmative, the pragmatic question would still remain as to the effect that such a use of power would have on the larger purposes of the Employment Act. This became a hot issue and is discussed in some detail in Chapter XIX.

The intent of Congress was clear, however, that the Council of Economic Advisers should be of high standing professionally and in their government rank. They should have a practical bent, not be spokesmen for any economic interest but, among them, should possess broad familiarity with all major economic groups. They should represent the "best talent in the nation" and be free to make their studies with entire independence. They were given no executive powers or responsibilities, but were made purely advisory to the President.

FOR THE JOINT COMMITTEE

The original intent in setting up a Joint Economic Committee in Congress was, both in S. 380 and in H. R. 2202, to provide a special review body to consider the National Production and Employment Budget. With the broadening of the purposes of the Employment Act and the calling on the President for a comprehensive economic report, the assignment of the Joint Committee was proportionately broadened. Section 5 (b) stated:

It shall be the function of the joint committee—

(1) to make a continuing study of matters relating to the Economic Report;

(2) to study means of co-ordinating programs in order to further the policy of this Act; and

(3) as a guide to the several committees of the Congress dealing with legislation relating to the Economic Report, not later than February 1 of each year (beginning with the year 1947) to file a report with the Senate and House of Representatives containing its findings and recommendations with respect to each of the main recommendations made by the President in the Economic Report, and from time to time to make such other reports and recommendations to the Senate and House of Representatives as it deems advisable.

In discussing the Joint Committee provisions of the bill, senators and representatives who approved the measure as a whole referred to this as an important part of the machinery for getting better study of and action on the problem of economic stabilization. The intent was "to analyze the President's economic report and attempt to co-ordinate the activities of the various committees of Congress affecting the full employment program."

Among those who were opposed to the legislation, the need of co-ordination was recognized. For instance, Senator Radcliffe:

... The provision for a joint committee of the House and Senate may be somewhat debatable; but it is certainly desirable that the House and Senate should keep closely in touch with what is going on, especially in regard to such an important matter as this. Whether the particular machinery of a joint committee is desirable or whether some other method should be suggested is something which is probably not of primary importance. But it is desirable that there should be fact-finding facilities in operation. It is desirable that estimates should be made, and that suggestions be presented as to what can be done in regard to relieving unemployment, and it is most assuredly desirable that in this matter the Senate and the House should co-operate closely in some suitable way.[29]

Others objected to the setting up of a new committee in the face of the demand for simplification. Representative Hoffman took a dim view of any possibility of real co-ordination, saying:

Then Mr. Speaker, after the President gets this advice he sends it down to Congress. And the Congress turns it over to the Joint Committee. This is one good thing the conferees did. They cut the committee from 22 to 14. Then after the committee searches around in several departments, they send it back to the Senate and the House and the President of the Senate and Speaker of the House split up that advice, and they give the various committees of the House and the Senate which have jurisdiction over the subject matters involved those parts of the report which the President of the Senate and the Speaker of the House think each committee ought to have, and then House and Senate are right back again where they were when the whole thing began, though we have chased the devil of unemployment around the stump, never quite catching him.[30]

Senator Murray had studied this phase of the conference bill with care as he had studied its other phases and gave by far the most com-

29 *Cong. Record* (79 Cong. 1 sess.) , Vol. 91, Pt. 7, p. 9026.
30 *Cong. Record* (79 Cong. 2 sess.), Vol. 92, Pt. 1, p. 978.

prehensive and penetrating statement of the intent of the joint committee. Of course, it was his intent rather than a consensus. But in view of the content of the debate and the unanimity of the vote by which the Employment Act was passed, it must carry great weight:

From the day this legislation was first introduced, the provision for a joint congressional committee to analyze the President's over-all program has been hailed as a distinct contribution to the improvement of congressional operations.

There is general agreement that such a committee could be extremely helpful in co-ordinating the separate and diverse activities of the many committees in the Senate and the House of Representatives. For example, let me quote from the Senate Banking Committee's minority report on the full employment bill:

"We believe there should be such a joint committee studying the effect of proposed legislation on economic stability. We question somewhat whether the standing committees will pay much attention to the report of the joint committee, but it should be helpful by revealing to these committees and the individual members of the Senate the relationship of this measure to an over-all economic program."

Accordingly, we must take care to establish this joint committee on sound principles.

First of all, careful consideration should be given to the idea of having the chairmanship and the vice chairmanship of the joint committee held by the majority leader of the Senate and the majority leader of the House of Representatives. Let us not forget the fact that this joint committee is to serve as an economic policy committee. Its chairman and vice chairman, therefore, might well be those members of Congress who are responsible for over-all policy. If any other members of the Congress were selected as chairman and vice chairman of the joint committee and if they succeeded in discharging their duties successfully, then they might find themselves, in large part performing certain functions of majority leadership. For the same reason, the leaders of the minority party in both Houses might well serve as the ranking minority members of the joint committee.

Second, the joint committee should submit regular reports on the progress of the full employment program in Congress. Both the general public and members of the Congress themselves need regular information on the status of the various measures that make up the President's full employment program. This information should be provided in a regular report of the joint committee explaining the status of each proposal and indicating what changes, if any, have been made by the various committees and houses of Congress.

Third, the members of the Joint Committee on the Economic Report should limit their activities on other committees. Effective work by congressional committees becomes impossible when individual members have too many committee assignments. In view of the importance of the Joint Committee on the Economic Report, therefore, the members of the joint committee should limit their activities on other committees. Since committee assignments in the Senate are much heavier than in the House of Representatives, this applies particularly to the Senate.

Fourth, more rapid progress is needed toward the general improvement of congressional organization. The successful operation of the joint committee would be merely a first step in the improved organization of the Congress. It cannot be regarded as a substitute for more adequate staffing in our legislative committees, for closer co-operation between committees dealing with related topics, for closer relationships between the two Houses, and for the many other fundamental improvements. . . . Unless we achieve a comprehensive strengthening of the Congress, I see little hope that the legislative branch of our Government will be able to do its part in maintaining an economy of full production and full employment. . . .

The Joint Committee on the Economic Report should be a tremendous contribution to the improved organization and operation of the Congress.[31]

To what extent Congress really intended to reform its own practices or has in fact done so under the leadership of the Joint Committee will be considered in Chapter XX.

TWO SCHOOLS OF THOUGHT

Representative Manasco, presenting the conference report to the House, said: "This is the first conference report I have ever seen where the proponents of two diametrically opposed views are in agreement that it is a good bill and that it meets the objectives of both their positions."[32] Mr. Church interposed to remind him that "The conference report is not signed by the minority members of the House." (They [Gibson, Hoffman, Rich—subsequently a member of the Joint Committee—and Church] presented a detailed dissent. As already stated, however, the Employment Act passed by sweeping majorities in both houses.)

In thus accepting the conference bill and putting Public Law 304 (79 Congress) on our Federal statute books, it seems clear that members of Congress viewed it in two quite different lights. Al-

---

[31] *Cong. Record* (79 Cong. 2 sess.) , Vol. 92, Pt. 1, pp. 1142–43.
[32] The same, p. 976.

though coming to substantial agreement that the features embodied in the statute were acceptable in and of themselves, there was sharp difference of opinion as to where this statute left the problem of dealing with unemployment.[33] This division of opinion was to be found also in other branches of the government and among persons outside the government who had been concerned in the act.

One school of thought clearly felt that a great deal had been accomplished in the Employment Act—perhaps all that should be undertaken in a general and permanent measure. This view was well expressed by Representative Cochran when he said:

When it [the conference bill] does become a law, Congress will have done two things. It will have made a solemn promise to maintain conditions under which there will be employment opportunities for those able, willing, and seeking work. It will have established procedures and machinery where these promises can be translated into reality. Again, we are passing legislation that is placing a new responsibility upon the President. I feel that this will be of benefit to the country as a whole.[34]

The other school of thought regarded the statute as a sound and essential but very short step toward dealing with the problem of unemployment or of national economic stabilization. They felt that, instead of relaxing in complacency now that the Employment Act was passed, no time should be lost in securing its effective implementation. One wing of this group was eager to move on

---

[33] "Mr. Patrick: Among those who voted for this bill in the House are some who feel they went a long way to support it at all. Some of you moderate gentlemen feel you came a greater distance than we who wished to put a stronger bill through and we feel that we had to go much further in your direction than you went in ours. At any rate we met near enough the middle of the field to pass a bill. The Senate came through with its version. Now, the conference has given us this piece of work and I am very happy to find it as good as it is. At least it lays out a piece of ground work and gives us something to build upon." *Cong. Record* (79 Cong. 2 sess.) , Vol. 92, Pt. 1, p. 984.

[34] The same, p. 890.

The most extreme phase of this interpretation was that of a few members of Congress who seemed to expect that the Council of Economic Advisers would come up with pat "answers" to the complex and ever-changing problem of economic stabilization. One such optimist said: "I am satisfied there is not going to be any substantial unemployment in the immediate future. There is a severe shortage of labor now which will doubtless continue for three years or more. By that time, I feel that the Council of Economic Advisers to the President, with broad powers and adequate funds granted, will have completed a full and unbiased investigation and will be ready to make recommendations for legislation which we all hope will encourage employment for every man and woman who wants to work, and at a fair wage." The same, p. 984.

promptly with a campaign to put specific implementing measures on the statute books. The thinking of this group was well expressed by Representative Outland:

I think we do have here a good start. I hope, however, we can bolster it with proper legislation to follow in these many fields. If we do not, and if this bill is not properly administered, we will be making a useless gesture here today. I hope that this House and the other body will follow up this conference report with useful legislation in all of these fields which the conferees mentioned. . . . Where we come to discriminatory practices, where we come to monopolistic practices, then I assume the conference report does mean that these and other causes of unemployment are to be eliminated. It is only through such additional legislation following up this conference report that we are going to bring about full or maximum employment to the people of America.[36]

Some members of this school of thought had quite drastic implementing laws in mind. They shortly came forward with two such measures—the Spence Economic Stability bill and the Murray Economic Expansion bill. (See p. 240 f.)

Both groups joined in the view that the character of administration of the act now became the paramount issue—whether to assure its terms being carried out under the most ambitious interpretation of the words in which the intent of Congress had been embodied or to see to it that the reservations expressed or implied in its final phraseology should be scrupulously observed.

Whatever hopes of some legislators and others had been squeezed into the labored phrases of the Employment Act, and whatever fears or antipathies of others had been met and satisfied or merely tricked by its verbal compromises, all realized that the "proof of the pudding would be in the eating." Some looked forward hopefully to seeing all or much of what they regarded as good put into the act by its administrators; others looked apprehensively forward to the possibility that safeguards that they had striven to have recognized might not be observed in the process of administration.

Even before the Employment Act had been finally passed by the Congress and signed by the President, interest began to focus on the matter of its administration. On February 8, Senator Murray called attention on the floor of the Senate to the importance of developing "a sound administrative structure in the Executive

[35] *Cong. Record* (79 Cong. 2 sess.) , Vol. 92, Pt. 1, p. 981.

Branch." "When new legislation is enacted," he said, "it often happens that many months and sometimes many years are spent in the trial and error process in developing an administrative organization. . . . It would be a tragic commentary upon the vast efforts that have been expended in attaining a sound Employment Act if the passage of this legislation were to be followed by the usual period of groping and fumbling." He went on to explain that, realizing this need, he had during the preceding year "had an intensive study made of the problems that must be faced in the administration of a full-employment program." He outlined under nine heads the major conclusions at which this study had arrived. This statement of Senator Murray's[36] will be referred to frequently as we go on to consider how the President, the Council, and the Joint Committee proceeded in interpreting and carrying out the law.

[36] *Cong. Record* (79 Cong. 2 sess.) , Vol. 92, Pt. 1, p. 1142.
The conclusion seems inescapable that Bertram Gross must have been familiar with this study, if indeed he had not been a participant in it. There is not in my files or in my recollection, however, anything to indicate that it was called to my attention when we began the task of setting up the Council and developing its work.

CHAPTER EIGHTEEN

From General Intent to Actual Operation—The President

The administrative task of the President, his Council of Economic Advisers, and the Joint Committee of Congress was to take the "tall opaque words" of the Employment Act and so interpret them and clothe them in action that the basic intent of Congress as an expression of "the will of the people" should be realized.

From our review of the legislative history of the act, we concluded that, as to the President's role, Congress intended to bring about more adequate staffing of the Executive Office and more explicit and consistent formulation of the President's economic statesmanship through the use of this staff aid. Congress also outlined certain criteria for the guidance of the President in selecting his economic advisers and using them as a resource of the Executive Office. In addition to this, the law clearly called upon the President to exercise his executive leadership toward proposing legislative programs designed to secure national economic stability and, as administrator, to carry out such policies as were authorized by Congress to this end. Finally, he was to do all this within the proviso that government action should be calculated "to foster and promote free competitive enterprise" and that consultation should be had with "representatives of industry, agriculture, labor, consumers, state and local governments," and other groups.

FROM SENATE TO WHITE HOUSE

As Senator, Mr. Truman had, from the beginning, been a supporter of the Murray "full employment" bill and, indeed, his name had been attached to one of the earlier bills that came forward as part of the move for legislation to avert a postwar depression.[1] After he became President, he lent Administration support to the more drastic S. 380 rather than to H. R. 2202, which largely superseded it in the conference committee. After a message to Congress calling for "a national reassertion of the right to work for every American citizen able and willing to work and a declaration of the ultimate duty of government to use its own resources if all other methods should fail to prevent prolonged unemployment," President Truman assigned John Snyder, then chief of the Office of War Mobilization and Reconversion, to organize Cabinet support for his legislative program.

For applying pressure on full employment legislation, Snyder recommended a four-man Cabinet committee made up of Secretary of the Treasury Fred Vinson, chairman; Secretary of Commerce Henry Wallace; Secretary of Labor Lewis Schwellenbach; and Secretary of Agriculture Clinton Anderson. This four-man committee was to meet frequently, figure out ways to maximize Executive pressure on Congress, and submit progress reports every two weeks to John Snyder. . . .

It was the intention of Secretary of the Treasury Fred Vinson to work out a compromise version of the Full Employment Bill which might, with the weight of the President behind it, be accepted in part or as a whole by the Congressional conferees. Vinson and his assistants produced such a draft, which provided, among other things, for a Cabinet committee under the directorship of the Secretary of the Treasury to replace the House-proposed Council of Economic Advisers. Vinson submitted his draft to Truman, who in turn, referred it to John Snyder for comment. Snyder, for reasons best known to himself, pigeonholed the Vinson draft, with the result that the Conference Committee had to proceed without the benefit of an Administration-endorsed substitute.[2]

In his speech recommending Senate acceptance of the conference report on the Employment Act, Senator Taft commented:

President Truman endorsed first the original bill containing all the provisions ["right to work," "full employment guarantee," Federal spending to "close the gap"] which have been completely eliminated. . . . On January 3, the President said: "A satisfactory full employment bill was passed by the Senate. Another bill was passed by the House of Representatives which was not at all acceptable and which does not accomplish any

[1] The Kilgore-Truman-Murray bill (S. 2061, 78 Cong. 2 sess.). See Stephen K. Bailey, *Congress Makes A Law*, p. 34.

[2] Bailey, pp. 162, 222.

of the purposes sought." There is a slight variation in the conference report bill from the House bill, but it is so slight that it can hardly be
recognized. . . . I am afraid that the President will have to accept a bill
which is substantially the House bill which he disapproved so strongly on
January 3.[3]

In spite of Mr. Truman's somewhat wayward course during the
legislative evolution of the Employment Act, he evinced considerable satisfaction that a measure that had so much support in both
parties had finally passed by sweeping majorities. The President
was clearly relieved at having a statute which promised something
definite toward combating recession if one should develop during
the term into which he had been catapulted. In signing Public Law
304, he said:

In enacting this legislation the Congress and the President are responding
to an overwhelming demand of the people. The legislation gives expression
to a deep-seated desire for a conscious and positive attack upon the ever-
recurring problems of mass unemployment and ruinous depression. . . .
Democratic government has the responsibility to use all its resources to
create and maintain conditions under which free competitive enterprise
can operate effectively.

In his statement announcing the appointment of the Council, the
President said: "I consider that this act constitutes a distinct and
vitally important new step in the history of this country."[4]

[3] *Cong. Record* (79 Cong. 2 sess.) , Vol. 92, Pt. 1, p. 1139.
[4] "The President repeated again a remark similar to those he had made on each
previous contact that I had had with him, to the effect that he was deeply interested in the work of the Council and attached great importance to its report.
'That,' he said, 'is why I worked so hard to get the act passed, although they cut
some things out and it wasn't as good as I hoped it would be.' " (*P. D.,* Nov. 26,
1946)
Right up to the time that I left the Council, the President continued to make
protestations as to the value of the agency. But it seemed to me that he valued it
only as a dignified "front" for his policies. As soon as we ventured to challenge
any of them, he retreated behind his Presidential prerogative and "put us in our
place." Thus, for example, when I tried to open up with him the issues involved
in the Brannan Plan, he dismissed the matter curtly, with "I think Charley's
[Secretary Brannan] got something pretty good there." No possibility was left for
me to analyze with him the nature of the problem and the discernible consequences of alternative measures for dealing with it. The President obviously did
not mean that, after careful study of these economic issues, he had come to the
judicial conclusion that the Brannan Plan would most effectively enable the
agricultural industry to contribute to the stabilization of the economy. It seemed
clear that what was "good" in the proposal was a political effectiveness in attracting votes from both rural and urban constituencies.

Thus it seems clear that President Truman welcomed the Employment Act, accepted its mandates, and intended—in his own way—to administer it effectively in the executive branch.[5] Some three and a half years later, however, after leaving the Council of Economic Advisers, the first chairman expressed the view that "In this Administration, the actual position of the Council has undergone such progressive attrition or debasement that it bids fair soon to be negligible."[6]

THE PRESIDENT'S CHOICE OF PERSONNEL

Those who were eager for immediate action under the law criticized the President's delay from February to late July in naming the Council of Economic Advisers, but it is readily explained by his preoccupation with a heavy legislative program in the first Congress with which he had Presidential responsibility. His problem was further complicated by an evident desire not to award these posts as political plums or make appointments in response to the urgings of pressure groups. Without any firsthand knowledge of qualified personnel in the economic field, he was seeking to make nominations of persons who would conform to the description in the law—"who as a result of training, experience, and attainments [are] exceptionally qualified to analyze and interpret economic developments, to appraise programs and activities of the Government . . . and to formulate and recommend national economic policy . . ." Quite a number of economists who were well qualified for the posts declined his invitation. His final choices, however, met with a large measure of public approval (see p. 109), and the nominees were confirmed by the Senate without hesitation.

When a vacancy on the Council was created in November 1949 by the resignation of the chairman, the President indicated a desire

[5] The memorial in support of the Employment Act submitted to the President on Feb. 11, 1946 by forty national civic, labor, and veteran groups (see p. 339) stressed the administrative responsibility of the President: "We hasten to add that the will to make the machinery work is more than the machinery itself. This is particularly true in view of the fact that the conference bill imposes upon you full and complete executive responsibility for carrying out the provisions of the bill. While the Council of Economic Advisers established by the bill is required to assist you and can, therefore, serve a most significant function, in the final analysis the success of the program in the executive branch of the Government rests squarely upon your shoulders, where it should rest."

[6] *American Economic Review* (Supplement) , May 1950, p. 190.

to secure an economist of outstanding professional qualifications to fill the post. After six months in which no accredited economist had been found willing to accept the position of chairman under the existing conditions, he moved the vice-chairman up and, three months later, named Professor Roy Blough as third member of the Council. Professor Blough was an economist of excellent training, recognized standing in the profession, and considerable experience with various government agencies. Over a period of some eight years, he had served in the Treasury Department as director of tax research and as assistant to the Secretary. His concept of the job will be discussed in the following chapter.

After Dr. Blough resigned in August 1952 to join the staff of the United Nations, the President quite promptly appointed Professor Robert Turner of Indiana University. Turner, though a relatively young man and unknown outside a certain government circle, was well trained professionally and had had a wealth of experience in government agencies closely connected with the work of the Council. Not only had he served the Executive Office at the operative level on problems with which the Council had to deal at the advisory level but had also worked as a White House aide in processing several of the Economic Reports of the President into the final form in which they were transmitted to the Congress.[7]

In brief, it may be said that the President tried to make good appointments to the Council but at the same time created conditions under which a really satisfactory personnel job could not be done. One distinguished economist commented on his own explanation of why he was refusing a proffered appointment as chairman of the Council in the spring of 1950: "This is the only time when, afterward, I have felt really satisfied with a statement which I had merely extemporized." The Council of Economic Advisers was a pioneer development of a government agency which was unique in character and raised delicate issues in the effective use of professional personnel. Hence the piecemeal procedure with even a small admixture of politics was most unsuitable.

Let us suppose that President Truman had sought competent advice, which would have been readily available, with which to

[7] This was simply an interim appointment, and Professor Turner retained his active status on the faculty of Indiana University, where he spent alternate week ends.

draw up a panel of names of economists of outstanding competence and the practical human qualities that would seem most suitable for the kind of agency intended by Congress. Let us suppose then that he had approached that one among these men who seemed to have greatest stature, making a forthright statement of the high importance he attached to the post and of his intention of using this staff service as a respected and valued preliminary to his practical decisions on economic policy matters. We suppose further that the President in due course secured acceptance by the economist of his choice and agreement to work with the White House in recruiting a full Council membership of men who represented some difference in fields of economic specialization but who also could work together in mutual respect, complementing each other's qualifications. In the course of such a procedure, much would have been accomplished toward visualizing problems of how the Council was supposed to serve the President. This understanding would have been very helpful to both sides during the ensuing months. I cannot believe that if in 1946 Senator Wagner's candidate (see p. 104) had been passed over under such a method of recruitment, the Senator would have been unwilling to subordinate his personal desires to the professional requirements of this pioneering agency.

STAFFING THE PRESIDENCY

When it came to using the Council as an intellectual staff arm of the Presidency in the sense clearly intended by Congress and remarkably well grasped by the public (see pp. 109, 111, App. A), the President was quite evidently at sea. His first admonition to us to "see that this national income stays at 200 billion dollars"; his failure to keep any touch with our thinking during the shaping of the first Economic Report; his lack of response to our request for discussion of this report; his unconcern with the Cabinet flare-up over the first Economic Report and its subsequent rewriting by the White House staff; and his relief at discovering that at the end he had a creditable state paper with which to discharge his first Presidential responsibility under the act—all these soon gave the measure of his capacity to make effective use of a professional staff arm of the character proposed in the Employment Act.

My early diary entries indicate that I very soon sensed what I afterwards came to experience as an impossibility of establishing a channel of communication with the President which would enable the Council to render him the service which I had envisaged when I accepted the post. (See pp. 103, 107.) On November 26, 1946, I wrote,

> He seems to me quite quick and brittle in his reactions, not at all attracted by a contemplative analysis of basic issues or impressed with the value that might derive from the work that we are attempting to do through the Council, using professionally trained economists to correlate the work of many government agencies, together with the judgment of experienced executives and leaders from the business, labor, and agricultural fields.
>
> This may perhaps be summed up by saying that I think the President feels that our service to him will consist in relieving him of the drudgery of preparing [supervising] a document called *The Economic Report,* which he must submit to the Congress, but that we either should draw this document in accordance with his [known] views or he will rewrite it so as to bring it into such conformity. I may have misjudged him in this matter and he may intend now or decide in practice to allow the character of his program and the specific form of his recommendations to be shaped in some real sense by the judgment of the Council. This, of course, is all in the cloudy future, but from now on each conference we have with him will give us a clearer notion as to whether we are to have any real influence during his Administration or be a sort of glorified secretarial force.

Some three months later, I noted that the President "seemed to indicate a great willingness to discuss with us at any time any matters which we wished to bring to his attention and was ready to toss off suggestions in the course of an interview but did not suggest or apparently contemplate turning to the Council for advice on matters of taxation, budget, or other subjects on which he is to take policy and action positions right along." (*P. D.,* Feb. 12, 1947)

As long as I remained on the Council, I continued to puzzle over this problem of how staff economists could use their professional training in the rendering of really effective service to the President. The Chief Executive, in the nature of the case, would not himself be trained in economics and in many instances not professionally trained in any field. He would likewise be under the constant drive of administrative matters, from the trivial to the momentous, and subject to intensive pressures from the various wings of the Executive Office and extensive pressures from the whole of Congress and the outside public. It is hard to suppose that any President could devote any great amount of time or achieve any high degree of mental detachment in deliberating on matters of national economic policy with a Council of Economic Advisers or its chairman.

On the other hand, it seems not too much to ask of the Chief Executive that, in his own interest, he delegate responsibility on operative matters and detach himself from pressure wielders to an extent that would make it possible for him to have recurrent periods of contemplation of the broad issues which underlie his ultimate decisions on practical policy. Nor does it seem too much to ask, in this day of heightened economic sophistication, that the President should make it clear to his official family that he believes it important that the executive branch have an internally consistent policy for dealing with the interests of business, of labor, and of agriculture, and with fiscal, monetary, and market processes in such ways as to promote national stability and well-being.

To this end he might properly call upon Cabinet officials and executive heads to accept or seek consultation with the Council of Economic Advisers on the question whether departmental policies were mutually compatible and geared to the over-all policy of high-level stability. He could expect the heads of several departments which are mutually concerned in a broad problem to do preliminary processing of these issues in consultation with the Council and with the use of top staff economists from all the participating agencies, so that only fully-considered alternatives are brought to his desk or to Cabinet meetings. This, admittedly, is an idealistic picture of Cabinet performance. But it is an ideal implicit in the terms of the Employment Act.

A limitation on the success of the Council during its first period has been that the President whom it undertook to serve had neither formal intellectual training nor a contemplative mind. After Mr. Truman had been in office five years, the *U. S. News and World Report* published an article based on careful research as to his strong and weak qualities for the post of President. It was a superb piece of reporting, based on intimate observation over the five-year period and extensive interviews with people in all branches of government and in nongovernmental relationships to the President. Brief excerpts from this report are pertinent here:

> The President, his intimates say, sees problems in terms of personalities, not of things or ideas. . . . He does not worry. Problems, no matter how

big, never get him down. He does not have much imagination. His mind is strictly factual. The President is good at figures, but not at interpreting what figures mean in their broad application. Details annoy him.[8] He doesn't like to deal with scientists and economists because they tend to be technical and exact. He likes to make "Yes" or "No" decisions on plans worked out by others rather than dig for the answers himself. He bases his decisions on snap judgment, sometimes, rather than on real facts. . . .

[8] A concrete instance of Mr. Truman's careless use of figures may be cited. In the summer of 1949, I was sent a draft of a fireside talk the President was scheduled to make that evening. Some figures which it contained were palpably distorted, and I promptly called this to the attention of the White House aides. I was so much concerned that I followed the matter up during the afternoon and was finally assured that changes were being made. That evening I listened to the radio address and was amazed to find the passage used exactly as first written. This led to the following exchange of letters:

July 14, 1949

Dear Mr. President:

My enjoyment in listening to your radio address last night was marred by hearing a statement near the opening which contained a serious error of statistics or their economic interpretation. Since I am sure that thousands of your listeners detected this error and that it weakened the otherwise favorable impact of the speech, I am venturing to write to inform you that I made every effort which seemed necessary or possible to prevent this highly misleading statement being put in your mouth.

The statement to which I refer is to the effect that national income during the last 40 years "has increased more than ten times as fast as the population. These figures are a measure of our rising standard of living, our increasing freedom from toil and poverty. They are the result of constant expansion in agriculture and industry."

It is, of course, obvious that if one magnitude rises from 30 to "well over" 200 while another rises from "between 90 and 100" to "nearly 150," the former increase is approximately ten times the latter, as a purely arithmetical proposition. But when it comes to talking of "a measure of our rising standard of living," adjustment must be made for price changes, and for this, the comparison would be *three times as fast*. When the draft of your speech was sent to the Council for comment yesterday noon, I advised Mr. Lloyd that this statement, as it stood, was highly vulnerable and suggested the revision. In the light of this comment, he informed me later that the passage had been changed to read "six times as fast." I told him that this involved a tricky arithmetical mistake and that I would check back with our statistical staff again to make sure our statement of "three times" was correct. I called him a third time to verify the figures, namely, 64.1 percent increase in population accompanying 196.6 percent increase in national income adjusted for price change, or a measure of our rising standard of living from 1909 to now equal to 3.1, instead of "more than ten."

I regret exceedingly that it was not possible to have this correction incorporated in the final draft of your talk, as the error will undoubtedly become the basis for considerable critical comment.

Sincerely yours,
/s./ Edwin G. Nourse

Individuals in his circle of advisers are classified in the order of their closeness and loyalty. The one considered nearest and most loyal is likely to win—unless political considerations are involved. . . . Mr. Truman does not have an inquiring mind. He does not ask many questions. But he has a good memory. It runs to facts about people. . . .

The President has no philosophy, doesn't think, doesn't read the things he would have to read if he were trying to understand the problems he's up against. . . . Even close friends shook their heads when asked about the President's knowledge of economics. . . . One close adviser declared: "Economics and banking problems are not his strong points. They seem to irritate him. Mr. Truman will tell you, himself, that he is a politician. His mind, almost automatically, gives a subject a political screening. But he thinks of a politician as being an adept at the art of government, in the best sense. . . .

A businessman who has worked with the last two Presidents said: "Mr. Truman is an economic illiterate. He won't concentrate. Try as you will, you can't get him to sit down and put his mind on a complicated problem. The late President Roosevelt had no real grasp of economics, business or fiscal policy. But he was a thinker. When something was explained to him, he put his mind to it and followed. He'd interrupt and say, 'Wait a minute now; let me get straight on that.' Mr. Truman hears you, or appears to, then says, 'O. K., that's fine.' But you know that he has not really grasped what you were saying. . . . When he follows my advice, I sometimes wish to heaven he understood why he does," this businessman lamented.[9]

THE WHITE HOUSE
Washington

July 15, 1949

Dear Dr. Nourse:

I appreciated your letter of the fourteenth very much and I think you are unduly alarmed over the statement in regard to the national income and the population increase. The figure really looks to me like ten and, I think, it looks that way to anybody else, unless he wants to go through a lot of statistical figures.

The facts in the case are, if you want to get right down to brass tacks, the thirty billion dollar income, as compared with the two hundred and twenty-five billion dollar income, is about seven and one-half to one. The population increase is about one and one-half to one, so when you figure it that way the relationship is about five to one.

I don't think any serious damage was done by the statement which I made in the speech.

I am glad you wrote me because that indicates to me that you listened to the speech.

Sincerely yours,
/s./ Harry Truman

[9] *U. S. News & World Report*, Apr. 14, 1950.

It is easy to see how a man of these mental characteristics would have seen in the mechanistic device of compensatory spending as embodied in S. 380 something that "looked pretty good" whereas an intellectual apparatus for continuous and comprehensive analysis of the complex factors involved in sustaining the economy on a high level of production and employment would be hard to understand and not congenial to his methods of work.

The inability to secure during its initial period of operation an effective intellectual relationship between the Council of Economic Advisers and the President then in office raises very sharply the broader issue whether the basic concept of a professional Council dealing directly with the President at the very top level of policy-making is practicable. One can run back in his mind to ask the question: How would such a Council have fared under Warren Harding or Woodrow Wilson, under Calvin Coolidge or Herbert Hoover, under William Howard Taft or Theodore Roosevelt? Its members might not have found it easy to serve a famous college president or a distinguished engineer or a great jurist in the manner vaguely outlined in Congressional debates or spelled out a little more precisely in my letter to the President when I went on the Council. One's mind can run still farther into the unknown and ask how it would have functioned under Thomas E. Dewey, Robert A. Taft, or Adlai Stevenson, and how it will function under Dwight D. Eisenhower.

The answer to this question is by no means clear. But it is clear that the success of the Council as an institution, the importance of the place it occupies and the value of its work will be just what the President makes them. This is not to minimize the professional competence of the members, but it recognizes the importance of the President's choice of properly qualified appointees.

WHAT PLACE IN THE "OFFICIAL FAMILY"?

Besides the question of the President's use or non-use of the Council of Economic Advisers as a means of informing himself as to the economic background or underpinnings of his policy decisions, its chances of success within the Executive Office were also dependent in very real ways on the official position which he accorded it or established for it in the executive branch. It was the evident intent of Congress that this agency should be established at the top policy level, not as a policy-making body but as a policy-analyzing body for the whole executive establishment. The relationship to at least five Cabinet members and the chairman of the Federal Reserve Board should be no less vital than that to the President.

The act itself defined the function of the Council as not merely "to assist and advise the President in the preparation of the Economic Report" but also "to appraise the various programs and activities of the Federal Government" in the light of the policy declared in the act and "to develop and recommend to the President national economic policies to foster and promote free competitive enterprise, to avoid economic fluctuations," etc. This would mean that the Council would be a review agency over the performance of all Cabinet departments and independent agencies and would criticize and suggest modifications in policies being espoused by such departmental executives if, in its judgment, they were not internally consistent and mutually contributory to national economic soundness and progress. A staff arm of the Presidency charged with such a duty cannot discharge it effectively from a place far down in the hierarchy of government. In the evident realization of this fact, the drafters of the Employment Act had specified that the members of the Council of Economic Advisers should have the same salary as Cabinet officers, and official spokesmen for the bill at the time of its passage explicitly said that it was intended that they should be of "Cabinet rank." (See p. 358.)

This intention of Congress was never accepted by the President. The first chairman of the Council was perhaps unduly impressed by it, but the air of Washington at the time the Council was launched fairly buzzed with this phrase "Cabinet rank." His concern was manifest in the struggle over the housing of the Council and less patently in his moves to establish personal relations with Cabinet members and agency heads in departments and commissions particularly concerned in economic matters. Even on what seems outside Washington to be the trivial plane of social protocol, he felt it incumbent on him to try to secure recognition for the Council at the level indicated by Congress. In September 1947, he brought this matter specifically to the President's attention

in view of the fact that the question had recently been raised with the Protocol Division of the State Department as to where my name should appear in any printed lists of Government officials. It had been the supposition of Protocol that we would rank as the newest of the independent agencies and thus would appear down below members of Congress, Under-secretaries, Assistant Secretaries, and independent agencies established prior to February 20, 1946. I referred the President to the committee reports on the Act and Congressional debate in which it had been stated that this agency was unique in character, set up in the office of the President, and to be rated "on the Cabinet level." The President said he was not at all interested in protocol but would look into the matter. He volunteered that he had regarded us as just like "the rest of the White House aides."

I pointed out that if we were to perform the integrating and co-ordinat-ing function provided in the Act, involving segmental and sometimes con-flicting departmental policies, it seemed to me essential that the Council be on the rank of the Cabinet officers with whom it must deal. There was no indication that the President was impressed by this point. In fact, he rather curtly told me to leave it with him, that he would look into it and that he thought I had felt satisfied with what he had done with reference to the Council in the past. (In fact, I have not been.)

As a matter of record of this date, I may state that I and other members of the Council have felt a considerable degree of disappointment and frustration as to the use that the President has made of the Council up to the present time. I feel that this statement for the first time clarifies the rela-tionship when he says that he has regarded us as in the same relationship as "the rest of the White House aides." After the lapse of a little more than a year, it can be said that there has been no single case when he has called upon us in any specific situation for counsel in his study of any matter of national economic policy.[10] While he has accepted the material which we have presented to him for use in the Economic Reports and passed it on without material change and with only minor omissions, there is no clear evidence that at any juncture we have had any tangible influ-ence on the formation of policy or the adoption of any course of action or feature of a program. A notable case of omission was when the President sent his rather comprehensive conservation report to the Congress last June. It was quite hastily drawn together by Mr. Steelman in consultation with army engineers, reclamation officers, and others, but without any partici-pation by or consultation with any member of the Council's staff. (*P. D.,* Sept. 25, 1947)

This matter of the Council's position in the Executive Office cannot be viewed in isolation. With the growth of the Executive Office of the President, a number of official positions have been

---

[10] This statement fails to note the request to the Council to prepare a study of the impact of a foreign aid program on the economy. But this involved a formal report to go to the "Citizen's Committee" and the public, not real study by the President of his policy line.

created at different times and in different ways and attached to this office or set up as independent commissions in the executive branch without any real consideration of internal consistency as to structure or rank.

This was notably true in the case of the Bureau of the Budget. It was originally established as a bureau domiciled in the Treasury Department (though reporting to the President), and the Budget Director, through legislative and administrative inertia, was continued at the rank and salary of a bureau chief after his agency had acquired considerable size, great administrative influence, and important status in the Executive Office of the President. Mr. Webb was drawing a salary of $10,000 while six members of the Council's staff and more than that number in the Bureau staff were receiving $10,400. On the other hand, the heads of such agencies as the National Security Resources Board, the Atomic Energy Commission, and the Economic Co-operation Administration, were given salaries well above those of Cabinet officers and, in the latter case, the Administrator participated more or less regularly in Cabinet meetings.

In the fall of 1948, the Senate Civil Service Committee under the lead of Senator Flanders undertook to clarify and systematize this situation by introducing in the Senate an "executive pay bill." A parallel bill was introduced in the House. While these bills were in the drafting stage, Mr. Truman said: "I will not have anyone of Cabinet rank who is not actually a member of the Cabinet." Thereupon a structure was proposed under which the chairmen of some nine agencies with important advisory or operative functions should each receive the same salary as that of an Undersecretary, Mr. Truman agreeing that these agency heads should, for purposes of protocol, outrank the Undersecretaries. This was a thoroughly sound proposal and would have produced a more workable arrangement for the Council.

As passed, the House executive pay bill (H. R. 1689, 81 Cong. 1 sess.) provided salaries of $25,000 for the Cabinet Secretaries and $20,000 for Undersecretaries, the Comptroller General, the Director of the Bureau of the Budget, the Chairman of the National Security Resources Board, the Federal Security Administrator, the Administrator of Veterans Affairs, the Administrator for Economic Co-operation, the Administrator of General Services, and two White House aides at the discretion of the President. Salaries of $18,000 were provided for the Chief of Staff of the Joint Committee on

Internal Revenue Taxation, and several other agency heads and deputy administrators. The Public Printer, the Librarian of Congress, the Assistant Federal Security Administrator, the Director of Central Intelligence, and members of the Council of Economic Advisers constituted a fourth bracket with a salary of $17,500.

The Senate bill put Cabinet officers at $22,500, the Deputy Secretary of Defense at $20,000, the Secretaries of Army, Navy, and Air Force at $18,000 and a large group of agency heads and deputies at $15,000. Members of the Council of Economic Advisers were not mentioned specifically, and so would remain at the $15,000 level provided in the Employment Act. In conference, the Senate provision for Cabinet officers and other defense executives prevailed, and Undersecretaries and a number of second-string officials were put at $17,500.[11] Members of the Council of Economic Advisers were put at $16,000 along with the Board of Directors of the Federal Deposit Insurance Corporation, the Chairman of the Civil Service Commission, the Federal Mediation and Conciliation Director, Deputy Administrator for Veterans Affairs, the Assistant Director of the Bureau of the Budget, Assistant Comptroller General of the United States, the Chairman of the Munitions Board, and the Chairman of the Research and Development Board.

This action carried out the President's proposal for a "little Cabinet" except that it dropped the Chairman of the Council of Economic Advisers and him alone out of this group. It thus abrogated the principle of differentiating the administrative head of an agency from its board members[12] and put the Council at the fourth

[11] These included the Comptroller General, the Director of the Bureau of the Budget, the Chairman of the National Security Resources Board, Federal Security Administrator, Administrator of Veterans Affairs, and Administrator of General Services, the Housing and Home Finance Administrator.

[12] Congress had, in setting up various agencies at different times followed a random practice, sometimes differentiating the chairmanship for administrative purposes, sometimes leaving it to rotate according to the vote of the members and sometimes, as in the case of the Council of Economic Advisers, absent-mindedly leaving the matter indeterminate. All members of the Council were to receive the same salary, and the President was to "designate one of the members of the Council as chairman, and one as vice-chairman, who would act as chairman in the absence of the chairman." In practice, the vice-chairman stoutly defended the thesis that this meant a co-ordinate council, with all members participating in official contacts and with intellectual positions as well as operating decisions determined by majority vote. This was an impossible administrative situation, from which he departed promptly after becoming chairman.

level below the Cabinet rank designated by Congress at the time the Employment Act was passed, outranked by five White House aides and both the other principal agencies in the Executive Office of the President, as well as other agencies in the executive branch. It may well be asked how much attention a Cabinet officer would pay to the voice of a Council thus constituted if they were to undertake to analyze with him the question of whether his department policies were compatible with a national stabilization policy or consistent with the policies and programs of other departments. It may be questioned also whether economists of the standing needed for such an agency would feel that its opportunities for effectiveness would justify them in leaving academic or other connections of a congenial and rewarding character to accept such a post.

Thus, under the first President who was called upon to administer the Employment Act, Congress, whether at the President's wish or simply with his acquiescence, and probably unbeknownst to most senators and representatives and only partially understood by a handful, has materially changed the original intent of setting up a Council of Economic Advisers at a level where they could deal effectively with Cabinet members and other top agency heads. Since this question concerns vitally the whole functioning of the Council, it will be discussed further in the following chapter.

Besides the problem of how the President would himself deal with members of his Council in arriving at policy decisions, there was the question of how he would infiltrate their work into the over-all policy-making function in which he must have the final say but in which it is desirable that he derive as much technical guidance and political wisdom as possible from those whom he has drawn about him as a Cabinet "team" or put at the head of other executive agencies. The question was early raised whether the Council or its chairman should sit in at Cabinet meetings whenever important economic issues were up for discussion or regularly so that he could be present whenever the economic aspect of an important policy came up.

It was—and still is—my view that regular attendance[13] would not

[13] It would be only reasonable, however, to expect the President to invite the chairman to attend particular Cabinet meetings when economic policies were to the fore. Such occasional attendance would give the Council a valuable "feel" of how Cabinet members acted and the President reacted when matters of national economic policy had to be faced.

promote the most helpful or harmonious relationship. It would make the Council a controversial figure in the strains between politically conditioned departments or agencies. More could be achieved toward economic understanding and political adjustment by analytical discussion between the Council and the given agency head in the privacy of his or the Council's office. It is notorious that the Cabinet room produces amazing sound effects in such places as the Drew Pearson column and that a Cabinet meeting is not a good intellectual forum. The Secretaries have a strong tendency each to follow his party line or to "clam up," awaiting private consultation with the President.

On only half a dozen occasions while I was on the Council were we invited to sit in a regular or special meeting of Cabinet officers and then largely to give its members a preview of a memorandum we were presenting to the President, asking their advice as to whether it should be given general publicity, or to inform the Cabinet and other invited agency heads of a line of inquiry in which we were to participate (such as budget ceilings or the impact of a proposed foreign aid program).

The most significant development in the area of Cabinet-Council relations was the request of the President (November 1948) that I serve as chairman of a Cabinet or executive-officer group for consideration of factual and analytical material to be prepared by the Council for use in the Economic Report of the President. (See p. 228.) This did not grow out of any constructive thinking of the President as to how Council work might be incorporated with Cabinet and other executive activities to promote more fully the purposes of nationally integrated policy-making. President Roosevelt's imaginative and venturesome mind was constantly thinking up new administrative moves and shuffling his line-up to get better utilization of talent or meet new situations. Mr. Truman, without much imagination, liked to continue with familiar arrangements and people who gave him "loyalty" instead of challenge.

While the suggestion for a Cabinet committee on stabilization policy likewise did not come from me (and was opposed by my colleagues), I regarded the arrangement as the high-water mark in the development of the Council into a position of unobtrusive but positive intellectual helpfulness within the executive branch. Nothing spectacular was accomplished during the two periods (prior to the annual and midyear 1949 Economic Reports) in which this committee arrangement was used, and the experiment has since lapsed. It is my belief, however, that if the Council of Economic Advisers is to be continued and revitalized, this is a device for policy review and co-ordination which holds the greatest promise.

INTEGRATING POLICY IN THE EXECUTIVE BRANCH

At several points during the Congressional debates on the Employment Act, a hope was expressed that the Economic Report of the President should be the means of getting a comprehensive statement of executive policy at one time and one place. It should offer a challenge to the President and his official family to produce an over-all national policy for the ensuing year (subject to revision as circumstances changed) that would be both adequate to the needs of the time and internally consistent as to its several parts. Beyond this, it was suggested that the very necessity of submitting such a report and conducting the studies that would lead up to it, on a basis of year-round study with the aid of a technical staff, would result in tightening up the relationships among the Cabinet departments and independent agencies of the executive branch.

This purpose was not stated clearly and explicitly in the final act, but it is implicit both in the declaration of policy and in the administrative machinery set up. How well it is accomplished will depend on both the zeal and the ability with which the President meets this challenge to his statesmanship and on the competence of the Council of Economic Advisers to give him adequate staff aid. Thus far the results have been quite disappointing. The shortcomings of the Council will be discussed in the next chapter. But part of the explanation is to be found also in the personality of the President.

The idea has been advanced from various quarters that a reasonable implication of the Employment Act is that we are moving toward a more tightly organized system of responsible party control or even Cabinet government of the British type. It is argued that it will be impossible to implement a stabilization policy and utilize the plans, functions, and resources of the government to that end unless we have the same party in control at both ends of Pennsylvania Avenue and party discipline within the executive branch and in the

Congress.[14] In fact some active sponsorship appeared within the President's own official family for the idea that, both by administrative action of the President and by legislation that would be acceptable to Congress, we might move appreciably closer to that situation. The name of Secretary Forrestal was most openly associated with the move. But the President rejected it and appeared to mistrust the motives of those who urged it.

The Employment Act represents a more conventional approach to the problem of administrative integration. It recognizes that there are numerous areas where problems of economic consistency and policy co-ordination call for vigorous Presidential leadership if the economy is to be safeguarded against unstabilizing forces or make a concerted effort toward offsetting such strains as the military build-up. The complex interrelation of Federal spending, taxation, private capital formation and investment, and consumer purchasing power present the outstanding issue or group of subissues. They have separate foci in the various branches of the executive establishment but should be brought to congruence in the President's office. The Economic Report and the Council of Economic Advisers have been set up as means to that end.

The one step toward removal of glaring inconsistency in national economic policy which has occurred since the passage of the Employment Act was the "accord" reached between the Treasury Department and the Federal Reserve System in the spring of 1951. It has from the start been a debatable question whether a "full employment" policy could be carried into effect without grave danger of inflation. It came to be widely accepted that this could not be done so long as government bonds were pegged at a low fixed interest rate, and the central bank required or constrained to support them at par. The Council was not united and effective in contributing to the understanding of this issue but the studies of the Douglas and the Patman subcommittees of the Joint Economic Committee were of outstanding value. When, eventually, the Treasury gave

[14] See Don K. Price, "Staffing the Presidency," *American Political Science Review,* December 1946, pp. 1154–68; E. A. Goldenweiser, "The Economist and the State," *American Economic Review,* March 1947, p. 1; Paul J. Strayer, "The Council of Economic Advisers: Political Economy on Trial," *American Economic Review* (Supplement), May 1950, p. 144; Charles S. Hyneman, *Bureaucracy in a Democracy,* particularly chaps. 21, 22, and 25. Though the latter volume was published in 1950, it contains no mention of the Employment Act of 1946.

recognition to the paramount duty of the Reserve System to promote monetary stability, not artificially low interest on government bonds, there was a notable *rapprochement* within our government policy.

Perhaps, if all the subtle influences could be traced, the President's final acquiescence to this development—reversing his long-held position in support of cheap money—may be credited to the Employment Act's concept of policy co-ordination. Let us look at the record. On February 26, 1951, the President presented a memorandum to the Secretary of the Treasury, the Chairman of the Board of Governors of the Federal Reserve, the Director of Defense Mobilization, and the Chairman of the Council of Economic Advisers, which expressed his great concern "with the problem of reconciling the need to maintain stability in the Government security market and full confidence in the credit of the United States, and the need to restrain private credit expansion at this time. . . . Both objectives must be achieved within the framework of a complete and consistent economic program."

Over the years, a number of important steps have been taken towards developing effective machinery for consistent and comprehensive national economic policies. One of the earliest steps in this century was the establishment of the Federal Reserve System before World War I. At that time, under far simpler conditions than those now confronting us, the Federal Reserve System was regarded as the main and central organ for economic stabilization. After World War II, in a much more complex economic situation and a much more complex framework of governmental activities affecting the economy, the Council of Economic Advisers was established by the Congress under the Employment Act of 1946 to advise the President and help prepare reports to the Congress concerning how all major economic policies might be combined to promote our economic strength and health. Still more recently, in the current defense emergency, the Office of Defense Mobilization has been established to co-ordinate and direct operations in the mobilization effort. In addition, some of the established departments, such as the Treasury Department, have always performed economic functions which go beyond specialized problems and affect the whole economy.

Consequently, I am requesting the Secretary of the Treasury, the Chairman of the Federal Reserve Board, the Director of Defense Mobilization, and the Chairman of the Council of Economic Advisers to study ways and means to provide the necessary restraint on private credit expansion and at the same time to make it possible to maintain stability in the market for Government securities. While this study is under way, I hope that no attempt will be made to change the interest rate pattern, so that stability in the government security market will be maintained.

This four-agency committee did not, in fact, report until May 31. But on March 4, only eight days after it was set up by the President, an accord between the Treasury and the Federal Reserve was announced. This has led some people to conclude that agreement was expedited by their desire to come to voluntary understanding between themselves without having to share responsibility (or credit) with other agencies.[15]

President Truman has on many occasions made it clear that he did not intend to see the dignity and power of the Presidential office shrink or be encroached upon while he was its custodian.[16] On the other hand, he was not consistently concerned about that independence of action and policy by Cabinet officers which has been a conspicuous feature of American practice. In his interpretation of the President's role, he apparently did not think of the Employment Act as supplying a touchstone of Presidential leadership within the executive branch. He did not see the institution of the Economic Report as a major state paper, prepared with the aid of a professional staff, as a means of arriving at integrated national policies which then would be the President's frame of national administration, to which all department and agency heads must conform their actions or be replaced. This possibility of significant tightening of administration in the executive branch without structural modifi-

---

[15] On February 28, the President requested the director of the Bureau of the Budget in co-operation with the Director of Defense Mobilization and the chairman of the Council of Economic Advisers to "reappraise" the programs of all Federal lending or loan-guaranteeing agencies from the standpoint of their contribution to defense needs and their consistency with the anti-inflation program. This committee submitted a report to the President in June 1951. It was never released to the public, but the setting up of the committee is interesting in view of the statutory function of the Bureau and the Council for reviewing policies and programs of all government agencies as to their internal consistency and their compatibility with the announced policies of the President and with the purposes set forth in the Employment Act.

[16] Not merely in the form of Congressional domination or the insubordination of Cabinet officers or agency heads. Mr. Truman reacted violently against the flouting of Presidential power or dignity by private power in the person of John L. Lewis in the coal strike of May 1948. But he appeared to be less sensitive on the point when Philip Murray took so intransigent a line in the steel controversy of 1951.

cation, envisaged by the Congress (see p. 348), remains to be explored by some later President.

General Eisenhower early announced plans for a thorough reorganization of the Executive Office of the President, which included several indications of an intention to secure better integration of policy. Thus the post of Assistant to the President, developed under Truman, is in effect expanded into that of Assistant President, with substantial responsibility for co-ordinating the policies and administrative programs of the various departments and commissions. Possibilities of further integration may be seen in the conferring of virtual Cabinet rank on the heads of the Mutual Security Administration and the Federal Security Agency, and a prospective realignment of the National Security Council.

No crisis of runaway inflation or of business collapse presented Mr. Truman with the necessity of facing a test of the Administration's ability to co-ordinate many lines of economic policy into an adequate program of stabilization. It seems highly improbable, however, that President Eisenhower will be equally fortunate. In a critical test of administration leadership against national danger, either inflationary or deflationary, it may be presumed that the skills and experience of one accustomed to the role of "supreme commander" will produce disciplined action among the various executive agencies. Will they then rely exclusively on the improvisations of experienced men of action? Or will they feel that economists have something better than this—or complementary to it—to offer? If so, will the Council of Economic Advisers be so reconstituted as to be a competent staff arm of the Executive Office? All this remains to be seen.

THE PRESIDENT'S VIEW OF THE ROLE OF GOVERNMENT

Last—and of great importance—comes the question of the extent of government intervention called for under the Employment Act. The "negotiated language" of section 2 stipulated that any action taken under it should be calculated "to foster and promote free competitive enterprise." To this was added in conference "and the general welfare." Whether this implies that the general welfare would be most effectively promoted by maximizing free competitive enterprise or whether these are two not fully reconcilable goals, either

of which could be taken as the ruling criterion of policy by the
President or by the Congress in any concrete economic situation,
will have to be clarified in the light of later experience. The divergent interpretations of the act given by different people in the
various branches of government and outside have been alluded to
in Chapter XVII. (See pp. 335, 364 f.)

President Truman carefully avoided any precise explanation of
his ideological position on this issue. He was never confronted with
any acute danger of large unemployment. Somewhat conflicting inferences may be drawn from what he has said and done at different
times during the last six years. In signing the act, he immensely
cheered the advocates of "positive government" by commenting:
"The Employment Act of 1946 is not the end of the road, but rather
the beginning. It is a commitment by the government to the people—
a commitment to take any and all of the measures necessary for a
healthy economy, one that provides opportunities for those able,
willing, and seeking to work. We shall all try to honor that commitment." He did not indicate then or later whether he considers an
economy healthy (1) only if the area of public enterprise is kept to
its present limits, (2) if it might with benefit be enlarged by further
construction projects or by actual government operation of facilities,
or (3) if it were curtailed by the withdrawal of government from
some bastions already occupied.

President Truman conspicuously supported the ambitions of the
Department of the Interior to expand its public utility empire. But
when the Spence Economic Stability bill and later the Murray Economic Expansion bill were pending he declined to give his sponsorship to the idea of government intrusion in the industrial field and
rapped the knuckles of a Council of Economic Advisers member
who was giving aid and comfort to these promotions. On the other
hand, he sponsored such use of government controls in peacetime
as stultify the process of real collective bargaining and, in an industrial crisis which many argued was government-induced, he
claimed "inherent powers" to take over private industry in ways
subsequently declared unconstitutional by the Supreme Court.

Thus the extent to which and the manner in which the Employment Act has modified our politico-economic system through Presidential interpretation of the intent of Congress in passing the act
remains uncertain. The real question is how this feature of the Act

will be interpreted by the incoming President—particularly if the incipient stages of a post-rearmament recession should appear. Some inferences may perhaps be drawn from General Eisenhower's Harlem speech on October 25, 1952:

. . . Let me say to you people what I have said time and again and with the full concurrence of all these associates of mine in this political crusade. Never again shall we allow a depression in the United States. The Soviet communism is looking for one great victory. That victory is the economic collapse of our country. They want to see us go broke. Why then would a nation such as ours refuse to mobilize all its resources to defeat a depression as we would mobilize all our resources to defeat an invasion? One is just as serious as the other.

So I pledge you this. If the finest brains, the finest hearts, that we can mobilize in Washington can foresee the signs of any recession, and depression, that would put honest, hard working men and women out of work, the full power of private industry, of municipal government, of state government, of the Federal Government will be mobilized to see that that does not happen. I cannot pledge you more than that.

CHAPTER NINETEEN

Actual Performance of the Council

If, as suggested in the preceding chapter, Congress imposed upon the President "full and complete executive responsibility for carrying out the provisions" of the Employment Act in the executive branch and the Council was merely to serve him as he might direct, it was perhaps expected that he would spell out for the new agency the character of the service which he would expect. Such direction, however, was hardly to be given by a heavily-pressured President little acquainted with the idiosyncrasies of the economic craft and only remotely in touch with the extended discussion by way of hearings, reports, and Congressional debates which had preceded the passing of the statute. In actual practice, President Truman's formal responsibility has been discharged chiefly in making nominations of Council members, in designating the chairman and vice-chairman, and in settling or straddling two or three other issues that arose. It devolved upon the Council itself to make interpretations of the intent of Congress and to decide, as situations unfolded, how it could most effectively serve the President and other top officials of the executive establishment in carrying out these intentions.

QUALIFICATIONS OF COUNCIL MEMBERS

It appears from the record that the President in making his appointments held fairly close to the criterion set by Congress, in the main nominating persons of professional training, experience, and standing to Council posts. He did not treat these positions as mere political plums or allow interest groups to induce him to place "their man" on the Council. In retrospect, however, it does not appear that he established appointment to the Council as, on the one hand, something that demands the highest qualities of technical competence, mature wisdom, practical realism, and intellectual objectivity that can be found in the country and, on the other hand, as the highest recognition and the greatest opportunity for public service that the most highly qualified economists in the country may aspire to.

Beyond a man's sheer technical competence, the question of general attitude is involved in judging the fitness of any economist to serve effectively on the Council. Some men of the highest professional standing would be quite unsuited because of their preoccupation with the pursuit of "pure science" and their unwillingness to work happily and effectively in the realm of applied economic science or economic engineering. Others are, in my judgment, unfitted by their desire to follow the career—noble though it is in its proper sphere— of economic politician. Such persons aspire to be themselves policy-makers rather than professional aides to the duly constituted makers of government policy. They would be restive and perhaps even supercilious as they saw their beautifully wrought analyses and recommendations adulterated, distorted, or completely ignored and would be thin-skinned at the thought that their professional brethren or the general public would be holding them accountable as the authors of whatever policies might emerge from the strange and wonderful process of political administration.

No unanimity has yet been arrived at among economists, even those who have served on the Council, as to the ideal or even the practically essential qualifications of a Council member. My own view was early set forth at a meeting of the American Economic Association as follows:

Some cynical people have alluded to the Council as "the Three Wise Men of Economics," standing at the President's elbow to give him smart answers to economic riddles or to tell him just what to do in every economic crisis or situation as it arises. Now I do not regard myself as $33\frac{1}{3}$ per cent of the Three Wise Men. I do not claim that the Council is composed of the three greatest economists in the United States or even that it includes any one of that sacred three. As I understand the matter, we have, by the vicissitudes of politics, been entrusted with the task of organizing an agency through which, over the years, the Chief Executive of the United States may see the economic situation and problems of the nation in their entirety and through professional eyes. It is the responsibility of this agency to process for his consideration the materials which should be of most use to him in laying out his policy and following his course of action with reference to the national economy. . . . I conceive this agency as the doorway through which the best thinking of systematic economics (not forgetting the lay brothers) may be brought into clear and effective focus at the point of executive decision as to national economic policy and action.[1]

With perhaps pardonable exaggeration, I said to a group of fellow economists during the very early days of the Council that I wished all my previous writings could have been obliterated at the moment I was sworn in as a member of the Council. Not that I wished to repudiate them, but I did not want it thought by the public that views previously expressed would commit me to any particular line of doctrine or impair my objectivity in considering the views of my colleagues, our staff, and our consultants in other branches of government or outside as we sought to explore every means by which the major stabilization purpose of the Employment Act might be most fully attained.

The qualification for membership which in retrospect seems to me still to be most important is (aside from technical competence) that the member shall not be "carrying the torch" for any special group or economic cult. This precludes a desire to make himself a figure of public prominence or an active factor in the effectuation of policies or programs.

Mr. Keyserling and Mr. Clark both seemed to me to lean somewhat to the "Three Wise Men" interpretation of the Council's role and to conceive their position on it as an opportunity to become directly influential on behalf of policies or causes to which they were already devoted or others which they might espouse as particular situations developed. I am unable to discover any place where Mr. Clark stated his view of the Council member's role explicitly. Mr. Keyserling's interpretation of the job can best be elucidated in connection with later sections of this chapter.

Mr. Blough, some months before he took a position on the Council, presented a very thoughtful analysis of its work before the American Economic Association. He stressed "sobriety of statement, tact, and the absence of partisanship and personal ambition" on the

---

[1] Edwin G. Nourse, "Economics in the Public Service," *American Economic Review (Proceedings)*, Vol. 37, No. 2, May 1947, pp. 22–23.

part of members as qualities that would make for the success of Council work but felt that there was an inherent dilemma between a proper independence for the Council and most satisfactory service to the President. I shall attempt later to resolve this dilemma, but here simply endorse Mr. Blough's characterization of intellectual independence combined with tact and with an absence of partisanship or personal ambition, as important qualifications for Council membership. During his two years of service he practiced these virtues.

What Mr. Blough calls "tact" is closely related to the emotional detachment which he also bespeaks. Since the Council members are not policy-makers, but are intended to condition the President, his Cabinet, and other executive heads for the wiser and better coordinated formulation of official economic policy for the nation, any influence which they wield should depend on the inherent reasonableness of the analyses they present and the persuasiveness with which they speak for the national viewpoint. Thus

the making of its economic synthesis demands of each Council member a broad and deep social philosophy. Only so can he weigh and scale the demands of the several parties to the economic process and display a calm judicial quality as the economic attorneys for one or another special interest group argue the claims of their respective clients for favored treatment in the matter of income, for special relief from effort or responsibility, or for exceptional security. These issues will frequently present economic dilemmas. So confronted, the Council must synthesize a policy which "on balance" holds greatest promise of practical workability. Furthermore, this must be presented in a way which will promote understanding and acceptance by the several contending parties.[2]

Senator Murray, in the outline of administrative problems under the Employment Act already quoted (p. 367), put as his second point:

The members of the Council of Economic Advisers must be wholeheartedly devoted to the principles of the bill. The employment bill as reported by the conference committee provides that the members of the Council of Economic Advisers be exceptionally qualified to "appraise programs and activities of the Government in the light of the policy declared in section

[2] Edwin G. Nourse, "Economic Analysis and Political Synthesis," R. A. F. Penrose, Jr., Memorial Lecture, *Proceedings of the American Philosophical Society*, Vol. 94, No. 4, 1950, p. 314. Since this paper deals with the Council's work in its broad aspects, it is reprinted as App. F.

2." This means that they must subscribe without reservation to the policy declared in section 2. It means that they must believe in the objective of full employment, in the basic responsibility of the Federal Government for maintaining conditions of full employment, and in the need for the Government to utilize all its resources for the purpose of discharging this responsibility.

I am sure that each of the five members who have thus far served on the Council of Economic Advisers would, without hesitation, feel that he met this qualification. In the first annual report of the Council to the President, we stated:

The three appointees who make up the initial membership of the Council, though no one of them had so much as met either of the others at the time of his selection, have found themselves in a gratifying state of like-mindedness on this matter. All of us believe wholeheartedly in the basic purposes of the act. We believe its broad enabling powers provide a device through which practical action can be suited to the demands of changing circumstances. In our judgment, too, there has come to be a broader understanding of the basic relationships among production, purchasing power, and employment, and an actionable degree of willingness to meet the requirements of better sustained general prosperity in the future. . . . The passing of the Employment Act by Congress would have been no more than a senseless gesture if it did not express a considered belief that, by mobilizing our capacity of economic reasoning and the brains and experience of business management, labor leaders, and others, we could moderate in the future the devastating periods of business depression.

This, however, does not mean that each member would, on close investigation, prove to be "wholeheartedly devoted to the principles" of the Employment Act as Mr. Murray himself would interpret them. As to ends, yes: as to means, however, there was an unresolved ambiguity in the act itself as set forth in its declaration of policy. This has already been noted in Chapter XVII (p. 364) and Chapter XVIII (p. 390). Senator Murray's support of the Spence bill and sponsorship of the Senate Economic Expansion bill in 1949 connote an interpretation of the Employment Act to which I could not personally subscribe. In fact, I would not be able to write in 1952, as I did in 1946, that the three initial members of the Council had as much "likemindedness" in their views of the proper implementation of the act as I then supposed or assumed. But on one interpretation of Senator Murray's criterion for Council appointment, all should be able to agree. No one should regard himself or be regarded as qualified to hold membership on the Council unless he believes wholeheartedly in that agency as a means of bringing scientific analysis of economic problems helpfully to the service of practical policy-making.

In all that has been said thus far, the implication has been that the choice of Council members and thus the criteria according to which their qualifications are to be judged rests entirely with the President. The act, however, provides for confirmation by the Senate. The legislative history shows that, in inserting this provision, the Senate had two somewhat mixed motives. One was that this review of the President's nominations would give the Senate an opportunity to assure and preserve the independent professional character of the Council and see that it was not "packed" with partisans of any particular interest group or type of ideology or with mere political hacks. Beneath the surface of this laudable purpose, however, there are traces of a second motive. This is a possible desire to put a Senate committee in a position to apply their own criteria of whom they would permit to serve the President rather than leaving to him the decision as to who could serve him most adequately.

At all events, Senate confirmation affords an opportunity for a few senators or a single powerful individual, either on his own motion or at the promptings of some interest group, to veto the confirmation of a prospective Council member whose past views or attitudes, however objective and worthy, have been found unacceptable.[3]

Confirmation hearings for the initial appointees of the Council were brief and almost perfunctory. When, at a later date, Mr. Blough's nomination came up, he was interrogated at a length of some two hours, but on a high plane. If Mr. Turner, now serving an interim appointment, comes up for confirmation on a permanent basis, it is quite possible that his past connections and relation-

[3] On April 9, 1947, Representative Clare Hoffman introduced a bill, H. R. 3000, to amend the Employment Act so that the term of one member would expire on December 31, 1947, one in December 1948, and one in December 1949, after which appointees should serve for terms of three years. Under such an arrangement, the Council would live under constant threat of interruption and periodic review of issues in an atmosphere surcharged with politics. Representative Hoffman had been a vigorous opponent of the Employment Act throughout the time that it was under consideration in the House.

ships in the White House staff might come in for close scrutiny. They might all too possibly interfere with his confirmation quite regardless of his professional competence and the character of his performance during his interim appointment.

For the longer future, it seems clear that the President should be free to make Council appointments according to his own criteria of qualifications and not run the risk that the confirmation hearing may become an occasion for discussion of the substance of the President's policy positions or of the nominee's economic beliefs rather than his professional competence and scholarly detachment. It is my view that the incoming President during the "honeymoon" period when desired Congressional action is most easily secured should have this provision of the Employment Act removed. Such a recommendation was made by the Hoover Commission.

Perhaps a final qualification for Council membership would be an ability to establish effective working relations with the President. Only limited success in this direction has been attained thus far.

RELATIONS WITH THE PRESIDENT

Personal and institutional relations of the Council with the President have been covered in considerable part by what has already been said about relations of the President with the Council. All this leads up to several questions on which the Employment Act was entirely silent, but which in practice have proved highly controversial. These issues center on whether the relation of the Council to the President is or is not to be "confidential."

In framing the Employment Act, the idea of a Council of Economic Advisers to the President won out over proposals for a National Economic Commission, reporting to the Congress and to the public—a sort of "supreme court of economics." Many senators and representatives felt that such an agency would not be so much an aid to the President as a check upon him, and thought that the latter function should be discharged by the Congress itself with the aid of the Joint Committee. But though the Council was set up in an advisory relationship, no language was put in the act which would enjoin it to make its appraisals and recommendations to the President confidential. And many people still clung to the idea of having the Council publish its separate analysis and policy recommendations on its own prestige and responsibility as a sort of external audit presented in "deadly parallel" to the President's Economic Report or special reports and messages.

Mr. Truman never faced—or perceived the real nature of—the issue. He fell into the trap, with members of the Council aiding and abetting. After repeated, but not very decisive, changes of stand on the form of the President's Economic Report, he insisted at midyear 1948 on a separate document over the Council's signatures—but added that this need not be permanent. He said that a separate document supplemental to and published with his Economic Report would "show that there were no politics" in the latter. This practice has since been followed and has resulted in creating a widespread impression among the public that there is a great deal of "politics" in the Council's document, without creating confidence that there is none in the President's Economic Report.[4]

Since the Economic Report is an official paper of the political chief of state, it is inevitable and entirely proper that it should blend political considerations with more rigorously economic ingredients in its formulation of practical policy. But there is no reason whatsoever why the Council should desire, or the President permit them, to present under their own names an economic analysis in the detail which clearly points to recommendations and still less reason to include explicit recommendations of their own in their document. With each successive report, however, assumption by the Council of the role of independent spokesmen on policy issues has appeared

[4] "Hopes that the President's Advisory Council would confine its activities to a dispassionate analysis of economic problems were dashed when two members of the Council became propagandists for Administration policies. The President's selection of Mr. Keyserling as chairman of the Council set the stamp of approval on this misconception of the proper role of an advisory group. Since the Council has given a political slant to its economic views, it was only to be expected that the findings and recommendations of the Joint Congressional Committee that examines the President's report would be influenced by politics. . . . The President and his Council are chiefly to blame for the failure of a promising experiment to substitute expert and unbiased discussion of economic problems and policies for partisan judgment." (Washington *Post,* June 21, 1950.)

"The forthcoming change in Presidents revives the hope that the Council of Economic Advisers may be put on a nonpolitical basis. It has been suggested that it can be nonpolitical only if its reports are made exclusively to the President and his immediate advisers; that when these reports are made public they must agree with the views of the President. That makes them political and betrays the purpose for which the organization was established, that is, to give the President objective, professional advice. In Washington some feel that reports as now published supply economic ammunition in support of administration policies; that the Council was not established for that purpose. Paul Wooton in *Dun's Review* (October 1952).

more clearly. Acute observers have not merely noted that the Council was thus making independent appraisals and recommendations, but some have pointed out what they regard as divergences in the two documents.

In a succinct but telling paragraph, Roy Blough has shown the self-destroying nature of this arrangement.

There is one proposal which would set up a Council that was both independent and powerful. The proposal is that the Council should serve as a sort of supreme court of economics. I can see no place in the American scene for such an organization. The "court" would presumably "decide" either economic policy or economic truth. Policy determination in a democracy is a function for persons whose responsibilities run to the people and not for independent authorities, however expert they may be. Truth in economics, as in all science, is established by running the gantlet of the widest professional criticism and standing the test of experience. It cannot be established by authoritative bodies except, of course, in totalitarian countries.[5]

By contrast, he visualizes a Council "doing nothing but advise the President . . . the only function that the statute now gives it. . . . The true adviser properly becomes anonymous. He has no publicity functions." This would mean no documents signed by the Council, no Congressional appearances, no public speeches of any sort—in other words, complete self-effacement. This was the extreme view taken by Franklin Roosevelt in connection with his ten special assistants in the White House "with a passion for anonymity." But it, too, has its dangers. So extreme a withdrawal from public contact leads to a certain amount of suspicion. "Who," it was asked concerning some of the economic advisers of F. D. R., "are these mysterious, even sinister, figures who flit, nameless and disembodied, in and out of the West Wing or indeed the 'oval office' of the President?"

Blough himself repudiated the anonymous role and even the middle course which I have sketched. He accepted the separately signed report procedure, spoke in public occasionally and with dignity and detachment, and defended the practice of Council discussion with the Joint Committee. While his appearances there have been constructive and not seriously controversial, his colleagues have become

[5] Roy Blough, "Political and Administrative Requisites for Achieving Economic Stability," *American Economic Review*, Vol. XL, No. 2, May 1950, p. 178.

involved in pronouncements and even verbal battles with committee members that have gone far to discredit the work of the Council in its duty to serve the President.

Mr. Blough saw the Council's situation as a dilemma. On the one hand, he believed: "There are important values to be derived from having an independent group of economists in a position of high visibility in the government. One result of this position is a dramatic impact on the public, the Congress, and administrators of the importance of economics as such, and of economic stabilization and growth. The results of this impact in developing the economic sophistication of the public and in promoting an integrated governmental policy directed toward stabilization may be immense." On the other hand, "if the Council acts in a very independent manner, it can scarcely be recognized as an advisory body to the President. And if it is not so recognized, it loses much of its value as a body of independent economists." But the dilemma immediately disappears if the Council forswears the mission of having "a dramatic impact" on the public and on government officials (which was not assigned it by Congress) and accepts the specific role which was assigned it by Congress, of helping the President, in the brief time at his disposal, to get at the basic economic issues involved in his political decisions.

The Council of Economic Advisers does not reallocate basic public responsibilities; it merely puts improved professional techniques and resources at the disposition of those who make national policy. Since the President must formulate his policies and shape his program within his own evaluation of the most varied and comprehensive political and social as well as economic influences and considerations, it is not to be expected that his Report to Congress will merely reflect the conclusions and recommendations of his Economic Council. He will simply use as he deems wise such economic analyses, appraisals, conclusions, and recommendations as they prepare for him.[6]

Adherence to this position would preclude all appearance before the Joint Committee or other Congressional committees. It would mean making the Economic Report of the President a single document that stated the President's policy and presented the line of reasoning or the state of facts on which it was based. Such a docu-

[6] Council of Economic Advisers, *First Annual Report to the President,* December 1946, p. 8.

ment would let the President's economic statesmanship stand out
in stark simplicity where it could be readily seen and be discussed
strictly on its own merits. Such an interpretation of the Council's
role, however, would not preclude some contribution by the Council to general information about broad economic issues or, in
Blough's phrase, "developing economic sophistication of the public."

There are two avenues of public communication which in my judgment are properly open to the Council within the limited role of
confidential advisers to the President which I visualize. One is
specifically mentioned but not elaborated in the act: "The Council
may constitute such advisory committees and may consult with such
representatives of industry, agriculture, labor, consumers, State and
local governments, and other groups, as it deems advisable."

At the outset, such consultative committees were set up. They provided a means for various business and non-Federal Government
units to express their reaction to the Economic Reports of the President or other expressions of his economic policy. They also provide
opportunity, as one of the members himself expressed it, to "needle
us" or, through us, to "needle the President" to take such lines of
action as they think desirable. But these groups also constitute small
and off-the-record centers where the Council can present such ideas
of its own or of the executive family on matters of policy and general
attitude as it deems desirable to have discussed on an educational
plane with these persons who occupy strategic places in the thinking
of their respective organizations. While this kind of deliberation is
not as withdrawn from the public forum as are confidential discussions with the President or other executive heads, it is still "off the
record" and subject to whatever safeguards the Council feels it
proper to place around it.

Another means of educational communication between the Council and the public comes in the members' publication of individual
articles, the making of personal speeches, or participation in certain
types of radio and television programs. Some people have charged
me with inconsistency in my position as to public appearances by
the Council. This does not in my mind involve any inconsistency,
but a rather precise distinction between unlike circumstances and
effects. The nature of this difference is that between a situation

under the speaker's control and one not under his control, with consequences which in the one case would be educational and in the other subject to political exploitation.

If a Council member responds to a request of a Congressional committee to appear as a witness on matters covered in the Economic Report of the President or on topics under investigation or review before standing or special committees, "the lead is in their hand." The committee can choose the area of questioning, phrase their interrogations, inject their comments, and suggest inferences in ways which will relentlessly draw out from the Council member any divergences or reservations that he may have as to the economic wisdom of policies advanced by the President or other branches of the Administration. As I put the matter crudely to Mr. Truman: "The opposition would like nothing better than to get you over a barrel and use us for a paddle."

The situation is essentially the same if one appears on one of the numerous panel-type radio or television shows. A smart reporter, a critical politician, or an irritated citizen can maneuver the hapless Council member into a position where evasion of the question or faint support of Administration policy is as embarrassing or mischievous as outright attack. I stubbornly refused to participate on such shows and appeared only on news broadcasts at the time of appearance of an Economic Report of the President, and then limited myself to a factual statement as to significant or newsworthy appraisals of the business situation which it contained or its recommendations of economic policy.

If the Council member elects to make a public address, he has entire freedom to decide which audience he will meet with, what topic he will discuss, and what scope and style of treatment he will use. It lies within his own discretion to decide whether or not he will respond to questions from the audience. If he does so, he should limit his answers to issues of general principle or statistical fact. He should not take a position on any pending issue of government policy or program.

I early raised with the President the question whether speeches by Council members should be "cleared" at the White House before delivery. He replied that that was not necessary as he had full confidence in our discretion in public statements. My first formal appearance as a member of the Council was at a luncheon session of the National Association of Manufacturers at the time of their annual meeting and Congress of American Industry. Their letter of invitation suggested that "both management and the Council stand to gain by the clearing up of any misunderstandings arising from hearsay reports or rumors about your organization. Particularly it would seem to us that you would want to underscore management's own responsibility in the matter because this is the greatest and most responsible audience of industrial management in action." The President expressed the view that this would be "a valuable opportunity to present the work of the Council to a large and influential business group. . . . I emphasized to him that I would limit my remarks to a statement of the Council's interpretation of the act and steps which it is taking to carry it out and not include any comments on the current business situation or prospective government policy." (*P. D.*, October 16, 1946)

On the one occasion when I was invited to address a labor union convention, I did not submit text of the speech for clearance but focused my remarks on broad economic issues and labor's responsibility in the national stabilization effort. The following paragraph is representative:[7]

We are dealing with a very delicate and complicated piece of machinery and we cannot safely operate as special interest groups or by using our sheer weight or fighting strength to force an economic adjustment merely to our arbitrary will or to our short-run or apparent advantage. Instead of such a militant or brute-force means of settling economic problems, we must, with the responsibilities that lie in our hands, turn to what I like to refer to as the engineering approach to problems of economic adjustment under free enterprise and collective bargaining. We cannot be content merely to be clever negotiators or ruthless fighters. We must acquire a basic understanding of the broad repercussions and long-run cause-and-result relationships involved in our business actions. Both the corporation and the union must be skillful in working out these relations when they set wage rates and working rules. Manufacturers and merchants must deal skillfully with these relationships when they mark price tickets and set service charges. Both individuals and corporate managers must deal intelligently with these relationships when they determine on their savings accumulations and their spending behavior. Public officials as well as citizens must show themselves economically literate when they decide on tax levies and public works expenditures.

[7] Text of this address in App. D.

When, however, I was invited by Secretary Forrestal to address the first Group Orientation Conference (see p. 172 n.), I felt that this pushed me out into a position where I could not escape being regarded as a spokesman for the Administration. I therefore submitted this manuscript to the White House and received clearance before it was delivered. It was limited to a statement of the issues involved in the increase by various hypothetical amounts in the size of the military budget.[8]

Since certain commentators who would have been satisfied with nothing less than a categorical endorsement of any increase suggested by the military, asserted that this had been cleared by the White House only in some merely *pro forma* fashion without coming specifically to the President's attention, I took further precautions when Secretary Johnson extended a similar invitation in connection with the second Orientation Conference the following April. After talking with Secretary Snyder and Budget Director Pace, I submitted the same paper to the President and said: "I have tried to sketch what seems to me the important background of economic analysis without using specific figures which should not yet be bandied about or become involved in any question of military feasibility, which lies outside my province." On April 5, the President sent me a brief note of thanks for this letter of explanation and copy of the talk, of which he said: "I think it is a good document."

Similarly, during the time that "the Brannan Plan" was a controversial issue, I was asked to address the Farm and Home Convention at the University of Kentucky (January 1949) and at Cornell in March. Speaking under the title, "Where Does the Farmer Stand on Agricultural Policy?" I limited my remarks on policy to a literal quotation from the statement of issues as contained in the current Economic Report of the President and sent my paper both to Secretary Brannan and to the President.

To the best of my knowledge, neither of my colleagues sought specific White House clearance on any of their public addresses. Mr. Clark made almost no speeches and did not become a conspicuous figure in this controversy. Mr. Keyserling, on the other hand, was in considerable demand as a speaker for labor meetings, before Americans for Democratic Action, and other "liberal" groups and business, academic, and civic organizations similar to those which I

[8] Full text of this address appears in App. E.

addressed.[9] He (and I think Clark, in principle) agreed with my view that it was both proper and useful for Council members to engage in public discussion of broad economic issues underlying or related to the effort to find ways of combining private and public enterprise in stabilization devices and practices. Beyond this, however, the record shows (pp. 248, 292) that Mr. Keyserling found no impropriety in appearing before political or even partisan groups as well as Congressional committees. In one instance, he took me to task for having overstepped the bounds of my own definition of what was proper for a Council member in connection with public addresses. I, in turn, felt misgivings as to the consequences of his participation either in party pow-wows or Congressional inquiries. Our respective views, as held at the time, are quite fully stated in the memoranda on pages 276 and 277.

Much of Mr. Keyserling's published material undoubtedly conformed to his statement that we should not "use a public meeting or the public press as a forum for expressing favor or disfavor of important proposals which the President currently has before him for decision." The reader will have to judge for himself whether Mr. Keyserling's participation in various labor meetings and party gatherings were consistent with such a criterion. On one occasion (p. 246), the President intervened to see that he did not fulfill an advertised speaking engagement.

I still believe that any Council member who so desires may engage in truly educational discussion of underlying economic principles and issues with thoughtful citizens through public speeches and printed articles without becoming involved either in business prophecy or discussion of specific Administration policies or economic programs. This I think is an economic service which tends to promote better understanding between the White House and the

[9] These included the National Farm Institute, the Northern California Management Conference, the First Annual Florida Business Conference, the Third Annual (Philadelphia) Bulletin Forum, the Institute of Trade and Commerce Professions (New York), the Economic Club of Detroit, the National Tax Association, the New York Herald Tribune Forum, the American Political Science Association, the National Planning Association, the University of Minnesota Industrial Relations Conference, and the Municipal Finance Officers Association. He also published articles in the *New York Times Magazine,* the *Nation, Harper's Magazine,* the *American Federationist,* the *New Republic, Banking Magazine,* the *Public Finance Journal,* and others.

public without impairing the relationship of the Council as confidential technical advisers to the President.

COUNCIL AND CONGRESS

The third aspect of the issue as to whether or not the Council should occupy a confidential relation to the President concerns Congressional committees. What has been said in the preceding section and also in our narrative chapters has covered many phases of the question of Council relations with the Joint Economic Committee and with Congress in general. These threads should now be drawn together into a final conclusion on the basis of three years' active experience and three more years of observation and reflection.

The case for public participation by Council members in the deliberations of Congressional committees (with special obligation to discuss the President's Economic Report with the Joint Committee) appears to rest on three propositions: (1) it is an explicit obligation of this post in the Executive Office of the President; (2) such an obligation is implicit in the statute or was clearly the intent of Congress; (3) it is a logical necessity for making the Economic Report of the President an effective instrument and the Council a truly useful staff arm of the Presidency.

In a lengthy "communication" to the Washington *Post* (November 1949) Senator Murray argued the legal, or at least formal, obligation of Council members to support the President's economic policies "publicly."

I have never heard the point made, in connection with foreign policy or domestic policy prior to the establishment of the council, that our Government could function effectively or in the manner to which our traditions have accustomed us if those who under established law advise the President in various fields shrink from the task of discussing with the Congress and with the people those policies which they have recommended and which the President has adopted. . . . The members of the Council of Economic Advisers should act as contemplated under the statute which created them, and should not be censured or ridiculed for so doing. To the best of my knowledge, every original sponsor of the Employment Act of 1946 contemplated that the members of the council, like other public officials, would assume that degree of trusteeship for programs which the President sent to the Congress with their advice as is assumed by other agencies of Government entrusted with specified functions under law. . . .

Who is better qualified to construe the intent of the law than those who wrote it?

The idea of men with a "passion for anonymity" has valid applicability to the immediate personal staff of the President, who advise him in a range of matters the content of which is unknown to the public. But officials of a permanent public agency, whose qualifications and duties are set forth in the statute under which they serve, who are confirmed by the Senate, and who under law work in a designated field and assist the President in sending to the Congress messages in that very field stand forth openly and in the public eye. They cannot exercise a "passion for anonymity" without being placed in a constantly compromising position, and without shirking their most basic responsibilities in the American traditions. The members of the Council of Economic Advisers are not "anonymous" and should not be shrouded in that pretense.

Here Senator Murray says that the Employment Act established the Council as "a permanent *public* agency whose qualifications and *duties* are set forth in the statute under which they serve," these duties including "trusteeship for programs which the President sent to the Congress with their advice." According to my reading of the act, the Council is not a public agency in the ordinary sense, but is a unique type of agency "created in the Executive Office of the President . . . to assist and advise the President in the preparation of the Economic Report" and for relevant service to him. There is not a single word about any responsibility of the Council to the Congress or any of its members or committees.

The only possible hint of such a relationship would have to be derived from the language of Section 5 (d) of the act, which says: "The Joint Committee is authorized to utilize the services, information, and facilities of the departments and establishments of the Government, and also of private research agencies." This provision was clearly intended to avoid duplication in the gathering and analysis of statistical and economic information of service to the committee, like the parallel provision that "the Council shall, to the fullest extent possible, utilize the services, facilities, and information (including statistical information) of other Government agencies as well as of private research agencies, in order that duplication of effort and expense may be avoided." From the start, I interpreted these two sections of the act to mean that the analytical work being done by the Council's staff should be fully open to examination and use by the staff of the Joint Committee (see p. 189). This interchange at the staff level has possibilities of useful co-operation and seems to be the only reasonable interpretation that could be given to the language of the Employment Act.

Mr. Keyserling apparently agreed fully with Senator Murray's reading of the act and went a little farther to interpret the acceptance or retention of a position on the Council as a formal obligation to appear publicly as spokesman for the President. In the first Council report after he became acting chairman, we read: "The signatories of this report have never found any reason to believe that our special service to the President under the Employment Act could be inconsistent with that degree of co-operative *servicing of Congressional committees*—particularly the Joint Committee on the Economic Report—which has become the traditional practice of policy advisers to the President who are set up under law, entrusted by law with a specified field of study and advice, and responsible under law for explicit *participation in* reports and recommendations transmitted to the Congress." (Italics added.)

In Mr. Keyserling's most recent and detailed exposition of the Council's duties and responsibilities, he said:

It is clear that the members of the Council are employees of and advisers to the President, and that they are not employees of and advisers to the Congress in the same sense. But this does not mean, in my opinion, that the members of the Council cannot or should not testify before, cooperate and consult with, and in a sense give advice to, committees of the Congress, just as this is done by heads of other agencies in the executive branch, and even other agencies in the Executive Office of the President such as the National Security Resources Board, who are appointed by the President and confirmed by the Senate under statutes defining their functions and responsibilities, and who are employees of and advisers to the President in the sense that they work under his direction as members of his "official family" and may, of course, be dismissed by him. . . .

In addition, it has been the almost universal custom and entirely appropriate for such officials [Cabinet Secretaries] to appear before congressional committees and to make analyses and give advice in the fields in which they operate under statute, even when this has not been preceded by a Presidential message covering the specific matters before the committee. In appearing before committees of the Congress in this role, I cannot see where the Council of Economic Advisers is doing any different or appearing in any different light from what is done by heads of other agencies working in different fields. And I have never seen any valid reason why the members of the Council, in view of the statute under which they operate and the nature of their role, should follow a contrary course or differentiate between themselves and the heads of the other agencies to whom I have referred above.[10]

Here Mr. Keyserling undertakes to identify the role of Council members with that of Cabinet officers or other agency heads in the executive branch and implies that the Council's "functions and responsibilities" are defined by statute as being the same as these others, who occupy executive as well as advisory posts. To put such an interpretation on the language of the Employment Act and the rationale of the Executive Office of the President completely negates the idea that the Council of Economic Advisers is or was intended to be something new within our frame of government—an intellectual staff arm of the Presidency devoid of any responsibilities or privileges of sharing in the official enunciation or implementation of executive policy.

Furthermore, to say that members of the Council may, like executive heads, be dismissed by the President implies in this context that they would be so dismissed if they found themselves unable or unwilling actively to support the President's policies before the Congress or elsewhere. This raises the issue not of legality but of practicality, to which we shall return later.

I am unable to find any role of active participation in the Congressional arena imposed upon the Council by the particular terms of the Employment Act or by the requirements generally applicable to the executive branch. This last point was made explicitly by the President himself (p. 270). We are thrown back, therefore, to a re-examination of the intent of Congress in this matter.

Senator Murray asks the rhetorical question: "Who is better qualified to construe the intent of the law than those who wrote it?" Who indeed—and what did they "contemplate" in their drafting? In the paragraph quoted above, Murray argues that Council members should give active sponsorship to the economic policies of the President, refers to himself as "the principal sponsor of the Employment Act of 1946," and adds: "To the best of my knowledge, every original sponsor of the Employment Act of 1946 con-

[10] *Monetary Policy and the Management of the Public Debt,* Hearings before the Subcommittee on General Credit Control and Debt Management of the Joint Committee on the Economic Report (82 Cong. 2 sess.) Mar. 10–31, 1952, p. 287.

templated that the members of the Council, like other public officials, would assume that degree of trusteeship for programs" of the President.

The reasoning here is a bit difficult to follow. The full employment bill of which Senators Murray, Wagner, Thomas, and O'Mahoney were original sponsors contained no provision whatever for a Council of Economic Advisers, and the Senate had not yet accepted this feature when the two bills went to conference. The House bill, which introduced the Council idea, contained no provision for its members to appear before Congressional committees. It did provide that the Joint Committee might request the President to make the Council's "various studies, reports, and recommendations . . . available" to it. Even this clause was eliminated by the conference committee, of which Senators Barkley, Taft, Tobey, and Taylor were members. In speaking in the House for the adoption of the conference bill, Representative Cochran referred to this deletion as "a distinct improvement because it emphasizes the fact that the Council is not an autonomous agency." Senator Murray in his speech strongly urging adoption of the conference bill, said: "If this provision [for making Council studies and recommendations available to the Joint Committee] had been maintained, it would have given the three economic advisers an independent status apart from the Presidency. Conference bill eliminates this provision, thereby emphasizing the fact that their function is to assist the President in discharging his responsibilities under the act." His letter to the Washington *Post* takes a position quite at variance with the representations he made to his fellow senators in arguing for the adoption of the conference bill.

During the evolution of the Employment Act in Congress, one proposal was for

an economic commission that would serve both the President and Congress and be composed of Presidential appointees, members of Congress, and representatives of the public. It was also proposed to create an independent agency responsible to Congress rather than the President, or a quasi-public body similar to the Federal Reserve Board. All recommendations of this type were rejected by Congress. The framers of the act approached their task in terms of developing governmental machinery that would fully gear into the constitutional separation of powers between the legislative and executive branches. Rather than ignore this separation or attempt to bestride it through the creation of a composite or in-between body, they chose to set up a council to advise the President and a joint committee to perform a similar function for Congress. The development of closer relations between the two branches of government was not sought through an agency that would somehow bring both branches together.[11]

Thus active participation of Council members in Congressional deliberations seems not to be established either by the language of the act or by its legislative history. Even so, there is nothing to estop the President from asking or requiring such service from a Council member nor to estop the member from engaging in such activities if invited by a Congressional committee and not instructed otherwise by the President.

Instead of appealing to any explicit requirement or implicit intention, it is probably safe to say that the real situation was that it was left up to the President or any future Chief Executive to decide, on this point as on some others, just how he wished to use the staff agency which had been set up to serve him. This brings us to the final issue, whether such participation would advance or impede the basic purposes of the act.

Let us concede at the start that the Joint Committee or other committees of Congress might wish to avail themselves of such service from Council members—either for lofty purposes of intellectual enlightenment or for less exalted political ends. It is argued, with good logic, that no outside individual or staff group can interpret and elucidate for the Joint Committee the conclusions in the Economic Report of the President and the methods of arriving at them so well as can the men who have advised and assisted the President in the preparation of this document. But it is quite beside the point if, in so doing, they can be put in a position to embarrass the President, compromise themselves, or bring about changes in Council personnel of such frequency or such character as to impair its usefulness in the Executive Office.

I cannot escape the conviction that it is both unnecessary and undesirable for the Council to accept or be assigned a duty of thus staffing Congress or even the Joint Committee.[12] It is unnecessary

11 Edwin G. Nourse and Bertram M. Gross, "The Role of the Council of Economic Advisers," *The American Political Science Review,* Vol. XLII, No. 2, April 1948, pp. 287–88.

12 I do not pause to discuss the "executive session" as a device for avoiding the dangers of publicity. After thirty years in the Washington scene, I am not so naïve

because Congress provided for the study of the problem of economic stabilization at the legislative level independently through a new special joint committee with staff, with full access to the facilities of the Library of Congress, and with favorable conditions for securing supplemental funds for special studies. It is undesirable because (a) it impairs the professional standing of the Council members and thus the public's faith that this agency does in fact furnish a source of objective analysis to the President; (b) it interferes with or prevents the establishment of a frank and comfortable intellectual relationship between the Council members and the President; (c) it tends to surround the Council member with the atmosphere of policy-maker in his own right.

(a) Pragmatically, it is evident that the zeal of the Council to be an active factor in Congressional formulation of policy has led to charges, whether right or wrong, that their positions are "political" rather than "scientific." This has brought popular demands for the abolition of the Council.[13] Congress in fact made a drastic cut in its appropriation, putting this in the form of a terminal grant which will expire in March 1953 unless action to continue the Council is taken.

Logically, it seems evident that if the Council member appears before Congress to elucidate the President's policies, he must argue in support of them or remain silent on any with which he is in disagreement. It is not reasonable to suppose that the President

---

as to think that what fourteen senators and representatives are privileged to hear will remain confidential beyond the evening's radio broadcast or the morrow's newspaper "column." To label a session "executive" puts the reporters and columnists on their mettle to get the "inside story."

[13] "Congressional economizers searching for ways to cut government spending are taking a long look at the Council of Economic Advisers. When the Council was created by the Employment Act of 1946, Congress intended that it should concern itself with a disinterested appraisal of economic trends and evaluation of economic facts. Many solons now think it is being used exclusively to promote President Truman's economic theories and his Fair Deal policies. This criticism comes from many Democrats as well as Republicans. *So, when the Independent Offices appropriation measure reaches Congress, an effort will be made to legislate the Council out of existence by denying it money to continue operation.* (Prentice-Hall, Inc., *What's Happening in Washington,* Jan. 21, 1952.)

"This year's economic report doesn't mean much. It's little more than an argument for Truman's whole program, Fair Deal and all. Congress has become used to this. . . . In fact, serious talk in Congress on the abolition of the Council of Economic Advisers, staffed with high-paid experts, seems certain at this session." (*Business Week,* Jan. 19, 1952)

will in all instances follow the advice of the Council or that its three members will at all times be in complete agreement among themselves. Silence on a controverted point cannot be passive but must take the form of active refusal to answer inquiries from committee members—generally keen, often unsparing, sometimes even malicious. Evasion or verbal subterfuge is likely to be detected, to be exposed, and to put the Council member in a ridiculous position.

In fact, there is an inherent inconsistency in having one who is ticketed as an economic adviser undertake to discuss the soundness of executive policy on economic issues. To accept such a role implies that he is fully informed as to the extra-economic (or, in a perfectly proper sense, political) considerations which the President and his Cabinet and White House aides have taken into account in arriving at the Administration position, and that it would be proper for him to reveal these politico-economic motivations and discuss them on their merits. If he is not both informed as to the circumstances and convinced of the propriety and wisdom of these adaptations of strictly economic findings, again he cannot speak in public without embarrassing the President or compromising himself.

(b) Unless the President feels that Council members will give him at all times their completely detached analysis of the cause-and-result sequences in any given economic situation, with a succinct statement of the issues as seen by economists and their divergent conclusions on occasion, and unless he feels that they understand the practical necessity of his weighing many factors in arriving at a final decision and knows that these advisers will not appear before the public either as pliant rationalizers of his statesmanship or personal challengers of his decisions, there can be no effective relationship of technical advisers and practical executive established.

It is not an answer to this difficulty to say:

What the individual in an inconsistent position like that facing the Council may do is to carry on as well as he can, thinking and speaking as independently as possible but being discreet and cautious, never abandoning his standards of integrity by saying what he does not believe to be true. Almost inevitably in the end, the inconsistency of the position will become too clear and he will be obliged either to withdraw from some aspect of his work or resign his position. I have no criticism of any economist who is not willing to put himself into such an inconsistent position, or who,

being in it, prefers to retire. That is clearly the most comfortable choice
and the most unequivocal position. But unless economists are willing to
carry on in the Council under the conditions I have outlined, I doubt if
we shall be able to achieve through the Council the various goals we would
like to see achieved. Perhaps we should look on Council members as expendable, each carrying forward the work as far as he individually can and
then retiring in favor of others who can carry it farther before they, too,
drop by the wayside. I suggest that even the institution of the Council
itself is expendable and that sooner or later it will be cut down politically
to be replaced by some other organization carrying forward the same functions in somewhat different ways.[14]

This problem is purely of the Council member's making. The
law does not require him to become a Congressional witness; nor
did President Truman request it. And if the member creates this
impossible situation for himself, the proposed remedy of official
suicide is as bad as the disease. If he resigns because he has, in
violation of the confidential character of his post, put himself in
a position where the fact that he believes the President's policies
to be bad economics has been revealed, then Council membership
will be limited to those who fully agree with such economics as the
President already has or with such compromises as he feels constrained to make. The essential purpose of the act will be defeated.

(c) If a Council member appears before the Joint Committee or
any other committee to support the President's program, it inevitably transfers him, in some subtle way, at least partially into
the role of policy-making official, not a staff technician in the
Executive Office.[15] This is true if he limits himself to the elucida-

[14] Roy Blough, "Political and Administrative Requisites for Achieving Economic
Stability," *American Economic Review*, Vol. XL, No. 2, May 1950, pp. 177–78.

[15] The suggestion that the Council member resign if the President's policy persistently departs from the member's beliefs seems to me to imply such an over-
ambitious concept of the Council member's role. The following quotation from
Mr. Keyserling, despite such escape clauses as "when under all the circumstances
he believes it to be in the national interest to do so" seems to me to carry this same
implication:
"Under our system, no *responsible* official in such a position, while working for
the President, parades before the public or before congressional committees the
differences of viewpoint that there may be between himself and the President
on matters under consideration by the Congress. If these differences are minor in
character, the responsible public official does not feel entitled to the luxury or
self-satisfaction of having the President agree with him in every detail: Government
could not function if that were expected. But *if the President*, in his recommendations to the Congress, *were to depart from the analysis and advice given him by
the official in question to the extent that it could be regarded as a fundamental*

tion and effectuation of policies with which he agrees and has indeed recommended. But it is equally and perhaps more true if, in some more or less recognizable way, he reveals greater or less divergences of his beliefs from the policies expressed by the President. In either case, what the President (a non-economist) says in the Economic Report has to share the stage with what the Council says in its signed document or in its oral presentation to the Joint Committee. Both cases present the possibility that a Council member, if disingenuous, may go some distance toward altering the impact of the President's actual policy or even tending to "force his hand."

Mr. Truman never resolved the issue for us or for himself. He expressed appreciation of my effort to see that the Council should not be made a means of embarrassing him in Congressional debate but saw no reason why they should not be regarded as combat troops to be thrown into the Congressional battle for his policies. His final position was that it was his policy to allow the Council to follow their own views as to whether to appear before committees. "If you do not desire to appear it is perfectly all right with me. If the other gentlemen feel that they should appear, I would not interfere with that procedure." Somewhat casually, he added the comment that "Other members of the President's staff do not appear before Congressional committees." (See p. 270 n.)

While I believe that it will prove possible to bring social science usefully to bear in the making of practical policy, I do not believe

---

repudiation of that official's views, the official of integrity should resign where under all the circumstances he believes it in the national interest to do so. . . . The view has been expressed in some quarters, that members of the Council of Economic Advisers, in order never to be faced with a choice based upon the situations described above, should solve the problem by advising the President but by refusing to appear before Congressional committees to analyze and support those recommendations by the President to the Congress which are in accord with the advice they have given him. I can see no more reason why the members of the Council should *duck their basic responsibilities* by so doing than why *other officials* should thus avoid their responsibilities." [Italics added.] (Leon H. Keyserling, *Monetary Policy and the Management of the Public Debt,* Hearings before the Subcommittee on General Credit Control and Debt Management [82 Cong. 2 sess.] Mar. 10–31, 1952, p. 288.)

So too Senator Murray when he says, "If the President repudiates [the Council member's] advice beyond the point of toleration, he is always free to resign." I do not believe he is free to resign merely because the President "repudiates his advice" *if* the President knows what that advice is, weighs it in making his final decisions, and calls upon his Cabinet group likewise to consider it. (See p. 457.)

that the unique service needed by the President to this end can be rendered by having the President's personal economic staff sent to the trenches of Capitol Hill. The more that economists of professional prestige, personal independence, and practical experience are listened to in Congressional hearings, the better. But this kind of public service can be rendered only by economists from universities, from research institutions, and from business, labor, and financial organizations. The moment a man accepts the President's invitation to become an Economic Adviser (or White House aide), he must either take on a confidential status or become a liability to his chief.

I would resolve the dilemma stated by Mr. Blough by saying that service to the President must outweigh any desire for an "independent" role as economic adviser to the Congress. The only independence that is needed by the economist, however eminent, is the opportunity to make intellectually uncommitted analyses of pending economic issues and have these materials considered by the President and his policy-making Cabinet before final decisions are made. This is a self-abnegating role equally unsuited to the savant who aspires to found a "school" or win "disciples" or be honored by a volume of memorial essays as it is to the economic attorney who aspires to enter the Executive Office as the "mouthpiece" for an interest group or for a "cause" or who is willing to be mouthpiece for the President's policies whatever they are.[16]

COUNCIL FUNCTIONS AND ORGANIZATION

As one looks over the first six years of the Council's life, he must realize that important issues as to the scope of its activities and its methods of work still remain unanswered. As Congress drew the Employment Act, it focused attention on the Economic Report of

[16] See *American Economic Review*, Vol. XL, No. 2, May 1950, pp. 187–89.

It was widely assumed that I resigned from the chairmanship of the Council in 1949 as a protest against the following by the President of policies with which I could not agree. By many people I was praised for this "courageous" action. But this approval was somewhat misplaced. I would have regarded personal agreements or disagreements as relatively unimportant or an inevitable part of the job if White House policy were crystallized only after serious economic analyses prepared by the Council had been really considered. Unless this is done, the Council member cannot function in the role for which the agency was set up by Congress in one of its more thoughtful moods. He then will naturally seek a place of usefulness elsewhere.

the President and the services of the Council of Economic Advisers in "assisting and advising" him in its preparation. But in the constructive task of analyzing the state of the nation's business and outlining measures to strengthen it, Congress recognized the great importance for good or ill of what the Government was already doing. Thus Sec. 4 (c) (3) of the act provided that a major function of the Council in serving the President would be

to appraise the various programs and activities of the Federal Government in the light of the policy declared in section 2 for the purpose of determining the extent to which such programs and activities are contributing, and the extent to which they are not contributing, to the achievement of such policy, and to make recommendations to the President with respect thereto.

Two things must be apparent in connection with this section. One is that some such appraisal of existing "programs and activities of the Federal Government" would be an integral part of any adequate diagnosis of present strong and weak features of the nation's economy and an invaluable preliminary to recommendations of steps which the Federal Government could most wisely take to sustain economic progress in the future or to furnish safeguards against stagnation or depression. The second fact that at once strikes one is that the task involved in a full appraisal of "the various programs and activities of the Federal Government" in the light of the purpose stated in the Employment Act would be enormous. Taken literally, the provision would call upon the Council to review and appraise the policies, programs, and practices of the Treasury and the Federal Reserve, the farm program, labor policy, tariffs, antimonopoly measures, hydroelectric development, and a host of others.

One is forced to the conclusion either (a) that this provision is inconsistent with the stipulation of the act that the Council should be a small agency with a staff payroll not to exceed $300,000 a year, or (b) that the intent of Congress was merely that the Council should, in its analyses, not overlook the possibility that dropping or revising past programs or correcting their administration might be more helpful than merely adding new activities.

In practice, the latter is about what has happened. Without having had time to make comprehensive or intensive reviews of the impact of existing institutional arrangements and administrative activities, the Council has still passed explicit or implicit judgment that "various programs and activities of the Federal Government are contributing" to the achievement of a maximum production, employment, and purchasing power policy and that others are "not contributing to the achievement of such policies." The selection of staff according to various areas of specialization, as outlined in Chapter IX, was designed to avail ourselves of the assistance of men long familiar with the programs and activities of the Federal Government in the problem areas most significant for the performance of the Council's duties to the President. Likewise our system of standing committees focused on strategic issues such as plant capacity, price and income relations, and stabilization devices. This would mean that Council work would, as thoroughly as time permitted, review what the Government was already doing in the areas most significantly related to the stabilization problem.

Even this modest interpretation of the Council's appraisal function was almost precluded by the pressure of report writing, the limitations of personnel, and the ceiling placed on our budget by the terms of the Employment Act and further lowered by the action of the Appropriations Committee. At the same time, it must be admitted that in its first six years, the Council has definitely failed to do all that might have been expected of it in formulating a philosophy of economic stabilization, drawing up a set of criteria which might be applied to the various activities of government in accordance with such a stabilization philosophy, and at least "spotting" the problem areas or the more egregious instances of nonconformity to such criteria on the part of government agencies.

The first chairman of the Council quite clearly failed "to get on top of this job," although he did visualize it after his own fashion. He hoped that it might be accomplished through the specialized staff, the staff committee set-up (with its foci on "stabilization devices," on "wage-price-profit relationships," and on "capital formation and plant capacity"), and the projected series of outside research-planning conferences. These were to include economic experts drawn from academic, business, and government staffs and to be focused on problem areas emerging from the Council's progressive exploration of the stabilization problem as posed by the Employment Act.

These plans went sadly awry for a number of reasons but primarily because of the basic differences in philosophy among the three members of the Council. The concept of a "co-ordinate" Council of three persons of diverse training, experience, and interpretation of the Employment Act made effective administration of the Council impossible. If the principle of a responsible administrative chairman had been accepted by Council members or enforced by the President, if it had been feasible to delegate the organization and supervision of staff work to the vice-chairman, and if the third member had "pulled his weight in the boat" in conformity with such a plan of operation, much more progress might have been made. Instead of an organized campaign for attack on the central problem, utilizing reasonably frequent and intensive staff meetings, our work fell apart into somewhat unrelated guerilla operations in response to the particular and sometimes temporary interests of single Council members and strong individuals within the staff.

If, in future years, the Council is to do an adequate job of bringing economics to the public service, it must become the center *par excellence* for perception and formulation of the basic problems of the functioning of the total economy. It must be skillful in communicating these problems (in their changing current manifestations) to the frontline workers in economic theory in government posts, in business posts, and in academic posts. It must work with these specialists and realistic generalizers in laying out and co-ordinating the studies of these many economists and their institutions or companies and bringing their findings (after review by competent groups) back to practical application to the persistent problem of national economic stabilization.

Such a procedure might, hopefully, produce a statement of substantial consensus among the specialists on a given phase of the problem. Where that proved impossible, it could clarify the issues and show the alignment of thinking among trained and experienced economists. In this collaborative effort, the Council and its staff would perform an important role of intellectual leadership in studying the problem of economic stabilization in the practical setting of government policy-making, institutional development, and administrative performance, by directing attention to the previously unsolved or newly emerged questions which require the most intensive study by economists of various connections.

In any program of intellectual co-operation such as this, the distinctive roles of the National Bureau of Economic Research, the Brookings Institution, the Food Research Institute, the Committee for Economic Development, the National Planning Association, and various other university and independent groups are evident. Outsiders should be alert to make and the Council cordial to receive sincere but searching criticism of all features of government economic policy, regardless of whether or not the Council had been responsible for some of their shortcomings or for failing to prevent their errors or omissions.

An interesting experiment in the direction of extra-governmental supplementation of the policy-analyzing function of the Council may be seen in the Economic Forum sessions of the National Industrial Conference Board. (See p. 161.) In these meetings a group of academic and business economists discussed the content of successive Economic Reports and the general body of economic theory which appeared to underlie them. They gave minor attention also to the machinery of the Council and the Joint Committee and the way in which it was functioning in bringing economic analysis to bear on policy-making at the executive and legislative levels respectively. Occasionally a session of some economic society would be given over to consideration of the work of the Council as an agency for spearheading the attack on the problem of sustained employment. But no systematic program has been developed for marshalling the intellectual resources of the profession to meet the challenge presented to them by Congress and the people in the Employment Act.

In the Council, we had begun to explore the possibility of convening groups of non-government specialists in particular economic issues which, as our work proceeded, appeared to be bottlenecks or problem areas in the development of a sound theoretical basis for advising the executive branch on matters of stabilization policy. The monopoly problem was the only one on which such a conference was actually held. But numerous others are crowding for attention, such as savings rates, investment incentives, tax level and price administration, wage policy, fiscal policy, debt management, and the like. As a member of the Research Committee of the American Economic Association, I tried on several occasions to get that professional body interested in making these realistic problems of the functioning of our economy the basis of systematic, though voluntary and decentralized, work in our universities and research institutes, but thus far without avail.

In some quarters it has been felt that the Council, even within its small organization, could have done more than it did toward getting understanding and action on the central problem of national stabilization policy if it had shown a clearer perception of the scope of its basic assignment. The view that it was undertaking to deal with too wide a range of minor issues was presented sharply in the critique of several of the economic reports of the President made by the Joint Committee. It was here stated as an issue between stabilization and "reform." This report on the second annual Economic Report of the President said:

> We are somewhat concerned about the scope of the President's report, covering as it does nearly every domestic policy other than questions of national defense. . . . While the language used in the Employment Act of 1946 is very broad, we conceive that its principal purpose is to maintain full employment in the United States and to avoid recurrent economic depressions which have brought unemployment, hardship, and suffering to its people. This task is sufficiently difficult, and we do not think that work under the act should be diverted from it by the study of all the important and complicated problems of social welfare, health, and education, nor should it be diverted to matters which cannot have an extensive effect on the over-all economy.

There are two quite different problems involved here—one operational, the other doctrinal. Both are important.

As to the first issue, I believe that the criticism of the Joint Committee (also expressed in other quarters) is well taken. The statute under which the Council was set up was called the Employment Act and it was focused on the maintenance of high-level economic activity. It was perhaps unfortunate that the President's annual report was called the Economic Report rather than the Stabilization-of-the-Economy Report, and the Council members were labeled Economic Advisers rather than Stabilization Advisers.[17] The present titles are, of course, much simpler, but it devolves upon all parties to interpret their scope and meaning strictly in line with the statute. I have indicated that we thus delimited our role in dealing with the Legislative Reference Service of the Budget Bureau. That is, we commented only on bills that were definitely pertinent to the stabilization issue, not on every measure having economic content. In connection with the Economic Reports, we did not do so well, perhaps did not try so hard to keep our task properly defined. From the President, from Council members, and from the staff came strong pressures to include many forms of economic or social betterment and to rationalize their inclusion by saying that only as all members of our population were well and happy could we attain maximum production and purchasing power. It was argued that only as all our resources, human and natural, are carefully conserved and fully developed can our economy attain its full potential.

But a practical limit must be found somewhere or basic policy will bog down among minor details. There are, no doubt, economic issues involved in deciding what we do about wildlife. But it could hardly be maintained that it would be a significant factor in our success in combating inflationary booms or in checking or reversing deflationary recessions. So of many other issues.

On the doctrinal side, although there has been lamentably little systematic discussion in the profession of what would constitute a professionally creditable and pragmatically useful theory of full employment, there have been numerous criticisms leveled at the Council for its failure to develop such a formal statement and to become an influential force in making it effective within the administrative area and having it effectively presented and urged in the Economic Reports and messages sent by the President to Congress. It is, I think, thoroughly in line with the interpretation of the Council's role in bringing economics to the public service that they should undertake leadership in this task. On the other hand, it would be a mistake to suppose that even the best of scientific mastery of the issues involved would yield any simple formulation of stabilization policy. I believe that oversimplification of fiscal policy

[17] Similarly I feel that there may be overtones of danger in the desire of the Joint Committee on the Economic Report to be known as the Joint Economic Committee—and to take jurisdiction in all economic issues that come before, or that they might bring before, Congress. (See p. 439.)

as a sovereign remedy was the great defect of the original Murray bill. And there is a tendency of some schools of economic thought still to believe that national economic stabilization might be effectuated by a combination of rigorously defined fiscal policy and monetary policy. These are, of course, basic functions of central government and can, within the area in which they operate, be reduced to relatively simple terms. But to get an adequate and well-rounded stabilization theory, we must have also as good grasp and formulation as possible of the principles which underlie market structures and managerial, labor, and agricultural policies and practices.

Thus the work of a council of advisers on the problems of economic stabilization in any realistic sense would have to cover many questions of institutional structure and executive and mass behavior. An attempt to deal with these parts of the problem has been responsible for some of the proliferation of Council materials which has carried through into the Economic Reports of the President. I believe this should not be abandoned in future work but should be tightened up and pruned of only vaguely related welfare matters so as to make a consistent philosophy of market adjustment integrated with the aggregative approach of fiscal and monetary policy.

There should be a better differentiation between what can be set forth clearly and usefully by the executive branch for the guidance of Congress and the public and what, on the other hand, should remain as "working papers" in the hands of the Council and its staff for further exploration with other technicians in government and outside. Thus revised, the Economic Report of the President would be a much shorter document,[18] better understood by the public and more effective in the Congress. The Council should have no policy document over their signatures, but should supply statistical and methodological appendixes to the President's report. "Staff materials" might from time to time be made available to fellow technicians working on the stabilization problem.

[18] Though the President's spontaneous reaction to the first body of materials for his Economic Report submitted to him by the Council was that it was "too long," his Economic Report, with its separated Economic Report of the Council rose to 278 pages in the report of July 1951, as compared with 54 pages in the initial report.

CHAPTER TWENTY

Some Neighborly Reflections About the Joint Committee

In the nature of the case my acquaintance with the affairs of the Joint Economic Committee has been considerably less intimate than that with the Council of Economic Advisers. The closeness of my contact with the latter may give my appraisal of their work and portrayal of their problems a subjective quality which would be a high price to pay for mere richness of detail. On the other hand, it would be pleasant to think that a certain detachment from the working details and personality aspects of the Joint Committee make for objectivity in my commentary on their work. Or, turning to metaphor, it may be easier for me to see the woods because I have not been too close to the trees.

STEPS TOWARD LEGISLATIVE CO-ORDINATION

It has been emphasized throughout our discussion that the Employment Act did not seek to crystallize an economic stabilization program but to provide machinery for systematic study of national economic policy and the co-ordination of its several parts. The Joint Committee on the Economic Report thus becomes one important part of a larger movement which has been going on for several decades to correct the traditionally disintegrated or diffusive character of our Federal Congress. For many years this legislative body had operated largely through a series of standing committees, each of which formulated policy and even determined expenditure with an amazing degree of independence. With the passage of the Federal Budget and Accounting Act of 1921, the centering of a review function over spending in the hands of an Appropriations Committee (and, to a lesser extent, a committee on Expenditures in the Executive Departments) in each House, and the progress made toward an omnibus appropriations bill, the fiscal operations of the Federal Government have been systematized and co-ordinated to a substantial degree. The establishment of a Joint Committee on Foreign Economic Co-operation did something toward unification of foreign aid policy. In the domestic economic field, there is still and will long remain a strong centrifugal pull of interest groups—labor, agricultural, banking, public works, merchant marine, small business, and others. Much remains to be done before it can be said that the Congress of the United States approaches its annual task of legislation from an adequate view of what constitutes the national interest and what measures would promote it.

Chapter XVII has shown that in passing the Employment Act of 1946 some at least of the members of Congress were thinking of this defect in our representative governmental machinery. Several of them voiced a belief that this act would do something significant toward removing it[1] (a) by requiring the President to furnish the legislature with a specific, formal executive program for advancing the national well-being, and (b) by assigning to a special joint committee the task of reviewing this economic program and reporting on it to the Congress and the public and conducting their own studies of these problems. The act did not confer upon this joint committee specific responsibility for drawing up a legislative program of its own or confer on it any power to intervene in the autonomous activities of the existing Congressional committees. The act explicitly stated, however, that a function of the Joint Committee would be "to study means of co-ordinating programs in order to further the policy of this act."

[1] Even Senator Radcliffe, who opposed the act as a whole, said: "The provision for a Joint Committee of the House and Senate may be somewhat debatable; but it is certainly desirable that the House and Senate should keep closely in touch with what is going on . . . that there should be fact-finding facilities in operation . . . and it is most assuredly desirable that in this matter the Senate and the House should co-operate closely in some suitable way."

Senator Murray was much more emphatic: "From the day this legislation was first introduced, the provision for a joint congressional committee to analyze the President's over-all program has been hailed as a distinct contribution to the improvement of congressional operations. There is general agreement that such a committee could be extremely helpful in co-ordinating the separate and diverse activities of the many committees in the Senate and House of Representatives."

Like the Council of Economic Advisers in the executive branch, the Joint Economic Committee was conceived as a "pondering" body. For this task it is given considerable resources for investigating unsatisfactory or menacing situations in the economy, examining the claims made for any proffered remedies, and adumbrating its own policy recommendations—which may or may not follow the lines proposed by the President. Another feature of the Joint Economic Committee's assignment that distinguishes it from other Congressional committees is that its point of view is to be that of national economic policy as such and not be limited to a particular area like agriculture or the merchant marine or a particular function like taxation or banking and credit.

One would be hard put to it to substantiate a claim that the Joint Committee has yet achieved notable success toward actually co-ordinating the legislative program which emerges from Congress. Six years is at best a very short time within which to look for change in the practices and attitudes of a legislative body with more than a century and a half of tradition behind it. But since there is now universal recognition that the work of Congress suffers from a lack of co-ordination and since the broad policy declared in the Employment Act gives a specific goal and point of reference for economic legislation, the mere act of Congress in setting up within its own organization an integrating joint committee constitutes a tangible step forward.

The very fact that its assignment is neither too definite nor too ambitious gives the Joint Committee time in which it can define a practical scope of operations, experiment with conventional or with novel methods of work, and gradually grow into a position of larger usefulness. At best, the difficulties inherent in the undertaking are quite considerable, but better co-ordination within the Congress and between the legislative and executive branches is a goal worth striving for.

To some as yet indeterminable degree it would seem that the setting up of the Joint Economic Committee reflects an intention to restore to Congress a more positive role of leadership in the determination of national policy. During twenty years of depression, war, and reconversion, there had been a strong tendency for the executive branch to enlarge its powers at the expense of the legislative branch. A dramatic check to this trend was recently administered by the Supreme Court in finding the claims of "inherent powers" of the President to seize private industry in time of "crisis" unconstitutional. In a quieter but more pervasive sense, the Employment Act distinguishes between the role of the President and that of Congress.

The act calls on the President for intellectual leadership in making a comprehensive draft of national economic statesmanship each year on the basis of his administrative experience during the preceding year. Then it emphasizes the duty of the Congress to provide machinery for the independent study of national economic stability and progress as an integrated problem and to consider the President's proposals carefully as to their fitness to the stated end. After Congress has followed the President's leadership to the extent it feels is wise and has made its own contributions to the shaping of a final program, the task of actual administration devolves on the President and his executive aides, who are to convert these general directives into specific actions. The purpose is not to have either executive or legislative branch dominate the governmental process but to have a well-balanced co-ordination of two mutually complementary agencies.[2]

This principle of the Founding Fathers was recognized by the drafters of the Employment Act with sufficient clarity that they set up two distinct and independent implementing agencies—the Council of Economic Advisers in the Executive Office and the Joint Committee in the Congress. They called for a new and distinctive state paper—the Economic Report of the President (and supplemental reports)—and a formal Congressional document analyzing, endorsing,

[2] Senator Murray clearly recognized this issue when he first introduced the "full employment" bill. Speaking of the proposal for a joint committee to study the "national production and employment budget" and for Congress by joint resolution to set forth a general policy with reference thereto, he said: "These provisions go a long way toward restoring Congress to its rightful place as the policy-determining branch of the Government. And this is done in a way which provides for active interplay between the Congress and the Executive, a way which makes the two branches of the Government really co-ordinate. The bill avoids the danger of delegating excessive power to the Executive, and the danger of involving Congress in administrative determinations (*Cong. Record,* 79 Cong. 1 sess., Jan. 22, 1945). Later, when the Council of Economic Advisers had been added in the Employment Act of 1946, Murray approved the giving to them of a confidential relationship to the President. (See p. 411.) It was only at a much later time that he came out for having the functions of the two agencies mixed.

or modifying the executive document and preparing a legislative outline for consideration by the whole Congress.

The result has not as yet by any means attained this full ideal. Many of the committee's reports on the annual Economic Report have partaken too much of the character of sniping at the President's economic proposals or of indiscriminate endorsement—generally some of both, divided in the main along the party line. Of this, more later. A second kind of retreat from the high ground occupied or at least envisaged during the legislative history of the act has been the effort to weaken the mutual independence of the two bodies by using the Council of Economic Advisers to reinforce the executive position in the area of legislative review. The chairman of the Joint Committee, the President, and members of the Council have all shared in responsibility for this confusion.

Exponents of "positive" government, party "discipline," or the British cabinet or European parliamentary system, have been irked at the delays entailed in a system of "checks and balances," and have seen in the Employment Act a possible opportunity of changing it—not only of promoting consistency of policy and program in the executive and in the legislative branch respectively, but also integration between the two. Though Mr. Truman at times sought to enlarge Presidential prerogatives at the expense of Congressional authority, he held back formally from endorsement of the cabinet-parliament proposal. The manner in which President Eisenhower deals with the administration of the Employment Act will shed light on what his attitude will be on this issue.

THE AMBIGUOUS ROLE OF THE JOINT COMMITTEE

The task of the Joint Economic Committee is as difficult as it is novel in our frame of government. If taken seriously, it entails long and painstaking work and does not carry emoluments of power or prestige (like the Appropriations, Defense, or Foreign Affairs committees). Its requirements are not met by the technical competence of the lawyer or the flair and experience of the politician. It calls for training and practice in the fields of economics, business, finance, and social psychology. The senator or representative who gives the needed measure of time and thought to the work of this committee must not merely curtail to that extent the effort given to legislative work and to rendering personal (and sometimes menial) service to the claims of his constituents or to mending his political fences. Beyond this, he is sure sooner or later, in larger or smaller measure, to find himself, in seeking to advance the national economic interest most soundly, to be refusing support to or actively opposing a pet project of his state or district or of a special interest group that is strongly represented among his constituents.

This invidious character of the Joint Committee member's task is manifest also in his relations to his colleagues. There is constant danger of stepping on sensitive toes in his own party as well as the opposition. In subscribing to a Joint Committee report, in his participation in the work of any legislative committee of which he is also a member, or in the course of general debate, he must from time to time take the position that this or that proposal is inconsistent with other positions being taken in the given House or that doing this or that for a particular interest group would contravene the over-all national interest. Protagonists of a measure will inevitably feel that these high-minded endeavors of the Joint Committee member brand him with a smug altruism or a doctrinnaire other-worldliness alien to the practical realism of normal Congressional processes.

Add to all this the fact that the separate issues raised in all these sub-areas must be covered under the wide canopy of "national interest" or economic well-being, and it would seem almost impossible for the scrupulous member to feel that he has become sufficiently informed and has pressed his analyses far enough so that he can himself be satisfied as to how the total national policy could be really integrated. The obvious answer is that no deeply perceptive and conscientious person fully attains his own ideals. "Not failure but low aim is crime," and Joint Committee service provides the opportunity of exercising an elevating influence on the work of Congress even without attaining full perfection in the economic analysis of all the issues involved.

Perhaps the ultimate strength of the Joint Committee as a co-ordinating agent will be found to reside in the very limited powers conferred upon it. The Committee as a merely advisory body may be expected in time to achieve a subtly permeating influence over the process of Congressional debate and legislative action. But this must derive from the innate propriety of the criterion which it appeals to—economic well-being of the nation as a whole or stabilizing *vs.* distorting actions—and from the impressiveness of the analysis of the problems which it presents.

This recalls an incident during the one appearance of the Council of Economic Advisers before the Joint Committee in which I participated—for there was one such. At Chairman Taft's invitation we met with them in their committee room in June 1948 as the session was drawing to a close and after it was clear how the Congress was responding both to the President's Economic Report and to the Joint Committee's critique of it. After we had discussed some phases of the Economic Report (especially its broad inclusion of "reform" proposals under its stabilization purpose [see p. 198]) Senator Taft commented somewhat wistfully on the imperviousness of the old committee structure and practices to the purpose of this new committee to give even a low-pressure kind of policy-integrating leadership. I ventured to suggest that they, like the Council, would have to exercise monumental patience and hope to gain influence unobtrusively through a long process of peaceful penetration on the intellectual level.

It seemed to me—and still does—that each member of the committee, by virtue of its basic assignment is committed to make two concepts the touchstone of his activities in whatever part he takes in Congressional debates. These two concepts are "national interest," to be argued against all claims of special interest; and "stabilization," to be safeguarded against the disturbing effects of all such special concessions. They can also brief their other committees on special aspects of the broad stabilization problems which lie in the province of a given standing committee and which might well be investigated by it rather than by a subcommittee of the Joint Committee—or in which the two might join.

COMMITTEE MEMBERSHIP AND CHAIRMANSHIP

With these general observations about the objectives of the Joint Committee and the difficulty of attaining them, we turn to consider the more detailed question of the committee's organization and methods of work. The act specifies seven members from each House, with party membership reflecting "as nearly as may be feasible the relative membership of the majority and minority parties in the Senate and the House of Representatives." In practice this has meant four majority and three minority members in each group and, unless one party attains a heavy majority, this will probably always be the ratio. The designation of members rests with the President of the Senate and the Speaker of the House, with no ex officio members but with individual senators and representatives free to exert their efforts to get on the committee and with the appointing officers consulting party leaders.

It has sometimes been suggested that effectiveness of the Joint Committee would be enhanced if it had the chairman or a prominent member of each of several important areal or functional standing committees included in its membership. One thinks at once of Appropriations, Agriculture, Labor, Banking and Currency, and Public Works, and (in the House) Ways and Means and Veterans Affairs.[3] Undoubtedly such a make-up would add to the prestige and the political power of the committee. On the other hand, it would mean that a large number of the members of the Joint Committee would be men already so burdened with operational duties that they would have little time to give to the studious work of this committee. It might mean also that they would be men little inclined by temperament or training to give it the kind of service which it requires.

This goes to the very heart of the concept on which the Joint Committee is founded. If, as I have suggested, it is designed to be a "pondering committee" rather than a direct action factor in the Congress, then it is of less importance that its members be in the influential chairmanships and more important that they be men with personal qualifications and aptitudes for the task of studying policy problems in a broad spirit and skillful in the slower process of education rather than the arts of political power. Leaving the make-up of the committee flexible at the discretion of the heads of the two Houses and the preferences of the members has worked well so far. The Joint Committee has attracted men of outstanding quality, men who by professional training and business experience

[3] S. 380 provided that "the chairman and ranking minority members of the Senate committees on Appropriations, Banking and Currency, Education and Labor, and Finance . . . and the chairman and ranking minority members of the House committees on Appropriations, Banking and Currency, Labor, Ways and Means" should be ex officio members of the "Joint Committee on the National Production and Employment Budget" together with seven members from each House not specified as to their connections.

are competent to make real contributions to the work.[4] While they
have sought or been willing to accept this post in lieu of others
which might have been available to them, they have had their share
of important places, even chairmanship, in some though not all of
the other standing committees whose work should be closely articu-
lated with that of the Joint Committee.[5]

However high the quality of the men appointed, it is an inherent
difficulty of our Congressional system that the life of a senator or
representative at best affords inadequate opportunity for doing all
of the many things required of him. It has been impossible to secure
attendance and attention by a sufficient number of committee
members, with sufficient frequency, or at sufficient length for them
to get real understanding of the problems they were grappling with
and to formulate their basic conclusions on them.[6]

Here we face a real dilemma. To secure adequate performance of

[4] Besides a strong Republican contender for the Presidency, a Democratic nominee for Vice President, and two successful candidates for State Governor, there are
included (1952) a former president of the Boston Federal Reserve Bank, a vice-
president of the University of Chicago, an Assistant Secretary of State, a university
dean, a past president of the American Economic Association, a newspaper editor
and publisher, a vice-chairman of the Committee for Economic Development,
two successful business men, a former staff member of the State Department, and,
of course, half a dozen able lawyers.

[5] Senator Murray in his advance memorandum on Congressional administration
of the Employment Act took the position that: "First of all, careful consideration
should be given to the idea of having the chairmanship and the vice chairmanship
of the joint committee held by the majority leader of the Senate and the majority
leader of the House of Representatives. Let us not forget the fact that this joint
committee is to serve as an economic policy committee. Its chairman and vice-
chairman, therefore, might well be those members of Congress who are responsible
for over-all policy. If any other members of the Congress were selected as chairman
and vice-chairman of the joint committee and if they succeeded in discharging
their duties successfully, then they might find themselves, in large part, performing
certain functions of majority leadership. For the same reason, the leaders of the
minority party in both Houses might well serve as the ranking minority members
of the joint committee." All this, of course, reflects the Senator's concept of the
Committee as playing an action role rather than study role.

[6] This appears to have been due in part to the fact that no regular meeting day
has been set for this committee. This means that members do not have the opportunity and pressure to arrange their schedules so as to facilitate attendance. A
regular meeting day once a month, carefully chosen to avoid conflicts with the
meeting days of other committees on which Joint Committee members also serve
might do a good deal to increase attendance and improve work. Under its recent
chairmanship there have been intervals of several months between executive sessions of the Joint Committee, and administrative actions have not even been reported to the committee fully or in detail.

the duties of a Joint Committee member would require that he take this as his exclusive committee assignment and even curtail other activities which are an almost indispensable part of a Congressman's life. To do this would so withdraw him from the actual work of the legislative body that he would lose most of his practical influence and opportunity to deliver the valuable product that would grow out of his Joint Committee work. This is a dilemma less easily resolved than that of a Council member. By definition, the Council member has only one career to serve, that of being a staff adviser and spending his full time in qualifying for the task. A member of the Joint Committee is, first and foremost, a legislator and a Washington representative of his constituents. This does not leave him leisure to be a full-time student of national economic policy.

The practical answer to this dilemma is, in part, that committee members like O'Mahoney, Wolcott, Taft, Hart, Herter, Douglas, Flanders, Sparkman, Rich, Boggs, Benton, McKinnon and others have brought a high order of qualification, a very lively interest, and an amazing amount of real work to the activities of the Joint Committee, setting standards which we can hope to see emulated, perhaps surpassed, in the future as the committee becomes more fully established.

A second phase of the answer is to be found in the leadership that can be and has been given to this committee by its chairman. Senator Taft as first chairman of the committee was recognized as one of the best-informed members of the Senate on economic questions and a phenomenal worker. Aside from the fact that he was breaking new ground, he was somewhat handicapped in the matter of time by virtue of the fact that he, for strategic reasons, had to retain the chairmanship of the majority party policy committee and that, for tactical reasons, he was unwilling to relinquish the chairmanship of the Labor Committee.

Senator O'Mahoney, who has been chairman of the Joint Committee for the past four years, has always had economic issues and national policy at the forefront of his interest and activities. He played a part in the drafting and passage of the Employment Act and, as was suggested earlier (p. 255) conceived the Joint Committee as a permanent national economic committee, continuing and enlarging the work of the Temporary National Economic Committee, of which he had been chairman and most active moving spirit. He has given tireless and imaginative direction to its work. At the same time, he has been a member of the Majority Policy Committee and the Defense Appropriations Committee and chairman of the Interior and Insular Affairs Committee, with all the prestige and opportunity for "follow through" on economic policy matters and all the drain upon time and energy that these positions entail.

The office of chairman of a standing committee in Congress is one of great inherent power and may be made almost dictatorial. Senator O'Mahoney has carried this tradition into this pondering committee with the laudable purpose of seeing that it should come to a position of fruitful activity within the legislative process, but also with a personal enthusiasm for promoting pet economic theories such as was manifest in his chairmanship of TNEC—particularly his fear of "concentration of economic power" and his concern for "small business." He has been inclined to use the Joint Committee as a sounding board for whatever economic causes he wished to serve (such as road building needs, the excess profits tax, or treatment of wool) regardless of whether his conclusions grew out of staff work of the committee or had the endorsement or even the knowledge of his fellow committee members. Since the committee as a whole embraces economic thinkers of no less competence or independent spirit than the chairman, his tendency to get it overcommitted has been checked without destroying the dynamic quality of his leadership. Frictions between the chairman and members even of his own party have at times been acute on administrative as well as economic issues.

Some criticism has developed also out of the fact that no organization meeting was held at the opening of the 81st Congress, thus permitting the committee, if it chose, to select a new chairman. Since Senator O'Mahoney failed to be re-elected, the opportunity is now afforded of considering this question on its merits. The idea has been advanced that the chairmanship should rotate at two- or four-year intervals from Senate to House and back. A joint committee always suffers from the fact or the fear of Senate domination, and it may be that the less active participation of House members in the work of this committee reflects this feeling and would be corrected by alternating House chairmanship from time to time.

RELATIONS WITH OTHER COMMITTEES

The impact of the Joint Committee on the Congress will depend not merely on what it does as a committee but, in perhaps larger degree, on how its individual members deal with segmental policy issues on other committees of which they are members. In such connections they can be expected to draw upon the broader understanding of the situation and functioning of the whole economy which derives from the staff work and committee deliberations of the Joint Committee and can help to keep the criterion of national well-being to the fore in the more specialized committee. Every Senate member of the Joint Committee is also a member of two (and occasionally three) other committees; each Representative will be a member of one and, occasionally, of two other committees. In a few cases, he will be in the powerful position of chairman. This provides an opportunity for him to bring the information and point of view of these other committees to bear on the deliberations of the Joint Committee as well as exerting its integrative influence in the opposite direction.[7]

To develop the two-way street within the committee structure of Congress has been a laudable purpose of the Joint Committee,

[7] The seven Senate members of the Joint Committee hold (in the 82nd Congress) thirteen memberships on eight of fifteen standing committees of the Senate—three on Banking and Currency, two each on Finance, Labor and Welfare, and Interior and Insular Affairs, and one each on Foreign Relations, Judiciary, Armed Services, and Appropriations. Besides this, Senator O'Mahoney is a member of the Majority Policy Committee, and Taft chairman of the Minority Policy Committee. Senator Sparkman is chairman and Benton a member of the Select Committee on the Problems of Small Business, and Benton is also a member of the Committee on Rules and Administration.

The seven House members hold seven memberships on four of the eighteen House committees—four on Banking and Currency, one each on Foreign Affairs, Judiciary, and Expenditures in the Executive Departments. Representative Patman is chairman of the Select Committee on the Problems of Small Business and McKinnon a member.

The large cross representation on the Banking and Currency Committee is noteworthy inasmuch as that committee has wide jurisdiction over economic questions. The presence of only one member of the Joint Committee on the Senate Appropriations Committee and none on either the House Appropriations or Ways and Means Committee is notable, although it should be remembered that a place on the House Appropriations Committee is, with rarest exceptions an "exclusive" assignment.

and they feel encouraged to believe that it is beginning to bring results. (See p. 271.) Efforts, however, to merge the work of one of the older committees with that of the Joint Committee when it is studying the same aspect of the functioning of the economy have not been successful. On one or two occasions a senator or representative who was chairman of one of these committees and also a member of the Joint Committee has sought to promote such practical co-operation but, at the last moment, vested interests have prevailed and the effort has had to be dropped. To ease such tensions, the Joint Committee makes a point of clearing with any other Congressional committee whose field covers matters on which the Joint Committee proposes to initiate an inquiry, and not proceeding unless or until the acquiescence of the other committee has been secured.

Experience seems to indicate that it is possible to have fruitful study-relationships even where the committees maintain their separate identities. This is notably true in the work which has been done on the problems of small business. Both Senate and House have a select committee on this problem, with Representative Patman the chairman of one and Senator Sparkman chairman of the other. The problem has not been merely its legal, financial, and technical aspects but is closely related to the broad issue of booms and depressions of the Joint Committee's problem of national economic stabilization.[8] In June 1951, an arrangement was made jointly by the chairman of the Senate Select Committee on Small Business and the Joint Committee on the Economic Report under which a spot check of the prevalence of price cutting of "merchandise marketed under price maintenance agreements" was made by Dun and Bradstreet, Inc. (at their own expense) and the results were made generally available through a report presented as a joint publication of the two committees.[9] This would seem to be a small precedent for a practice which might be

[8] Senator O'Mahoney, as chairman of the Defense Appropriations Subcommittee as well as chairman of the Joint Economic Committee held a combined hearing of the two groups when Defense Secretary Lovett and others were testifying just following the panel hearings on the Economic Report of the President in January 1952.

[9] Likewise the Joint Committee staff collaborated with the staff of the House Select Committee on Small Business in a study of Constitutional Limitation on Federal Income, Estate, and Gift Tax rates, which was published in February 1952 as a Joint Committee print.

considerably enlarged in the future. The staffs of two or even more Congressional committees might contribute to a piece of research in a field of common interest, and the resulting report be put out under the sponsorship of both committees as a factual and analytical product, leaving all parties free to make their own recommendations as they saw fit.

A particularly interesting phase of the relationship of the Joint Committee to standing committees has come up in connection with the matter of monetary policy and debt management. First under the Douglas subcommittee and more recently under the Patman subcommittee, the Joint Committee has made quite exhaustive investigations of the problem of monetary and related fiscal policy, particularly as to the conflict in policy and action between the United States Treasury and the Federal Reserve System. In this area the factual and analytical results of these two investigations and the voluminous published material which they produced are widely regarded as the most important contribution that has been made in this difficult area in some time. There appears to have been no serious feeling on the part of the Banking and Currency, Finance, or other committees of either House that this activity of the Joint Committee encroached unduly on their preserves. On the other hand, the general set-up and mandate of the Joint Committee enabled them to pursue the matter in its wide ramifications and interrelations with the whole question of economic stabilization.

The way in which membership on the Joint Committee affords opportunity to study complex economic problems intensively and thus equip the member better to perform his responsibilities on legislative committees is illustrated also by the problem of low-income families. A subcommittee of the Joint Committee has, over the past three years, been making systematic inquiries into this problem, which have included a variety of fields in broader relationship than would be covered by any one of the legislative committees.

This suggests a possibility that in its final development the Joint Committee might grow to be a central research or investigation center for many phases of economic policy which formerly have been pursued along somewhat more narrow lines by various standing committees. This would lead both to economy and to a more objective and comprehensive exploration of the problems. There has been a laudable expansion during recent years in the staffing of the various standing committees, but it creates the possibility, particularly where the direction of the work has fallen to persons of legal rather than economic training, of something of a partisan approach and a poor use of funds and personnel because the questions raised in one area overlap into adjacent areas. Growth of the Joint Committee staff as a sort of pool or GHQ of broad-viewed economic research for Congress would not supersede the proper specialized work of the various standing committees but would simplify the research function which, more and more, runs parallel to the political process of Congress. Such a development on a well-balanced basis has thus far been impaired by the majority-minority differentiation within the staff of the Joint Committee itself.

"AS A GUIDE TO THE SEVERAL COMMITTEES OF THE CONGRESS"

In a review of the first year's work of the Joint Committee[10] Senator Flanders referred to its task as "(1) reporting to the Congress on the President's report by February 1 and (2) guiding substantive committees of the Congress on legislation throughout the year." The latter duty is a more ambitious statement of the role of the committee than it has developed up to the present time or than was explicitly called for in the act. The full expression was "guide to the several committees of the Congress dealing with legislation relating to the Economic Report." This raises the same point of interpretation that Chairman Taft made in connection with the central theme of economic stabilization. It is obvious that there are many matters of a politico-economic nature which would be discussed by substantive committees which would not be covered in any reasonable interpretation of that particular policy focus. If the President's Economic Report covers the waterfront, it is perhaps incumbent on the Joint Economic Committee to spread itself over the same ambit. As a practical matter, however, it seems a wiser procedure for the Joint Committee to focus its labors as strictly as possible on the stabilization problem.

This general issue must be considered in the particular context

[10] Ralph E. Flanders, "Administering the Employment Act—the First Year," *Public Administration Review,* Vol. VII, No. 4, Autumn 1947, p. 226.

of methods by which the Joint Committee could seek to guide legislative committees. The act specifies that the Joint Committee's "findings and recommendations" with respect to each of the main recommendations made by the President in the Economic Report would serve such a purpose. But beyond this, they authorized the committee also "from time to time to make such other reports and recommendations to the Senate and House of Representatives as it deems advisable." Fairly numerous and distinctly valuable reports of this kind have been made by the Joint Committee as described in Chapters XIII and XVI. They are addressed to the Congress as a whole rather than to any specific committee. But where a member of the Joint Committee is also a member of a standing committee concerned particularly with the area in which the special report falls, or if the chairman of the standing committee is impressed by it, he can make it an influential factor in the deliberations of his committee.

In one instance in the first year of the Joint Committee's life, Congress passed a special resolution (and granted special funds to the Joint Committee) to hold hearings and report on the cost of living and specifically authorized the appointment of additional members of Congress to sit with the Joint Committee in these hearings and the writing of the report. This would seem to be an example which might fruitfully be repeated in the future. Or Congress might pass a resolution (or amend the act) authorizing the committee to co-opt additional members of particular qualifications to work with them on any of their special studies.

Some persons interested in effective implementation of the act have hoped to see the time come when legislative committees would submit pending bills to the Joint Committee for its judgment as to their consistency with or value for a national purpose of economic stabilization. Thus far no committee has turned in this manner to the Joint Committee for "guidance."[11] Nor has the Joint Com-

[11] But when the Congress in December 1947 passed legislation for the stabilization of commodity prices, it included in a joint resolution (S. J. Res. 167) a provision that when the President had made a finding of critical shortage and a recommendation for allocation or restrictive use of such scarce commodity: "Within fifteen days after the submission of such proposed conservation measures, the Joint Committee on the Economic Report shall conduct public hearings thereon and shall make such recommendations to the Congress for legislative action as in its judgment the recommendations of the President and any additional information disclosed as the public hearings may require."

mittee had the temerity to intervene in any formal way in the "guid-ance" of any legislative committee. Senator Flanders early com-mented: "To avoid any possible criticism on the part of other committees, the few recommendations made during the first year were informal—members of the Joint Committee carried the word to members of the committee having primary jurisdiction over the subject bill," but added:

> While this informal procedure may have been justified during the first year because of lack of staff and in order to allay criticism by the standing committees, it is too piecemeal as a regular proposition. Rather definite procedures should be established whereby an enlarged Committee staff would analyze the principal pieces of legislation which it, or members of the Committee, believe have important economic implications. Follow-ing the analysis, a staff memorandum should be submitted to members of the Committee. This memorandum should contain a brief statement of the economic effects of the subject piece of legislation and specific recom-mendations as to what action the Committee should take. At each meeting the Committee should have a place on its agenda for consideration of these pending bills. Committee action could take the form of a report to the substantive committees including an economic appraisal and recommenda-tions. Alternative Committee action could take the form of a report to the substantive committees containing merely the staff's economic appraisal with no Committee recommendation.
>
> When Committee recommendations are given it may be expected that majority and minority reports could and should be made. The purpose of these reports should be to indicate the economic implications of the pend-ing legislation. Admittedly, other considerations, such as military, ethical, and political, would be involved. All factors, of course, would be weighed by the substantive committee, the majority and minority policy commit-tees, and each individual member of the Congress in taking final action on a bill.[12]

While it would appear that there are potential values to be cap-tured by having pending bills referred to the Joint Committee for comment, such a procedure would require a much larger staff and might engender strains that would prove to be the committee's undoing. Such "clearance" relationships must be developed with discretion and cannot move at a pace more rapid than that set by the chairmen of the other committees. For the present it seems

[12] Ralph E. Flanders, "Administering the Employment Act—the First Year," *Public Administration Review,* Vol. VII, No. 4, Autumn 1947, p. 226.

safer to be content with the influence that individual members can exert through cross membership on other committees or in floor debate, rather than having the committees as such take a formal position on specific measures. The attempt to do this would probably only accentuate party alignments within the Joint Committee.

As to the use of materials prepared by the Joint Committee's staff or of reports formulated by the Joint Committee itself, the committee's report of January 1950 stated hopefully: "The standing committees of the Congress have made use of [Joint Committee] reports and hearings in connection with the consideration of specific legislation and arrangements have been made to supply these committees with all material of special interest to them." There is no question that the Joint Committee is thus willing—indeed anxious—to make all materials prepared under its auspices freely available to committees and to the public. Its staff also responds to numerous specific inquiries from individual senators and representatives. There is, however, wide variance of opinion among members of the Joint Committee itself and even between the same individuals at different times as to whether the work of the committee produces any real difference in the course of Federal legislation.

Perhaps the strongest case that can be made for positive results came shortly after the Korean outbreak. In July 1950, the chairman of the committee submitted to the members a four-page mimeographed communication presenting a "review of current economic pressures and the outlook" prepared by the staff, with a three-page analysis of his own of the question "whether we should hold an executive session to discuss economic policy in the present world situation." Such a session was in fact held and resulted in the Joint Committee's taking a rather positive lead in securing the prompt passage of three measures substantially increasing Federal taxes as a means of preparing for a defense effort and forestalling as far as possible the inflationary effects of the Korean outbreak.

In this instance, action of the Joint Committee not only influenced Congress, but the executive branch as well. Up to the time that the Joint Committee took an aggressive position on this matter, the President and the Secretary of the Treasury (along with the chairman of the two tax committees of the Congress) had publicly stated that January 1951 would be early enough to increase taxes. After Chairman O'Mahoney went to the White House with the unanimous recommendation of the Joint Committee, the President reversed himself and sent a message to Congress calling for immediate increase in taxes. Undoubtedly also, the work done by the Douglas Subcommittee on Monetary, Credit, and Fiscal Policy contributed importantly to the change in attitude of the Secretary of the Treasury and the President which made possible the "accord" between Federal Reserve and Treasury in 1951.

For myself, I would ascribe considerable importance to the hearings conducted by the Joint Committee in January 1952 on the Economic Report of the President. Following these hearings the Committee took a forthright position with reference to the reassessed military and industrial situations in their interrelations and pointed to the necessity and feasibility of a reduction of 10 billion dollars.[13] While Senator Douglas, in a minority report, disparaged the caution and vagueness with which this recommendation was put forth (spelling out at the same time a detailed and specific program to this end) and although Congressional action fell short of the 10 billion dollar goal, this use of the Joint Committee attracted wide public attention and seems to me to be a creditable example of the kind of positive leadership that the Joint Committee should be expected to manifest increasingly in the future.

THE ROLE OF THE JOINT COMMITTEE STAFF

In spite of the great amount of economic competence, business experience, and personal interest that have been assembled in the membership of the Joint Committee, it is clear that much of its success will depend on the work of its staff. This staff is even smaller than that of the Council of Economic Advisers—six professional and eight secretarial-clerical employees. But it has extensive supplementary resources on which it can draw according to its needs.

First among them is the Legislative Reference Service of the Library of Congress. This branch of the library has grown from a budget of $166,300 in the fiscal year 1944 to a present budget of $866,300. It has a sizable staff of "senior specialists" covering most branches of economics and statistics. From time to time these ex-

[13] However, as chairman of the Senate Defense Appropriations Subcommittee, Chairman O'Mahoney did not appear to follow a line consistent with the Joint Committee report.

perts are assigned to the Joint Committee at its request (sometimes
on a reimbursable basis, sometimes remaining on the Library pay
roll). Or special studies needed by the Joint Committee will be
taken over by the Legislative Reference Service as part of their own
working program. Since the basic concept of the Legislative Reference Service is that it shall provide the best factual data and well-
balanced *pro* and *con* analysis for the use of Congress, this agency
supplies an invaluable source of material for the Joint Committee
and its staff without the necessity of maintaining a large shop of
its own.

Useful also, but sometimes less objective at the policy-analyzing
level, is the aid which can be drawn from the staffs of the various
executive departments and agencies and those of the standing committees of Congress. Much of this collaboration is with technicians
who are concerned with factual materials and statistical manipula-
tions, not policy matters.

Besides these intra-governmental sources of professional help, the
Joint Committee from time to time employs economic specialists
from the universities to direct or to assist in staff or subcommittee
studies of particular problems. In one case a professor on sabbatical
leave from his university made a detailed study of the taxation of
corporate surplus accumulations at no cost to the committee but
published by them as a committee print and widely distributed by
the Government Printing Office. Thus the regular full-time staff is
a sort of skeleton organization that gives continuity and general
direction to the work of the committee, with considerable powers
of expanding in particular directions as special problems come up
for study and as special funds are provided by Congress. This arrangement not only makes for economy and flexibility but gives the
challenge of fresh viewpoints.

Since the membership of the Joint Committee includes only one
professional economist and since all its members have a variety of
other duties and distractions, the staff of the committee enjoys a
greater degree of independence of action and more opportunity for
intellectual leadership in the activities of the committee than does
the staff of the Council of Economic Advisers. This situation has
produced two observable results—both of which have made some
contribution to the success of the committee's work but both of
which also entail possibilities of abuse. One of these results is the
exploration of new or modified methods for accomplishing the pur-

pose of the Joint Committee in implementing the Employment Act. The other (not completely separate) is the preparation and publication of a staff product distinct from the committee product.

To understand the problem of staff work in the Joint Committee, one must bear in mind the difference in character between the Council of Economic Advisers and the Joint Committee. The Council is not a policy-making body but is designed to provide to the President the economic background or underpinning for his politically synthesized policy. For this task the methods of economic and statistical research are indicated. The Joint Committee, on the other hand, seeks to correlate in the Congress a politico-economic policy of the same general scope and focus as that presented by the Executive. For this work, methods already developed by Congress and others to be fashioned in the light of unfolding experience are needed.

The public hearing is a relatively new method of investigation employed by Congressional committees.[14] It is basically suited to the purposes of formulating Joint Committee reports, and is capable of extension and refinement. This the staff has undertaken through several lines of experimentation. First was the use of itinerant hearings somewhat after the manner of the British Royal Commission of Inquiry. Second, it has used carefully prepared questionnaires sent to different groups to elicit a detailed factual picture and objective analysis preliminary to the holding of a public hearing, which then takes on much of the character of a university seminar rather than a legal proceeding. Third, it has experimented with the conference of professional specialists to seek "areas of agreement" and, so far as possible, a "consensus statement" in concise form on basic issues. Finally, it has combined several of these features in a series of topically organized panel discussions among professional and lay students of the issues presented in the President's annual Economic Report, with Joint Committee members first as auditors and then as participants in the panel discussions as a preparation for the formulation of their own report. These methods of staff-committee work are still in their developmental stage but have already shown promise of improvement in Congressional techniques for germinating national economic policies.

Besides the factual and interpretative material brought out at

[14] Ernest S. Griffith, *Congress: Its Contemporary Role,* p. 63.

Joint Committee hearings, the staff undertakes continuously to locate and bring together in convenient form materials they think would prove useful, or that committee members indicate a desire for, in connection either with the preparation of the committee's report on the Economic Report or with the special investigations conducted by subcommittees. Some of this material is drawn from private rather than government sources, and it is worth noting that in some cases the prestige and latent authority of the Joint Committee has made it possible for their staff to secure information which even the staff of an executive department had found it difficult or impossible to get.

A distinctive characteristic of the work of the Joint Committee staff has been its freedom to push ahead as an operating agency identifying problems, proposing methods of attack, producing draft "materials" which they make available for the service of the Joint Committee members, other Congressional committees, and executive departments. Some of these staff products are eventually published either separately or as parts of the Joint Committee Report on the President's Economic Report. (See pp. 195, 259, 314, 321.)

The staff's service in assembling documentation and preparing memoranda which are put in the hands of all committee members is of great importance. It is a means of partially overcoming the difficulty of securing adequate attendance of members at meetings of the committee. But it also supplements committee meetings in another way. Members who find themselves somewhat out of their depth in the technical economic questions which frequently come before the committee can do "home work" on these staff materials and so feel better informed when they attend committee hearings or deliberative meetings or when it devolves upon them to sign or dissent from a committee report or to pass upon plans for subcommittee investigations.[15]

[15] If at times it seems as though the staff is giving undue independent publicity to its own findings, one point must be borne in mind. The conditions under which the Joint Committee works make it practically impossible to maintain the desirably confidential character of staff materials in their preliminary form. Many of the topics dealt with and the figures developed by the committee's staff are of the liveliest public interest. While it is helpful to have these put promptly in the hands of committee members, such distribution on a confidential basis would inevitably lead to "leaks," with data appearing in incomplete and possibly garbled form. This has led to the practice of making the full text of much of this material in mimeographed form available to the press.

The staff of the Joint Committee has had two courses open to it. It could have sat back and waited for requests for information or assignments of work from the committee, which in the nature of the case would have been piecemeal and probably infrequent. On the other hand, they could show initiative in assembling pertinent information in the field of work assigned to the Joint Committee, in suggesting lines of research that would develop these fields of inquiry more adequately, and in devising more effective methods (such as the "panel" hearings) for conducting its work. It was the latter course which commended itself to the staff director and his colleagues. As a full-time professional group they have tried to service the committee in constructive ways to capture whatever values seem to them to have been intended by Congress in setting the committee up—this with the approval of the chairman and at least some members of the committee.

The distinctive manifestation of this concept and practice of Joint Committee staff work is to be seen in the "Staff Materials" which are included more and more prominently in recent Joint Committee Reports on the President's annual Economic Report. It appears also in special topical reports that sometimes attain only the formality of a "committee print" but sometimes become regular Congressional documents. The Joint Committee divests itself of responsibility for staff views expressed in such papers but at the same time makes it possible for free exploration of the problems to go on.

These practices obviously "have the defects of their virtues." There is the possibility that "the tail may wag the dog"—that the staff may come, in effect, to direct the committee rather than merely serving it, or that they might implement and magnify the dominance of a particular chairman. The latter has large powers in choosing the staff director, selecting topics to be dealt with, calling and conducting committee meetings, and scheduling publications. He is likely to be very responsive to the suggestions of a staff director whose general approach and attitude appeal to him, and he has little time to study the trend and consequences of what is going on in the subtle phases of substance and method. The character of the committee's findings can, for example, be greatly influenced through the use made of public hearings, questionnaires, or panels. The choice of topics, time, and personnel, and the framing of questions may tend to produce a partial or distorted picture for the committee members and the public. Or, on the other hand, they can give a comprehensive and well-balanced view of the major shades of competent opinion. It is of the utmost importance that such a staff shall not be permitted to become protagonists either of a cause or of a doctrine.[16] The panels conducted in January of each of the last three years have won increasing respect for the committee as have also the hearings and reports of several of its subcommittees.

A gravely complicating factor here is the inevitable intrusion of political partisanship into questions of economic policy. This has been conspicuously present in the reports of the Joint Committee on the President's annual Economic Report, which have usually divided along party lines. It is hardly to be expected that a bipartisan committee will arrive at a unanimous report. Nor indeed is it desirable that the Joint Committee should present a single line of interpretation of national issues or recommendations of national policy to their Congressional brethren. But it is highly desirable that the reports shall show sincere and carefully considered divergences, discriminations, and value emphasis, not mere party alignments.[17]

This inherent difficulty cannot be entirely overcome by even the most able of staff work. But it would seem that it might be lessened by a more complete pooling and better balance of the various schools of economic thought in a staff organized to serve all members of the committee equally. The present staff prides itself that, before it gets very far on an idea, it secures permission from the committee as a whole or at least its key members as well as from the chairman, and certainly that they do this before they release the findings of their studies. They pride themselves also on a democratic procedure

[16] Personally I feel that they have crowded unduly on the use of their "projections" technique, although I would not suggest that they drop it from their own intra-office analyses. There should be division of labor here between the staffs of the Joint Committee and the Council of Economic Advisers—not overlap or duplication.

[17] On this point, the Staff Director comments: "In the early years, the Committee automatically issued majority and minority reports which were primarily statements of economic policy of the two parties. In the last two years, however, real progress has been made in the direction of threshing out within the Committee these economic issues, and arriving at a larger area of agreement. It means, in many instances, however, footnote dissents and weaker language than we would always like." Grover W. Ensley, "The Work of the Congressional Joint Committee on the Economic Report," Associated University Bureaus of Business and Economic Research, Oct. 14, 1952.

under which, both at its inception and during its progress, staff work is reviewed and each member has an opportunity to express himself freely rather than merely take instructions from the director. A point is made also of the fact that services of the staff are equally available to all members of the committee and that they do receive calls from minority as well as majority members. Even so, it seems anomalous that the publications of the Joint Committee should habitually refer to the staff as a unit and then differentiate one individual as "minority" economist. Along with this invidious designation goes the fact that this economist does not participate in the democratic conferences of the staff nor see their product except or until it is mimeographed for distribution to all members of the committee.

This may perhaps be counted a minor defect in the work of a staff which on the whole is very creditable. But just at the present juncture it seems timely to suggest that caution should be taken not to reorganize the Joint Committee work in such a way as to staff it with economists of a generally different outlook or economic philosophy but to secure a group so representative and establish procedures so eclectic that the best of analytical service will be available to committee members of all political faiths and economic predilections, thereby removing any occasion for change in personnel accompanying a shift in administration from one party to another. Political partisanship is deeply ingrained in our Congressional system. But it seems not too much to hope that the unique purpose and structural position of the Joint Committee may be made the entering wedge toward more bipartisan or nonpartisan dealing with basic economic issues.

CHAPTER TWENTY-ONE

Evolution or Episode?

The six chapters of Part I presented a thesis about economics in the public service. Briefly stated, that thesis was that we have developed the techniques of statistical fact-finding and economic analysis and have raised the economic sophistication of our leaders of thought and action, in government and outside, to a level where it is practicable as well as desirable to apply economic science systematically to the making of practical policy for the nation's economic well-being. The last three chapters of Part I traced successive steps toward national policy-making from the Federal Reserve Act of 1913 to the Employment Act of 1946 and the increasing use of the professionally trained economist as economic adviser as those steps proceeded. Against that background, Part II peopled the foreground with those persons in the Executive Office and in the Congress who have been the players in Act I of the first full-dress performance under the Employment Act. In Chapters XVII–XX I have ventured to speak frankly as critic of that performance. This closing section of my appraisal will turn to the even more hazardous attempt to judge whether "the show will fold" after a rather brief career or have a long and successful run.

In other words, does a study of the case history here recorded lead to the conclusion that the philosophy expressed and the machinery set up in the Employment Act mark a logical evolution from the institutions and the traditions of our past, soundly adapted to the changing conditions of our present and outlook for the future? Or is it already apparent that this was a brave try against impossible odds or even an ill-conceived venture and that, on either judgment, it should be abandoned, writing this off as merely an episode in the history of a free people constantly experimenting with new ways to better the common lot?

This question cannot be answered by a single generalization. The Employment Act has four major aspects, and it is quite conceivable that one of its features might be highly successful and permanent while others might prove disappointing and be dropped. Furthermore, any part of the machinery setup might prove to be so promising as to be unhesitatingly accepted for continuance but require more or less drastic redesigning. The four aspects of the Employment Act on which separate judgment is both possible and needed are: (1) its basic declaration of Federal policy, (2) the mandate for an Economic Report of the President, (3) the Council of Economic Advisers, and (4) the Joint Economic Committee.

THE FEDERAL GOVERNMENT AS SERVANT OF ALL

Since this book is addressed to administrative aspects of the Employment Act rather than its economic or political justification, this first question may seem to be outside my province. But the suitability and probable permanence of administrative machinery can be fully judged only in relation to the purposes which it is supposed to serve. Therefore a few words may properly be said about the basic policy declared in the act.

At several points on previous pages I have expressed or clearly implied my personal judgment as an economist (that is, as a social scientist specializing in economic problems) that the policy declaration contained in Section 2 of the act is both technically sound and logically consistent with our national traditions and institutions. It makes explicit the "mixed system" of politico-economic life characteristic of these United States. This way of life is grounded on "free competitive enterprise" and sheltered under the canopy of the democratic government process. To this government we must look for market structures, financial facilities, and a necessary minimum of business policing. The Employment Act defines the general objectives of these legal institutions and the practices of government as being to maximize "employment opportunities for those able, willing, and seeking to work." This system has very aptly been called "assisted laissez faire."

We faced in Chapter XVII and elsewhere the bald fact that in the wording of the Employment Act (truly reflecting the state of our national thinking) there was a vast uncertainty as to how far we are prepared to go along the road of Federal job-making in case of an unemployment crisis. In my judgment, however, it is not likely that the declaration of responsibility enunciated in this statute will be retracted. The real question is how broadly the law will be interpreted and by what sort of programs it will be implemented. Where would you find a Congress with the political temerity to repeal a statute which is dedicated to the purpose of safeguarding the country against massive unemployment or designed to "promote employment opportunities . . . and maximum production"?

The statement of policy could, and perhaps will, for a long time stand precisely as it does in the present act and yet the actual scope of government action be curtailed to less than what we have seen over the last twenty years. Or, without the change of a single word, supplementary legislation and administration might bring the country on to intervention of government in the operative aspects of business to an extent even greater than that of the Labor Government in Great Britain. We are not, by statute, estopped from making wise and helpful changes nor protected against making foolish or reckless changes. If sensible public policy, paralleling sophisticated private business policy, fails to prevent a business recession, it is almost certain that drastic Federal action to *cure* it will be forced by our democratic process.

As for the near term, President Eisenhower's creed has been quoted on page 391. It strikes a note that is reassuring to some of the people under any interpretation and to all the people under some interpretations of what might be done in time of real depression threat. It must be read in context. The incoming President has surrounded himself with a Cabinet of great talents, wide experience, and practical vigor. While the outcome of this total Administration leadership cannot be foreseen, I believe that the declaration of policy in Section 2 is no mere episode in our history, but marks an irreversible—though as yet indeterminate—step in the evolution of our politico-economic life.

A MAJOR STATE PAPER

Whatever our philosophy of government and economic life and whatever the economic dangers that may confront us in coming years, it is of great importance that their emergence be noted when the cloud on the horizon is "no larger than a man's hand," that the force and direction of coming storms be measured with the most reliable instruments available, and that the best of talent and judgment be applied to shaping measures for meeting these dangers. To the extent that adverse forces are of a sort that can be corrected or turned aside, it is important that those in positions of responsibility shall have the readings currently charted, that they be studied in their totality, and that there be a consistent as well as an adequate program that avoids both blind inaction and panicky meddling.

The Economic Report of the President to the Congress at its opening (with supplemental reports as needed) seems to me an admirably conceived means to the ends just stated. It calls upon the Chief Executive to review the past year and to preview the coming year or years with the best of technical aid, and to map an explicit policy and program of action in consultation with the heads of all administrative divisions of the government.

I cannot believe that the emergence of this new state paper in a position of top-rank importance and periodic appearance is a mere episode of New Deal days. It seems to me as natural an evolution of modern practices of large-scale business management and growing economic literacy among the public as is our Federal budget and just as sure to become a permanent feature of our economic life. As such it would continue its evolution in form and content under the efforts—even though intermittent—of successive Administrations to make it more and more adequate to its purpose. That purpose is to outline successive annual programs under which government action would be so ordered as to promote maximum stability of the economy at the highest practicable level of private production. The Economic Report should be the state paper that gives to future historians the most definitive measure of our Presidents' statesmanship.

TECHNICAL STAFFING OF THE PRESIDENCY

To staff the office of the President for doing the best possible job on the Economic Report, any one of several methods might have been chosen. Congress hit upon a three-man Council, to be manned by economists of great eminence, accorded a position of high prestige in the Executive Office. They were to act as confidential technical advisers to the President and the heads of departments and agencies concerned with economic matters, and to be untouched by personal ambition or political activity. This would have been a logical culminating development in the use of economic experts as advisers at the policy-making level which had been developing in government for more than two decades and also in the most broadly managed corporations and the most progressive farm and labor organizations.

This phase of the Employment Act has not met with conspicuous success. The Council of Economic Advisers was launched with considerable fanfare, with emphasis on the "Cabinet rank" of the members, and with popular expectations that it would produce Einsteinian formulas for the combating of depressions, the repulse of inflation, and the perpetuation of prosperity. The first appointments to the Council (though not conforming rigorously to the qualifications envisaged by Congress) met with a large measure of public approval as among "the President's best." Over a six-year period, the momentum of this early start has largely been lost. Recent reports of the Council and of the President have received little attention, and its counsel has not been sought or even tolerated either by the mobilization agencies or by "old line" departments. Almost nothing has been said about it in connection with the reorganizations of the executive establishment instituted by the new Administration. Its present appropriation will expire on March 31, and unless President Eisenhower decides to revamp and revitalize it, the proposal for using top-level technical staffing in the preparation of national economic policy will have become only a short-lived episode.

Causes for the decline of the Council of Economic Advisers are not far to seek. The President did not in his initial appointments succeed in finding three economists of the stature needed for the task; he did not accord them the status in the Executive Office requisite for success; he did not make effective use of them or influence his official family to do so; he did not establish a confidential character for their advisory service or recognize a distinction between economic service and political involvement. The superimposing of mobilization agencies on the executive structure introduced complications that neither the guidance of the President nor the leadership of the Council were able to cope with. The general verdict seems to be "Too much politics and not enough economics. So interpreted and so operated, this device of the Employment Act is at best superfluous and at worst mischievous."

If a real reconstruction job is undertaken, two courses are open to the President. One would call for such replacements as he thinks would make the Council most helpful to him, and restoration of this three-man group to a position of prestige in the Executive Office. The other course would be to have the law modified so as to provide for a single Economic Adviser to the President (with staff similar to the present). Such a change was recommended by the Hoover Commission, saying:

> Just as the budget is the responsibility of the President and not of the Office of the Budget, the annual economic report is the report of the President, not of the Council. Like the Office of the Budget, the Council should advise the President as a professional staff agency and should not take public leadership on issues of policy in its own right. . . . It seems clear that, at least potentially, it is handicapped by being a multiheaded body, with the requirement that its members be confirmed by the Senate. To put a full-time board at the head of a staff agency is to run the risk of inviting public disagreement among its members and of transplanting within the President's Office the disagreements on policy issues that grow up in the executive departments or in the Congress. It also makes co-operation with related staff agencies more difficult.
>
> The Commission recommends that the Council of Economic Advisers be replaced by an Office of the Economic Adviser and that it have a single head.[1]

Such an arrangement would have several obvious advantages. It would avoid conflicts of philosophy, economic or administrative, and the possibility of personal frictions. The thought in Congress that having a three-man Council would assure breadth and balance in the advice given the President was somewhat mistaken. The President wants to have a single judgment rather than three to choose among, and the Economic Adviser should be able to secure all the desirable comprehensiveness of view and balance of judg-

[1] The Commission on Organization of the Executive Branch of the Government, *General Management of the Executive Branch* (A report to the Congress, February 1949), pp. 16–17.

ment by making suitable staff appointments, by inviting uninhibited staff discussion, and through the use of outside consultative committees. It would give the President complete freedom to bring in a man in whom he had great confidence and, in many cases no doubt, who had already worked with him in some similar capacity.

This would be a comfortable but not a very challenging situation. It would mean that the Economic Adviser would come to his post along with the President's entry into office and would depart with him. There would be only such continuity of experience and familiarity with the needs and resources of the job as could be supplied by the staff, and that would not reach up to the administrative level. It would personalize the position to the greatest degree, whereas it seems to me, ideally, to call for being institutionalized so that there would be a continuing and largely depersonalized staff service to the Presidency rather than too "cozy" a personal relation with a particular President.

If the present three-man Council is continued, the President should be free to select and to replace its members without the complication of Senate confirmation. The chairmanship should be recognized as a responsible post in the Administration and should be restored to the position in the "little Cabinet" from which it was dropped by the Executive Pay Act of 1949. Perhaps the Congress was groping for a concept of Cabinet *stature* rather than insisting on actual Cabinet *status* when it set up the Council, but certainly the chairman of the Council of Economic Advisers could not function effectively from a position four grades down the scale, to which he has now been relegated.[2]

---

[2] A study of reorganization of the Executive Office just completed, under the auspices of the National Planning Association (Bradley D. Nash, *Staffing the Presidency*) proposes (p. 39) an "office of Policy and Program Development—this office should absorb the duties and personnel of the Council of Economic Advisers, the National Security Resources Board, and the Legislative Reference Division of the Bureau of the Budget." The precise character and the probable consequences of this "absorption" are not made clear. If merely a matter of administrative blueprinting, it might be a sound suggestion. If it implies that the Council were to become an active factor in formulating the politically synthesized policies and programs of the President and if they were to work with one of three administrative assistants to the President rather than "having the right to be heard" on the economic issues by the President himself and his Cabinet advisers before policies were crystallized, I should feel that the possibilities of the unique type of service envisaged in the Employment Act had been foreclosed.

If the Council is to serve the President and the Executive Office effectively in the future, I believe that the new President should make it clear to each prospective nominee that he will be accorded an opportunity for real economic advisership by the President and members of the top policy-making group; that all matters of specific recommendation will be treated as confidential on both sides; that members will not appear as spokesmen for the President or for themselves before Congressional committees; and that public writing or speaking will not be barred but will be limited to broad issues of economic analysis designed to promote better understanding of the real nature of pending economic issues rather than pointing to specific conclusions of public policy.

Of course the Council of Economic Advisers could be abolished and the mandate of the Employment Act formally complied with by having the President's Economic Report drafted by one or more White House aides, drawing their materials from various statistical and economic agencies of the Government. If this were done, there would be no chance for economic issues to be considered on their merits before political expediencies were weighed. There would be no continuous center for consideration of national policy out of the ex parte atmosphere of the separate departments with their special constituencies and their (properly) political headship. It would not in future be possible for several top-flight economists to gain the most intimate and realistic view of the overall problem of keeping a total economy in such a state of dynamic equilibrium that reasonably full and continuous use of our resources might be maintained. There would be no "sending station" through which progressively more adequate formulation of the central problem of economics could be disseminated to economic workers. There would be no "receiving station" through which the best—and ever-improving—appraisals and insights of those who have both the most adequate qualifications for judgment and the greatest degree of objectivity or immunity from political pressures could be brought back into government thinking at the highest policy-making levels.

Imperfectly as these objectives have been realized in these last six years, they are ideals easily discernible in the provisions for a Council of Economic Advisers and ideals well worth striving toward

SURVIVAL VALUE OF THE JOINT COMMITTEE

The Joint Committee has the possibility of becoming a permanent and valuable feature of our Congressional system. It represents a natural evolution toward better functional specialization in the legislative process and the use of social science methods consonant with our modern economic and political growth. Beginning on a level of rather limited activity and casual participation, the committee has progressed to an organized but flexible program of work. There are accumulating evidences of growing, even if still moderate, influence won merely through intellectual leadership. The intensive investigations of special topics by one or two of its subcommittees have already produced results of national importance. Its staff has shown that old Congressional techniques of inquiry can be perfected and new ones devised that will bring economics more effectively into the public service at the legislative level.

If upon this promising foundation the Joint Committee is to rear an expanding structure of Congressional service, it would seem timely now for its chairman, and in lesser degree its members, to appear in all committees dealing with economic legislation as qualified and vigorous spokesmen for conclusions and recommendations derived from its study program. To this end it is desirable that the positions of chairman and vice-chairman of the Joint Committee shall be held by persons of such stature in their respective Houses and of such personal drive that they can command careful consideration of Joint Committee findings throughout the course of all important economic legislation.

As long as the submitting of an Economic Report at the opening of Congress continues to be a duty enjoined on the President by Congress, the Joint Committee is called for as an agency for seeing that it is given full attention and competent review. The Employment Act also assigns an independent role to the Joint Committee, parallel to that of the President, to study national policy as an integrated whole and to raise the level of its economic statesmanship above local and pressure-group politics. As long as senators and representatives peculiarly qualified by training and experience seek membership on and, particularly, chairmanship of this committee there is little danger that this will become a mere episode in the history of our government.

"THE SPIRIT OF '46"

In a previous volume I ventured to evaluate the Employment Act
in terms of historic, even epochal importance, in our national life
comparable to "the spirit of '76."

"The spirit of '76" is a phrase of almost hallowed significance in the
book of American patriotism. That was the Year 1 of our national freedom.
The Declaration of Independence launched us on our career of discovering
whether men of many races could live together in peace and could evolve
an art of self-government. We are still struggling with that task, and we
need all the best of the spirit that animated our ancestors if we are to
meet the challenge now hurled at free government.

To the economist, the year 1776 has a double connotation of freedom
and progress. For that was also the year of Adam Smith's *Wealth of
Nations,* generally taken as the Declaration of Free Enterprise.

If 1776 was an epoch-marking year and the spirit of '76 symbolizes personal freedom and economic progress for the United States, it is quite
possible that 1946 will, in the long perspective of history, become no less
an epoch-marking year. "The spirit of '46" may by future generations
attain, if not equal, at least very great significance. It may signalize the
crowning of our centuries-old faith in private enterprise with a more
adequate grasp of the nature and the complementary potentialities of public enterprise. . . .

The attempt to co-ordinate the best of our practical economic thinking
around the central problem of avoiding depressions or maintaining high-
level production calls for intellectual sweat and co-operative action. But
it does not demand the impossible or a higher order of performance in the
economic field than we are achieving right along in the technological area.
It seems to me quite comparable to what we long ago demonstrated and
now take for granted in developing our electronic and chemical technology, in operating our great assembly-line industries, and in synchronizing
our air transport or communication operations.[3]

One reviewer—not unkindly—noted that I entertained an "exalted" estimate of the Employment Act. In a quite sober sense I
do take an exalted view of what is potential in that statute. I believe that, with its declaration for private enterprise and government responsibility, with its call for a major state paper of integrated economic policy, with its staff of professional economists in
the Executive Office and its newly devised pondering committee

[3] Edwin G. Nourse, *The 1950's Come First,* pp. 7–8, 9.

(with trained staff) in Congress, it may translate a growing economic sophistication of our country into practical means of checking runaway boom, supporting incipient depression, and stabilizing high-level use of our resources to a degree comparable to our achievements in the field of technology.

So interpreted and so realized it would indeed be evolution under the guiding hand of science, not a mere political episode.

Appendix A

EXCERPTS FROM PRESS COMMENTS ON THE
APPOINTMENT OF THE COUNCIL OF
ECONOMIC ADVISERS

Press comment was voluminous and covered both the commentator's concepts of the Council's work and their estimates of the appointee's qualifications.

The Boston *Herald* (July 31) had a hopeful approach:

The United States now has, pending Senate confirmation, an Economic Advisory Council, containing or able to mobilize the best brains in the country to warn us when we are drifting toward depression and to chart our course toward consistent prosperity. President Truman evinces high hopes that it will succeed in deflecting booms and busts; at least he believes our country can maintain an even keel.

If confirmed cynics feel less sanguine than the President, it is not because of the calibre of the council. Chairman Edwin Griswold Nourse, vice-president of the Brookings Institution; John Davidson Clark of the University of Nebraska, and Leon H. Keyserling, general counsel for the National Housing Agency, are as competent as any other triumvirate to guide our economic destinies.

But for a democracy to know what it ought to do is not the same as doing it. Depression preventives are often too unpalatable to large and powerful blocs. How many therapeutic measures like credit restriction would the nation have accepted in 1928? How many cities and towns are willing to spend in depressions and save in booms? How often would labor forego pay increases for the sake of stability?

Yet the "Act to declare a national policy on employment, production and purchasing power, and for other purposes" does have the virtue of introducing one of the social sciences into government. Not only does it set up the advisory council, but it provides for a standing joint committee of Congress to make a continuing study of the President's economic reports on the nation, to survey means of co-ordinating policies and to guide other com-

461

mittees. The truth may not make us free at once, but it will help us to recognize the false.

The American correspondent of the *London Economist* wrote, on October 12:

Earlier doubts notwithstanding, it does seem clear that Congress from next year onwards will be in a far better position to align fiscal policies with broader economic trends. Under the joint influence of the Congressional Reform Act and the Full Employment Act, there may one day emerge something like an economic General Staff; meanwhile, Congress itself will for the first time on record, be in a position to relate both revenue and expenditure programmes to the over-all economic picture. . . .

The Economic Tribunal (or Council of Advisers) established by the Full Employment Act is expected to do its work quietly, and with little of the publicity suggested by initial fanfares heralding an almost omniscient body. Indeed, its members are reported to be in some considerable doubt concerning their precise stature in the role of advisers to the President. Its main task at the moment is to establish and strengthen coordination between the various departments—more especially the Treasury, the Federal Reserve Board, the Department of Commerce, and the Bureau of Labour Statistics. But it will also be able to draw on the resources of any Federal agency, business institutes, and such private bodies as the Committee for Economic Development and the [National] Bureau of Economic Research. It may in the longer run—clearly, it should—supersede separate agency reports on the economic outlook. . . . There is any amount of room for friction between the new Economic Council and the established agencies. But a valuable start has been made, and the new Council seems to have won the approval of many responsible observers.

Printer's Ink on September 27, observed:

The President's Council of Economic Advisers, set up under the modified pro-free-enterprise version of the so-called Full Employment Bill, is going to come through with some important material one of these days. But you, a mere citizen, won't get a chance to read it. It is understood that the Council . . . will make its report available only to the President. Out of this great mass of data, covering government fiscal policies and all segments of activity affecting the economic health of the nation, Mr. Truman is supposed to draw up a set of recommendations to Congress. Dr. Nourse and his associates will hardly presume to instruct the President or even give him their own interpretation of what they are finding out. They will give him the consensus of informed opinion and let him draw his own conclusions. Proceeding on this basis, the Council will not have to weigh political considerations in arriving at its answers—something the President can do much better for himself. But how long this independence of thought will survive is another question—especially since the President's recommendations will go to the joint Committee on the Economic Report, headed by the politically minded Senator Joseph C. O'Mahoney (D., Wyo.). You can just about count on it that before long Mr. O'Mahoney's group will be summoning the Council members—Messrs. Nourse, Clark, and Keyserling—to ask whether they agree with the President's views.

Frank Kent prophesied failure for us.

. . . there is a great deal of skepticism as to usefulness and value. . . . The board's job is to serve as a sort of economic crystal gazer for the President, forecasting economic conditions from a year to a year and a half ahead, and advising how to meet them. Further, it is supposed to consider unemployment and depression causes and to advise the President how best to strengthen the federal financial structure—and in other ways.

But the President does not have to take the board's advice—not at all. It is purely an Executive [Office] agency and is empowered only to study and make recommendations. This sounds well, but it does not mean much because its recommendations can be ignored entirely by Mr. Truman. . . .

The board does not report to Congress, which next year, under its contemplated reorganization, should be better informed fiscally than ever before, and is to have a legislative budget that, in theory, will be scientifically devised. So the Economic Advisory Council will advise the President, who can make its recommendations public or not as he pleases and act upon them or not as he desires. As it is seen here, the board can make recommendations either along sound lines or unsound lines, but in either it hardly can produce anything that has not been recommended before. . . .

There is a feeling here in the highest fiscal circles that the new board, for a number of years, will produce long, dull and deep reports, which will attain considerable publicity but otherwise not affect anything at all. And after a few more years it will become a target for the economizers in Congress as a useless government bureau the somewhat costly existence of which cannot be justified.

The Washington *Post* said on August 6:

President Truman deserves a vote of thanks for having made all his appointments to the Council on the basis of merit. The pressure to award these high-paid jobs to the politically deserving was undoubtedly great. Had the President yielded to that pressure, the hope of making any substantial progress toward the goal of full employment by the research route would have gone glimmering.

The *Daily Worker* of July 30 felt that labor had not been adequately considered.

"Full employment" law was finally fished out of an obscure pigeon hole by President Truman, who announced he has appointed Edwin G. Nourse, vice-president of the conservative Brookings Institution, as chairman of the Economic Council to administer it. The other two members, chosen last week, have been approved without a scrap by the Senate Banking Committee. They are Leon Keyserling, a New York attorney, and John Davidson Clark of the Nebraska University College of Business Administration. Nary a trade unionist or well-known advocate of liberal job policies in the lot!

A personality critique was supplied by the writer of "Washington Viewpoints" in *Buffalo Business* for September.

It has been said here in Washington that the selections of the three Council members were made according to President Truman's "second-policy-phase." Bluntly, it is meant that the Council is well-balanced from the standpoint of political and economic thinking. . . . Keyserling, New Dealer, is balanced off with such men as Clark, conservative ex-businessman-professor, and Nourse, middle-of-the-road researcher, on his new Council.

All three men on the Council are colorful personalities. Clark's career is an odd reversal of the usual professor-to-business economist route. Clark was at one time lawyer for Midwest Refining. Then, he became vice-president of Standard Oil of Indiana. After some years of business success, he decided he wanted to get into the field of education. Resigning from Standard of Indiana, he returned to college for three years, got his doctor's degree in economics, and took on a professorship at the University of Denver. When tagged for the Council by Mr. Truman, Clark was dean of the College of Business Administration, at the University of Nebraska. In the years between, he'd also tucked service in the Wyoming legislature under his belt, as well as several banking directorships, and committee memberships on a number of governmental and defensive advisory groups. (As a matter of fact, Clark is not too keen about being considered a "conservative." He is a Democrat—and served on some rather liberal policy committees. It has, indeed, been said of him, even, that he was a real liberal—but not a "whole-hog" New Dealer, as one of his friends put it.)

Leon H. Keyserling is perhaps the best known of the three men, here in Washington, and over the country, too. Keyserling is a liberal, and a "devout" New Dealer. (However, contrary to Clark, Keyserling is to some extent rather anxious to side-step the left-of-center label, and, indeed, there is some evidence that he has mellowed into a more middle-roader this past year.) He, too, has a background of college association, having been on the staff of the Economics Department of Columbia University in the early 'thirties. Later, he became legislative assistant to Senator Robert Wagner, from which association came his first relationship with National Housing. He served as deputy administrator and general counsel for the United States Housing Authority for five years, and became acting administrator in 1941. In 1942, he was appointed general counsel for the N.H.A. and served in that capacity for the next four years. His position on the Council, which he serves as vice-chairman, doubtless springs, in part, from the fact that he assisted in drafting the bill which ultimately became the Employment Act of 1946.

Mr. Keyserling was further characterized in *Washington Close-Up* of August.

Mr. Keyserling probably would be classed among the economic planners— at least among those who advocate a greater measure of government control and direction over the national economy. His essay which won the second prize of $10,000 in the Pabst Brewing Company's postwar employment award contest, was along that general line, with many specific suggestions for government action. He also is reported to have assisted in the drafting of the original version of the full employment measure and to have drafted the Wagner-Ellender-Taft general housing bill which would have extended broad government controls over the entire national housing industry.

We were all rated by the Gannett papers (September 9).

All three have written papers and made speeches. All are scholars. All have been concerned with the public welfare.

Stimulation of business activity appears to be the main aim of Dr. Nourse. He feels that government taxing, monetary and credit policies should be designed to this end. Full use of the nation's natural resources, is essential, he believes. Lending of money to businessmen, farmers and foreigners is essential, he feels, to spur business. There, however, he stops.

Mr. Keyserling goes further to suggest wise public spending for worthy projects, if needed, to make jobs. Central thought to him is jobs for all. Jobs must be at good salaries and under decent conditions, he feels. The production of scarce commodities should be stimulated by government guarantees to write off any losses a business may suffer in producing them.

The views of Dr. Clark are less well known. From Wyoming, he is a protege of Senator Joseph O'Mahoney, a New Dealer. Persons close to Dr. Clark feel he favors more government planning and more government control than do his colleagues.

The *Christian Science Monitor* on August 7 introduced us thus to its readers:

Edwin G. Nourse, Chairman: formerly Vice-President of the Brookings Institution, a highly respected economic analyst who believes profoundly in the free enterprise system and who wants the Government to help make it work; he certainly doesn't want to doctor it for the sport of it. His approach to deficit spending will be "show me," but, if shown, he will favor the Government's taking a part in sustaining a stable economy.

John D. Clark, a Dean of the University of Nebraska College of Business Administration, who took up teaching not because he failed in business but because he was successful in it.

Leon H. Keyserling, formerly General Counsel of the United States Housing Administration; a careerist in Government service; a sincere New Dealer unconnected with the pre-Truman White House economic planners.

Clark "took a bow" in the St. Louis *Post-Dispatch* on July 31.

The most colorful member of the board is John Davidson Clark, who in 1928 got tired of being an "oil millionaire" (he was vice-president of Standard Oil of Indiana) and determined to give the rest of his life to the study, teaching and public practice of the economics of government.

Clark took his Ph. D. in economics at Johns Hopkins in 1931 and then became a professor of economics—usually without pay. He is now dean of the College of Business Administration of the University of Nebraska, his first Alma Mater. On the side, he has been a member of the legislature of Wyoming. He was a warm, but not uncritical supporter of President Roosevelt's policies. He should give the Economic Council the balanced view of a progressive, hard-headed business man.

We evoked "practical interest" from the Phoenix *Gazette* on August 3.

What might otherwise be dismissed as a studious undertaking by visionaries to combat a trend that has become almost as sure as death and taxes, assumes practical interest in the present because Nourse has emphasized a new factor in the attack—the "intelligent co-operation by management and labor with government." Without an effective merging of these three elements, the closely related problems of prices and employment cannot be solved. On the satisfactory solution of those problems, economic stability depends.

Nourse thinks of "business leaders" as including union leaders. This is the kind of approach to the problem which the country needs. As long as our economy is hog-tied by recurrent struggles for power between labor and management, we will go from one crisis to another. Once a system has been devised in which labor and management can attack a common problem as partners rather than as mortal enemies, the nation can hope for some measure of that economic utopia in which booms and busts are unknown.

Another major depression, Nourse believes, would so endanger the private enterprise economy that prevention of a slump should be the primary effort of American business. It must also be the aim of American labor, which depends on private enterprise.

A Canadian neighbor (Victoria *Daily Times,* August 15) also was interested and illuminating.

One of the chief keys to the United States Employment Act of 1946, enacted last March, is the Economic Advisory Council. It was to be composed of three men chosen by Mr. Truman as trustees of the public interest. Two of these, Mr. John D. Clark and Mr. Leon Keyserling, were appointed a few days ago; but the President's choice for the chairmanship of the Council—which he believed could solve the differences between political expediency and economic necessities—wavered between recommendations, some conceivably too tainted with politics or too inflexible in their economic doctrines. Finally, the chief executive's choice fell upon Mr. Edwin G. Nourse, Director of the Brookings Institution, a society "devoted to Public Service through Research and Training in the Social Sciences," whose "first purpose is to aid constructively in the development of sound national policies." For three days Mr. Nourse hesitated, later accepting it, probably to the great relief of President Truman.

The Chicago *Times* of July 30 rated me nonpolitical.

Nourse considers himself an independent in politics and has not been affiliated with any party. He told an interviewer today that he is an advocate of retention of the private enterprise system, adding, however, that private enterprise must be used to the broad ends of national welfare.

The New York *Times* of July 31 gave me to the farmers.

Mr. Nourse presumably answers the requests of large farm organizations for one member of the Council familiar with agricultural matters.

And the widely syndicated *Washington Farm Reporter* said: "Farm leaders in Washington generally applauded the appointment by President Truman of Edwin G. Nourse as head of the new Economic Advisory Council."

Walter Locke in his "Trends of the Times" was our most enthusiastic booster.

John D. Clark, who quit the "oil millionaire" business to study and teach the business of government is picked by the President for the Economic Council job. Business, educators—everybody that knows him—says: "A fine appointment!"

So said the Senate, too, in confirming him. . . .

Nourse is to be chairman of the "economic council," charged with keeping industry right side up. If anybody can tell us how to do it, says the chorus, Nourse can. What a team, Nourse and Clark! So the Senate, confirming them decides.

Leon H. Keyserling is general counsel for the National Housing Agency, a recognized authority in this field. He makes the third member of the Economic Council and everybody says Hurrah. Nourse and Keyserling and Clark can find ways to keep the nation right side up if it can be done. The Senate confirms Keyserling with the rest. From nowhere in the country comes complaint. With such an Economic Council we shall know the way to go. If we insist on going otherwise, that will be our own suicide and funeral.

President Truman will note: Only praise from press and country follows these appointments of men clearly fitted for their special posts. When the office goes out to seek the man, it generally gets a good one.

Appendix B

THE COUNCIL'S PLAN OF STAFF WORK

ORGANIZATION OF STAFF WORK

June 17, 1947

I. FIELDS OF OPERATION

The principal members of the Council's staff are selected both because of their understanding of the workings of the economy as a whole and their specialized knowledge in certain major fields of economic activity and study. These fields are as follows: (1) labor force and labor relations; (2) plant capacity, investment, and management; (3) agriculture and consumer economics; (4) flow of income, goods and services (Nation's Economic Budget); (5) price relations and policies, monopoly and competition; (6) international economic relations; (7) development of human and material resources; (8) construction, housing, and public works; (9) veterans, social security, and welfare; and (10) taxation, debt, and banking.

II. DIVISION OF RESPONSIBILITY AMONG COUNCIL MEMBERS

To the end that staff work may progress in the most orderly and expeditious manner, the Council members have allocated among themselves responsibility for initial follow-up of the progress of Council work and for primary contact between the Council and each of the members of the top staff in his respective area of work. The individual members of the Council will undertake respectively with each individual top staff member and his assistants to keep the individual staff member informed of general Council policies affecting or influencing his work; to explore and tentatively outline areas and programs of inquiry and report these proposals back to the Council for approval. When plans have been so approved, the individual Council member will take primary responsibility for carrying forward the work in those areas of responsibility allocated to him. He shall undertake to organize and develop the external as well as the internal relationships and contacts necessary for these areas of inquiry; to keep the Council as a whole informed as to the nature and progress of the work going forward, and see that product is presented at a suitable time for the Council's consideration and use. This apportionment has been made on the following basis:

Mr. Nourse

(Besides responsibility for general administration and special contacts)
Plant capacity, investment and management
Price relations and policies
Development of human and material resources
Operations of wage-price committee

Mr. Keyserling

Labor force and labor relations
Nation's economic budget and its components
Construction, housing, and public works
Veterans, social security and welfare
Operations of stabilization devices committee
Operations of economic round-up committee

Mr. Clark

Agriculture and food
Monopoly and competition
International economic relations
Taxation and debt management
Money and banking
Operations of Federal grants-in-aid committee

The above division of labor is to be carried forward, subject to these considerations: (1) it shall not impede freedom of access between any member of the Council and any member of the staff, or vice versa; (2) all fundamental matters of economic policy, adminis-

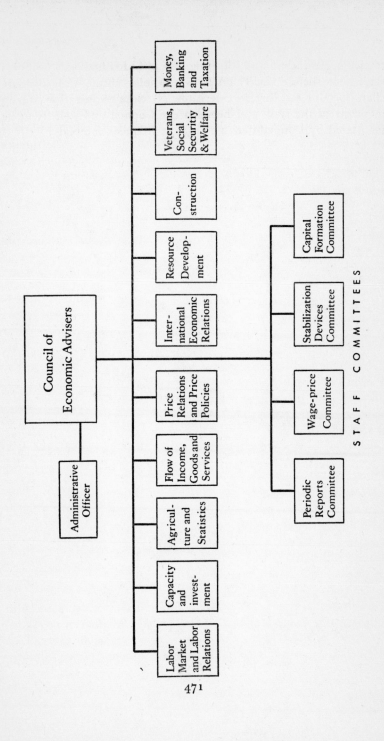

Council of
Economic Advisers

Administrative
Officer

Labor
Market
and Labor
Relations

Capacity
and
invest-
ment

Agricul-
ture and
Statistics

Flow of
Income,
Goods and
Services

Price
Relations
and Price
Policies

Inter-
national
Economic
Relations

Resource
Develop-
ment

Con-
struction

Veterans,
Social
Securitiy
& Welfare

Money,
Banking
and
Taxation

Periodic
Reports
Committee

Wage-price
Committee

Stabilization
Devices
Committee

Capital
Formation
Committee

STAFF COMMITTEES

trative organization, and job programs of·individual staff members
shall come before the Council as a whole (through appropriate
channels) for scrutiny and decision; (3) close co-operation among
members of the staff, and between the Council and staff, is to be
facilitated by Council-staff meetings at frequent intervals.

Appendix C

Honorable Joseph C. O'Mahoney
Chairman, Joint Committee on the Economic Report
United States Senate
Washington, D. C.

My dear Senator O'Mahoney:

Your telegram of February 4, inviting the members of the Council to appear at hearings of the Joint Committee yesterday has only now reached me. I was out of town attending several meetings important to the work of the Council on Saturday, Monday, and yesterday.

I understand that Mr. Keyserling and Mr. Clark freely and gladly accepted your invitation to appear before the Committee. If I had been here, I would have had, in good conscience, to ask that I be excused.

I think you are aware that I have always taken the position that the Council occupies a unique role of intimate and essentially confidential professional staff service to the President. It is my belief that this agency cannot, over the years, discharge this function effectively and without embarrassment either to the Chief Executive or to Council members if it is drawn out of the Executive Office into the political atmosphere of the Hill to discuss specific issues of policy on which the President has made his own recommendations. However perfect our agreement on these recommendations in the past or in the present instance, it is clearly foreseeable that the Council or individual members of the Council sooner or later will be in quite frank disagreement with some policy recommended by the President. We would then be confronted by a difficult and dangerous dilemma. Either we would have to "go down the party line," supporting this position by the most plausible arguments we could devise, regardless of our honest professional beliefs; or else we would have to debate and in the end criticize positions taken by the President.

I would be much disturbed, here in the latter years of my professional career, to be put in the position which would be created by the first line of action. As chairman of this agency, I am desirous of demonstrating the

473

unique staff service that it is capable of rendering to the Chief Executive. Therefore, I would strongly regret being put in a situation where my testimony could be used to embarrass or weaken the position of the President.

In the past, I have outlined these views to the President and to Senator Taft, when he was chairman of the Joint Committee. The Senator said that, without committing himself in principle, he respected the position which I took and, in the light of that fact, would not request my appearance at hearings of the committee. The President likewise expressed himself as believing that my position was taken on high professional grounds and not through any lack of a desire to co-operate in every way. He therefore would not instruct or request me to appear before any Congressional Committee. I hope that you will take a similar view.

I am confident that there will be active and useful developments in the work of the Joint Committee under your chairmanship. We desire to have our staff co-operate in every possible way with your staff. Committee members also may wish to discuss various economic issues with Council members in private. I shall be happy to participate in this way and believe that in time we may develop a practice which you and your Committee will find eminently satisfactory.

Sincerely yours,

/s./ Edwin G. Nourse
Chairman

Appendix D

ORGANIZED LABOR AND ECONOMIC STABILIZATION[1]

When Mr. Harrison invited me to attend this Grand Lodge Convention of your Brotherhood, I accepted with genuine pleasure. I wrote him: "This is the first invitation from an international union that has been extended to any member of the Council of Economic Advisers. I shall therefore regard the meeting as an occasion for a major statement on behalf of the Council" as to how the policies and actions of organized labor fit into the objectives and means for obtaining them outlined in the Employment Act of 1946.

That act proposed that the Federal Government shall "co-ordinate and utilize all its plans, functions, and resources for the purpose of creating and maintaining conditions [of] maximum employment, production, and purchasing power." This positive program for economic stabilization and the maintenance of sustained prosperity is to be carried out "in a manner calculated to promote and foster free competitive enterprise and the general welfare," thus recognizing our established system of corporate and union organization and of free collective bargaining between them. Furthermore, the Congress clearly states that this policy and program are to be carried out "with the assistance and co-operation of industry, agriculture, labor, and state and local governments." It suggests further that the Council of Economic Advisers to the President shall consult with such representatives of industry, labor, agriculture, and consumers as it deems advisable.

We promptly decided that it was advisable for the three members of the Council and those of our top staff who were particularly concerned with labor matters to sit down with representatives of the principal labor organizations, at least quarterly, for a frank exchange of views. We have also met with management, agriculture, and consumers. As a matter of record, the first such consultative conference that we held, soon after our work got

[1] An address by the Chairman of the Council of Economic Advisers, International Union Convention, Brotherhood of Railway and Steamship Clerks, Cincinnati, Ohio, May 14, 1948.

under way and before we made our first report to the President, was with
Mr. Harrison, Mr. Lyon, and five other representatives designated by the
Railway Labor Executives Association. I am glad now to broaden my
acquaintance with your membership and to consider with you the principles under which we both must work in promoting the economic welfare
of our great country.

THE EMPLOYMENT ACT DECLARES RESPONSIBILITY

Now there is one point about the policy set forth in the Employment
Act of 1946 and the working relations and program of the Council of
Economic Advisers which I think it is most important that everybody
have clearly in mind at all times. The Employment Act recognizes and
underscores the responsibility of existing and long-established organizations
in the field of private business; but, at the same time, it accepts and clarifies a reciprocal or complementary responsibility of the Federal Government for promoting high and continuous use of our country's productive
resources.

I undertook to drive this point home in the first formal address that I
made as chairman of the Council of Economic Advisers. This was on
December 6 last, when I was invited to address the National Association of
Manufacturers assembled in their 51st Congress of American Industry. A
single paragraph will give you the point of view from which I urged them,
and I now urge you, to approach this great new development in our institutions of free government. I said:

"It now devolves upon each of us, whether in the executive or legislative
branch of the Government to see that, in carrying out the purposes of this
law, we study wisely and with due counsel as well as acting decisively and
promptly when occasion demands. To this end, we of the Council sincerely
hope that you of the House of Business no less than those of the House
of Labor and the House of Agriculture will join actively and sincerely
in our studies of causes that impede the attainment of maximum production, employment, and purchasing power and in the making of recommendations which would operate effectively toward the removal of these
impediments."

All this simply reflects my general economic philosophy and understanding of how an economic system works and can be made to work more efficiently and steadily through the guidance of intelligent men who occupy
official or administrative positions in economic organizations, private or
public. It reflects the view that in these relationships we are dealing with
a very delicate and complicated piece of machinery and that we cannot
safely operate as special interest groups or by using our sheer weight or

fighting strength to force an economic adjustment merely to our arbitrary will or to our short-run or apparent advantage. Instead of such a militant or brute-force means of settling economic problems, we must, with the responsibilities that lie in our hands, turn to what I like to refer to as the engineering approach to problems of economic adjustment under free enterprise and collective bargaining. We cannot be content merely to be clever negotiators or ruthless fighters. We must acquire a basic understanding of the broad repercussions and long-run cause-and-result relationships involved in our business actions. Both the corporation and the union must be skillful in working out these relations when they set wage rates and working rules. Manufacturers and merchants must deal skillfully with these relationships when they mark price tickets and set service charges. Both individuals and corporate managers must deal intelligently with these relationships when they determine on their savings accumulations and their spending behavior. Public officials as well as citizens must show themselves economically literate when they decide on tax levies and public works expenditures.

Economics is really a particular species of engineering—wealth engineering. Your union officials and likewise corporation officials and government officials must, if they are to be successful in the long run, bring scientific analysis to bear upon the study of business forces, market values, and high real incomes, much as the mechanical, electrical, or chemical engineer brings scientific methods to bear in dealing with the forces and materials of nature. Like these other engineers, they seek to find what is wrong with the mechanisms and practices through which we are currently utilizing these forces and materials. And they should contribute to their more effective utilization.

This engineering approach to your business and the Nation's Business comes to a sharp focus today. We stand at the end of a war of unprecedented magnitude and severity, in which swift, skillful, and massive industrial production has been a decisive factor. It was a great engineering or technological achievement. But it was not a great business or economic achievement or a demonstration of our ability to run an industrial system at high efficiency in peacetime. It was a highly artificial episode of industrial production, in which motives of patriotism or even fear largely supplanted ordinary motivation and in which government orders were financed out of a national deficit and we rolled up a gigantic debt. The basic problem of reconversion is to keep the momentum of this high-level economic activity but convert it to orderly market transactions on a self-sustaining basis. To stabilize such high-level production and consumption is the basic purpose of the Employment Act of 1946.

In the world of normal bargaining relations to which we have now returned, several goals have to be jointly attained. The consumer has to be satisfied that he is getting proper value for his dollar. The capitalist or saver has to be satisfied that he has enough prospect of interest or dividends and certainly enough safety for principal so that he keeps investment flowing in at the rate needed for efficient equipping of labor and for necessary growth. Labor has to be satisfied that wages correspond reasonably to actual productivity and that special skills or extra effort can win financial recognition and lead to advancement.

Businessmen are fond of saying that it is the task of management to do all these things. For myself, I think they cannot really be accomplished unless other parties to the processes of business intelligently and conscientiously play their part also. I am not here to talk about management's responsibilities or the means by which they can be most fully met. Nor am I here to claim that they have been or are being met as fully as is necessary if we are to demonstrate the superior efficiency of the private enterprise system. Among businessmen there is right now considerable complaint that the Council of Economic Advisers and the President are putting too much heat on them for solving current economic problems and relieving present business difficulties and that we are putting little or no responsibility on agriculture and labor, where they say it belongs. Personally, I see no reason for stopping, or indeed moderating, our statements as to the responsibility of management at this juncture in the return to postwar private business.

I said to the N.A.M. audience:

"It is up to you to show your capacity to do business in a buyers' market. Unless you can allow the full volume of productivity of our capable labor force, our ample plant, and our marvelous technology to continue unabated and absorb within your long-time accounting, financing and managerial system such price declines as result, you will not have shown a capacity of the competitive free enterprise system adequately to serve the Nation's needs.

"You can't pass the buck to labor any more than labor can pass the buck to you. They also regard themselves as part of the system of competitive free enterprise, and you must both of you find a way of getting together to hammer out a mutually sound adjustment. I hope some day I'll have the chance to say these things to a labor audience."

UNIONISM AND ECONOMIC STABILIZATION

Well, I now have my chance to talk to such an audience, and there are just three points I want to make. The first is that organized labor settlements must be the parent and not the child of economic stabilization. The great purpose of the Employment Act of 1946 is to promote economic stability or high continuous utilization of our natural resources and the maximum purchasing power for the whole consuming population that would go with such high production. It is a mistake to think that the Act provides any trick device for guaranteeing business stability or full employment. It commits the government to provide favorable conditions, but within these conditions labor and management must work out the actual arrangements under which high production can be attained.

A very distinguished labor leader once said to me: "We are strong for the Employment Act and the Council of Economic Advisers. You just go ahead and stabilize business, and we'll get ours." I have no doubt as to the second of these propositions. But I would simply be seeking to deceive you if I left the impression that the Council for a moment supposes that it can stabilize the economy or even point the way in which it could be stabilized except through the sound action of labor as well as management in their collective bargaining settlements. Under wage rates and working practices, labor must put as much into the creation of products as it arranges to take out in the way of consumer goods. In other words, the settlement must be one that creates both the opportunity and the inducement for business—jobs—to go on.

It is sometimes pointed out that the maintaining of full employment is the same as making a perpetual sellers' market for labor. You may reply: "Well, is that bad? Isn't it just what the whole labor movement is for?" My answer would be: Whether it is good or bad remains to be seen. It will depend upon how wisely union members and union officials can use the power that is theirs in a sellers' market. At the least, I would have to say that it is dangerous.

We have just seen a demonstration of the dangers of a sellers' market for commodities, which has caused you as consumers a good deal of anguish and threatened the country with spiraling inflation. I am somewhat reassured that that danger is now being averted, in part through the self-control of some businessmen and in part through the corrective effect of increasing production. It is hardly to be supposed that a sellers' market for labor would be protected against abuse by the stimulative effect that it would have on the production of new laborers. Hence all the more responsibility devolves on labor policy and adjustment practices if you are to keep from engendering an inflationary spiral of annual wage increases followed by annual price increases which promptly extinguish the gains for the consumer.

In this connection it seems to me that the greatest danger that the Council will have to face in its study of wage-price stabilization is that particular groups of workers will feel strong enough to secure a substantial wage increase in an industry whose product does not enter directly into their consumer budget or which is only an insignificant item in it. Thus they feel that they stand to gain more in wages than they lose in prices and are ready to ignore the losses that they are putting on the rest of the community, mostly wage workers like themselves, or on farmers—who, in the last analysis, are no less wage workers. This seems to me to call for a greater integration of policy in the whole labor movement, so that particular crafts or groups will not be seeking to promote their own advantage at the expense of other workers. This idea of union members' responsibility has been powerfully stated by two union groups, and I believe their words will carry more weight with you than anything that I might say.

In the *United Rubber Worker* for May 1946, President L. S. Buckmaster said:

"Industrial labor in America has emerged from a state of helpless, spineless submission and from the status of second or third rate citizenship to a position of power and influence in this country. . . . Now that Joe Worker has become a first-rate citizen and a power in the community, he must make sure that he behaves as a first-rater should behave. He must accept this thing that we call responsibility. He must adjust himself to fit in with this whole scheme of things sometimes referred to as society. He must learn to be tolerant lest he become a tyrant. He must be unselfish lest he be classed as an exponent of greed. He must play life's game according to the rules lest he be banned as a menace to the other players.

"In other words, we must use this new-found power of ours in a clean and decent manner if our unions are to survive. That does not mean that we should revert back to our old position of spinelessness. It means that we must begin to mix a higher percentage of intelligence and moral courage into the batch than we used to do. The end result of this sort of mixture will be a product of finer quality. It will look better and wear longer, as the advertiser would say. It will give you a union that fills your needs and makes you proud to be a member of that union."

And two years earlier, the International Brotherhood of Paper Makers, after an elaborate special study of union problems, reported:

"Wages in the paper industry as a whole have been comparatively high since it first became one of the *organized industries*. Although many believe our wage rates are not as high as they should be today, the paper industry is still a high wage industry. Average annual earnings rank high among all other industries on the North American Continent. Many professions, even in these war times, are not providing comparable earnings. There are today many millions of employees of other industries earning 40¢ an hour and less. . . .

"When unions fight for wage increases, with a blare of trumpets, they are fighting for something for themselves only. The public doubts it is going to benefit from the fight, and often is worried lest any increase will be passed on to them in the form of increased prices.

"A reduction in the cost of living should benefit the public as well as the members of the union. Should unions put up a determined fight to get the cost of living down, they would have the public in their corner, cheering them on. If the unions win, the public wins also."

It was not strange that when labor undertook to correct the abuses of early industrialism through union organization, it relied exclusively on militant methods—on trying to get as much strength as the employer, or even more strength. That was the only tool at hand—and a perfectly proper tool for establishing the institution of collective bargaining. But the time was bound to arrive when unionism, through its organizing ability supplemented by the political resort to government aid, should catch up with and might perhaps even pass capitalistic organization in the race for power.

I suppose that if we could get an absolute equilibrium of size, strength, and skill between the two parties, that condition might assure that wage contracts from then on would reflect a true economic equilibrium. But the attaining and maintaining of any such precise equality of bargaining power is the purest figment of a theorist's imagination. What actually takes place is an endless and destructive struggle of each party to get a little bigger than the other—or a little stronger—or a little more deeply entrenched in government protection. In all probability, the end of that struggle would be marked by the trading of independence and private enterprise for complete paternalism and bureaucratic control.

This would mean the end of unionism and, I fear, the beginning of totalitarianism. To avoid such a disaster, it would seem imperative that both labor and management abandon the race for each to get strong enough to beat the other and that, instead of gang fighting, they adopt in good faith the method of collective adjustment of the economic process in which they are both partners.

MAXIMUM PRODUCTION OUTLAWS RESTRICTIONS

My second proposition is that restriction of production must be definitely opposed and not even silently condoned by organized labor if the great objectives of the Employment Act of 1946 are to be achieved. We could have all those able and willing to work actually on the pay roll and even employed 40 hours a week and still not attain "maximum production and maximum purchasing power" if the bricklayers were only laying 300 or 400 bricks per day, if the painters insisted on narrow brushes and no spray guns, and if we had to march a band in to stand by every time a juke box played or a high-school orchestra tuned up. Featherbedding and every make-work or work-spreading policy of unions is based on a fear that there won't be enough work to go round. On the other hand, the whole philosophy of the Employment Act is that there shall not merely be a full number of jobs but that workers shall work at high efficiency so that real wages or purchasing power shall be raised until a point is reached where people prefer more leisure rather than additional goods. The only limitation that would be acceptable would be in adjusting the length of the work week to the level of high productivity—not low consumption.

It is a matter of common knowledge that there is also a restrictionism on the part of employers. It is no less prevalent than that of labor and no less threatening to the objectives of high production and purchasing power. Producers match workers' fear that there won't be enough work to go round with their own fear that there won't be enough market to go round. This leads to curtailment of output in order to support price instead of simply guiding full productive effort into those channels which reflect consumers' relative preferences and then accepting the price that balances that supply with the demand available when employment is sustained.

Now in fact there is enough work to go round and enough market to take the full product if only we poor ever-struggling and often stupid agents of the business process would just relax and woo rather than coerce the price-making and wage-setting process. So you see I get back again to my basic proposition that economic adjustment via collective bargaining has to become an engineering matter strictly on the scientific up-and-up if we are not to get ourselves again into a stalemate and force the resort to authoritarian settlements. This may quite possibly be the last chance for voluntary bargaining in the private market.

IS THE OUTLOOK BRIGHT OR DIM?

Probably some of you are beginning by now to feel a little impatient with me. You may accuse me of being a bureaucrat who lives in an ivory tower or a professor content "to lecture on navigation while the ship is going down." To this latter jibe, I might reply (1) that the good ship America is not going down, and (2) that sound practical knowledge of the principles of navigation will do a lot to bring her to the ports we seek as our journey continues.

Even so, I daresay you are primarily interested in the wage demands you are about to present to the railroads and on the likelihood that you can in the end get the "pattern settlement" of "a buck a day" or perhaps of 15 cents an hour. Secondarily you are no doubt interested in whether the level of prices or the cost of living is headed up or is likely to remain stationary. As a third issue you are probably wondering whether there is going to be a recession of enough magnitude to affect railway business seriously and, if so, how long it will last. And then what?

Well, I am not going to indulge in any specific forecasts or record any detailed prophecies. I don't know whether you are going to get to ride in the 12½-cent surrey with the 2½-cent fringe on top. But in your own interest as embedded in the economic interest of the country as a whole, I shall hope that you will seek and win the settlement which adjusts your wage rate most equitably within the total price structure and your wage level in best equilibrium with prices and transportation charges as a factor in manufacturing costs, market prices, and consumers' cost of living.

As an economist—a wealth engineer—I cannot but deplore the way in which we have allowed ourselves in the last few years to drift into the acceptance of over-all formulas and pattern settlements. And this applies to 10 per cent price cuts "across the board" just as much as to "pattern" wage increases. This kind of thing is definitely alarming to an agency like our Council which is devoted to the attainment of true economic stability in the nation's economic mechanism. The mechanics adjusting a machine don't say that, just because one nut needs to be tightened by 1½ turns, all the other nuts must or can be tightened by the same amount. Some may need to be loosened. The only sound question is: Why is the present adjustment wrong and what will happen if we put on more pressure or less?

As to the cost of living, I don't know just how that line is going to run either. But I believe that there is solid ground for relief in the way in which union negotiators and employers have been able to get contracts without strikes and in the present prospect that the dreaded wage-price spiral will not get out of hand in a process of runaway inflation. Frankly, I see real hope that the tide of inflation is being stopped and that we shall see a flood of efficient production engendering market competition that makes more goods available to more people at distinctly lower prices.

And so to the third question: Are we headed for a recession or depression that would cut railway traffic seriously, and hence employment? Well, that is the kind of thing the Employment Act of 1946 is designed to prevent. But it will not achieve that end except through the intelligent and determined participation of organized labor, of corporate management, and of farmers and their associations.

Why should we not have sustained prosperity? We have "the makin's." To be sure, the war imposed some drain upon our natural resources and some impairment of our manpower—beyond the losses we regularly sustain even during four years of peacetime operation. On the other hand, it stimulated industrial training and important additions to our industrial plant even after allowing for those types of building and equipment that were adapted only to military uses. There can be little doubt that the productive potential of the United States today is higher per capita than it has ever been before. We still have intact our system of democratic government and free competitive enterprise which we believe provide an independent, ambitious, and intelligent people the greatest opportunity for putting their powers into productive effort and thus producing for themselves a living on the highest possible standard.

In terms of opportunity, then, I do not see how any one of us can feel that the economic prospects of this country are other than bright. The real question is: Are *we* bright? Are we smart and tolerant and well disciplined enough to work together in a democratically organized program to realize those productive possibilities?

The prime purpose of the Employment Act of 1946 and the objective to which the work of the Council of Economic Advisers is to be directed is to secure the highest *real* wages—that is, the largest package of goods and services—for all the men and women "able, willing, and seeking to work." The rewards are to be as nearly as possible in proportion to the true productive value of their several contributions. But as I have said before, that end cannot be accomplished unless every individual and every organization within this complex and interrelated system is willing to accept the verdict of the most scientific means of measuring productivity that can be devised, and to forswear the struggle to force a settlement in its own favor regardless of the consequences to the delicately adjusted machine of which it is a part.

If I understand the Employment Act of 1946 correctly, it declares more specifically than this government has ever before declared its policy for the continuance of a system of free competitive enterprise. It likewise declares more specifically than ever before the intention on the part of the government to take these complementary lines of policy and action which are necessary to sustain a high level of national production and employment opportunity. In so far as that dual system of economic life succeeds, we shall attain the goal of maximum purchasing power for those who work with hand and brain in the mines, forests, fields, workshops, and offices of the Nation.

Appendix E

ECONOMIC IMPLICATIONS OF MILITARY
PREPAREDNESS[1]

Members of the military profession are technicians in the science of defense. Their major premise is that the economy and the social structure, hardly less than the political state, are lost if the system of military security should fail. Like the engineer, they feel the need to include a substantial margin for safety in their calculations but, unlike the engineer, they have no means of knowing in advance the loads or strains that will have to be dealt with. Hence the plan they offer must be one that provides every technically available safeguard against any and all foreseeable threats. In a word, they think of the total resources of the country as potentially available for implementing the security effort.

The economist's thinking is definitely cast in a different mold. His basic problem is: how can scarce resources be most efficiently administered toward the attaining of specified objectives? These objectives are steps toward attaining higher standards of consumption and a freer and richer cultural life for the whole population. Ideally his field of work would concern the efficient administration of economic resources in peacetime, with security assumed or, at least, with military insecurity adequately guarded against by a relatively minor allocation of men and materials.

There is, however, a common ground on which the military man and the businessman or economist can and must meet. This common ground is likewise the field of decision on which the President, the Congress, and the thoughtful citizen must take their stand during the next few months and over the ensuing years. The common problem in whose solution both points of view and both types of professional competence are required is that of the needed balance between the military striking force and the civilian reservoir of men, morale, and machinery upon which the actual fighting force must depend in this day of industrialized war. The old adage that "an army travels on its belly" has to be enlarged to the form, "travels

[1] An address by the Chairman of the Council of Economic Advisers, National Military Establishment Joint Orientation Conference, Nov. 10, 1948.

on the economic machine that maintains the physical and psychological well-being of the soldier and keeps him supplied with efficient weapons." In providing the means of modern war the whole structure of economic society is involved.

I appreciate the opportunity afforded me by Secretary Forrestal to consider with you how the economic factors may be brought into proper working relationship with the military factors in the security equation. In the well-worn phrase of economics, it is the question of economic *supply* and military *demand*. This issue can be considered at two levels, first as it was posed by the President's Message to the Congress on March 17, 1948 and, second, as it will confront the country when the 81st Congress convenes. It is to the latter that I will primarily address my remarks.

What the President said last March was that "the critical situation in Europe" required that we not merely arrest the process of disarmament but promptly enlarge defense preparations. A few days later, this general recommendation was given definite dimension by a proposal that the military budget be enlarged by about 3 billion dollars.

The economic implications of that development in national affairs were briefly but quite definitely appraised by the Council of Economic Advisers in the closing paragraphs of their quarterly memorandum to the President on April 9. We there said:

"At this early stage of the defense plan, two points should be clearly recognized and made plain to the public:

"1. We are in a peace economy, not a war economy. The maintenance of an armed force is as much a part of the peacetime system as is the maintenance of a police force by states, counties, and cities, or the employment of railroad detectives and factory guards. The last two years have given us a fuller measure of the productivity of our resources when aggressively used. We were not staggering under the load of 11 billion dollars for our protective forces, and the rise in this item to 14 or 15 billion dollars will not swamp our economy nor require us to pass from free enterprise to regimentation. Some rather systematic and vigorous discipline, however, must be exercised to redirect our economic effort so as to meet the new goal in an orderly and economical manner.

"2. Every citizen must recognize that further diversions of productive effort to military uses inevitably involves some sacrifice of civilian types of consumption. It is our particular application of the old alternative of 'guns or butter.'

"Our people had—and we believe quite properly—looked forward to a postwar period in which larger numbers of people would achieve higher standards of living than had ever been realized before. These hopes are not nullified by the defense program. But they must in some measure be postponed or for the present revised downward. During this period if any group insists that its income shall be advanced in proportion to every advance in prices or that it shall be in a position to pay up to whatever level is needed to bid its accustomed amount of goods away from other users, it is in effect demanding that it be exempted from sharing in the common burden of protecting our country. These economic facts of life should be proclaimed along with every step in working out the practical details of the defense program."

Personally, I still believe that that statement correctly defined the major economic implications of the limited defense program to which the President has thus far held the line. In amplification of that statement, however, I should like to review quite briefly the situation of the economy at the time when mounting international tension caused this preparedness program to be launched. This involves considering not merely the situation of the economy at a certain point in time but also something of where we had been coming from and where we thought we were going. What had our people been demanding or expecting of the postwar economy?

The war period had been preceded by a severe depression, in which the use of the Nation's productive resources dropped to less than half their capacity. Millions of men and women able, willing, and seeking to work had not been provided with work opportunities, and the national standard of living suffered. From this depression we had made so disappointing a recovery that concern began to be felt lest we grandchildren of the pioneers might allow ourselves to accept a condition of chronic economic stagnation.

War changed all that and ushered in a period of intense and brilliant national effort. The beginnings of this effort moved much more easily and swiftly by reason of the fact that our resources were not already being fully utilized. There were large numbers of unemployed persons and under-utilized facilities. The defense effort therefore got under way with a minimum of disturbance to the civilian economy. In the end, however, attainment of military success required the subordination of ordinary consumer interests to the requirements of military production, though we were never compelled really to learn the meaning of the word "austerity." While individual deprivations and family losses were grievous, it could be said of the Nation as a whole that we lost some blood, shed a few tears, and got up a healthy sweat.

When President Truman presented his defense message to the Congress last March, we had had two years and a half of vigorous postwar reconversion. During this period we were still feeling the tremendous economic momentum of the war influence, with its creation of superabundant monetary purchasing power and its accumulation of enormous unsatisfied wants, public and private, from highways, dams, generating plants, factory equipment, and operating inventories to houses, passenger cars, electric toasters, and bed linen. What we were witnessing in the market was an inability of end products to satisfy simultaneous demands of the market for capital goods, current consumption goods, and exports on the level that unprecedented savings, high current earnings, and foreign demand made possible. Hence we were being swept along in the grip of a strongly inflationary current, inadequately stemmed either by Government policies or by private self-restraint.

At this point, I may perhaps be permitted a modest reference to the Employment Act of 1946 and the dual implementation which it provided through the Council of Economic Advisers and the Joint Committee in the Congress. The declaration of national policy made in this act was for such wise use of free competitive enterprise and such prudent discharge of public functions by government as would prevent a return to the baffled waste of productive resources of the 30's and, on the other hand, transmute the momentum of the war and reconversion period into a long-sustained period of high-level peacetime production and the broadly rising standards of living that would go with vigorous and efficient use of our rich resources.

This was a large order, but I for one have never felt that it is beyond the powers of a people possessed of as much ingenuity as ours, with such highly developed institutions of public information and discussion, and with the degree of economic literacy that we have attained. Perhaps the most important requisite for success would be that we also be animated by good will and a spirit of practical co-operation. Individuals and groups must accept the necessities of practical working adjustments between themselves and other parts of a complex productive mechanism. Otherwise, they slow down the machine in the stubborn effort to gain immediate personal or group advantage.

If the nations of the world had been willing to disarm and devote themselves to restoring and subsequently expanding domestic production and enlarging the flow of mutually profitable trade, the years 1947 and 1948 would have at least gone far toward completing the process of physical reconversion and catching up with activities and rates of growth interrupted by the war and the preceding depression. As was stated in several successive Economic Reports of the President to the Congress, the practical problem to be met in successfully completing the catching up process would have been to adjust the several relationships of prices, wages, savings, taxes, and investment one to another so that the great flood of products resulting from high employment with efficient equipment and direction would move promptly into use.

This would have to be worked out through the competition of the market, the policy decisions of executives, the rulings of regulatory bodies, and the process of collective wage bargaining, together with the financial operation of bankers and the Federal Reserve and the economic program of the Government. All together, these economic adjustment processes would have to work out a new and internally consistent set of money relationships which would realistically reflect major changes in industrial techniques and plant capacities, in tastes and habits of consumption, and in government commitments, all this in the face of tenacious patterns of economic behavior. To quote from two sentences in the Economic Report of July 1947: "At present we are in the process of seeking to find a workable pattern of income and price relationships on a new price level but with continuing high production and employment. It is generally conceded that this new price level will be higher than prewar." Probably this should have read "substantially higher."

If prospects for peace had improved, or even not grown worse, throughout 1947 and 1948, our ability to adjust our economy to the requirements of sustained peacetime prosperity would progressively have been put to the test in one industry after another as each passed from a condition of scarcity to one of abundance, from a sellers' market to a buyers' market— or true competitive enterprise. If the practitioners of communism had not thrust us back into the danger of war, we would soon have been thrust forward into the difficulties of peace.

These difficulties are of various sorts. There is the danger that, taking fright from weakening markets, business would sharply curtail its investment plans and bankers unduly tighten credit. There is the danger that business managements would attempt to hold up prices and profits at the cost of restricted production. There is the danger that labor would make excessive wage demands, contributing to unemployment and loss of production. There is the danger that consumers, hoping for lower prices, would limit their purchases unduly or, on the other hand, that they might spend so lavishly that savings would not provide adequately for capital needs. And there is danger that Government, faced with some or all of these threats to continued prosperity, would not use its powers with sufficient vigor to offset or correct the elements of instability by which our type of free economic system is beset.

The level of defense expenditures for which the President and the Congress made provision last spring tended to avoid or defer these dangers. They are still further limited by the very widespread expectation in business circles that that level will be raised. If the scale of military expenditure does in fact increase substantially, they may be postponed indefinitely, and the country confronted by quite another kind of problem.

This brings me to the second part of the question of economic *supply* and military *demand* which I raised earlier in my remarks, that of prospective enlargement of military expenditures. How will this question look to the President and to the 81st Congress in discharging their responsibility for providing an adequate defense program? Both the Congress and the public will need to understand the economic implications of a defense budget 2 or 5 or possibly even 10 billion dollars above the level presently provided.

Superficially it may seem plausible to say that a 2 or 5 billion dollar item cannot seriously disturb an economy in which total production amounts to 250 billion dollars annually. But it is equally important to remember that to the economist, no less than to the physicist, the chemist, and the physician, there are "critical points" where relatively small changes of actual magnitude have decisive influence. Hence we must look not merely at aggregate sums but at strategic spots in the delicate process of economic life which would be affected by the monetary disbursements and the monetary withdrawals.

You are well aware that the country's productive resources are now being used at peak levels. You realize too that already a substantial portion of our productive resources are being used for military and foreign aid purposes—approaching 10 per cent of national product. These uses do not give rise to the production of domestic consumer goods or capital goods. Inflationary forces, though checked at various points, have by no means disappeared.

Even if the defense program were limited to 15 billion dollars, the expenditure of that amount would exceed by at least 3 billions the present annual rate of cash outlays for national defense. If to this are added further increases, to a level of 18 or 20 billions, there are bound to be important repercussions on the operation of the economy.

The specific effects on our business world that can reasonably be foreseen in 1949 and 1950-plus can conveniently be discussed under four heads: inflation, labor diversion, materials shortage, and controls. Within the short time available, I must state my conclusions on these points quite dogmatically without much supporting data or analysis.

Inflation. There appears to have been increasing agreement during the last few months among professional economists and experienced business leaders that, in the absence of the foreign aid and enlarged defense programs, deflationary influences would by this time have become clearly evident. As current expenditures have developed under these programs and, as expectations for the future have become more clear, inflationary forces have tended to outrun deflationary developments, and the trend of both wholesale and consumer prices is still rather steadily upward. If against this background we project a substantially larger scale of military expenditures for rearming ourselves and perhaps Western Europe and some other countries, it is clear that new forces of inflation would be unleashed. They would operate through monetary mechanisms, technological situations, market processes, and psychologic reactions. To some extent, the inflationary impact would be moderate or strong according to the amount of outlay. But to some extent also, they might prove erratic or disproportionate to the financial sums actually involved. We must face the possibility that if the trend toward inflation became generally discernible at the present juncture, it might develop a strongly marked cumulative or spiraling force unless strong anti-inflationary policies were promptly declared by the Government. There would also be needed a strong will on the part of influential business leaders and economic groups to resist inflationary temptations.

A major physical problem of the increased defense program is to get production resources transferred from civilian to military uses. The related economic problem lies in devising financial methods by which this transfer can be effected and still avoid the potential inflation.

To some extent higher prices and higher wages would increase the government's tax revenues, but they would also raise military procurement costs, probably necessitate further advance in military pay and allowances and a compensating reclassification of the Civil Service. It seems doubtful that, as a practical matter, offsetting economies in government expenditures could be worked out in the face of the demand for additional civilian services ancillary to the war effort. We must remember that public works, at least in such areas as transportation and electric power, would have to be materially enlarged.

At present tax levels, Government revenues would be insufficient to finance any large increased cost. Resort to deficit financing through bank borrowing would at once enlarge the stream of money demand and start an upward movement of prices. Rising prices would not only push up the cost of living, giving rise to demands for higher wages. It would also create a speculative interest in markets which would be well designed to force prices upwards.

An inflationary spiral initiated and re-enforced in this manner is by no means unavoidable. To prevent it, however, the program must be financed by drawing the cost out of the pockets of the people. It must, in other words, be financed out of higher taxes and larger savings, voluntary or involuntary. And, even so, it may call for other types of control to meet the physical problems to be noted.

Shortages of men and materials. Passing from the monetary to the physical implications of an enlarging military program, we need to distinguish between over-all demands and particular points of impact. The military efforts that we are talking about are estimated to divert somewhere from

1 million to 2 or 2½ million workers from the civilian labor force. Out of a total of some 62½ million workers, this is not a crippling drain. We anticipate a rather abnormally large increase in the labor force of a million or even a million and a quarter next year as against an annual gain of some 700,000 in recent years. The point, however, is that the withdrawals for military service would be persons of more than average physical and mental capacity. Even with the most skillful procedure in granting exemptions, they would withdraw appreciable numbers from areas where scarcities (particularly of skilled workers) already exist. At the same time, the character of the equipment and materials required in the military effort would increase the pressure of demand on areas of manufacturing and mining, where even now there is real shortage of skilled personnel.

Much the same can be said as to the demand which an expanded military effort will make upon our supply of materials and equipment for producing finished goods. Unlike the expansion of our military program at the beginning of World War II, we must now start our effort from a level of very high utilization of our productive resources. Today there are bottlenecks in steel and non-ferrous metals, in coking coal and petroleum, ore-carrying boats and pipeline capacity, and at numerous other minor spots. The progress of military stockpiling of strategic and essential materials is being slowed down by such shortages. While there is some present easing in various food, clothing, and non-durable goods industries, the chief impact of a rearmament program would be at the very points where we are still far from being caught up. In general, military demands could not be met by the stimulated use of reserve resources but would have to be at the expense of withdrawals from other claimants whose wants have not yet been satisfied.

These points of present shortage and of special military demand for skilled labor, materials, and facilities would be the first focal points for the inflation referred to earlier. Even if general measures were taken to stem the inflation, there is no assurance that the physical transfer of resources from civilian to military production could be made with sufficient promptness and completeness to meet the need without the introduction of more direct methods of controlling the flow of resources. And if this promptness and completeness were not achieved, we would have breakdowns in the physical process by which adequate military production could be maintained. Since our money and banking system is now so elastic as to permit such market forces to be readily reflected in the price level, we can expect the specific impacts of an enlarged military budget to produce an accelerated inflation unless strong offsetting measures are taken. If the sources of monetary inflation were not severely curbed, direct controls would be needed so much the more to prevent the progressive and senseless bidding up of prices and to assure the scheduled level of military production.

Controls. A program of military expenditures at any level much above the present would, in my judgment, force us out of the free market procedures of a peacetime economy and drive us to the acceptance of a number of direct controls. Otherwise, the strength of the inflationary pressures, the confusion and delay in the defense effort, and the friction and hardship in the civilian economy would create demoralizing conditions both in market processes and in the public mind.

The central and certainly the first feature of a system of controls to facilitate military production would be the allocation of key materials, re-enforced by limitation and conservation orders and inventory controls. Even at the present time, some need for allocation controls is recognized. So far, only voluntary methods are available, and even in the limited field where they have been tried, they have not been conspicuously successful. It is easy to see that a mounting program of defense would soon call for more authoritative methods of broader scope.

Second, there would undoubtedly be early need of considerable placement control for scarce types of skilled labor and a more extensive employment service. Finally, to prevent the spiraling of living costs, wages, and production costs, price control of a quite extensive scope might well be necessary, unless severe fiscal measures were invoked to curtail civilian demand.

Over against this view as to the need of controls in an increasingly inflationary situation, it is clear that businessmen, workers, and farmers have a basic aversion to limitations on a free enterprise system in the areas where they are respectively affected. Mr. Grether yesterday indicated to you that at M-Day, the full panoply of wartime controls far beyond those of World War II would have to be invoked. How far lesser or partial controls would be accepted in the twilight zone between the present state of preparedness and actual mobilization is anybody's guess, but certainly an issue which will be fought out in the next few months and must be considered in parallel with discussion of and decision on scale of military expenditures in the immediately coming months. It is not clear that a control program could be introduced piecemeal, but it is possible that even business leaders who would have to bear the brunt of responsibility for delivering the goods specified in a military expenditures program only a few billion dollars above the present level would find at least materials controls necessary to keep their operational program from bogging down.

The issues of economic controls cannot be divorced from other policies of the Government. A very severe fiscal policy of taxation, and possibly forced saving, would minimize the need for price control. It would also to a degree lessen the problem of allocation by driving civilian demand out of the market. The extent of the need for direct controls is therefore in part directly related to the extent to which the Government permits inflationary pressures to develop.

So much for my suggested answers to the question of the specific effects that a continued and rising scale of military expenditures would have on our economic life in the near term. It is clear that this would not mean the onset of economic disaster. For the next few years it would guarantee maximum employment in some sort of activity and maximum production of some sort of goods and services. But it certainly would not provide the maximum standard of living that our men, money, and management are capable of producing. It would indefinitely postpone the time when we can organize our economic life for the production of maximum real purchasing power for our people—and that was the purpose for which the Employment Act of 1946 was designed and which we had thought we could really get down to business on in these postwar years.

This clear economic implication of rising military expenditures raises a much more fundamental question. Would such a development simply defer the attainment of peacetime economic objectives, or will it make them more difficult of attainment over an indefinitely long future period? There are several respects in which the latter appears definitely to be the case. I shall touch briefly on only four.

This diversion of national resources to war goods rather than peace goods would bring a new threat to the educational interests of this country. Few people appear to realize how great was the accumulation of deferred maintenance in our total school system during the war and the further deterioration both plant and personnel have suffered during postwar inflation. Much the same can be said as to streets and highways and other types of public facilities. This type of problem is further aggravated by the fact that the accelerated rate of family formation in the war and early postwar years has brought more than normally increased demand on community facilities and is just beginning to bring larger numbers of infants to the schoolhouse door.

A second type of persistent harm to the economy is that a military effort results in building expensive kinds of equipment—and to some extent plant—highly specialized to the uses of war engineering which have no use in civilian production or which are in excess of peacetime needs. This sort of economic distortion is aggravated to the extent that the military effort results in accelerated drain on natural resources which are already scarce and for which no equally good or equally cheap substitutes are available.

The third danger of economic scar after the period of actual military effort could be the further distortion of price and income relationships that would result from a further and perhaps more extreme phase of inflation. The impacts of this process are very unevenly distributed. The strong, the favorably situated, and the ruthless or unscrupulous can often protect themselves against adverse effects or even reap positive benefits from extreme price and income disturbances. The weak or unfortunate not merely suffer deprivation but even create maladjustments which make the problem of ultimate stabilization still more difficult.

Finally, the return to controls and their continuance for some years would present a two-pronged danger. As a free people, we are always fearful that economic controls may prove habit-forming and develop a spirit of acceptance of authority over larger and larger areas of life and weaken the reliance of the people on free bargaining. If that danger is avoided, there is the opposite danger that in avoiding it, we develop evasion or defiance of constituted authority, black markets, and a lowering of the moral fiber of our people. In any event, by giving legal sanction to certain structures, procedures, and property rights for a period of years, controls build up greater or less vested interests on the part of beneficiaries of these arrangements to have them perpetuated and vested claims of those who have been hurt by them to secure some offsetting benefit. Either way it complicates the return to smooth operation of the economy.

What I have been saying involves no judgment as to what is the scale of military expenditures the country could wisely and safely undertake at this time. It is simply an attempt to look frankly at the actual costs, present and future, of a military effort of stated magnitude.

If any moral is to be drawn from the objective analysis of this problem, it would go to these points: (1) that those who are entrusted with our foreign relations must be wise as serpents and harmless as doves so that the need for military effort shall be held or reduced to the lowest possible point; (2) that those who are entrusted with the military effort display the prescience and the abnegation that will direct every dollar to the point of greatest effectiveness, and forego every outlay based on traditional practice, corps pride, or dispensable ceremony; (3) that the Government stand ready to introduce those measures of finance and control which will minimize the disturbing effects upon the economy; and (4) that the people at large face the necessities of the situation, make the sacrifices, and accept the disciplines which are entailed.

Appendix F

ECONOMIC ANALYSIS AND POLITICAL SYNTHESIS[1]

The distinctive thing about the Employment Act is its recognition of the need for comprehensive and internally consistent economic policy as among government agencies and activities, as among private agencies and activities, and between governmental and private parts of the economy. It does not conceive our modern economic process as merely a private enterprise system seeking to attain efficiency and preserve individual freedom under voluntary representative government. It recognizes the subtle fact of an ubiquitous interpenetration of our economic and political systems. It was probably recognition, at most subconscious, of this advanced stage of evolution in our economic affairs that caused certain imaginative citizens and legislators to push at that particular time for such a development within our frame of government as the Employment Act of 1946.

The elaboration of our corporation and union institutions in the industrial field, the peculiar requirements of our family farm system of agriculture, and the adventitious forces of war and its financing with our new central bank machinery for monetizing a debt however large, conspired to create an irresistible demand for a much better administrative machinery for the economy.

SCIENTIFIC METHOD IN POLICY MAKING

In some quarters, there was a broad understanding of these courses of our economic evolution and a groping for more adequate means of responding to or dealing with them. In others, there was the more limited and definite feeling of need for a specific remedy to meet the threat of a postwar business depression. It was this latter influence which produced the Murray "full employment" bill, later superseded by the Employment Act of 1946. The Murray bill proposed a fiscal specific for the undulant fever of boom and depression, which it was widely feared would display a typical and critical postwar manifestation. This first formulation of the stabilization proposal met sharp and widespread opposition. After a multitude of coun-

[1] Edwin G. Nourse, *Proceedings of the American Philosophical Society* (R. A. F. Penrose, Jr., Memorial Lecture), Vol. 94, No. 4, 1950.

selors had contributed their joint wisdom, the final act was framed in much more eclectic terms.

So revised, the Employment Act of 1946 formulates a general goal and pattern of satisfactory achievement in the economic field and provides two specific devices to aid in attaining it. Its objective is somewhat more than moderating or even curing the malady which threatened to become chronic in modern industrial society, namely, the business cycle. The act demands of an intelligently administered economy not merely a steady level of operation but likewise a high level of sustained use of the nation's resources, human and material—in the phrase of the act "maximum employment and maximum production."

As to the attainment of the goal thus defined, there is in this measure an at least latent assumption that we have now gained scientific knowledge and practical competence which should enable us to perfect our institutional machinery, clarify our policies, and improve our practices in handling our national affairs so that the desirable results envisaged in the preamble to the act could be reasonably approximated. In a word, the act invites economic science—or, if that be an over-ambitious term, scientific methods as applied to the subject matter of economics—into an ancillary position of recognized importance within the frame of voluntary government. Nor is this service to be rendered merely as the government's own fiscal, monetary, or regulatory operations. It is conceived also as furnishing intellectual leadership and co-ordination in the reciprocal area of private business policy and practices.

By inviting economics into a larger place in the public service, the Employment Act opens the door to professional economists through the Council of Economic Advisers to apply all their techniques of analysis to the affairs of the economy. Economic (and statistical) techniques are to be used by the Council also to synthesize an ideal policy for the economy as an integrated whole. This synthesis is to be presented for consideration by the President and his official family.

Through the Joint Economic Committee of the Congress, economists are likewise to participate in an independent analysis of the problems and the President's proposals for dealing with them and to synthesize the Committee's own program as a frame of reference for co-ordination of the legislative process in so far as it touches economic matters. Space does not permit examination of this institutional development here. Reference to one or two phases of its work will be made later in my paper.

There are thus two separate and successive levels or patterns of synthesis. The first is to be seen in the confidential report of the Council to the President, appropriately labeled "materials for the use of the President in the preparation of his Economic Report to the Congress." The second is to be seen in the state paper which the President, with the collaboration of his Cabinet officers and agency heads and with the assistance of the White House staff, prepares and submits to the Congress. The former of these documents embodies the economic scholarship of the Council members as surrogates for their staff and for the profession as a whole. The latter embodies the politico-economic statesmanship of the chief executive of the Federal Government and the titular head of the incumbent party. I wish to describe briefly what seem to me the ideal possibilities of both documents, and also the possibility or danger that either or both of these works of art may fall slightly or seriously below levels presumably attainable in the present "state of the arts"—of business and of government.

The policy statement that the Council prepares for the President's consideration must deal with many aspects of the economy. It must make proposals for dealing with all of them simultaneously and in interaction in ways that are mutually consistent and that would, together, promote the well-being, that is the sustained productivity, of the economy to the highest degree possible. The attainment of such an economic synthesis calls for exceptional intellectual capacities and personal qualities. They may be classified under three heads.

First, it presupposes technical competence of the first order on the part of each Council member (and likewise skill in selecting and organizing a specialized but co-ordinated staff to supplement such competences as the Council itself possesses). Besides sheer technical ability, there is required the greatest possible frankness and objectivity. Each member of the Council (and top staff) must be able and willing to lay all the premises and the processes of his analytic and synthetic thinking unreservedly on the Council's work table for the searching scrutiny of his fellows.

Second, synthesis of a sound and workable national policy requires the greatest realism in fitting the mechanics of economic theory to the human peculiarities of the persons through whom the actual economic process is conducted. The economist is dealing, in the future tense, with the mass behavior of 150 million technically free but variously conditioned human beings and the individual behavior of a much smaller, though still considerable, number of executives who wield greater or less degrees of administrative power or influence.[2] His cannot be an exposition which traces cause

[2] Insight into the psychological processes of business executives, labor officials, farm leaders, and organized consumers was promoted through a number of consultative committees set up by the Council. As these representatives of the various groups sat around our Council table, it was possible first to draw out their criticisms of government policies or the action of rival groups and to have them elucidate their own objectives and the means they proposed for attaining them. It was possible also to get their reaction to difficulties as revealed in Council analyses and the

and result sequences with the mathematical precision of the natural scientist, who deals with inert and tractable materials and orderly and measurable forces. He must show in his synthesis a realistic grasp of whatever the psychologist has taught about normal and abnormal psychology plus such insights about incentive, motivation, and revolt as he has been able to gain from empirical labors in his chosen field. Here is a fine line, to attain psychological realism and yet not be swayed by subjective judgments.

Third, the making of its economic synthesis demands of each Council member a broad and deep social philosophy. Only so can he weigh and scale the demands of the several parties to the economic process and display a calm judicial quality as the economic attorneys for one or another special interest group argue the claims of their respective clients for favored treatment in the matter of income, for special relief from effort or responsibility, or for exceptional security. These issues will frequently present economic dilemmas. So confronted, the Council must synthesize a policy which "on balance" holds greatest promise of practical workability. Furthermore, this must be presented in a way which will promote understanding and acceptance by the several contending parties.

Having sketched what seem to me the limits of proper economic synthesis and the qualities required of the Council members in reaching or approximating that ideal, I now turn to two comments on how or why that level of attainment may not actually be reached. They concern first the availability of material from which to choose, and second the lack of understanding of needed qualities on the part of the President in appointing, or the Senate in confirming, candidates for the Council.

One of the greatest shortcomings in my profession is a superindividualism which causes many of its members to develop each his own economic system or philosophy, expressed in a trick vocabulary. There has also been a deplorable willingness of some members to become the attorneys for certain vested interests or interests aspiring to become vested. It may likewise lead to more or less active identification with a political party. Third, and related to the points just mentioned, is an unwillingness on the part of many persons of scholarly pretensions to accept the anonymous and self-abnegating role which is called for by the peculiarly confidential relationship of a professional staff post in the Executive Office.

If we are to have economic synthesis developed calmly but vigorously on its side of the line, in such a way as to have greatest practical helpfulness and, at the same time, greatest disciplinary value to political synthesis on

---

probable workability of policies under consideration by the Council or by particular government agencies. Finally, it was possible to get from them some expert counsel as to the reasoning, attitudes, and probable behavior of the rank and file in their respective groups.

the other side, the economist must be spiritually capable of bringing the choicest pearls of scientific work to cast before the politically motivated and politically conditioned policy makers of the executive branch. He must be prepared to see these carefully fabricated materials rejected or distorted, and still carry on the same process of preparation and submission again tomorrow, unperturbed and unabashed. He must all the while be aware that his professional brethren and the public will hold him accountable for the final compromised product while he, by virtue of his relationship to the Executive Office, is estopped from saying anything in explanation or vindication of his own workmanship. Many an able economist refuses such an affront to his "academic freedom" and professional dignity.

Much also devolves upon the President if a Council is to be provided which will cap the most competent economic analysis with the most adequate economic synthesis. The Employment Act stipulates that the Council "shall be composed of three members . . . each of whom shall be a person who, as a result of his training, experience, and attainments, is exceptionally qualified to analyze and interpret economic developments, to appraise programs and activities of the government . . . , and to formulate and recommend national economic policy." This implies that the President shall have a real grasp, direct or vicarious, of the qualities needed for scientific performance and a sensitive desire that service shall be kept on that plane. It requires also that he shall subsequently in every way emphasize and preserve the non-political character of the agency. Since members will only in exceptional cases have been entirely free of active affiliation with political or other policy-promoting organizations, the President should insist that, after appointment, they regard Council membership as enjoining withdrawal from these connections to an extent comparable to that expected, in their somewhat analogous area, of Justices of the Supreme Court. For the President to permit or encourage intervention of Council members in any manner in the legislative process or in the public promotion of measures or policies is to make them politically expendable and to destroy the unique usefulness of the Council as an institution designed for scientific service to the executive branch.

FROM ECONOMIC SCIENCE TO PRACTICAL POLICY

The title of my paper, in the interest of brevity, was compacted to the form "Economic Analysis and Political Synthesis." The scheme of treatment in fact involves three concepts: economic analysis, economic synthesis, and political synthesis. Among these three I make a two-way comparison. The first comparison is between economic analysis and the synthesis of a comprehensive, realistic, and objective many-faceted policy based strictly on criteria of economics as a social science. The second comparison is between such a policy and an active political policy designed to combine strictly economic considerations with others which cannot be ignored. This second level of synthesis, which enters into the making of a national economic policy under the objectives set and with the devices provided in the Employment Act, inevitably is the personal responsibility of the President.

Under our system, the President is not merely the chief executive of a democracy. He is also the titular head of a political party under a two-party system, and this we hold to be the best system yet devised for free government. It is obvious that the President cannot, as a practical matter, adopt and effectuate a policy drawn up exclusively in accord with economic criteria even in the realistic view I previously referred to. I used often to say to staff members: "If you were translated from your relatively comfortable office chair to the hot seat occupied by the President, you would not find it wise or safe as political head of the state to make your statesmanship conform precisely to what, strictly as an economist, you would be profoundly convinced was the desirable course."

I recognize that the line between the realistic economist and the scholarly politician is so vague as not to be drawn with even an approach to precision. It seems to me, however, that it is quite possible to perceive the qualitative difference between (a) political synthesis of a statesman's policy based on a conscientious study of the economic synthesis of competent technicians on his staff and (b) the political disregard for or debauchment of economic data, analysis, and objective evaluation. Synthesis is an orderly process which observes rules of evidence, scientific canons, and strict logic to test cause-and-result relations. It is very different from the cunning of a politician seeking to capture votes by specious or venal appeals in order to remain in power, synthesizing a plurality by the additive process of placating special interest groups. In the vernacular, this might be called "drawing to fill an inside straight."

There is one quite simple and obviously valid criterion of a proper political synthesis: What combination of segmental policies will integrate into an over-all policy which will be not only economically self-consistent but will, "on balance," be best calculated to promote the welfare of the whole people—while preserving their basic freedoms? In the search for such a national political synthesis the Council's position in the Executive Office must be vitalized not merely as toward the President; it must be active and intimate also as to Cabinet officers and other agency heads. The Council must challenge the policies of those political lieutenants of the Chief Executive if they seem designed or to tend toward promoting any special interest rather than maximum production or continuing well-being for the whole people. The President must be willing to preside over, and the Cabinet officers willing to participate in, a genuine seminar session for the final resolving of conflicting policies.[3]

BASIC DIFFICULTIES IN GETTING A SOUND POLITICAL SYNTHESIS

In commenting on criteria of an ideal political synthesis, I have clearly implied some of the difficulties to be encountered in reaching that high plane of statesmanship. These difficulties inhere not only in the personality of the President and of the aides whom he selects but also in certain features of our government structure and general policy. Some of the latter are deeply embedded in tradition. Examining them would require time far beyond what is available for this paper. Some of them, on the other hand, are indigenous to the current situation.

This is particularly manifest in the present drift toward central governmental planning in the implemented blueprint sense. Present political policy-making seems to be infused with a great zeal (a) to get quick results and (b) to have these results conform to a certain philosophy of "what is good for the people" rather than a desire to facilitate their working out that kind of life which they themselves will, in the long run, find good. This is much too large an issue to open up at the close of a brief paper. It is, however, interesting to conjecture whether this trend will persist and grow stronger in the future. It would seem to me both to negative the town meeting concept of democracy on which the United States was founded and to negative also the teachings of the scientific method which I hoped the Employment Act would make much more effective in our executive and legislative processes.

The potential usefulness of the Employment Act, with its professional Council of Economic Advisers, has not yet been given a real test. Its lack of success has, in addition to the Council's own internal shortcomings, been due to the fact that even such materials as it has prepared were not studied and debated as a preliminary to making those compromises among rival desiderata that are a part of the art of free government. It seems to me self-evident that the Council will be accepted within the government and by the public only in the light and at the level indicated by the President.

But there are difficulties also in getting economists to recognize and accept the distinction between economic analysis and political synthesis. Several years ago a gentleman who aspired to nomination for the Presidency of the United States made a pilgrimage to one of our leading universities.

[3] As I presided over the meetings of the Cabinet committee on stabilization policy (see p. 228), it was very interesting to observe the way in which executive heads of other agencies would argue against policies proposed by a brother secretary or chairman when he overreached himself to serve his constituents through ex parte proposals that threatened the general welfare.

He invited a group of its top economists to meet with him that he might get the best of their wisdom on certain pending economic questions. He said: "Just give me the economic facts and analysis. If I have to act on these matters in the political milieu, I have, and expect to rely upon, my own techniques for making political evaluations and executive decisions." As the session proceeded, he had to become schoolmaster to the schoolmasters to keep them from spilling over into political—perhaps they called them social—value judgments far beyond the cause-and-result relationships on which he sought their technicians' aid.

It would, I think, have great value for us economists to deal with a political executive who saw this distinction clearly and enforced it as a frame of reference for the work of his economic advisers. I am not presuming to make a nomination for President or assuming that this is the only qualification. But I do suggest that not until we have a President with that kind of mind and not until he finds economists who can make professionally wise economic synthesis and refrain rigorously from political synthesis will the Employment Act and its Council achieve the high purposes which are latent in it.

In closing I repeat an observation I have made on a previous occasion: "It will take time for successive Presidents to learn how to use a nonpolitical advisory staff agency effectively. It will take time for successive Council members to learn how to bring the most competent and realistic analysis of economic problems simply and effectively to the President's aid."

Index